THE LOYALISTS *of* New Jersey

Their Memorials, Petitions, Claims, Etc. from English Records

By E. Alfred Jones

With New Appendix of Additional Loyalists by
A. Van Doren Honeyman

HERITAGE BOOKS
2008

HERITAGE BOOKS
AN IMPRINT OF HERITAGE BOOKS, INC.

Books, CDs, and more—Worldwide

For our listing of thousands of titles see our website
at
www.HeritageBooks.com

A Facsimile Reprint
Published 2008 by
HERITAGE BOOKS, INC.
Publishing Division
100 Railroad Ave. #104
Westminster, Maryland 21157

Originally published in 1927 as
*Collections of the New Jersey Historical Society
Volume X*

— Publisher's Notice —
In reprints such as this, it is often not possible to remove blemishes from the original. We feel the contents of this book warrant its reissue despite these blemishes and hope you will agree and read it with pleasure.

International Standard Book Numbers
Paperbound: 978-1-58549-791-1
Clothbound: 978-0-7884-7047-9

WILLIAM FRANKLIN

LOYALIST GOVERNOR OF NEW JERSEY, 1763-1776

Taken from proof of a medallion by (probably) the sculptor, John Flaxman, and used for reproduction in Wedgwood Ware. Date about 1784.

PREFATORY NOTE

My first duty is to acknowledge the invaluable help accorded to me in the preparation of these notes, now published for the first time from the original material in the Public Record Office in London, on the New Jersey Loyalists, by Mr. A. Van Doren Honeyman, Corresponding Secretary of the New Jersey Historical Society, at whose invitation they have been published.

Not only has Mr. Honeyman corrected the proofs—no mean task in view of the fact that he and I are separated by the Atlantic—but has also contributed many additions of real importance and interest from historical material in New Jersey especially Appendix III, as well as the Index.

Acknowledgment of notes from other correspondents has been made in the text.

The following printed sources have been freely consulted in the course of the work and will be found with abbreviated titles throughout:

Lawrence and Stockton, "The Judges of New Brunswick and their Times."
Sabine, "The American Loyalists," 2nd. ed., 1864.
Stryker, "The New Jersey Volunteers."
"The Royal Commission Reports on the MSS. of the Earl of Dartmouth; and on the American MSS. in the Royal Institution," 4 Vols.
"The Royal Commission on Loyalists' Claims," 1783-1785. Ed. by H. E. Egerton for the Roxburghe Club, 1915.
"Second Report of the Bureau of Archives for the Province of Ontario," 1904.

To this list may be added Archdeacon W. O. Raymond's account of certain Loyalist Regiments and lists of Officers from the original rolls, in the "Collections of the New Brunswick Historical Society," No. 5, 1904. The dates of commissions there differ in some cases from half-pay lists (unpublished) in Ind.: 5604-5-6.

A few other American sources are named in certain of the notes.

In the following records reference by way of letters signify: A. O.—Audit Office; W. O.—War Office; T.—Treasury; F. O.—Foreign Office; C. O.—Colonial Office; Ind.—Index (War Office).

E. ALFRED JONES.

INTRODUCTORY NOTE

THE GENESIS OF this original matter may be explained at the outset. In July, 1782, that benevolent and high-minded statesman, William, second Earl of Shelburne, previously Secretary of State for Foreign Affairs and then Prime Minister, appointed two men to enquire into the cases of the American refugees, victims of the War, many of whom had sought an asylum in Great Britain as early as 1775. This large number of Loyalists was considerably increased after the Declaration of Independence. Lord Shelburne's choice fell upon two men of probity and independence, both members of Parliament and trained lawyers, namely, J. Eardley Wilmot and Daniel Parker Coke. The demand was imperative for some more satisfactory method of alleviating the distress of the exiles in Great Britain than the grant of temporary allowances, previously made by the Treasury, which had already amounted to over £43,000 annually.

Under this scheme Commissioners were to be appointed "to enquire into the losses and services of all such persons who have suffered in their rights, properties and professions during the late unhappy dissensions in America in consequence of their loyalty to His Majesty and attachment to the British Government." The loyalty and conduct of the claimants for compensation for their property confiscated by the various States were to be the foundation of the enquiry. "Though, in general, the Commissioners found the loyalty of the party uniform and unequivocal, yet there were some who had not been early in the part they had taken, and others who had at first taken part with the Americans; and, as the Commissioners thought it was their duty to place them in separate classes, not knowing whether Government or Parliament might or might not make any distinction in this respect, it became a necessary but an invidous and arduous part of the enquiry in some of these claims." So said J. Eardley Wilmot in his "Historical View of the Commission . . . with an Account of the Compensation Granted to the American Loyalists . . . by Parliament in 1785 and 1788."

Accordingly, the Loyalists were divided broadly into six classes. Included in the first were those who had performed exceptional services on behalf of Great Britain. The second consisted of those who had borne arms against the Revolution. In the third were men of uniform zeal and loyalty throughout. The fourth were Loyalists resident in Great Britain. In the fifth and sixth classes were those who took oaths of allegiance to, or bore arms for, the American States, but afterwards joined the British forces as civilians or combatants.

Difficult, and indeed impossible, was the task of the Commissioners in maintaining a hard-and-fast rule between these classes, for the simple reason that many men of high character and ability, who were Whigs or of Conservative political views in the early stages of the Revolution, were compelled by their opposition to the Declaration of Independence to transfer their support to the side of the Crown.

In A. O. 13 are the original memorials and petitions of the Loyalists, with letters, certificates to their military service, and loyal conduct, original commissions in many cases, great numbers of official documents relating to their estates, special copies of the inquisitions in New Jersey into the affairs and political views of the Loyalists, conveyances of properties, copies of wills and other papers of interest. A. O. 12 consist of the volumes of evidence taken before the Commissioners, and copies of the memorials, the originals of which in several cases have been lost, or are damaged beyond recognition.

In A. O. 12:85 (ff.61-4) is a list of about 658 Loyalists, whose estates had been confiscated. This volume also contains the reports and remarks of John Anstey, barrister-at-law, who had been sent out to America by the Commissioners of American claims to investigate questions of confiscation and debts due to the Loyalists. There are also copies of official documents from New Jersey, relating to Loyalists' property.

It has been supposed that most of the Loyalists were recent emigrants; but such is not the case in New Jersey or in the other Colonies. In New Jersey's list will be found the names of no fewer than 237 who were born in America, mostly in New Jersey, and 36 others who were probably American-born. The birthplaces of 68 Loyalists are not recorded. Englishmen born rank next in point of numbers, with a total of 36, followed by 23 Irishmen. Fifteen were Scotsmen, three were Germans and one was a Portuguese.

The Loyalist papers were unknown to Bancroft among American historians, and to Trevelyan among English. The popular view of the character and attitude of the Loyalists in the Revolution has undergone considerable change in recent years, in consequence of these and other valuable historical documents.

The notes from W. O. 42 (American), with extracts from birth and marriage and other certificates, are now published for the first time, with the summaries of the other papers.

In these main pages will be found the names of about 130 officers of the New Jersey Volunteers, a Loyalist Regiment which was raised mainly by the exertions of General Cortlandt Skinner. The Regiment consisted at first of six Battalions, commanded by Elisha Lawrence, John Morris, Edward Vaughan Dongan, Abraham Van Buskirk, Joseph Barton and Isaac Allen, which were reduced, in or shortly after 1777, by casualties and other causes, to three Battalions. Scattered notices of engagements of the Regiment are noticed under officers' names.

The clergy of the Episcopal Church in New Jersey would seem to have been Loyalists, all. At their head stood the venerable Thomas Bradbury Chandler, who afterwards declined the new Bishopric of Nova Scotia, and among the others was that resolute supporter of the Crown, the Rev. Jonathan Odell, perhaps the most polished satirist on the Loyalist side.

Among many Loyalist-lawyers were several of distinction in their profession. First on the list is that pathetic figure and eminent jurist, regarded as the most highly educated lawyer in New Jersey in the early stages of the Revolution, leader of the Provincial Bar and Judge of the Supreme Court, David Ogden, whose appropriate family motto was, *"Et si ostendo non jacto."* As with many other prominent families, the Ogden family was divided in its allegiance in the great struggle, for David Ogden himself and three of his sons were Loyalists, while two other sons were staunch supporters of the American cause.

Governor Franklin's name may also be added to the roll of Loyalist-lawyers, as the proud claimant to membership of the Middle Temple and of the Bar of England, an honor which was shared by his successor, Governor William Livingston. Cortlandt Skinner was a successful lawyer, Attorney-General and Speaker of the House of Assembly, and was held in such high esteem by the British Commander-in-chief as to be appointed Brigadier General of the New Jersey Volunteers, a Regiment which included among its officers such lawyers as Isaac Allen, Edward Vaughan Dongan and Daniel Isaac Browne.

The list may be strengthened by the inclusion of Bernardus La Grange and of John Taylor, a prominent lawyer and father of two lawyer sons, Joseph and William, who carried on the family tradition of zealous supporters of the Crown. William Taylor was rewarded for his loyalty by the dignified appointment of Chief Justice of Jamaica. Prominent also in the legal annals of New Jersey was Philip Kearny, the father of no fewer than four sons as adherents of the British. Nor must the name be forgotten of Daniel Coxe, fourth bearer of a name honored in the history of the Province.

Loyal Quakers include the families of Hinchman, Woodward and Williams. The honorable profession of schoolmaster is represented by two or three Loyalists.

Many surgeons, physicians and apothecaries were steadfast Loyalists, as well as several pensioned officers of the regular British army, who had retired to New Jersey after the peace of 1763. Indeed, all ranks of Colonial society are represented —yeomen, laborers, men of leisure, and representatives of such conspicuous families as Kennedy, Van Cortlandt, Jouet, Lawrence, Leonard and Van Buskirk, in addition to those already specifically mentioned.

In the main text will be found 419 Loyalists regularly treated, and in Appendix III 1308 more, making in all 1727.

Of most of the Loyalists, not only in New Jersey, but also in other Colonies, it may well be said with Milton:

> "Their Loyalty they kept, their love, their zeal,
> Nor number, nor example with them wrought
> To swerve from truth, or change their constant mind."

E. ALFRED JONES.

THE LOYALISTS OF NEW JERSEY IN THE REVOLUTION

ISAAC ALLEN (Lieutenant-Colonel)

A Trenton lawyer, who was ever a uniform and loyal subject of Great Britain and took an early and active part in favor of that Government by joining his Majesty's troops under the command of Sir William Howe in New Jersey in December, 1776. Soon afterwards he raised, and was commissioned Lieutenant-Colonel Commandant of the 2nd New Jersey Volunteers, and ever after performed most arduous and active military duty in New York, the Jersies and particularly in Georgia, South and North Carolina. He was present at the taking and defense of Savannah and was afterwards on duty at Charleston, where he acted as Commandant previous to and on the evacuation of that city and of the province of South Carolina. Upon the final reduction of his corps at the Peace he went with a large family to form a settlement near Annapolis, in Nova Scotia, where he labored under a debility of constitution contracted on military duty in the South. In consequence of his loyalty he was attainted in Pennsylvania and proscribed in New Jersey, and his whole estate in both Colonies seized, confiscated and sold.

With this memorial (in A. O. 13:17), written by Daniel Coxe (q. v.), March 19, 1784, are the following documents:

A schedule and an estimate of his losses in property, including his dwelling house of stone, two stories high, in Trenton; a farm on the river Delaware, within half a mile of Trenton; a brick house of two stories on the west side of Fourth street, between High street and Chestnut street in Philadelphia; and a property in the Northern Liberties, called Spring Hill, or Bleaching Green, within two miles of the centre of Philadelphia.

An affidavit to the valuation of his real property, signed by Abraham Hunt, merchant, and Isaac de Cow, High Sheriff of Hunterdon county.

An account of his estate in Hunterdon county, confiscated and sold for £5,076 currency, March 25, 1779.

An affidavit that his estate in Hunterdon county had been seized, confiscated and sold, signed by Jared Sexton and Nathaniel Hunt, dated October 10, 1783.

A signed valuation of the property in Philadelphia, which had been bequeathed to Colonel Allen's wife, Sarah, by her father, Thomas Campbell, merchant, of Philadelphia, signed by Charles Jervis and Thomas Canby, October 18, 1783.

A long description of the Allen property in New Jersey and Philadelphia is in A. O. 12:16, ff. 212-222. He was granted £925 from his claim of £2,400. (A. O. 12:109).

His grandfather, Isaac Allen, emigrated from England. His father, John Allen, born in 1718, married, in 1738, ———— Watson, who had two other sons, John and William, and one daughter, Hannah. An Isaac Allen became counselor-at-law of New Jersey, May 16, 1765.

Upon the organization of the Canadian Province of New Brunswick, Colonel Isaac Allen was appointed a member of the Council and, on November 25, 1784, a puisne Judge of the Supreme Court. He died in October, 1806. His only son, John (born June 27, 1784), was for many years a Judge of the Inferior Court of Common Pleas for York county, New Brunswick; for over 25 years a member of the House of Assembly; Captain and Colonel of militia, and a member of the Executive Council before his death in 1875. His grandson, Sir John Campbell Allen, was Chief Justice of New Brunswick.

Colonel Allen's spinster daughters, Charlotte, Margaret, Anne, Sarah and Frances, were put on the Compassionate Fund in 1821 and 1822 (W. O. 25:3087, 3088).

Captain Peter Campbell (q. v.) was his brother-in-law.

(Ind.: 5604-5-6; A. O. 12:63, ff. 82-3; "Ontario Archives," pp. 248-250; Lawrence & Stockton, "Judges of New Brunswick and their Times," pp. 3, 59, 77, 141, 507; Sabine).

JOHN ALLEN

Of Hackensack was an active Loyalist, and no person was allowed by the Whigs to trade or to correspond with him. His four sons served with the British, three of them in the New

Jersey Volunteers. (A. O. 13:21). He settled at Burton, Province of New Brunswick.

JOSEPH ALLEN

He was of Lawrence Neck, Dover township, Monmouth county, and was the owner of 490 acres of land bought of Peter Benson in 1770. Here he remained on and off until 1780, though frequently arrested as a Loyalist. In the latter year he escaped from prison and went to New York, where he joined Major Ward and served in the Associated Loyalists. Joseph Allen succeeded in raising a Company of Loyalists, which he commanded at Bergen Neck from 1781 until the evacuation of New York by the British, when he went into exile at Quinte Bay in Canada. He was alive there in 1788. His property in Monmouth county, N. J., was forfeited February 9, 1784. The following is an abstract of affidavits in A. O. 13:17:

James Allen, April 20, 1786, states that he and others had surveyed the property of Joseph Allen and found it had contained 1,326 acres.

Margaret Runnelds and William Gifford, April 18, 1786, declared that Allen was plundered in October, 1779, by about 30 men commanded by Major Reuben Randolf, and that in March, 1780, he was taken prisoner by Captain Bigelow and 29 men, but escaped.

Affidavits of John Stillwell, 1784, and William Howel and Joseph Miller, 1786, regarding his property.

There is also a schedule of his property, including a sloop of 30 tons, cattle and horses, valued at £4,760 currency, equal to £2,856. 2. 11 sterling.

Joseph Allen was allowed £1,050 from his claim of £2,856. (A. O. 12:109; "Ontario Archives," pp. 262, 1270-'1).

ASA (or ASHER) ALLWARD

Lived with his father in Woodbridge; he was at St. John, New Brunswick, in 1787. The sum of £25 was allowed from his claim of £105. (A. O. 12:16, ff. 270-2; A. O. 12:63, f. 91; A. O. 12:109).

BENJAMIN ALLWARD

Of Woodbridge, farmer, a zealous Loyalist, fled to New York in an old and infirm state. He had proposed an Association of Loyalists in New Jersey, which was signed by many, including all his sons. His former neighbors, John Ford and Steven Kent, swore on oath at New York on June 18, 1783, to the value of his property. There is an affidavit to the sale of his confiscated estate in 1779. (A. O. 13:17). In 1787 he was living at Manowagonish, New Brunswick. (A. O. 12:16, ff. 170-6; A. O. 12:63, f. 80).

He was allowed £706 from his claim of £1,361. 16s. (A. O. 12:109).

SILAS ALLWARD

A farmer, of Woodbridge, fled from home and joined the British troops on Staten Island in July, 1776. He was living in New Brunswick, Canada, in 1786. His claim was rejected. (A. O. 13:21).

JOHN ALSTON (Captain)

He was born in America about 1740 and served in the New Jersey Volunteers. He was on the seconded list in 1783. (Ind.: 5605).

There were three of the name whose estates were confiscated in Middlesex county, N. J., on September 22, 1778, viz., David, Jonathan and Lewis, all of Woodbridge, and Capt. John probably belonged to that family. (Midd. Records).

PETER ANDERSON

He was born in America about 1750 and on December 15, 1776, was appointed Ensign in the 5th New Jersey Volunteers, from which he was transferred to Major [Robert] Rogers's King's Rangers in June, 1779, on the nomination of Captain Samuel Hayden (q. v.). He died about 1827. (Ind.: 5605-6).

Stryker states that he was a member of Governor Franklin's Board of Associated Loyalists at New York and that he died at Fredericton, New Brunswick, aged 95.

OZIAS ANSLEY

He was born in America about 1743, and had a plantation of 100 acres in Sussex county, N. J., which was confiscated and sold. On August 25, 1780, he was appointed Ensign in the 1st New Jersey Volunteers, after four years service as a private in a Loyalist corps. He acted as Adjutant and Quartermaster of this Battalion. He settled in Sussex Vale, King's county, Province of New Brunswick, on his free grant of land and his half-pay, and was there a magistrate and a Judge of the Court of Common Pleas.

Ozias Ansley was married, as a widower, to Elizabeth Johnson, widow, in the United Brethren's Moravian Church, at New Dorp, Staten Island, New York, by the Rev. Nathaniel Brown, on October 23, 1805. Here he died on September 5, 1828. (W. O. 42:A8; Register of Births and Marriages, p. 63). His son, the Rev. Thomas Ansley, an Episcopalian, died at St. Andrews, New Brunswick, in 1831, aged about 65.

(Ind.: 5605-6; A. O. 13:90; Sabine; Am. MSS. in Roy Inst., iii, 348).

JOHN ANTILL (Major)

Major John Antill was the son of Hon. Edward Antill, of Perth Amboy, N. J., and was born about 1745. He was admitted to the New Jersey Bar in 1767. He held several public offices with general approval before the War, namely, Secretary of the Supreme Court of Judicature, Surrogate, Keeper of the Records and Clerk of the Council, all of which were obtained by purchase for the sum of £2,900 sterling and yielded an annual income of £600. He was also the holder of other offices before and during the War, such as Clerk of the General Post Office in America from 1775 to 1778, agent for the packet boats, and one of the six Clerks of Chancery.

As an "obnoxious Tory" this lawyer was under the necesity of taking refuge on board H. M. S. "Phoenix" in March, 1776, and remained there until the arrival of the British Army. With his brother-in-law, Lieutenant-Colonel John Morris, of Shrewsbury, New Jersey (a retired Lieutenant in the 47th Regiment of Foot in the British Army), he was instrumental in raising in 1776 the Second Battalion of the well-known Loyalist Regiment, the New Jersey Volunteers, commanded by Cortlandt Skinner. To his mortification, Major John Antill, as he then was, was later cashiered (Aug. 15, 1780), for making false returns and drawing provisions for more men than the effective strength of his battalion, but was shortly afterwards re-instated.

With Lieutenant-Colonel Elisha Lawrence, Antill was one of the accredited agents of the seconded officers of the Loyalist Regiments to secure settlements for them in Nova Scotia. Parr, the Governor of that Province, was dissatisfied with his conduct there, and wrote, on August 15, 1783, to General Sir Guy Carleton, complaining of his "unreasonable demands and illiberal ideas" on behalf of the seconded officers. Carleton, in his reply, expressed regret that those officers had "made choice of so improper a person as Major Antill to act as their agent."

John Antill married (1) on April 21, 1770, Margaret, daughter of Alexander and Elizabeth (Nicholls) Colden, of New York, who died in Canada, in 1783; and (2), his deceased wife's sister, Jane Colden. By his first wife he had three children.

For the loss of his real estate in New Jersey he was awarded by the British Government the sum of £2,900, as well as £340 for the loss of his annual professional income. In addition to these grants he received a pension and half-pay as Major until January, 1813, when they ceased, probably after his death.

Major John Antill was also the owner of about 9,000 acres of land in his own right in the Province of New York, and between 3,000 and 4,000 acres in right of his first wife, valued by him at £3,000 sterling, besides a large tract devised to him by Cadwallader Colden, late Lieutenant-Governor of New York. Debts due to him on bonds and notes amounted to about £3,500 sterling. The Commissioners reported on his case that he had lost very fair prospects as a lawyer in America. The Revolution drove him into another profession, in which he made his way very well. (A. O. 12:100, f. 248).

John Collins Antill, eldest son of John Antill and his first wife, Margaret Colden, became Major in the 76th Regiment and died in Ceylon, without issue. Henry Colden Antill, another son, born in 1779, left America at an early age and served in the army in India, receiving a medal for courage at the battle of Seringapatam. He returned to England at the end of the campaign and within a few months went out to Australia as aide-de-camp to John Macquarie, Governor of New South Wales. There he settled and married Eliza Wills in 1818.

(A. O. 12:14, ff. 281-7; 12:109; 13:108, 113; Ind. 5605-'6. Also in "Hist. MSS., Com. Rep. on the American MSS. in the Royal Institution," Vol. IV, pp. 60, 280, 334; Stryker's "N. J. Volunteers (Loyalists)," p. 31; "N. J. Archives," Third Series, Vol. 11, p. 47, and authorities there cited).

JOHN ATCHISON

An Englishman, born about 1752, who had seen service with the British army before the American Revolution. In 1781 he was appointed Ensign in the Loyal Foresters and on November 10 in the same year he was transferred to the 1st New Jersey Volunteers, becoming Adjutant on May 25, 1782.

He was married on February 22, 1788, at Maugerville, New Brunswick, to Sarah Cranmer, of St. John, and the certificate was signed by Captain Peter Campbell (q. v.). He died on November 2, 1810, at Fredericton, New Brunswick, and was buried with military honors, the service having been conducted by the Rev. Jonathan Odell (q. v.). (W. O. 42:A11; Ind.: 5605-6).

DR. ABSALOM BAINBRIDGE

Born at Maidenhead (now Lawrenceville), New Jersey, in 1742, son of Edmund and Abigail Bainbridge, and a descendant of Sir Arthur Bainbridge, of Co. Durham, England. He was graduated at Princeton College in 1762. He is said to have practised medicine in his native village of Maidenhead until 1773, when he removed to Princeton, and at the outbreak of the War was "happily and independently" settled there in a very extensive practice as a physician and surgeon. Dr. Bainbridge joined the British army on the first invasion of New Jersey in 1776 and his house became the headquarters of the Commander-in-chief, Sir William Howe. In consequence, he was declared guilty of high treason against the State and all his considerable property, including a plantation of 400 acres in Princeton, described in a schedule, was confiscated and sold.

With this schedule and his memorial is a copy of a conveyance in 1729 of land in Maidenhead township from John Bainbridge to his son, Edmund; and an extract from the will dated July 17, 1763, of Edmund Bainbridge, (who died in 1770), leaving property to his son, Absalom, this Loyalist, whose share, if he died before the age of 21, was left in equal shares to his (Absalom's) brothers and sisters, John, Peter, Edmund, Abigail and Sarah. (A. O. 13:107; A. O. 13:108).

Absalom Bainbridge went in 1777 to Flatbush, L. I., and later to New York City. He was appointed surgeon to the 3rd New Jersey Volunteers in 1778.

This early President of the Medical Society of New Jersey (in 1773) died in New York on June 23, 1807, and, with his wife, was buried in a Trinity Church vault. He had been supported in part upon his pension and his half-pay and upon the interest or capital of £2,250 granted to him as compensation by the British Government from his claim of £5,762. His loss of professional income during the War was also met by a grant at the rate of £140 a year. (A. O. 12:109).

His wife, Mary, was the daughter of John Taylor, of Monmouth county, and sister of William and Joseph Taylor (q. v.). His son, Commodore William Bainbridge, was in command of the frigate "Constitution," and another son, Joseph, was also a Captain in the United States Navy. His great-grandson, the Rev. Dr. John Maclean, became alma mater, i. e., President of Princeton College. (A. O. 13:83; A. O. 12:14, ff. 139-144; A. O. 12:101, f. 255; Ind. 5605; Stryker; Sabine; Wicke's "Hist. of N. J. Medicine," p. 131).

JOHN BAKER

He was an Englishman of Bergen county, and not only bore arms, but acted as guide and spy for Lord Cornwallis. In 1787 he was living in the 4th township, above Cataraqui, in Canada. (A. O. 13:17; A. O. 12:16, ff. 432-4; A. O. 12:63.

f. 127). He was granted £15 from his claim of £20. (A. O. 12:109).

DANIEL BANCROFT

He was born in Westfield, Mass., Nov. 2, 1746; his wife was Mary Magdalen Valleau. He served for six years on the Loyalist side in the American Revolutionary War. There is no record of the name of the corps in which he had served before his appointment as surgeon to the 3rd New Jersey Volunteers in February, 1781. Daniel Bancroft remained on half-pay as a surgeon of the 2nd Battalion until 1804. (Ind.: 5605-6). Wickes, however, says he died in Philadelphia in 1796. (Wickes' "Hist. of N. J. Medicine," p. 133).

JAMES BANKS

Ensign from October 24, 1781, in the 3rd New Jersey Volunteers, was alive at the Peace and was in receipt of half-pay. (Ind.: 5604).

WILLIAM BANKS

An Englishman, born about 1732, who had served in the army for fifteen years as a private and non-commissioned officer before the Revolution, in which he served on the British side from the outbreak of hostilities. He was rewarded for his services by a commission as Ensign in the 2nd New Jersey Volunteers and was on the half-pay list until 1810, when he probably died. (Ind.: 5605; Stryker).

WEART BANTA

He was of Hackensack, born in New Jersey, but had settled as a carpenter and joiner in New York. In 1774 he was obliged to quit this city "for being a Tory" and for assisting Alderman Blagg to remove a Loyalist, one Moore, off a cart when about to be tarred and feathered by a mob who were using him "very rough." Banta himself escaped from the mob to Albany and there remained in peace for some time, until requested by the committee to sign an Association. Having refused he was taken up as a Tory and imprisoned for ten months. He escaped to New York, then in possession of British troops, and was employed in recruiting and in procuring intelligence. Among other active services rendered by Banta was that of capturing "the infamous Brown," the murderer of Captain John Richards. He also captured with the aid of only five men, the American General Ward and Colonel Bradford, after first disarming the General's guard of a sergeant and 16 men.

Weart Banta would seem to have been of a courageous and enterprising nature; he was on several expeditions to intercept the Colonial mails and was sent by General Sir William Howe to reconnoitre Fort Montgomery, a service successfully accomplished, and afterwards was present with the British force which took that fort. As a guide he was with the Light Infantry which once fell upon and is said to have "destroyed" Gen. George Washington's Light Horse. In all these services he was considered most useful, but the promised commission was not given to him until February 2, 1779, when he was appointed a Lieutenant in the King's Militia Volunteers. On March 28, 1779, he was severely wounded in an engagement in New Jersey and permanently disabled. Inquisition against him in Bergen county, N. J., was found in October, 1780.

He was working as a carpenter at Shelburne in Nova Scotia in 1786, and from 1788 to 1804 he was in receipt of a military allowance of £70.

Sieba Banta is mentioned in A. O. 12:110, ff. 23-4.

Captain John Richards, mentioned above, was a native of Barbadoes, but long a resident of and Loyalist in New Jersey, where he inherited a "genteel estate." He was foully murdered in 1778 and his murderer rewarded with a Captain's commission. (T. Jones: "Hist. of New York in the Revolution," I, 280-1).

(A. O. 13:17; A. O. 12:15, ff. 200-4; A. O. 12:102, f. 162; Ind.: 5606; "Am. MSS. in Roy. Inst.," ii, 98).

JOHN BARBERIE (Captain)

He was born in 1751 and was the son of John Barberie and his wife, Gertrude, daughter of Andrew Johnston of Perth Amboy, and a brother of Major Oliver Barberie (q. v.). He served as Captain in the New Jersey Volunteers; was taken prisoner at Staten Island in 1777 and sent to Trenton, N. J.; was wounded in the memorable siege of Ninety-Six, on May 22, 1781, and at the battle of Eutaw Springs on September 8, 1781. At the end of the War he settled with his brother, Oliver, on their grants of land in New Brunswick, Canada, where he was married, at St. John, on July 21, 1784, to Mary Ann Stockton, daughter of Major Richard W. Stockton (q. v.) of the New Jersey Volunteers. Captain Barberie became a Colonel of militia and a magistrate of York county in this Canadian province, while his son, Andrew, became a member of the Provincial Assembly. He died on June 19, 1818, in the parish of Sussex, King's county, New Brunswick.

John Barberie, his father, was a descendant of French Protestants. He died July 23, 1770, at the age of 50, and was buried in the graveyard of St. Peter's Church, Perth Amboy. He was Collector of the Port of Perth Amboy.

Andrew Barberie, a brother (Sabine says, "son") of Captain John and Major Oliver Barberie, was (according to Whitehead's book) placed in the Royal Navy and was shot on board a War vessel in the course of the American War of Independence. (W. O. 42: B2; Ind.: 5605-6; Sabine; Stryker; Whitehead's "Early Hist. of Perth Amboy").

OLIVER BARBERIE (Major)

He was a brother of Capt. John Barberie, above named, and son of John and Gertrude Barberie, of Perth Amboy, and was born in 1756. He had studied law under Cortlandt Skinner (q. v.) before joining the New Jersey Volunteers in December, 1776. On February 15, 1778, he was transferred from the rank of Ensign in the New Jersey Volunteers to that of Lieutenant in the Loyal American Regiment, commanded by Colonel Beverley Robinson, and in 1780 he was transferred to the Provincial Light Infantry. Oliver Barberie served for about eighteen months in the arduous campaigns in the Southern colonies. A blank now occurs in the military career of the young Loyalist, but, on September 25, 1787, he appears in the rank of Ensign in the 41st Regiment of Foot, and in January, 1788, he was in London on the way to join his Regiment at Portsmouth. His service in the regular army would seem to have been short, for in 1788 he returned to half-pay as Lieutenant of American Provincials.

Oliver Barberie married an American lady from his own birthplace, Euphemia Skinner, daughter of his former legal mentor, Brigadier-Gen. Cortlandt Skinner. The marriage took place on June 17, 1801, at Holyhead, in North Wales, while he was holding the office of Barrackmaster and Major in the army. She died at that place, in the house of her brother, Captain John Skinner, in 1830, aged 64. Major Barberie died in London on May 2, 1824. Their two sons, John and Cortlandt Barberie, were legatees under the will of their maternal uncle, Lieutenant-General Philip Kearny Skinner (q. v.). Oliver's and also Captain John's shares in the Barberie property in New Jersey were confiscated. (A. O. 13:13; A. O. 13:22; A. O. 13:108; W. O. 42:33; Ind.: 5604-5-6; A. O. 12:102, f. 185).

JOHN BARNES (Major)

This Loyalist lived for many years as a distiller in Queen street (now Greene street), Trenton, N. J., before the Revolution. He had taken an active part in the military affairs of the State, first as a Lieutenant, from August 23, 1746, in the Company of Captain John Dagworthy, Junior, in which he was granted a commission on the representation of that officer to John Hamilton, President of His Majesty's Council and Commander-in-chief of the Province of New Jersey, as an acknowledgment of his services in recruiting men for the intended Expedition to Canada. His original commission, in which he is described as "gentleman," is preserved in the Public Record Office in London. (A. O. 13; 108).

He was afterwards appointed by Governor William Franklin to the dignified office of "High Sheriff of Hunterdon County," a lucrative office, which produced him an annual income of about £600 in fees, in New Jersey currency, and which he held until the Declaration of Independence. Having espoused the Loyalist cause he was deprived of this office at that time. We next hear of him with the British army at New Brunswick, N. J., in November, 1776, when he was appointed Major in the First Battalion of the New Jersey Volunteers. He lost his life in the attack on the British posts on Staten Island, New York, by General Sullivan, being wounded on August 22, 1777, and dying nine days later.

This Loyalist's house at Trenton is described as a large and commodious mansion, two stories high, with stables and other buildings, the whole of which property was confiscated and sold by the State. In his will he left his estate to his wife, Mary, and, after her decease, to his niece, Sarah Hooton Barnes, whom failing, to the daughters of his sister, Rachel Stelle (perhaps the wife of Pontius Stelle, a member of the Assembly of New Jersey and a Commissioner for the Disbursement of the funds for the Expedition to Canada, for which Major Barnes had been so zealous in recruiting). His widow lived upon a Loyalist pension granted by the British Government until her death, April 14, 1807.

Stryker describes this Loyalist as "much lamented as a worthy man and a gallant soldier." (The references for the official documents in this case (in London) are: A. O. 12:14, ff. 260-267; A. O. 12:100, f. 147; A. O. 12:109; and Ind.: 8229. Another source which may be consulted is the "Historical MSS. Com. Report on the American MSS. in the Royal Institution," Vol. IV, pp. 284, 318. See also Stryker's "N. J. Volunteers (Loyalists)" in the Rev., p. 31).

ELLIS BARRON

He was born at Woodbridge, N. J., and lived on his own property. He served on the Committee of Observation of Middlesex county, N. J., from Woodbridge, in January, 1775, and became Captain in the First Regiment in Middlesex county, serving thus on the American side until the entry of the British troops in New Jersey, when he became a Loyalist. With his memorial are an account of his real estate and an official affidavit to the sale of his confiscated property. In 1786 he was living in the United States. (A. O. 13:17; A. O. 13:90; A. O. 12:15, ff. 383-8; A. O. 12:63, f. 50; "Min. of Prov. Congress").

JAMES BARTON (Ensign)

This Loyalist was born in America, probably in New Jersey, in or about 1763, and was commissioned Ensign in the 1st New Jersey Volunteers, in September, 1780, or August 14, 1781. He was put on half-pay at the end of the War. (Ind.: 5604-5-6). How closely he was related to Lieut.-Col. Joseph Barton (q. v.), of Sussex county does not appear.

JOSEPH BARTON (Lieut.-Colonel)

He was a farmer of Newtown (now Newton), Sussex county, N. J., and was born in America about 1723. He was an agent for the East Jersey Proprietors. From 1775 until the Summer of 1776 he was a member of the House of Assembly for Sussex county, and not only opposed the measures of the Provincial Congress in the early stages of the Revolution, but was "the only member of Assembly who voted against Governor Franklin's imprisonment as an enemy to the liberties of his country." He joined the British army in 1776, and was appointed by General Sir William Howe to raise a Battalion for the New Jersey Volunteers, and took command of the First Battalion from November 7, 1776. He was captured on Staten Island, Aug. 22, 1777.

Peter Hopkins, formerly a member of the House of Assembly of New Jersey, and James Broderick, of Sussex county, both presumably Loyalists, testified on oath to Barton's property before David Mathews, last Mayor of New York under the Crown, on September 10, 1783. (A. O. 13:90).

With the Barton papers are a copy of the inquisition and proceedings against him in New Jersey as a Loyalist; the original certificate of Governor Franklin to his loyalty, dated September 1, 1779; a list of his losses; schedules of his property, and lists of bonds, with the names of his debtors and the amounts. His son was in possession of part of his property in New Jersey in 1786, while he himself was an exile at Digby, in Nova Scotia. This son was probably Henry L. Barton, born about 1761, who was Ensign from 1780 in the 1st New Jersey Volunteers and Lieutenant from 1782, and who was on the half-pay list until 1802. (Ind.: 5605-6, and Stryker).

Col. Barton was on the list of Seconded officers, Prince of Wales' American Volunteers from 1792 (W. O. 24:711; Ind.: 5605). The sum of £1,814 was granted to him as compensation from his claim of £3,955. 6s. (A. O. 12: 109). A long list of his confiscated properties and the names of the previous owners is in "Ontario Archives" (pp. 600-5), together with the names of some purchasers. Evidence in his favor as "an honest and loyal subject" was given by Oliver de Lancey and Governor Franklin, April 30, 1781. ("Am. MSS. in Roy Inst.," II; 273; A. O. 13:17; A. O. 12:15, ff. 274-291; A. O. 12:63, ff. 35-6; "Am. MSS. in Roy. Inst.," I:150; Stryker.

Rev. DANIEL BATWELL

This English-born clergyman appears to have had no ministerial association with New Jersey, and finds a place in this account solely from his appointments as Chaplain, first to the West Jersey Volunteers and, from October 25, 1778, to the 4th New Jersey Volunteers. Previously, from 1774, he had been a missionary of the Society for the Propagation of the Gospel to three congregations in Pennsylvania, at York, Carlisle and Huntingdon, and was the owner of 265 acres of land in Cumberland county, Pa. By a resolve of Congress, dated December 27, 1777, he was given the alternative of taking the oath of allegiance to the State of Pennsylvania or removing into the British lines. As a staunch Loyalist he chose the second course. He declared he had already suffered much for speaking his loyal principles; that a loaded musket was levelled at him with threats of violence, and that he was thrown into the river by the populace and imprisoned for five months, while his wife was insane.

This clergyman was educated at Corpus Christi College, Cambridge, and was for some years a distinguished preacher in London before the American Revolution. He received a pension and half-pay as military chaplain before his death, on April 2, 1802. His widow, Bithia, died on April 5, 1803. (A. O. 459:7; A. O. 463:23; A. O. 461:18; A. O. 13:70; A. O. 13:83; A. O. 12:42, ff. 306-310; A. O. 12:106, f. 75; T. 50:6; Ind.: 5604-5-6; Venn, "Alumni Cantab.").

STEPHEN BEDELL

An American-born Loyalist, who joined the British army in 1777 and his property was confiscated. He is described in one paper as late of the county of Richmond, New York, and in another as of New Jersey. (A. O. 13:90). There were Bedells in both Morris and Essex counties, N. J., but this Stephen yet remains unidentified.

JOSEPH BEERS (Ensign)

He was born in America about 1753 and served throughout the War in a Loyalist corps, as Ensign in the 5th New Jersey Volunteers and in Major Robert Rogers's King's Rangers. Once more he took up arms in defence of Great Britain, on this occasion at the beginning of the French War in 1793, when he was commissioned Lieutenant in the Prince Edward Island Fencibles, in which he served until the reduction of that corps upon the Peace of Amiens. He appears to have settled in this Island in the St. Lawrence soon after the Peace of 1783, and was there married, on August 16, 1795, to Margaret Hayden, by the Rev. Theophilus Desbrisay, Rector of Charlotte Parish and Chaplain to the garrison of the Island. Here he died on March 22, 1810, at Cherry Valley, near Charlottetown, leaving a widow and six children, namely, Joseph, born in 1796; Matilda, born in 1798; Henrietta Christina, born in 1799; Margaret, born in 1802; Thomas, born in 1804; and Maria, born early in 1810. His wife was probably a daughter of Captain Samuel Hayden (q. v.). She received a pension from the British Government after her husband's death and his five daughters were put on the Compassionate Fund for £8 a year each in 1820. (W. O. 42: B9; Ind.: 5605-6).

WILLIAM BEERS

He was of Woodbridge, joined the British army and consequently his property was confiscated. "Godbeer" would seem to have been his correct name. He was at Maugerville, New Brunswick, in 1787. He claimed £414. 11s., and was allowed £107. (A. O. 12:109; A. O. 12:16, ff. 324-8; A. O. 12:63, f. 99).

ANDREW BELL

He was born in Philadelphia, Pa., June 4, 1757, the son of John Bell, of Withern, England, who died in 1778, and he was living on an estate called "Bellfield," Bridgewater township, Somerset county, N. J., at the outbreak of the War. At the same time he was studying law under Cortlandt Skinner (q. v.). In December, 1776, he was appointed a confidential clerk in the office of the British Commander-in-Chief in New York and remained in that service under different Commanders until the end of the War (A. O. 12:15, ff. 322-6), although, from June 17 to July 2, 1778, he was with the army of Gen. Sir Henry Clinton in its march across New Jersey from Philadelphia to New York. During that march the Battle of Monmouth occurred. It was this period during which he kept a "Journal," which was published in the "New Jersey Historical Society's Proceedings" in 1851. (Vol. VI, First Series, p. 15).

In A. O. 13:17 are copies of the inquisition and proceedings against him, and official documents concerning the sale of the Bell estate, confiscated by the State of New Jersey at the January Term of Court in Somerset County, 1779. He was residing in New York in 1786, but was about to remove to Nova Scotia. (A. O. 12:63, f. 42).

According to his own sworn statement on file in London, his father, John Bell, left considerable property, real and personal, by will, to the son, viz., about 50 acres of land, including house and barn, in Bridgewater township, also a negro and furniture, all of which were confiscated. He placed their value at £1,110. He also states that at the end of the War, wishing to have some permanent provision, he applied to Sir Guy Carleton (in whose office he was) for an appointment. Carleton said he had so few offices to dispose of that it might be impossible to serve him, but recommended him to go to England, which claimant intended, and a friend, Captain Cochran, had promised him a passage, but he was prevented from going by the death of a near relative. However, Sir Guy Carleton, as a mark of approbation, gave him money to bear his expenses in England. He intended to have gone the next Spring, but did not. In 1783 he was a petitioner for lands in Nova Scotia.

He was then included in a survey of lands in the Province of Sissiboo. Claimant paid his proportion of expense in sending an agent. Claimant's share was to be 1,000 acres. The grant was not made out when his affidavit was made at Halifax, Nova Scotia, May 8, 1786. His statements as to value of property were corroborated by Dr. James Boggs (q. v.) and William Drake (q. v.). It seems the claim actually made for loss of property was £624. 7s., and there was allowed and paid to him £456. It is doubtful if he obtained the 1,000 acres sought in Nova Scotia; at all events in 1786 he settled at Perth Amboy, N. J., became Collector of the Port (1800-1801), Surveyor-General of East Jersey Proprietors (1804-1842), and an active officer in St. Peter's church in that city. He was married in New York City, Sept. 23, 1782 to Susannah Moore, a widow, who had been an O'Brien, daughter of Daniel and Margaret O'Brien. They left no children.

Andrew Bell died in Perth Amboy, July 19, 1847, aged 92 years, and in that city was greatly respected. He had one sister, Cornelia, who became the first wife of Hon. William Paterson, Attorney-General and Governor of New Jersey, Justice of the U. S. Supreme Court, etc. (See, in addition to previous references, A. O. 15:473-9; "Calendar of Original Memorials," Vol. 1, pp. 277-8; Jones' "St. Peter's Church, Perth Amboy," pp. 201-2).

MATTHEW BENSON

This Loyalist was born in America and lived in Bergen county, N. J. He bore arms in the King's Orange Rangers. His estate in Bergen county was confiscated at the January Term of Court, 1780. In 1787 he was living at Cataraqui in Canada. With his memorial is a list of his losses. (A. O. 13:17; A. O. 12:63, f. 126). He claimed £142. 17s. and was allowed £39. (A. O. 12:109).

NICHOLAS BICKLE (PICKLE)

He was of Alexandra township, Hunterdon county, N. J., and said he "escaped from prison loaded with irons" in October, 1777. He was, no doubt, of the well-known Pickle family of that county. An account of his losses is preserved in

A. O. 13:17. He was at Kingston, Province of New Brunswick, in 1787. The sum of £62 was granted to him from his claim of £521. (A. O. 12:109; A. O. 12:16, ff. 248-251; A. O. 12:63, f. 87; Chambers "Early Germans").

WILLIAM BLAIN

This Scotsman emigrated to New Jersey in 1774 and bought a plantation at Woodbridge. In 1776, he said, the Americans conceived that he had great influence over the natives of Great Britain, particularly the recent emigrants from Scotland, and requested him to raise a Company of Scotsmen to oppose the British, "with cogent promises of future preferment, emoluments, etc." But, "actuated as he was with a warm attachment to his Majesty's Government and person," he not only refused to comply with these requests, but also disapproved of and censured the rebellious proceedings, though well aware of the hardship and distress which would be inflicted upon him, as well as the loss of his property. He was cast into prison and suffered much. Upon his release he fled to the woods and concealed himself, receiving food by stealth.

This Loyalist joined the British army in New Jersey in 1777, although 52 years of age, and took up arms as a volunteer. Later he joined the Volunteers commanded by Major Stephen Skinner (q. v.) in New York. He claims to have been the first Loyalist in New Jersey to suffer for his loyalty. (A. O. 13:108). The Commissioners reported on his case that, if he had been a native American, they would have been called upon to recommend a larger allowance. (A. O. 12:100, f. 318).

William Blain died on July 26, 1784, leaving a widow, Barbara, who had remained in New Jersey for two months after her husband's flight, until at last she, too, was "obliged to quit by threats of violence from, and of the destruction of her home by the Rebels, if she persisted in remaining there." Her father was Samuel McKenna (q. v.). ("Loyalist Claims," pp. 207-8). She was awarded £253, from her claim of £1,164. 10 s. (A. O. 12:109).

THOMAS BLAKENEY

An Irishman, who was resident in the English Neighbourhood at Fort Lee, Bergen county, N. J. He joined the British in 1776 and acted as a guide to the army under Lord Cornwallis in New Jersey; he served as an Express for 17 months and was pressed into the Royal Navy, in which he served until the end of the War. His father-in-law was Thomas Moore. His wife remained in New Jersey and married there in his lifetime. (A. O. 12:14, ff. 254-8).

The Rev. Garret Lydecker (q. v.), in evidence in London on November 22, 1786, was doubtful of Blakeney's ownership of the house and land which he claimed, as his father-in-law, Thomas Moore, had taken possession of this property before the Revolution because of a dispute between Blakeney and his wife, who had since married again. The pastor had a bad opinion of the Irishman's conduct as a "private man." His memorial of March 14, 1788, is endorsed: "The Board cannot do anything for him" (A. O. 13:108), and his claim of £465 was disallowed. (A. O. 12:109).

URIAH BLEAU, or BLAAU (Ensign)

He was born in New York City; in 1777 was commissioned Captain, but in 1777 was appointed Ensign in the New Jersey Volunteers. His father, a Loyalist, was possessed of considerable property and died before July, 1784, leaving ten children. (A. O. 12:100, f. 336). He was taken prisoner at the Battle of Eutaw Springs by the forces under General Greene. (Stryker).

WALDRON BLEAU, or BLAAU (Captain)

He also was of New York City, where he signed the address to Admiral Howe and General Howe on their occupation of the city in 1776. He first joined the New Jersey Volunteers in November, 1776, and was commissioned Captain in the 4th Battalion of that Regiment on July 24, 1781. (Ind.: 5604). He served through all the War. All his New York City property was confiscated, but was later restored to his widow and daughter. He died within a week of his arrival at St. John, New Brunswick, in 1783. (Stryker). A widow, Eleanor

Blaau, of an officer in an American Loyalist corps, is on the widow's Index in Ind.: 8229.

JOANNA BLUNT

She was the widow of an officer in the New Jersey Volunteers and was, as such, put on the pension list in 1804. (W. O. 24: 847-854).

Dr. JAMES BOGGS

A native of Delaware, son of Ezekial Boggs, who came thither from Ireland. He was born Jan. 22, 1740, at New Castle, Del., studied medicine in Philadelphia and located as a physician at Shrewsbury, New Jersey, about 1764. His real property there, bought in 1773 from Stoffel Loggan, and valued at £450 sterling, was confiscated by the State, May 18, 1779. When the War broke out he joined the British and was taken on board the sloop of war "Swan." In 1779 he received a commission as surgeon's mate in the General Hospital in New York City. He was also the same in the 2nd New Jersey Volunteers and later was promoted surgeon. In September, 1783, he was appointed by Sir Guy Carleton, Commander-in-Chief, an assistant surgeon on the Staff. He was granted compensation £530 for the loss of his real estate and for the loss of his professional income. (A. O. 12:109).

Dr. James Boggs was described by the Commissioners for American Claims in London as a "meritorious Loyalist". He had a large family, his wife's name being Mary, dau. of Robert Hunter Morris, Chief Justice of New Jersey, whom he married Nov. 24, 1765. After the War he accepted the appointment, first as mate and afterwards (Nov. 22, 1798) as surgeon, to the garrison at Halifax, Nova Scotia, where he died, July 8, 1830, at the age of 90. There is an account of the sales of his confiscated property in 1779, and a copy of the conveyance of property by the above Stoffel Loggan, blacksmith, and his wife, Cornelia, of Shrewsbury, to James Boggs. (A. O. 13:17). He had five children. (A. O. 12:15, ff 1-6; A. O. 12:63, fl; A. O. 13:83; "Ontario Archives," pp. 35-6; Stryker; Kemble Papers in "New York Hist. Soc. Colls.", 1883, p. 469; Wickes "Hist. of N. J. Medicine," p. 160; "The Boggs

Family," Halifax, N. S., 1916, p. 10 et seq.; Jones' History of St. Peter's Church, Perth Amboy, N. J., 1924, p. 204 et seq.).

ISAAC BONNELL (Lieutenant)

He was born in New Jersey (perhaps being the son of Nathaniel, of Elizabethtown), and lived at Perth Amboy, where he was appointed in 1770 Barrackmaster for the Province. In June, 1775, he was appointed Sheriff of Middlesex county, but was removed from this office in 1776, when, in July, as a Loyalist, he was arrested and paroled to reside at Cranbury and not to depart from there. He subsequently was released upon taking the oath not to bear allegiance to King George, and it is said he served once in the American militia. He, however, joined the British army the same year (1776), and in 1777 was commissioned Lieutenant in the Prince of Wales's American Regiment, raised in that year. He was the partner of Abraham Veal in the sloop "Lively," which was impressed by Cortlandt Skinner (q. v.) for the use of the army. His estate in Perth Amboy was entailed on his three children and, therefore, saved from confiscation; but there is an official account of the sales of other property confiscated, in A. O. 13:17.

His wife, Grace, whom he married in 1763, was the daughter of Thomas Fox, who gave her a house and other property in Perth Amboy. His son, William Franklin Bonnell, was the godson of Governor Franklin. In 1786 Isaac Bonnell was living at Digby, Nova Scotia, and was a Justice of the Peace and Judge of the Common Pleas. His small pension of £15 was paid to him until 1805, probably the date of his death. He had been granted compensation of £210 from his claim of £635. 12s., and at the rate of £30 a year during the War for the loss of his income as Barrackmaster. (A. O. 12:15, ff. 119-123; A. O. 12:63, f. 13; A. O. 12:74, ff. 279-281; A. O. 12:109; "Min. of Prov. Congress").

DANIEL BOWEN (Captain)

This Captain was born in America about 1742 and was a joiner at Rhodes Town, Cumberland county, New Jersey, where his property was confiscated and sold. He joined the British army in August, 1777, at Philadelphia, and acted as a guide on several occasions; furthermore, he raised a Company of Loyalists for the West Jersey Volunteers, whose Commandant, Major John Vandyke (q. v.), described him in a certificate as a vigilant and brave officer. This Corps having been united with the New Jersey Volunteers, Daniel Bowen was given a Captaincy in that Regiment by Sir William Howe on March 21, 1778, and he continued on service on Long Island for the remainder of the War.

Captain Bowen settled with his wife (born about 1749) at Wilmot, Nova Scotia, at the Peace and was granted half-pay; he died at Burford, district of London, Upper Canada, on September 4, 1819, at the age of about 78. He was married on December 31, 1766, to Sarah Daniel, in Hopewell, Cumberland county, New Jersey, by the Rev. Robert Kelso [Kelsey]. He was compensated to the amount of £180 from his claim of £240. (A. O. 12:109; W. O. 42:B18; Ind.: 5606; A. O. 13:17; A. O. 13:90; A. O. 12:16, ff. 18-20; A. O. 12:63,f. 69; "Ontario Archives," p. 708).

EDWARD BOWLBY

Born in New Jersey, the son of George Bowlby, and lived on his own property in Morris county. He joined the British army in 1777 and served until the Peace. His brother, Richard, died in service with the British. Another brother was John. A kinsman was Thomas Bowlby, leather cutter, of London Wall in London. In A. O. 13:17 are a schedule of his property and a copy of the inquisition. He was granted £518 from his claim of £1,048. 12s. (A. O. 12:109; A. O. 12:15, ff. 389-395; A. O. 12:63, f. 52).

RICHARD BOWLBY

This Englishman settled in Sussex county, N. J., about 1746 and was Justice of the Peace there. The list of stock on his farm, which is said to have been the best in the county, would seem to indicate that he was a considerable farmer. It was confiscated and at the sale was bought by Benjamin McCulloch. Bowlby declares that he was compelled to sign the Association agreement by a man forcibly drawing his hand across the paper. He joined the British in December, 1776, at "Pennytown," bringing with him 80 neighbors. He refused a commission on account of his advanced age. That uncompromising Loyalist, Joseph Lee (q. v.), was commissioned on his (Bowlby's) recommendation. A witness to his loyalty was one Philip Marchinton, probably a Loyalist himself.

Richard's brother (name not stated), although a Loyalist, remained in New Jersey throughout and after the War with his wife and children, who were "Rebels." Richard's son, Abraham, served at first in the American militia against the will of his father, who sent him to Philadelphia. The son later joined the 80 Loyalists mentioned above, with his father.

Richard Bowlby and his son, Abraham, were at Annapolis in Nova Scotia, in 1784. The grant of £1,400 from his claim of £1,962. 5s., indicates ownership of considerable real estate. (A. O. 12:15, ff. 141-6; A. O. 12:63, f. 17). A valuation of his property, with official papers concerning confiscation, is in A. O. 13:17.

JAMES BRITTAIN (Lieutenant)

He was probably of Sussex county, N. J. He was born in 1752, served first as a private in the 1st New Jersey Volunteers and was promoted Ensign in 1779, and, on February (or April) 25, 1782, Lieutenant of that Battalion. He served throughout the War and is said once to have been taken prisoner and sentenced to death, but escaped. At the end of the War he sought refuge in the new Province of New Brunswick, where he settled on the free grant of land granted to the officers of this Regiment in what is now Kingsclear Parish. His military experience in the American Revolution entitled him to take service in the militia of New Brunswick, in which he held the rank of Lieutenant-Colonel. He was also a magistrate. He died at Greenwich in that Province on October 10, 1838, aged 86.

James Brittain married Eleanor Butler, at Knowlton, Sussex county, New Jersey, on February 24, 1773, the marriage ceremony having been performed by the Rev. Jabez Collver. She died at Greenwich in 1846, aged 94. His brother was Joseph Brittain (q. v.). Sabine mentions another brother, William, as a Loyalist and an exile in New Brunswick. One Israel Brittain was an Ensign in the 1st New Jersey Volunteers. (W. O. 42: B21; Ind.: 5606; A. O. 13: 17; A. O. 12: 16, ff. 351-4; A. O. 12: 63, f. 105; Stryker; Sabine).

JOSEPH BRITTAIN (Ensign)

A brother of James Brittain, above named, and was born in America about 1759 and served throughout the War, first as private and, from Oct., 1782, as Ensign in the 1st New Jersey Volunteers. He was taken prisoner with his brother James and also escaped. He died on May 26, 1830, aged 72, in King's county, New Brunswick, Canada. (Ind.: 5605-6; Stryker; Sabine).

JOHN BROWN

A cooper by trade, who was born in New Brunswick, N. J., and was at first a Commissary in the American army. He deserted and joined the British forces, in which he served as guide until his death in 1779, or 1780, from exposure in the North river. His widow, Margaret, who was born in Martinique in the West Indies, and whom he married in 1763, kept a shop for the sale of earthenware in New Brunswick, while he followed his trade as a cooper.

The Commissioners refused Margaret Brown an allowance or pension as a Loyalist's widow, on the ground that her husband was, like the Vicar of Bray, indifferent as to which army he served, and, moreover, his losses by the War were more than counterbalanced by the money he had made by the War. She was, however, granted compensation of £345, from her claim of £709 for the loss of his real estate, and was allowed £25 to defray her expenses to Nova Scotia in 1786, whither she was accompanied by her only daughter, Elizabeth, and the latter's husband, Captain James Kerr, a Loyalist, of the Queen's Rangers, who had been married in 1782. (A. O. 12: 14, ff. 113-9; A. O. 12: 101, ff. 164, 316; A. O. 12: 109).

DANIEL ISAAC BROWNE (Major)

He was of Hackensack, N. J., and was the son of the Rev. Isaac Browne (q. v.), and was born in 1739 or 1740 on Long

Island, New York, and was Clerk of the Court of Common Pleas in Bergen county from 1771 and Surrogate of the Eastern Division of New Jersey from 1774. He is said to have practised law, and he may be the "Isaac Brown" admitted as attorney in New Jersey in 1760.

According to his evidence in London, two Association papers were directed at a County Committee in Bergen county to be drawn up, one by Mr. Morris, "who was violent for the Rebels." Browne himself drew up the other by which it was engaged to comply with the legal orders of Congress, and this Association was adopted at the meeting against the violent one of Morris. His reason (as given by him) for drawing up this Association paper was to prevent people from signing a worse. He remained quiet until the arrival of the British troops in New Jersey, having been exempted from serving in the militia by reason of his profession as a lawyer.

Mr. Browne was a "Committeeman" and a member of the Provincial Congress in June, 1776, a course taken by him on the advice of Governor Tryon of New York, whose letter of May 13, 1777, advising this course, was produced before the Commissioners in London. He could not be a member of the new Legislature in September, 1776, because he would not take the oath of abjuration of the King. He claimed that a majority of the inhabitants of Bergen county were Loyalists. The records of that county were carried away by him to New York at some personal expense and danger. His commission as Major of the 1st New Jersey Volunteers is dated November 17, 1776.

In A. O. 13:17 are the following papers: (1). A letter from Richard Varick, of New York, dated April 20, 1786, regarding monies due to Major Browne in New York and New Jersey, and stating, *inter alia*, that, according to the confiscation laws of New Jersey, debts must be first paid, but the monies must in the first instance be paid into the State Treasury, out of which none, to his (Varick's) knowledge, had yet come to creditors, and that it is supposed that none ever would come from thence to those Loyalists who resided in New York during the War. (2). Browne's power of attorney to Isaac

Ogden, January 2, 1784. (3). Copy of the inquisition into his property in New Jersey by order of the State in 1779, with the names of the jurors. (4). Certificate of James Board, August 21, 1786, to the sale of Browne's confiscated property. (5). Schedule of his real and personal estate, which includes several bonds. (6). List of the names in support of his claim for compensation as follows: James Van Buren (q. v.), John Francis Ryerson (q. v.), Hendrick Lutkers (Lutkins), Lawrence Roome and Major Thomas Millidge (q. v.).

John Francis Ryerson (q. v.) stated in evidence in London that at the first meeting in Bergen county on the troubles about Associations, some were violent and others moderate. Ryerson himself was opposed to all Associations. Eighteen voted for a "mild Association," as the best way to prevent violent measures. He says of Browne that he was not so clever as other lawyers in speaking, but was much employed in giving advice; he had heard him blamed for giving bad advice, which often tended to promote unsuccessful suits, while producing fees for himself.

Major Browne's estate was confiscated in Bergen county in 1779. He received half-pay of £133.9.1; £335 as compensation from his claim of £3,056.11; and compensation at the rate of £200 a year during the War for the loss of his income from his public offices. (A. O. 12:109). He accompanied the refugees to Annapolis, Nova Scotia, at the end of the War. (A. O. 13:83; A. O. 12:15, ff. 98-110; A. O. 12:63, ff. 14-15; Ind.: 5605; "Ontario Archives," pp. 541-3).

Rev. ISAAC BROWNE

He was born in New Haven, Conn., March 20, 1709, his parents being Daniel and Mary (Edwards) Browne. His grandfather, Francis Browne, emigrated from Ratcliffe, England. He was educated at Yale College (class of 1729). He had ministered in another communion 14 years (at Brookhaven, or Setauket, L. I.), before his appointment as Rector of Trinity Church, Newark, New Jersey, about 1747. Here he served for about 30 years, until 1777, when this Church was closed by the Revolutionary party, and he became a refugee in New York until May 10, 1778, when he accepted the chaplaincy of the New York Volunteers. He had been a medical practitioner as well as preacher. With other Loyalists he sought refuge in Nova Scotia in 1783 and was there a missionary of the Society for the Propagation of the Gospel (which had previously appointed him to Newark) until 1785. He is said to have died in 1787 at Windsor in that Province, though his name appears on the half-pay list until 1791. He was granted £145 from his claim of £282.18. (A. O. 12:109). His letter to the Rev. Thomas Bradbury Chandler (q. v.) commending to him the conspicuous loyalist, James Moody (q. v.), is printed in Moody's "Narrative," 2nd edition, p. 8 of the Appendix.

His papers in A. O. 13:17 include an account of his property; several notes of hand for money from his parishioners towards his stipend; and documents relating to the confiscation of his estate in 1778. His sons were Major Daniel I. Browne (q. v.) and Dr. Peter Browne (q. v.), and a son-in-law was Isaac Ogden (q. v.). (A. O. 13:83; A. O. 12:15, ff. 415-420; Ind.: 5604-6; W. O. 24:750; A. O. 12:63, f. 58; "Ontario Archives," p. 688; Dexter's "Biog. of Yale Graduates;" Wickes' "Hist. of N. J. Medicine," p. 167).

Dr. PETER BROWNE

This son of the Rev. Isaac Browne (q. v.) was a physician and surgeon and acted as a surgeon's mate in the army and afterwards in the hospitals in Nova Scotia. He was at Annapolis in 1786. (A. O. 12:15, ff. 420-6). A list of his property in Newark (inquisition against him was of June 12, 1778), and of debts due to him by his patients in New Jersey, are in A. O. 13:17. He was allowed £290 from his claim of £2,676, which doubless included debts; and he also received compensation at the rate of £150 a year during the War for the loss of his practice. (A. O. 12:109).

There were apparently two medical men of this name, Loyalists, from New Jersey.

WILLIAM BURKITT

A native of Philadelphia, resident at Billingsport in Gloucester county, N. J., was a farmer. He joined the British forces in 1777. He died at Digby, Nova Scotia, soon after his exile there, leaving a widow, Hannah, and several children. (A. O. 13:17; A. O. 12:16, ff. 61-5; A. O. 12:63, f. 88). She claimed £343 and was allowed £180. (A. O. 12:109).

ANN BURNET

She was the daughter of Dr. Lewis and Martha (Heathcote) Johnston, of Perth Amboy, N. J. She had an estate valued at £9,000, shared by her brother, Heathcote Johnston (q. v.), at Perth Amboy. Her husband was Captain John Burnet, of the 8th Regiment, British Army. She and her one daughter lived after the War with her father-in-law at Plymouth in England, and from 1783 to 1831 she was granted a Loyalist pension of £30. (A. O. 13:90; A. O. 12:99, f. 246; Whitehead's "Perth Amboy").

WILLIAM BURTON

An Englishman, who sold an estate in England and emigrated in 1772 to New Jersey, where he bought property in Somerset county on the banks of the Raritan river, one mile from Brunswick, for £1,500 sterling, from Anthony and Elizabeth White, the same now known as Buccleuch Park. He appears to have fled from his new home in 1776 for New York, and from 1778 he was Commissary-General of Naval Stores and Prisoners to the British army. In January, 1779, his estate in Somerset county was forfeited. The same year he sailed for England and remained there. In evidence in London he stated that he had money invested in English funds which produced an income of about £200, and that he had expectations of a legacy of about £5,000 at his mother's death. He was obliged to support his wife's mother and daughter, both Loyalists. His wife was the daughter of the Rev. Samuel Auchmuty, the distinguished Rector of Trinity Church, New York. William Burton expressed a wish to return to America and reëstablish himself there, presumably at his former home in New Jersey. (A. O. 12:13, ff. 351-6; A. O. 12:104, f. 18). His Loyalist pension of £200 was reduced to £90 in 1785. (T. 50:6 and 9. See also Benedict's "New Brunswick in History").

ABRAHAM CADMUS

He is mentioned as a spy employed by Pierre de Peyster (q. v.) in the evidence of this Loyalist in A. O. 12:14. He was, doubtless, of the Bergen or Somerset county, N. J., Cadmus family.

DONALD CALLAGHER

An Irishman who emigrated to New Jersey in 1759 and there served his time to a farmer, subsequently renting a small farm for himself. He joined the British army in 1775 and served until his departure for England in 1782, when he left two children in New Jersey. In 1784 he was granted £20 for his expenses to New Jersey. (A. O. 12:100, f. 244).

JOHN CAMERON

He was of Ringwood, Bergen county, N. J., and had served in the 26th and 55th Regiments of the British army in the War with the French in America. He joined the British forces at New York in 1777 and served in the Royal Highland Emigrants for five years. In 1786 he was at Sorel in Canada, and his claim was rejected. (A. O. 13:81).

WILLIAM CAMERON

Nothing is recorded of this Loyalist, supposed to be from New Jersey, except that he bore arms and that he was living on the "River Raisine" in 1788. (A. O. 12:63, f. 130). He was granted £30 from his claim of £93.10. (A. O. 12:109).

COLIN CAMPBELL (Lieutenant)

An attorney-at-law from May, 1773, and a Master in Chancery from 1774, at Burlington, N. J., where his father, the Rev. Colin Campbell, was the predecessor of the Rev. Jonathan Odell (q. v.) at St. Mary's Church. In February, 1775, he was appointed on a Committee of Observation for Burlington county, and in May and August was a member of the Provincial Congress. In December, 1776, however, he joined the British troops. He returned to Burlington in April, 1777, from exile in Pennsylvania, with the object of recovering his valuable private papers. On the next day he was arrested, taken before the Governor and the Council of Safety and the oath of allegiance to the United States tendered to him, which he refused to take. He was then bound over to appear at the next Court of Quarter Sessions in May, with Abraham Hewlings as surety, in £300, when he duly appeared and the oath was again administered and met with the same refusal. Campbell was fined and forthwith fled to Philadelphia, and there remained until the evacuation of the city by the British forces, which he accompanied to New York. Here he practised as an attorney and was Secretary to the Commissioners for settling debts. Sabine says he was also an Ensign, Quartermaster and Lieutenant. He was appointed in 1785 Clerk to the Supreme Court of the Province of New Brunswick, where he died in 1801.

Colin Campbell (who left his mother, wife and a child at New York at the Evacuation) was granted a Loyalist pension of £40 until 1797 and was allowed compensation at the rate of £80 a year during the War for the loss of his professional income. (A. O. 12:109). The son, Colin, went later to Charlotte county, New Brunswick, and died at St. Andrew in that Province in 1843. (A. O. 13:108; A. O. 12:13, ff. 120-5; A. O. 12:100, f. 226; "Loyalists' Claims," pp. 174-5; Sabine: "Judges of New Brunswick," pp. 22, 35; "Min. of Council of Safety," N. J.).

DONALD CAMPBELL (Captain)

Born in Scotland in or about 1754, he served for seven years in the Loyalist forces, from December, 1776, as Captain in the 2nd, and from July 24, 1781, in the 3rd New Jersey Volunteers. He was married, apparently in New York, on August 2, 1815, to Margaret Euphemia Campbell, by the Rev. John Stanford, in the presence of Charles Campbell, gentleman, and Margaret, his wife, the latter of whom was the bride's family relative. He died on August 18, 1825, at New York, on half-pay as Captain in the 3rd New Jersey Volunteers, and was buried in St. Stephen's churchyard. His will was admitted to probate at New York on August 31, 1825. (W. O. 42:C2; Ind.: 5604-6).

PETER CAMPBELL (Captain)

He was born about 1756, the son of Thomas Campbell, a prosperous merchant of Philadelphia. He lived at Trenton and was the brother-in-law of Lieutenant-Colonel Isaac Allen (q. v.). He joined the British army in 1776 in New Jersey and received a warrant from Isaac Allen to raise a Company for his Regiment, and served as Captain of the 2nd New Jersey Volunteers. For twelve months (1777-'78) he was a prisoner and upon his release he rejoined the New Jersey Volunteers, with which he was ordered to Georgia under Colonel Archibald Campbell and in which he had a Company. Captain Campbell served at the reduction of Savannah and of Charleston, in the memorable defense of "96," in the Battle of Eutaw Springs, and in other engagements in the South. (A. O. 13:17). Stryker says he was killed "on Brewton's Hill, near Savannah, Ga., Dec. 29, 1778," which must be an error.

Accompanying his papers are an attested copy of a summons to this Loyalist, who is described as a practitioner of physic, formerly of Philadelphia, to appear before the Judges of the Superior Court, or Justices of the Peace, to attend his trial for high treason; and an original conveyance of property to Mary Harrison, widow of Henry Harrison, in Philadelphia, in 1776, in which Peter Campbell is described as of Nottingham township, Burlington county, New Jersey. He settled on a grant of land in Kingsclear Parish, in the Canadian Province of New Brunswick, where he died, February 21, 1822, and was buried at Fredericton with Masonic honors. (A. O. 12:16, ff. 204-211; A. O. 12:66, f. 32; Ind.: 5605-6; "Ontario Archives," pp. 832-4; Sabine).

Thomas Campbell, in his will of October 11, 1762, bequeathed property to his son (this Loyalist) and to his daughter, Sarah, wife of Isaac Allen (q. v.), and, in the event of the death of both without issue, the estate was left to his brother, John Campbell, residing near Liverpool in England. Legacies were left to another brother, Bayan Campbell, at Maydown, County Armagh, Ireland; and to his kinswoman, Margaret Campbell, tailoress, in Germantown, Pennsylvania. The Pennsylvania Hospital and the College of Philadelphia were beneficiaries.

ROBERT CAMPBELL

A merchant and surveyor, he lost his plantations, valued at £1,484 currency, by confiscation. He took an active part for the Crown from the beginning of the Revolution and was obliged to quit his home in New Jersey (not stated where) and seek refuge on board the "Asia" man-of-war. He raised a Company in the Guides and Pioneers. At the Peace he settled at St. John, New Brunswick, as a surveyor and was a Captain in the Provincial Militia. Campbell received a military allowance of £40 from 1788 to 1816. (A. O. 13:21; A. O. 12:102, ff. 129, 214; Ind.: 5606).

Rev. THOMAS BRADBURY CHANDLER

He was of Elizabethtown, N. J. His memorial (in A. O. 13:108) shows that in 1766 he received the degree of D. D. from the University of Oxford, *conspirantibus omnium suffragiis*. A year later he was selected by the clergy of New Jersey and New York to plead the cause of the Church in the Colonies and to defend it against the assaults meditated against it. In 1772, "finding that the evil spirit in the Colonies, which broke out on occasion of the Stamp Act, and which had not subsided on the repeal of it, was still treating the British Government very indecently and disseminating the principles and a general disaffection," he endeavored to counteract this "evil spirit" by contributions to the newspapers, etc.

This eminent divine declares that he wrote three pamphlets, namely: (a). In 1774, on the appointment of the delegates to the General Congress, in which he endeavored to persuade the people to leave their political affairs to their chosen agents. (b). In October, 1774, showing the dreadful consequences of a war between Great Britain and America. (c). In February, 1775, to prove that, as Congress had exceeded their instructions, their constituents were not bound, in justice or honor, to execute their resolves. This third pamphlet was regarded by him to have done more good in New York and New Jersey than any other written during the controversy.

As the missionary of the venerable Society for the Propagation of the Gospel at Elizabethtown from 1751 to 1775, he wrote (in 1776) to the Society that, if "the interest of the Church of England in America had been a national concern from the beginning, by this time a general submission in the Colonies to the Mother Country, in everything not sinful, might have been expected . . . and who can be certain that the present rebellious disposition of the Colonies is not intended by Providence as a punishment for that neglect? . . . The Nation, whether sensible of it or not, is under great obligations to that worthy Society." That the Government might become "more sensible of the Society's services" and at length co-operate with them "as the most probable means of restoring the mutual happiness of Great Britain and her colonies, was his 'Dayly prayer'." ("Two Hundred Years of the S. P. G.", 1701-1900, p. 55).

Mr. Chandler was born April 26, 1726 in Woodstock, Connecticut; was educated at Yale College, being graduated in 1745. He had been a Congregational "Dissenter" before ordination in the Church of England. He was one of the champions of Episcopacy for the American Colonies. In 1775 he was a refugee in England, and in 1776 petitioned the King for a grant of 100,000 acres of land in Canada; during the War was the friend, advisor and helper of many of the distressed Loyalist exiles in London, consoling them with help in divers ways and helping them with their claims for compensation and applications for temporary allowances from the British Government. He himself received a pension of £200 from 1782 until 1788.

That one so respected and beloved by the American clergy and by many conspicuous Loyalists was selected by them for recommendation as the first Bishop of Nova Scotia is not surprising. Advanced age and declining health obliged the eminent divine to decline the appointment, which was offered to and accepted by the Rev. Charles Inglis (q. v.), the well-known Rector of Trinity Church, New York, and Chaplain to the 1st New Jersey Volunteers. (Ibid. p. 751). His son was William Chandler (q. v.). A daughter, Mary Goodin Chandler, married, in 1800, the American Bishop Hobart. Another daughter married Gen. E. B. Dayton. One of his pupils was Cavalier Jouet (q. v.).

He died June 17, 1790 in the New Jersey town, from whence he was obliged to flee in 1775 and to which he returned in 1785—Elizabethtown, where the silver cup in which he administered the Sacrament for 24 years is still preserved. (T. 50:6; T. 50:10; A. O. 12:104, f. 25; Sabine; Dexter, "Biogs. of Yale Graduates"; Hatfield, "Hist. of Elizabeth," which see for some other particulars of him).

Inquisition against him in Essex county, N. J., was returned April 19, 1779, and judgment entered July 6, 1779. (Essex Forfeited Estates Records).

WILLIAM CHANDLER (Captain)

He was a son of the Rev. Thomas Bradbury Chandler, above named, and was born in Elizabethtown, N. J., May 23, 1756; was graduated at King's College, N. Y., in 1774, and was educated to be a physician. He received a warrant as Captain in the New Jersey Volunteers on April 10, 1777, serving for two years on Staten Island. (C. O. 5:116, f. 223). General Sir Henry Clinton, Commander-in-Chief, recommended him for consideration by the Government. (T. 1:339). He was put on half-pay as Captain at £70, and for two years from 1784 received a Loyalist pension of £40. (Ind.: 5605-6; T. 50:8; T. 50:9). His name disappears from the half-pay list in 1786. (W. O. 24:748). According to Stryker and Hatfield, this Loyalist went to England and died there on October 22, 1784. (See also Wickes' "Hist. of N. J. Medicine," p. 199, and Sabine).

WILLIAM CLARK

His name is recorded in A. O. 12:110, f. 123, and it may be he was the Loyalist of New Jersey of this name who was shot in June, 1782. Sabine terms him "a noted horse thief," who "stole upwards of 100 valuable horses from New Jersey, which he sold to the Royal Army."

GEORGE CLARKE (Captain)

He was the son of a man of property in Salem county, N. J., first joined the British in 1777 and received a Captain's commission in the West Jersey Volunteers on March 24, 1778. He received a Loyalist's pension of £30 from 1784 until 1788 and, apparently, went to Nova Scotia; whether permanently is not disclosed in the available papers. (A. O. 13:108; A. O. 12:101, f. 67; T. 50:8; T. 50:10).

JONATHAN CLAWSON

The son of John Clawson (who died in 1779), he was born in America. He was settled as a farmer at Woodbridge, N. J., where his neighbor was Dr. Samuel Barron, and, though brought up as a Quaker, was confirmed in the Church of England. He joined the British army in New Jersey in 1776 and served until the end of the War. His eldest son, aged 19, was put to death by the Americans by order of General Maxwell as a spy; he had served in several engagements under the command of Thomas Crowell (q. v.), who described him as a smart and active lad. This Loyalist settled in Nova Scotia with his wife and children. (A. O. 12:13, ff. 402-8; A. O. 12:101, f. 207, "Loyalists Claims," pp. 378-9). Compensation to the amount of £1,400 was granted to him for the loss of his property from his claim of £1,674. (A. O. 12:109).

In A. O. 13:108 are a schedule of his property and certificates of confiscation, his property being confiscated in Middlesex county, N. J., June 20, 1778.

JAMES CLENDENNING

A farmer of Sussex county, N. J., who served in Butler's Rangers from 1778 until the end of the War, as did two sons. He had hoped to go into the United States after the War to obtain compensation for his losses, but, having heard on the journey of "the rigorous ill-treatment of those Loyalists who had travelled thither on a similar errand," he thought it more prudent for his own safety to return to Niagara in Canada, his home in 1787. He claimed £309. 13s., and was allowed £138. (A. O. 12:109; A. O. 13:17; A. O. 13:81; A. O. 12:16, ff. 415-9; A. O. 12:63, f. 123).

JOHN CLOUD (Quartermaster)

An Irishman, born about 1744, emigrated in 1772 and settled at Cupars Ferry in Gloucester county, where he "taught school." He "rendered every service in his power to suppress the Rebellion," in consequence of which his property was confiscated and sold. For the brief period of service of the West Jersey Volunteers he served from March 20, 1778, as Quartermaster. He died in July, 1784, leaving a widow, Rebecca, and three daughters, who were at Aylesford in Nova Scotia in 1786. (A. O. 13:17; A. O. 12:16, ff. 39-41; A. O. 12:63, f. 63). She was awarded £40 from her claim of £284. 8s. (A. O. 12:109).

RICHARD COCHRAN

A Scotsman, who was born in Edinburgh and emigrated to America about 1749, settling in New Jersey in 1764. A year later he bought a plantation in Somerset county, within a mile of Princeton, and soon became the owner of four houses and lots in Princeton itself. Here he imported occasionally some goods for sale, but kept no store. Governor Franklin stated that the Scotsman lived very comfortably as a country gentleman and appointed him a Justice of the Peace and a Judge of the Court of Common Pleas on February 22, 1772. Dr. John Witherspoon, President of Princeton College, in an affidavit of June 2, 1784, declared that his fellow countryman had lived "in the state of a gentleman and in good repute, kept a chaise and a four-wheeled carriage," and that he had a valuable library. He lost cattle, houses, furniture and a library of over 300 volumes, mostly plundered by the King's troops and the Americans, to the value of about £8,340 in New Jersey currency, equal to between £4,000 and £5,000 sterling.

Richard Cochran joined the British army in Princeton and there administered the loyal oaths to recruits and others and acted as Deputy Commissary for nearly four months, as well as performing other functions in support of the British. In consequence the State of New Jersey forfeited his estate late in 1778. Before his flight from America he left vouchers for debts due to him with one Lewis Pintard, merchant, of New York, who joined the Americans some time after. He left his wife and a daughter in New York and two sons were in New Jersey in 1784, when he was earning a scanty living as a clerk in Glasgow, and was in receipt of a Loyalist pension of £60, which was reduced to £44 in 1785, and which ceased in or just before 1786.

One John Cochran, doubtless a kinsman, made an affidavit before the Lord Provost of Glasgow that he was present at the sale of Richard Cochran's plantation and property in New Jersey. The plantation on Stony Brook was sold by the State to David Hambleton (*vide* certificate of Elias Boudinot). He was granted £1,912 from his claim of £2,554. (A. O. 12:109; T. 50:6; T. 50:8; T. 50:9; A. O. 12:13, ff. 136-151; A. O. 12:104, f. 4; "Loyalists Claims," p. 190.)

THOMAS COLDEN (Major)

He served for about two months as Captain in the 2nd New Jersey Volunteers from September, 1777, until November, when he was transferred to the Pennsylvania Loyalists, commanded by Lieutenant-Colonel William Allen. In September, 1781, he rejoined the New Jersey Volunteers as Major of the 1st Battalion. Meanwhile, on February 16, 1781, he had married Anne Willett, in the presence of Jane Antill, of Coldenham, Orange county, New York, widow of John Antill. He died on March 30, 1826, at New York, where his widow resided. (W. O. 42:C21; Ind.: 5604-5-6).

This Loyalist, born in 1754, was the son of Cadwallader Colden, of New York, and grandson of Lieutenant-Governor Colden of that Province. His wife was the daughter of William and Alice (Colden) Willett. It was probably his brother, John Colden, who was Major of the 2nd New Jersey Volunteers and (from 1782) of De Lancey's Brigade.

JAMES COLLINS

He was born in New Jersey and describes himself as "gentleman," of New Brunswick. In the copy of the inquisition taken and made in Middlesex county, N. J., June 16, 1778, and containing the names of the jurors, it is stated that Collins joined the British army in June, 1777. There is also a schedule of his property, including ready money, bonds and notes, "taken away by violence when his house was broken open Dec. 1st, 1777." Nathaniel Munro and Frederick Weiser (q. v.) declared their faith in Collins's statements of loyalty and property. At Shelburne, in Nova Scotia, in 1786, the Rev. William Walter, the Loyalist from Boston, stated in a certificate that Collins was a tradesman and a conscientious member of the Church of England in that place. He claimed £336. and was allowed £180. (A. O. 12:109; A. O. 13:17; A. O. 12:15, ff. 244-8; A. O. 12:63, f. 32; "Ontario Archives," p. 142).

DENNIS COMBS (Adjutant)

He was, apparently, a coachmaker in Middlesex county, N. J., and was born in America. His service in the War included that of Adjutant of the 3rd New Jersey Volunteers. He was married in New Brunswick, Canada, on February 22, 1784, to Martha Vail, by the Rev. John Beardsley, the Connecticut divine and Loyalist refugee. His claim for compensation was rejected. (A. O. 13:21; W. O. 42:C22). He died on April 10, 1827. (Ind.: 5605-6).

JOHN COMBS (Lieutenant)

He was born in America about 1752 and was given a commission as Lieutenant in the 3rd New Jersey Volunteers on September 10, 1778. He died about 1828 on half-pay in the same rank, in the 2nd Battalion of that Regiment, to which he had been transferred in 1781. (Ind.: 5604-5-6). He died in 1827 in New Brunswick, Canada. (Stryker; Sabine).

NATHANIEL COMBS (Ensign)

He was born in America about 1757 and appears to have served as a private before the grant of a commission as Ensign in the Third Battalion, New Jersey Volunteers, on July 29, 1778; later, 1780, was transferred to the Second Battalion. He was married on August 25, 1806, to Alice Oliver, of Woodbridge, New Jersey, who is described in the official document as the mother of Charles Oliver of the same place, and, therefore, probably a widow. He died, on half-pay of the 2nd New Jersey Volunteers, on March 22, 1813, at Allentown, New Jersey, and was buried in the graveyard of the Episcopal

Church. His widow resided after his death at New Brunswick in the same State. Nathan Combs, their son, was born on February 13, 1809. (Ind.: 5605-6; W. O. 42:C23).

A Loyalist brother, in Georgia, changed his name for political reasons at the Revolution. Another brother, Nathan, who is described as of New York during or after the Revolution, was possibly the man of this name, of Amwell, New Jersey, who appears to have been an apprentice of one Thomas Skelton, whose (Skelton's) claim was declared as fraudulent. ("Loyalists' Claims," pp. 4-6).

CHARLES COOKE

He emigrated from Ireland in 1766 and was in partnership with his brother, Robert (q. v.), as a general merchant at Crosswicks, Burlington county, N. J. He was captured in December, 1776, in an endeavor to raise recruits for the New Jersey Volunteers and was detained for over three years. He had a plantation on the Susquehanna. From 1783 to 1786 he received a Loyalist pension of £80, and from 1786 to December, 1816, a military allowance of £100. (A. O. 12:14, ff. 400-6; A. O. 99, f. 69; Ind.: 5606; T. 50:7; T. 50:8; T. 50:9).

ROBERT COOKE (Major)

This sturdy Loyalist emigrated from Ireland a year or two later than his brother and partner, Charles (above named). He served at the Battle of Monmouth, where he was of "singular service." From May, 1780, he was an Assistant Commissary of prisoners and, later, was appointed Major of a Corps, probably the Duke of Cumberland's Regiment, which was intended for service at Jamaica in the West Indies. He was in London in 1788, subsisting in part on his military allowance of £50, granted to him in 1787. The brothers were awarded £200 from their claim of £1,385, which doubtless included debts not allowed by the British Government because they were recoverable under the Treaty of Peace. (A. O. 13:108; A. O. 12:14, ff. 400-6; A. O. 12:74, ff. 249-264; A. O. 12:100, f. 258; A. O. 12:109; A. O. 12:111, ff. 61-2; Ind.: 5606; T. 50:8; T. 50:9).

Rev. SAMUEL COOKE

He was born in England in 1723, the son of Thomas Cooke, Collector of Revenue at Yarmouth, and was educated in that town, at Charterhouse, and at Gonville and Caius College, Cambridge, of which he was scholar, 1743-8. After ordination he was curate at Beccles in Suffolk. He appears to have gone out to America in 1750, or 1751, as missionary of the Society for the Propagation of the Gospel, and from 1765 to the Revolution was in Monmouth county, N. J., in charge of the Episcopal parishes at Shrewsbury, Middletown, Freehold and other places. In 1760 he received the honorary degree of M. A. from the College of Philadelphia.

This Loyalist divine returned in 1775 to England "on private business," and in 1776 sailed back to America as deputy chaplain to the Brigade of Guards. His property in Shrewsbury, New Jersey, was confiscated May 15, 1779; but this, or part of it, was conveyed later to his daughter, Mary, by the Commissioners of Confiscated Estates. At the end of the War he went into exile in New Brunswick, Canada, and there was appointed chaplain to the garrison at St. John, on August 25, 1784, and in 1785 became missionary there of the venerable Society which had sent him to New Jersey. In the following year he became first rector of the Episcopal Church at Fredericton, the present capital of New Brunswick. This respected exile was drowned by the upsetting of a canoe in crossing the St. John River to Fredericton, May 23, 1795, and his son, Michael, lost his life in trying to save him, to the grief of the whole Province. He received compensation for loss of property and a pension during his lifetime.

His wife, Graham Kearny, born 1736, daughter of Michael Kearny, of Perth Amboy, New Jersey, died in 1771. In all they had 10 children. Isabella Cooke, his daughter, married, in 1791, Lieutenant-Colonel Harris William Hailes, Canadian Regiment of Fencible Infantry. (W. O. 42:H2; T. 50:9; T. 50:11; A. O. 461:15-16; A. O. 12:13, ff. 376-382; A. O. 12:100, f. 183; A. O. 12:101, f. 279; A. O. 12:109; "Judges of New Brunswick," p. 117; Sabine; "Loyalists Claims," p. 357; Venn., "Alumni Cantab."; Stillwell's "Hist. Misc.," Vol. III, p. 389).

RICHARD COOPER (Lieutenant)

He was American-born (about 1756) and served throughout the War, first as a private and, from August 25, 1780, as Ensign in the New Jersey Volunteers, and, later, as Lieutenant. His name disappears in 1802 from the half-pay list as a Lieutenant in the 3rd Battalion. (Ind.: 5604-5-6).

JOHN CORDUE

A tailor of Trenton, N. J., who enlisted in the British army in 1777 and joined in 1778 the 3rd Battalion of the militia in New York, commanded by Colonel Isaac Low. He was settled at New Carlisle in Chaleur Bay in 1786. (A. O. 13:81).

WILLIAM CORLIN

He was of Shrewsbury, N. J., and is mentioned in A. O. 13:97.

JOHN COWGILL, or COUGLE (Captain)

Born in New Jersey, about 1748, he was a planter in Newtown (now Newton), Sussex county. Early in the Revolution he signed an Association in support of the American cause and was employed in raising recruits for the New Jersey Brigade. "Fear," he assigned as his reason for taking the part of the Americans. In February, 1777, he joined the British army in New York and brought with him 36 recruits, receiving for this act of service a Lieutenant's commission. He succeeded afterwards in recruiting 51 more men and was awarded a Captain's commission in the 1st New Jersey Volunteers on July 29, 1778. Cowgill settled on the Kennebecasis River and was on half-pay until 1802. (A. O. 12:16, ff. 163-8; A. O. 12:63, f. 114; Ind.: 5605-6).

George Ross, in a letter dated Elizabethtown, April 10, 1787, forwards to this Loyalist, his "old loyal acquaintance," certificates of the confiscation and sale of his estate. (A. O. 13:17). He was allowed £138 from his claim of £660. (A. O. 12:109). According to Stryker he died in New Brunswick, Canada, in 1819, aged 73.

HUGH COWPERTHWAITE (Captain)

He lived in the township of Pittsgrove, in Salem county, N. J., until January, 1778, when the oath of allegiance to the

American States was tendered to him and, having refused to take it, he fled to Philadelphia. Alderman Melville, of St. John, New Brunswick, stated that he was his fellow-member of a garrison of Loyalists at Billingsport on the Delaware river. Into this garrison, then commanded by Major John Vandyke (q. v.), Cowperthwaite brought between thirty and forty Loyalists, whom he commanded as Captain, and took them out on all excursions of reprisals against the enemy. Among the prisoners taken by this force were several Continental officers. Later, upon the evacuation of Philadelphia by the British, he went to New York and served as a private in the Loyalist corps of Colonel de Lancey, probably De Lancey's Brigade. An estimate of the loss of his property is given.

In 1787 this Loyalist was living at Sunbury, New Brunswick. He was allowed £444 from his claim of £964. 15s. (A. O. 12:109; A. O. 13:17; A. O. 12:14, ff. 97-111; A. O. 12:16, ff. 193-8; A. O. 12:63, f. 84.)

James Harrison (q. v.) married a Charity Cowperthwaite in Sunbury county, New Brunswick, in 1788.

Major Gabriel de Veber, a Swiss, (appointed, March 19, 1778, Major of the West Jersey Volunteers) would seem to have been in command of Billingsport Fort, for, on March 31, 1778, he wrote to Daniel Coxe (q. v.) that the fort had been completed and that he had taken prisoners, some "very bad and dangerous." He expected to have a force of 194 strong and "Captain Hugh Cowperthwaite 50 more." (A. O. 13:108). Major de Veber became Lieutenant-Colonel of the Prince of Wales's American Volunteers in December, 1781.

JOHN COX (Captain)

This Loyalist had a plantation in Woolwich township, Gloucester county, N. J., which was sold to Felix Fislar for £2,100. With his papers is a copy of the inquisition taken at Swedesboro, New Jersey, August 5, 1778, with the names of the jurors, which states that Cox, on or about March 20, 1778, joined the British army and assisted in "taking the good subjects prisoners and destroyed their property." There is also a description of his estate, and an affidavit of Captain Daniel Cozens (q. v.), dated Quebec, May, 1787, that Cox was his former neighbor, was taken prisoner by the Americans in 1778, escaped and went into the post at Billingsport, then commanded by Cozens, and took part in many expeditions against the Americans. Cox was at St. John's in Antigua in 1787. In one document he is described as Captain John Cox, mariner. Miles Union, late of Woolwich, in his affidavit, dated from St. John, New Brunswick, adds that he had known him from infancy. (A. O. 13:17). He claimed £1,017.12s., and was awarded £699. (A. O. 12:109; A. O. 13:97; A. O. 12:16, ff. 406-414; A. O. 12:63, f. 120; "Ontario Archives," p. 929).

DANIEL COXE

A Trenton, N. J., lawyer of eminent family, who, in his long memorial, refers to his ancient connection (the fourth generation of the name) with New Jersey. His grandfather, Colonel Daniel Coxe, a member of the Inner Temple, settled there in 1702, became Speaker of the Assembly and a Judge of the Supreme Court of the Province, and his great-grandfather, Dr. Daniel Coxe, was Governor and Chief Proprietor of the Province of West Jersey. With his memorial are a great number of documents and the following:

1. A minute schedule of his property in the counties of Hunterdon, Burlington, Sussex, Somerset, Salem and Cape May, all in New Jersey, and also in the Province of New York. 2. A printed extract of a letter, published by order of Council of Safety, from an officer of distinction (not named) in the American army, on the "horrid depredations" and brutalities committed by the British force stationed at "Pennytown" under Lord Cornwallis. He refers to the burning of the elegant house of Daniel Coxe at Trenton by the British. 3. A printed copy of the proclamation of Lord Howe and Sir William Howe, September 19, 1776, Commissioners of Peace, and their proposals.

While the extract from the printed letter, mentioned above, accuses the British troops of the burning of his house, Coxe himself is careful to state that his houses and property were taken possession of by the Hessians and that, notwithstanding his well-known character as a Loyalist and the remonstrances of his friends and servants, his rooms, stores and cellars were broken open, ransacked and pillaged, and all the furniture, china, glass and liquors were plundered, destroyed or taken away, leaving the place a scene of wanton desolation. (A. O. 13:108, 111).

In A. O. 13:93 is a summary of the sales of the Coxe real estate, many papers relating to his property, correspondence, and his original commission as a member of the Provincial Council, May 4, 1771.

Daniel Coxe swore in evidence in London on November 29, 1784, that he was in the highest degree in the profession of the law, namely, Serjeant, with a professional income of £400 a year; likewise, he was one of the "Mandamus Counsellors." He said he not only refused many offers by the Americans, but took an invariable opposition to their measures, and never in one instance gave them reason to think that he was wavering. Upon the invasion of New Jersey by the British troops in 1776 he escaped to Pennsylvania. In the Winter of 1777 and the Spring of 1778 he raised the West Jersey Volunteers. During the British occupation of Philadelphia he acted there as a magistrate of police without emolument. He accompanied the army to New York and was there a member of the Board of Associated Loyalists. He disapproved of the execution of Huddy, the American soldier, mentioned later under Governor Franklin. ("Am. MSS. in Roy. Inst.," II: 529).

Cortlandt Skinner (q. v.) in evidence said that Daniel Coxe was instrumental in raising the West Jersey Volunteers, but that Major John Vandyke (q. v.) was principally concerned in recruiting the men, a statement which was confirmed by Vandyke on the same occasion. Bernardus La Grange (q. v.) added that Coxe was not "one of the most eminent" lawyers in New Jersey. According to the evidence of Governor Franklin, this Loyalist lawyer "never took any oaths to the Rebels, but that when he was in the country he made interest with some of the Rebels to let him remain quiet," a statement in contradiction to Coxe's assertion that he had never in one instance wavered in his opposition to the measures of the Americans.

His claim for ¼ of the land exchanged for the Province of Carolana was rejected, as was the claim of his mother, Abigail Coxe, for £480. He was allowed £9,997 from his claim of £41,305; and, at the rate of £360 a year for the loss of his professional income during the War. His pension was £180. (A. O. 12;109).

Daniel Coxe was Secretary to the Peace Commission to America in 1781. He was born in New Jersey about 1741. He married, June 5, 1771, Sarah, daughter of Dr. John Redman, of Philadelphia, and died in London March 10, 1826. In his long will, dated January 8, 1825, and proved in London April 18, 1826, he left legacies to his wife, Sarah, and to his daughter, Anne, in Philadelphia, and his estate in America to his son, John Redman Coxe, Doctor of Physic. At the death of his wife his property was to be divided in five parts, going to his said son, Dr. Coxe, to Leonard Street Coxe, to George Coxe, and to his said daughter, and to his two grandchildren, Maria and Harriet Phillis Lockhart, daughters of his deceased daughter, Maria. (P. C. C.). His widow in 1828 brought suit in New Jersey for her dower rights in his confiscated property and recovered judgment. She died in Brighton, England, in 1843, aged 91. (See A. 12:74, ff. 39-60; A. O. 12:100, ff. 117, 285; "Loyalists' Claims," pp. 274-7; Sabine; "N. J. Hist. Soc. Coll.," Vol. III, p. 84, where many facts and American references appear).

DANIEL COZENS (Captain)

Born in America about 1746, he was a planter on his own property in Gloucester county, N. J., fifteen miles from Philadelphia. He was also the owner, in right of his wife, of the toll bridge, with a large tavern attached, in the town of Gloucester, within four miles of Philadelphia, on the post road from that city into the counties of Salem and Cumberland. The toll bridge was bought in 1768 from Samuel Blackwood, High Sheriff, by Samuel Shivers, father of this Loyalist's wife, who was also the owner of Shivers Island. The property would seem to have descended to Mrs. Elizabeth Cozens and her sister, Mary, by will of their father, dated May 1, 1777.

Daniel Cozens joined the British early, after taking the oath of allegiance to the Americans under threats of imprisonment, and it was said that through his influence 100 of his neighbors and friends followed him in the autumn of 1777 to Philadelphia and put themselves under his command, he victualling them at his own expense. In January, 1778, he was commissioned Captain, and in March he and his Company took command of Billingsport Fort on the Delaware, where he was joined in June by Captains Hugh Cowperthwaite (q. v.) and Hutton. Soon afterwards Major John Vandyke (q. v.) was appointed to command this force, with the title of West Jersey Volunteers. At the reduction of this corps, Captain Cozens and his Company joined the 3rd New Jersey Volunteers. In November, 1778, he accompanied Colonel Archibald Campbell's Expedition to the Southern colonies and served in Georgia at the capture of Savannah and in South Carolina for four years (except for the term of his captivity) until Yorktown, where he was among the prisoners taken. There are long schedules of his property in A. O. 13:108, with certificates to his military services from Cortlandt Skinner (q. v.) and Captain George Clarke (q. v.)

Daniel Cozens was the son of Jacob Cozens and brother of Joshua Cozens (whose wife was Martha). His wife, Elizabeth, and four children were living in February, 1786, in the "Rebel country," at Philadelphia. He was granted £997 from his large claim of £41,305 and at the rate of £360 a year for the loss of his income during the War. (A. O. 12:109). He also received a pension of £180 and half-pay as Captain in the 2nd New Jersey Volunteers until 1808, when he probably died. (Sabine and Stryker are in error in their statement that this officer was killed at Savannah in 1779). (A. O. 12: 14, ff. 97-111; A. O. 12:74, ff. 19-71; A. O. 12:101, f. 189; Ind.: 5604-5-6; Stryker).

JAMES CREIGHTON

Born in the province of New York, he was admitted to the Bar there in 1774. He was imprisoned early for his loyalty. In February, 1777, he was commissioned Captain in the 3rd New Jersey Volunteers, a commission which he resigned on his appointment as Secretary to the Police on Long Island. At the Peace he sailed to Dominica with his wife and four small children, and thence, in July, 1789, to Halifax, Nova Scotia. (From a memorial by Captain Robert McCrea (q. v.) in F. O. 4:1).

RICHARD ROBERT CROWE (Captain-Lieutenant)

An Irishman, who was commissioned Lieutenant in the 48th Foot in 1754 and Captain-Lieutenant on November 10, 1755. He accompanied Braddock to America, was present and was wounded in the defeat of that officer, and served in the taking of Quebec, Louisburg, Martinique and Havana. At the end of the War in 1763 he sold his commission in the army and for his services was granted free land in the Province of New York and settled near Perth Amboy, New Jersey, where he bought land for himself and his brother, Captain Eyre Evans Crowe, who had not, however, set foot on American soil. Early in the Revolution he was offered the rank of General by the Americans. He preferred, however, to serve with the British forces, in the inconspicuous ranks of furrier to the army and Captain in the Black Pioneers. Subsequent to the offer of this high rank in the American army, he was subjected to the resentment of the adherents of Congress, by whom he was apprehended and detained a prisoner for several months.

Captain Crowe was a signatory to the memorial for the establishment of a Masonic Lodge at Digby, Nova Scotia, in September, 1784. ("Hist. of Digby Lodge, No. 6 and St. Mary's No. 5, Digby," by R. W. Bro. Rev. Wm. Driffield). He settled at Parrsborough, Nova Scotia, and was living there on half-pay from 1792 and on the interest of the sum of £515 allowed from his claim of £794. 5s. (W. O. 24:751; Ind.: 5605; A. O. 12:63, f. 140; A. O. 12:109; "Ontario Archives," pp. 1276-8).

The particulars of his estate in New Jersey include a kiln for making stoneware; there are also a copy of the inquisition in 1778 into his affairs and into his loyalty, with the names of the jurors; and an affidavit of Samuel Warne, of Digby, Nova Scotia, dated July 24, 1787, testifying to the loyalty of Captain Crowe and to his personal knowledge of the Crowe property in New Jersey. (A. O. 13:17).

His brother, Captain Eyre Evans Crowe, served in the War against the French, and in the East Indies in several important engagements. (A. O. 13:17; A. O. 12:63, f. 139). He claimed £1,200 for the loss of his American property and was awarded £700. (A. O. 12:109).

JOSEPH CROWELL (Captain)

He is said to have been "of Middletown," but with property in Sussex county, N. J. He was born in New Jersey about 1745. He served for most of the War in the New Jersey Volunteers, from 1776 as Captain in the 5th and 6th Battalions and from 1778 in the 1st Battalion. In 1777 he was attainted of treason and his property was confiscated and sold in 1779. There is a list of his property sold at this time, with the names of the buyers and the prices realised, the total amount being £7,444. 8s. 4d., in New Jersey currency. With these papers is an affidavit, dated July 7, 1783, of Nathaniel Pettit, Samuel Crowell, Andrew Willson and Amos Pettit, all Justices of the Peace in 1776 in Sussex county, regarding his property there. (A. O. 13:17).

He appears to have settled at St. John, New Brunswick, Canada, and received half-pay until 1798. (Ind.: 5604-5-6). The sum of £450 was allowed him from his claim of £534. 7s. (A. O. 12:109). His son, Thomas, died at Shelburne, Nova Scotia, in 1845, aged 80. His only daughter married Luther Wetmore. His uncle was Thomas Crowell (q. v.). (A. O. 12.15, ff. 266-272; A. O. 12:63, f. 33; Stryker; Sabine; "Ontario Archives," p. 596).

THOMAS CROWELL (Captain)

A native of New Jersey, born in 1724, and for twenty years a master mariner near Sandy Hook. In 1764 he bought 240 acres of land near Middletown, Monmouth county, and was the owner of a house and a lot in Amboy, all of which property was confiscated on May 15, 1779. For his loyal services he was appointed a Captain in a corps of Loyal Volunteers in New York and Warden of that Port. He received a Loyalist pension from 1784 to 1788, when he was put on the military establishment for an allowance of £70. Cornelius Hatfield (q.

v.), his neighbor, describes this Loyalist as "no two-sided man" in the Revolution. His only son was at Elizabethtown, New Jersey, in 1786. His nephew was Joseph Crowell (q. v.). He was allowed the substantial sum of £1,247 for his valuable estate, from his claim of £1,562. (A. O. 12:109; A. O. 13:108; A. O. 12:14, ff. 21-30; A. O. 12:100, f. 121; Ind.: 5606; T. 50:8; T. 50:10).

GEORGE CYPHERS (Adjutant)

He was born in America and served, first, as a Sergeant in the 2nd New Jersey Volunteers and, from September 7, 1783, as Adjutant of that Battalion. He may be the same as the "George Cyphers, Jr.," ordered to be apprehended in New Jersey, June 26, 1776. ("Min. N. J. Council of Safety").

According to the account of William Mills, farmer, of Douglas, York county, New Brunswick, "George Cypheus" and he were present at the battles on Staten Island and Egg Harbor, in the taking of Savannah in Georgia, and elsewhere. Cyphers also took part in the successful siege of Charleston, South Carolina, and both he and Mills were besieged in the siege of Ninety-Six. They fought in what Mills describes as the most severe battle of all, that of Eutaw Springs.

Cyphers was married, on April 8, 1790, to Sarah Estey, at Kingsclear Parish, New Brunswick, in the presence of her sister, Ruth Everitt, of Fredericton, and of her brother, Aaron Estey, of Douglas, York county, all in the Province of New Brunswick. He died on July 18, 1828, and was buried in the graveyard of the Episcopal Church at Fredericton. (W. O. 42:C33; Ind.: 5605-6). Sarah, his widow, received £10 to relieve her in her distressed circumstances in 1846. ("Journals of the House of Assembly of New Brunswick," February 24, 1846).

JOSIAH FRANKLIN DAVENPORT

A High Sheriff of the County of Burlington, N. J., appointed Jan. 8, 1773, and Collector of Customs, who was deprived of his offices on account of his loyalty and died towards the end of the War. (A. O. 12:17, ff. 43-4). During 1776 he received from the State of New Jersey money for boarding Governor Franklin, then held at Burlington as a prisoner. ("Min. Prov. Cong.," pp. 482, 575).

WILLIAM DEBNAM

He was an English shoemaker, a Loyalist, settled at Mansfield, in Burlington county, New Jersey. (A. O. 12:100, f. 363).

DAVID DEMARE

A small farmer of the Demarest family in Bergen county, N. J., who served for three years in the 2nd New Jersey Volunteers. (A. O. 13:81).

WILLIAM DEMAYNE

He was of Morristown, N. J., but a native of Yorkshire, England, and, with Thomas Gummersall, was agent to the English firm of Kent & Company in the management of a farm, iron works and a merchant's store in Morris county. In the Winter of 1777 he had a warrant from General Cortlandt Skinner (q. v.) to raise a company in the New Jersey Volunteers, with Joseph Cunliffe as his Lieutenant; but in consequence of the heavy losses sustained by the British in the attack on Staten Island by General Sullivan on August 22, this Loyalist brigade was reduced from six to four Battalions. To his mortification, Lieutenant Cunliffe was the one who was promoted Captain. (According to Sabine, Cunliffe served as a Lieutenant from Jan. 25, 1777). Demayne afterwards served as a guide and, later, in one of the gunboats under Captain Hatfield, "which were a great annoyance to the enemy." He was unable to cultivate his bounty lands in Nova Scotia because of ill-health. In 1788 he was at No. 2, White Hart Row, Kennington, London, at the age of 49. (F. O. 4:1). He claimed with Thomas Gummersall £2,096 for the loss of his property in New Jersey and was granted £1,078. (A. O. 12: 109). From June, 1788, he received a military allowance of £25. (Ind.: 5606).

Thomas Gummersall emigrated to New York in 1771 with a cargo of merchandise, accompanied by Demayne. He provided the money for the purchase of a plot of land at the corner of the cross roads on Wantony Plain, near Morristown, and built a store there and in Elizabethtown. Joseph Cunliffe and Robert Morris were in the employ of the firm. Although a Quaker, Gummersall took a commission as Captain in the 2nd King's Royal Regiment of New York. His long memorial gives an account of his troubles and adventures in the Island of Jamaica, Savannah in Georgia, at Albany, New York, and in Philadelphia. (A. O. 12:16, ff. 223-247; A. O. 12:63, ff. 109-110; "Amer. MSS. in Roy. Inst.," IV, 48).

JOHN DE MENEZES (Captain-Lieutenant)

He was born in Portugal about 1754. No information is available in the documents as to the reason for his presence in America or for his motives in accepting a commission as a Captain-Lieutenant in the Second Battalion, New Jersey Volunteers. He was on the Seconded List of that Regiment in 1783. (Ind.: 5605).

PIERRE DE PEYSTER

He describes himself as a "gentleman," born in New York, and settled at Newark in New Jersey, where his estate and mills produced him an annual income of £400 sterling. On the advice of friends he went into the American Committee at Second River and was obliged "for his own safety" to sign an Association to support the American cause and to take an oath of allegiance to the United States in 1778. He had previously, in 1777, served in the Quartermaster-General's Department in New York City and, later, rejoined this service, in which he was employed in obtaining intelligence until 1782.

In A. O. 12:14 is a copy of his long letter to Sir Guy Carleton, Commander-in-Chief, referring to the unstable conditions of American banking affairs in New York, under Morris, and urging a blockade of the Chesapeake and the Delaware, and giving a long account of the positions and condition of the American army. Extracts from this letter (he says) were published in the newspapers. The letter had been intercepted in May, 1782, and Pierre de Peyster was then seized as a traitor and imprisoned, but escaped death by procuring the flight of the hostile witness. For these valuable services to the British army he claimed £1,000.

Pierre de Peyster was concerned in April, 1782, to the extent of half in a merchandise transaction made for him in New York by Philip Schuyler. The goods were sent to him in New Jersey, and thence for sale to Philadelphia, but they were seized by the Americans and sold.

In his memorial to Lord North, dated May 5, 1783, he relates his services in, and losses by, the War, and complains of the inadequate allowance granted to him by the Government, which was insufficient to bring his wife and six children from America to England, while he himself was not allowed by the Americans to return to his native country. (F. O. 4:1). He was in reduced circumstances in England after the War and was keeping a small shop in Hull, his wife and six children being there with him. His sister, Catherine, married one Dubois, a New York magistrate, who died in 1781, childless (A. O. 12:99, f. 320).

The sum of £200 was allowed to Pierre de Peyster from his claim of £1,656 (A. O. 12:109); and he was granted a pension of £100 from 1789 to 1806. (T. 50:11; A. O. 462:21). In his memorial he makes no mention of his family connection with Captain Abraham de Peyster of the King's American Regiment, who succeeded to the command of the Loyalist force at King's Mountain, upon the death of Major Patrick Ferguson, or of this officer's brothers, Frederick and James de Peyster, of New York, both officers in Loyalist Regiments.

EDWARD VAUGHAN DONGAN (Lieut.-Colonel)

He was the youngest son of Edward Dongan, of Elizabethtown; was born on Staten Island and was married on April 4, 1773, to Frances, daughter of Bernardus LaGrange and sister of three loyalists, Lydia, wife of Dr. Henry Dougan (q. v.), Susannah, wife of Captain Arthur Wadman (q. v.), and of James Brazier LaGrange (q. v.).

The young Loyalist was a lawyer admitted to the New Jersey Bar Nov. 15, 1770, and earning £300 a year in practice, first in Elizabethtown and then in Rahway, where, in 1776, he bought a house, which was converted into a "Rebel barracks." In the summer of this year he was forcibly taken from his bed in the dead of night, in the presence of Dr. Samuel Barron, by a body of armed men and carried six miles away. On the following day Governor Livingston ordered him to be removed to a plantation of his father-in-law, Bernardus La-Grange (q. v.), a distance of thirty miles.

It would seem that his first military experience in the Revolution was in the rank of Lieutenant in the 26th Regiment. On November 5, 1776, he was appointed Lieutenant-Colonel of the 3rd New Jersey Volunteers, and as such was in the memorable engagement of August 22, 1777, near Richmond, on Staten Island, and there received a wound from which this "young gentleman of uncommon merit, both as a man and a soldier," died within three days, at the age of 29, after making his will on the 23rd, attended in his last moments by his brother-in-law, Dr. Henry Dougan. His wife, who had been at headquarters on Staten Island, fled with her baby son and only child, Walter Townley, aged 18 months, "through marshes and ditches and mire frequently up to her knees," under a heavy American fire for over three miles, until she reached a boat by which she was conveyed to New York. The baby died from the results of these hardships, on the same day as his father, and was buried in the same grave. Cortlandt Skinner's tribute to his memory was that he was "an active and sprightly young fellow and very zealous." His widow was granted £422 from her claim of £2,232 and an annual allowance as the widow of a Lieutenant-Colonel and a Loyalist pension until her death. (A. O. 12:109, T. 50:8; T. 50:28). The Middlesex county, N. J., Court records show property of his was confiscated April 18, 1778. (A. O. 13:109; A. O. 12:13, ff. 259-273; "Am. MSS. in Roy. Inst.," III: 4; "Loyalists' Claims," pp. 281-2; Sabine; Stryker; Middlesex, N. J., Records).

Dr. HENRY DOUGAN

An Irishman by birth and, from September 17, 1761, surgeon's mate (i. e. assistant surgeon) in the 29th Regiment of Foot, stationed in New Jersey, before settling about 1773, as a surgeon and physician and "man midwife" at Elizabethtown. He had already been admitted a "surgeon in the Colony of New Jersey" on September 7, 1773, and had married, on October 26, 1771, Lydia LaGrange, daughter of Bernardus LaGrange (q. v.), at Christ Church, New Brunswick, and sister of Frances, wife of Lieutenant Colonel Edward Vaughan Dongan (q. v.) and of Susannah, wife of Captain Arthur Wadman (q. v.).

On December 20, 1776, Henry Dougan was appointed surgeon to the 3rd New Jersey Volunteers and, at the close of the War, was put on half-pay of that Regiment. He was in County Armagh in his native country in 1788 and died, probably in Ireland, in or about 1805, when his pension ceased. He was compensated the full amount of his claim of £216, and also at the rate of £200 a year for the loss of his professional income. His widow was living in London in October, 1814, with her granddaughter, Frances Lucy LaGrange Dougan, aged 10, only daughter of her son, Lieutenant James Dougan, of the 48th Foot from 1793 to 1802, afterwards of the East Yorkshire militia and the 2nd Garrison Battalion.

Susannah, daughter of Dr. Henry and Lydia Dougan, married, in 1809, one Julius Wynne, who was afterwards discovered to have been a married man, with a child living. She was in child by this "inhuman monster" and subsisted on needlework for a living and on an allowance from the Government Compassionate Fund. (W. O. 25:3074; W. O. 25:3076; W. O. 25:3077; W. O. 25:3084; W. O. 25:3094).

There is evidently some close family connection between this family and Lieutenant B. Dougan, of the Antrim militia, an active and meritorious officer who died from fatigue on service against the rebels in the Irish rebellion in 1798, leaving a widow, Margaret, and a daughter, Lydia Maria Dougan, the latter of whom was put on the Compassionate List and died shortly before June 19, 1820. (W. O. 25:3081; A. O. 462:20; A. O. 13:83; A. O. 13:109; A. O. 13:137; A. O. 12:14, ff. 369-374; A. O. 12:100, ff. 116, 125; A. O. 12:101, f. 356; A. O. 12:109; "Army Lists").

THOMAS DOWDESWELL

An Englishman, born at Sedgeberrow in the county of Worcester, England, and had been for many years an English trader, resident at Shrewsbury, New Jersey, until 1777. Having espoused the cause of the mother country he states he was plundered of his personal property by a Company commanded by Brigadier-General David Forman. After five days' imprisonment he sought refuge in New York, at the age of 63, and was granted a free passage home to England. (A. O. 13:96; A. O. 13:110).

BENJAMIN DRAKE

He joined the British army in 1776 and in the same year was attainted. He was born in New Jersey and was a farmer at Piscataway. He died in exile at Digby, Nova Scotia, intestate, leaving an only son, William (q. v.), and two daughters, Rachel, the wife of Peter Holton (q. v.), and Mary Frazer, who lived in New Jersey with her husband, a citizen of the United States. (A. O. 12:15, ff. 131-9; A. O. 12:102, ff. 147, 186). In A. O. 13:17 are a schedule of his real estate in New Jersey and three original indentures of sales of land to him, in 1742, 1751 and 1774.

WILLIAM DRAKE

A son of the above Benjamin Drake. He resided in Somerset county, N. J., served for a while with the British and was captured. Upon his release he returned to New Jersey and took the oath of allegiance to America and abjuration of Great Britain, as well as serving with the American militia. He settled at Digby, Nova Scotia. (A. O. 13:17; A. O. 12:15, ff. 131-9; A. O. 12:102, ff. 147, 186). He and FitzRandolph Drake claimed £5,256 for the loss of their property in New Jersey, which was ordered forfeited in 1778, and William Drake was granted £800. (A. O. 12:109). His claim of £1,603. 8. 2. was disallowed, because he had taken the oath of allegiance to the State of New Jersey and resided there after the Peace. (A. O. 12:63, f. 16).

WILLIAM DRAKE

Only child of Fitz-Randolph Drake. He was a Loyalist. (A. O. 12:17, ff. 140-9).

ROBERT DRUMMOND (Major)

He was born about 1736 in New Jersey and was a general merchant and shipper at Acquackanonk Landing (now Passaic). He was one of the Loyalists who joined the British upon the arrival of the army in the Province and was commissioned by Sir William Howe to recruit men. Success attended his efforts and 120 recruits joined the New Jersey Volunteers, in which he was appointed Major of the 3rd Battalion on November 20, 1776, and with which he served on Staten Island; later was of the 2nd Battalion to the end of the War.

Robert Drummond's political career is of some interest, for, as he declared in London, he had become a member of the Provincial Congress of New Jersey "out of fear," and had signed an Association to support the magistrates. Another version of his conduct was that he had been urged by loyal friends to take a seat in that body and oppose all "Rebel" measures. A record states that he was a member of the General Assembly of New Jersey from 1770 to 1774 (but this is not confirmed by the official N. J. "Legislative Manual"), and a deputy to the Provincial Congress in May, 1775, and again in October, 1775, and in January and June, 1776. On a momentous day in the history of America, namely, July 2, 1776, he voted against the adoption of the Constitution of the State of New Jersey. In August, 1776, he is noted down in an American bill of expenditures as "Captain Robert Drummond." ("Min. Prov. Cong. of N. J.," p. 574).

Major Drummond saw much active service in the South. He accompanied his Regiment in November, 1778, to Georgia, where he remained on duty until August, 1780, when he was ordered from Savannah to Augusta, a well-known fortified town in that colony, and thence to the Fort of Ninety-Six in South Carolina, which he helped to defend during the memorable siege. Thence he removed to Charleston and there served until the evacuation of South Carolina by the British in 1782. Later he served on Long Island and in New York, and at the conclusion of the War sailed for England. He died in 1789 in Chelsea Hospital, founded in the reign of Charles II and built by Sir Christopher Wren for the old warriors of England, and was buried in St. Luke's churchyard close by, on February 3.

The sum of £1,286 was granted to him as compensation, which was in excess of his claim of £1,091. (A. O. 12:109). His property was confiscated in Bergen county in 1778, (but not sold until 1784). He had married Jennie, daughter of Elias Vreeland, on April 1, 1759, and inquisition against her was entered Sept. 21, 1779. His portrait, in the uniform of a British officer, is said to have been painted in London in 1784. A sketch of his life is in the "Paterson (N. J.) Press" for January 31, 1877. (A. O. 12:14, ff. 193-205; A. O. 12:100, f. 327; Ind.: 5605-6; "Am. MSS. in Roy. Inst.," IV: 374; Sabine; Stryker; Bergen Co., N. J., Records).

PETER DULYEA (alias PIERRE DOLEAY)

He bore arms in the War and was a refugee on the Bay of Quinte in Canada in 1788. (A. O. 12:63, f. 132). He was awarded £42 from his claim of £54. 12s. (A. O. 12:109). New Jersey residence not stated.

JOHN DUMONT (Captain)

He was born in New Jersey, where he was the owner of property, including three-fourths of a brewery on a lot in present John street, New Brunswick, bought as late in the Revolution as 1776, the other fourth being owned by William Van Deursen, who seems to have got possession of this and other property after the War. The Middlesex county, N. J., records show confiscation of property, belonging to him, Feb. 20, 1779.

On November 15, 1776, he was appointed Lieutenant in the New York Loyal militia and in February, 1777, he was promoted Captain. In March he sailed for England, with what object is not stated, and in September, 1777, returned to New York, again sailing to England in 1780. Here he settled in business. His first commission (in A. O. 13:109) bears the arms of Governor Tryon, of New York, and is signed by Tryon and by Edmund Fanning, the conspicuous Loyalist and Colonel of the King's American Regiment. (A. O. 13:112; A. O. 12:14, ff. 381-4). His claim of £850 was disallowed (A. O. 12:109).

DENNIS DUNCOMBE

He was a silversmith in New York City before 1775, where he had property left to him by his grandmother. Having been banished for his loyalty, he sought refuge in New Jersey, where he endeavored, with the help of two comrades, to enlist men for the Loyalist forces. The three were captured and his two comrades were hanged. He, however, was reprieved, or otherwise escaped the fate of death. He afterwards joined the Royal Navy and served in H. M. S. "Pegasus." (A. O. 12:99, f. 275; A. O. 13:109).

ASHER DUNHAM (Captain)

He was born about 1745 in New Jersey, where he lived on a small farm at Hanover, Morris county. He had seen considerable military service in the previous War in America as a volunteer in the 80th Regiment of Foot, being present at the defeat of Ticonderoga and in the reduction of Canada. He joined the British army in November, 1776, and within a month received a warrant to raise a Company for the New Jersey Volunteers. Dunham was ordered, under the command of Major Richard W. Stockton (q. v.), to take post at Bennets Neck, with a small party of the new levies. In February, 1777, the party were taken prisoners by a superior body of the enemy and Dunham was marched in irons from Princeton to Philadelphia jail. He was detained a prisoner in different jails until August, 1778, when he was exchanged for Captain Nathaniel Porter, of the New Jersey Continental Regiment. To his great astonishment he found, on his release, that all the Companies of the New Jersey Volunteers were filled with the required officers, and, on December 24, 1779, he was put on the Seconded list as Captain. His name appears on this list after the War, when he had gone to St. John, New Brunswick. (A. O. 13:21; Ind.: 5605; Sabine).

ISAAC DUNHAM

A farmer, of Woodbridge, and a native of New Jersey, who joined the Royal army in 1776. In A. O. 13:17 are a certified valuation of his estate by Asa Morris and Josiah Dunham,

Auditor of Accounts of New Jersey, and an account of his confiscated estate, signed by the same Josiah Dunham. He was living on the Kennebecasis River, Province of New Brunswick, in 1786. His cousin, Daniel Dunham, and one John Dunham, are mentioned. He was allowed £155 from his claim of £507. 1s. (A. O. 12:109; A. O. 12:16, ff. 135-140; A. O. 12:63, f. 77).

BENJAMIN DUNN

He was of Piscataway, New Jersey, and fled to the garrison at New York in December, 1776, and remained within the British lines, often as a guide, until the end of the War. An affidavit of Hugh and James Dunn, dated Middlesex county, New Jersey, April 3, 1786, states that this Loyalist bought a plantation of 180 acres at Piscataway in 1772 from Colonel Azariah Dunham, who took possession of it during the Revolution. There is a schedule of his confiscated property. He was allowed £487 from his claim of £842. (A. O. 12:109; A. O. 13:17; A. O. 12:16, ff. 378-381; A. O. 12:63, f. 118).

Dr. CHARLES EARLE

A Scotsman, born in 1754, who served throughout the War in the Loyalist forces, as surgeon to the 2nd New Jersey Volunteers from 1777, and from 1782 to the 1st Battalion. He was put on half-pay of this Regiment. (Ind.: 5605-6).

Dr. Earle was appointed first surgeon to the King's New Brunswick Regiment, formed in 1793 upon the declaration of war by France against England. Of the four Captains of this Regiment one was from New Jersey, namely, Joseph Lee (q. v.), and three of the Lieutenants were John Jenkins, William Chew and William Turner, late of the New Jersey Volunteers. Later in the year John Simonson (q. v.), of the 4th, and Xenophon Jouet (son of Cavalier Jouet (q. v.), of the 1st New Jersey Volunteers, were added to the Lieutenants. Peace having been declared between Great Britain and France on October 1, 1801, this Regiment was disbanded in the following year, only to be reorganized as the New Brunswick Fencible Regiment in 1803, on the renewal of war with France, in which Dr. Earle continued service as surgeon. This Regiment was incorporated with the 104th Foot in 1811. (For these two Corps, see Jonas Howe's account in the "Collections of the New Brunswick (Canada) Historical Society," Vol. I, pp. 13-59).

EDWARD EARLE (Captain)

He was born at Hackensack, New Jersey, on November 27, 1757, the son of Silvester Earle, whose will was made in 1768. Here he was a farmer at the outbreak of the War. From 1776 to the end of the War he was a Captain in the 3rd Battalion, New Jersey Volunteers.

He was married on January 19, 1784, to Sichy Van Dine [Van Dyne], at Maugerville, New Brunswick, by the Rev. John Beardsley, himself a refugee, who married more than one New Jersey Loyalist exile. Captain Earle died on July 5, 1825, in New York, where his widow remained and where his son, Silvester, was living in 1827. His eldest brother, John, born on January 21, 1744, was living in 1827 at Lodi (formerly New Barbadoes) in Bergen County, New Jersey. His widowed sister-in-law, Mary Heaton, aged about 60, was at New York in 1826, while his wife's brother, Cornelius Van Dyne, was a grocer in Brooklyn, New York, in the same year. (W. O. 42:E1).

With the account of the losses of Edward Earle and his brother, Justus, are copies of the official documents relating to the confiscation of their property in Bergen county, N. J., in 1778. (A. O. 13:18). The brothers claimed £1,750. 5s., and Justus was awarded £300 and Edward £200. (A. O. 12: 109; A. O. 12:16, ff. 177-180; A. O. 12:63, f. 81; "Ontario Archives," p. 814).

JUSTUS EARLE (Lieutenant)

Born in 1749, he was the son of Silvester Earle, of Hackensack, New Jersey, and brother of Captain Edward Earle (q. v.). He served, first, from 1775, as a volunteer, but appears to have rejoined the Americans, from whom he and his brother Edward (q. v.), deserted on November 26, 1776. On April

16, 1777, he was appointed Ensign in the 4th New Jersey Volunteers. In August, 1779, he was a prisoner in Philadelphia, but was exchanged. He was promoted to be Lieutenant on December 18, 1781. He was living on half-pay in Queen's county, New Brunswick, in 1787, and died on September 21, 1825, probably in that county. Of his three sisters, one was dead and another, Hannah, married William Sorrell, at Shelburne, Nova Scotia, in January 1787, perhaps the New Jersey Loyalist of this name, mentioned later, or a son. (A. O. 12: 16, ff. 181-6; A. O. 12:63, f. 81; Ind.: 5604-5-6; "Ontario Archives," pp. 814-5).

Dr. WILLIAM FARQUHAR

He is described in the Loyalist papers as a "physician of great repute practising in New Jersey" until the beginning of the War, when he removed to New York. At the end of the War he was in New York, at the age of 80, but intending to sail for England to join his son, Major William Farquhar, of the 20th Regiment of Foot.

Dr. Farquhar resided for a time, in New Brunswick, New Jersey. He married, first, Elizabeth Farmar, daughter of Major Thomas Farmar of New Brunswick, and, second, after he removed to New York City, Jane Colden. (A. O. 12:99, f. 321; A. O. 13:54; Benedict's "New Brunswick (N. J.) in History").

RICHARD FINNIMORE (Ensign)

An Ensign in the West Jersey Volunteers, who was on half-pay after the War. (Ind.: 5606).

DAVID FITZ RANDOLPH

Owner of a plantation of 150 acres at a very noted ferry, known as the Old Blazing Star, in Middlesex co., N. J., his birthplace. He was the eldest son of Nathaniel FitzRandolph, grandson of Joseph FitzRandolph and great-grandson of Nathaniel FitzRandolph. He "exerted himself at the commencement of the late unhappy Rebellion," and consequently was proscribed and his estate confiscated, Sept. 22, 1778. During the War he resided at Staten Island and was embodied in the militia of the Island, serving in many severe actions in the defense of the West side. (A. O. 13:18).

His description of his property was witnessed by Robert FitzRandolph (q. v.). With a copy of the inquisition is an affidavit of Joshua Wright and Nicholas Stillwell, dated New York, October 21, 1783, to their knowledge of FitzRandolph's estate. His confiscated property was sold for £1,900. 14s. in 1778 and 1779. (Ibid). He was at Sissiboo River, Nova Scotia, in 1786. He was allowed £745 from his claim of £956. (A. O. 12:109). His brothers, Joseph and Asher, took the American side in the War. (A. O. 12:15, ff. 259-265; A. O. 12:63, f. 29; Middlesex Records).

Some other member of the FitzRandolph family, a Lieutenant in the Royal militia, was killed in service with the Queen's Rangers in New Jersey. (Sabine).

ROBERT FITZ RANDOLPH

Born in New Jersey, he was a Quaker, farmer, distiller and merchant in Woodbridge and was clerk of the records of that township in 1776, when he refused to surrender these records to "the Rebels." He also had property in Elizabethtown, which was confiscated in 1779. He also refused to sign the Association against the British Government and, having been suspected by the Americans of giving information to the British, he escaped, first, to the army at Perth Amboy in January, 1777, and, later, to Staten Island, where he was employed as superintendent of men building a redoubt. He settled at Annapolis, Nova Scotia. (A. O. 12:15, ff. 74-80; A. O. 12:63, f. 9). Several papers concerning his property are in A. O. 13:90. His notes and book debts were assigned to James and Edward FitzRandolph. With certain papers are a copy of the inquisition and a list of the debts due to him, with the names of the debtors and the amounts. Jonathan Dear was his greatest debtor, for £100, with £51. 6. 8. extra for interest. (A. O. 13:18). He was allowed £575 from his claim of £675. (A. O. 12:109).

JOHN FORD (Lieutenant)

He was born in New Jersey about 1746; was a tanner in a large way and a planter at Woodbridge. He "relinquished all the comforts of a private and independent life" for the sake of his loyalty. His father, Samuel Ford, by his will of 1768, left all his lands to this son, except a life interest in his homestead to another son, Oswald, who died during the War. His uncle, Oswald Ford, bequeathed to him (John Ford) by his will of 1777, all his property. He served as a Lieutenant in the N. J. Volunteers in 1777, and, according to Stryker, was dismissed from the service May 3, 1778.

His property was confiscated and sold and fell into the possession of Ebenezer Ford, James Taping and Reuben Porter. In 1786 he was a refugee on the Kennebecasis River, fifteen miles from St. John, New Brunswick. He died at Hampton in that Province in 1823. His claim of £966. 7s. was met by an allowance of £580. (A. O. 12:109; A. O. 13:18; A. O. 12:16, ff. 104-8; A. O. 12:63, f. 72; Sabine).

Oswald Ford, of Woodbridge, the brother of John, had his property confiscated Sept. 22, 1778. (Middlesex Co., N. J., Ct. Records).

EZEKIEL FORMAN

A native of New Jersey and a planter. On July 1, 1776, he was taken before the Provincial Congress of New Jersey to answer charges of being a Loyalist and gave bonds in £500 to remain friendly to the United Colonies, and on August 20 was fined £3. ("Min. of Prov. Cong.," pp. 486, 545). He must then, almost at once, have joined the British army, which he served from 1776 until 1778, when he was taken prisoner and was adjudged to suffer death for his active loyalty. He was, however, released and resided in Pennsylvania. His wife had been deprived of her property because of her father's activity as a Loyalist. She and her seven children were living in New Jersey in 1788. (A. O. 12:102, f. 143).

ARTHUR FORREST (Commodore)

He commanded the squadron of the Royal Navy at Jamaica from 1769 until his death on January 1, 1770. He was possessed of a considerable share in large ironworks and iron mines in New Jersey and New York, known as the "American Company," which he bequeathed to his son, Thomas Forrest, afterwards a Lieutenant in the Royal Navy, who was killed on board H. M. S. "Ajax" in the defeat of the Spanish by Lord Rodney off Gibraltar.

Commodore Arthur Forrest, having been killed in an insurrection of negroes in Jamaica before the American Revolution, should not himself find a place here; but as the memorial of his five granddaughters, Julia, Cecilia, Margaret, Harriet and Augusta Forrest, daughters of his son, the above Lieutenant Thomas Forrest, is included with the Loyalist documents in A. O. 13:90, the family should doubtless be included, especially as he was, perhaps, a former resident in New Jersey.

The iron and copper mines in New Jersey cost the Commodore £20,000, in purchase and in expenditure. They descended to these five ladies by the will of their father; but no information is available in the documents as to whether they recovered any part of, or were compensated for, them.

The commissions of Arthur Forrest were:

Master and Commander, seniority, May 25, 1741; and Captain, March 9, 1744-5. (Commission and Warrant Books). April 8, 1760, Captain to "Centaur," and, June 26, 1760, Captain to "Augusta." (Ad. 6:19). Appointment as "Commander-in-Chief of H. M. Ships & Vessels employed at and about Jamaica and in the Gulf of Mexico, from the River Mississippi to Cape Florida." Empowered to hoist "a broad pendant," May 16, 1769. His ship, the "Dunkirk," sailed from England on June 6, 1769. He died at Port Royal, Jamaica, at 2 a. m. on Saturday, May 26, 1770, in H. M. S. "Dunkirk." (Ad. 6:20, p. 23; Commission & Warrant Bks.). As will be observed, there is a discrepancy as to the date of his death between the family account in A. O. 13:90 and the official account just quoted.

Thomas Forrest, then over 20 years of age, was examined by the Navy Board and by certificate it was shown that he had been to sea for more than six years in the following ships: In the "Augusta," as Captain's servant, for three years; in the "Dunkirk," as midshipman for nearly seventeen months; in the "Phœnix," as able seaman, for four months; and in the "Modeste," as midshipman, for seventeen months. He produced Journals kept by himself in the "Dunkirk" and "Modest," and certificates from Captains Stirling and Wheelock to his diligence, etc.; he could "splice, knot, reef or sail, and was qualified to do the duty of an able seaman and midshipman." Date May 11, 1774. His seniority as Lieutenant is dated September 27, 1775. Thomas Forrest was appointed Second Lieutenant to the "Cerberus," March 4, 1776; to the "London," September 13, 1779; and to the "Ajax," October 16, 1779. On Monday, January 17, 1780, during an engagement with the Spanish fleet off Cape St. Vincent, nine men of the "Ajax" were wounded, three of whom lost a leg, one of them being Second Lieutenant Thomas Forrest. (Captain's Log, H. M. S. "Ajax"; "Adm. Navy Bd.," Passing Certificates, Vol. 4; Commission & Warrant Books).

EBENEZER FOSTER

This Loyalist lived as a farmer in Woodbridge, N. J., and was Judge of the Inferior Court of Common Pleas. He was on a Committee of Observation in Jan., 1775, but his situation as a Loyalist became every day more "unquiet" after January 1, 1776, and he states he was kept a prisoner from July to December of that year, having previously been paroled in £1,000 of bonds.

The schedule of his property indicates prosperity and includes a Bible with a silver clasp. He refers to the property of his grandfather (not named); to his mother, Margaret Heddon (died February 9, 1767), whose only child he was; and to his aunt, Catherine Loofborrow. The names of the persons from whom Foster bought his property are recorded in one document. With this is the original indenture of March 25, 1773, of Benjamin Thorp, a poor child, of Woodbridge, to Ebenezer Foster, farmer, with the original signatures of Samuel Barron and David Alston, both Justices of the Peace. He was living at Kingston, New Brunswick, in 1787, with two sons, Stephen and Lawrence. Compensation to the amount of £906 was awarded to him from his claim of £1,937. 3s. (A. O. 12:109; A. O. 13:18; A. O. 12:16, ff. 312-22; A. O. 12:63, f. 98; "Minutes of N. J. Council of Safety").

Governor WILLIAM FRANKLIN

The original documents of Governor Franklin are few in number, though his name is of frequent occurrence in the Loyalist papers as a witness in favor of, or against, the claims of certain Loyalists. His original memorial is not preserved, but an official contemporary copy survives (A. O. 12:17, ff. 27-65), in which he declares that, on June 19, 1776, he was seized by an armed force by order of the Provincial Congress of New Jersey, an order which was confirmed by the Continental Congress, and having refused to give his parole the Governor was sent as a prisoner into Connecticut. There he was detained until the end of October, 1778, and treated with "extraordinary rigor and severity." For over eight months he says he was confined in a loathsome room previously used as a dungeon for common felons and overrun with vermin. He was deprived of the use of pen, ink and paper, debarred from conversation except with the sheriff or gaoler, and often subjected "to the grossest insults from the Rebel soldiery and others."[1] Meanwhile, in consequence of the evacuation of New Jersey by the British troops, he stated his wife was obliged to remove with his effects into New York, where the difficulties encountered and the uneasiness of mind under which she labored, on account of his long absence and of his ill-treatment, occasioned Mrs. Franklin's death.

During the Governor's imprisonment he contrived to send a letter to General Sir William Howe, offering himself for active military service, by which means he hoped to effect his exchange as a prisoner of war, but he never received any re-

---

[1] Sabine says (on what authority is not stated) that he was indulged in selecting the place of confinement and selected Connecticut, where he was quartered in the house of Captain Ebenezer Grant at East Windsor.

Sir George Otto Trevelyan, in his book on the "American War of Independence," goes further and gives a picture of freedom from restraint, by saying that the Governor was not only permitted to choose his own place of sojourn, but also led a free and jovial existence in Connecticut, giving tea parties to ladies of the neighbourhood. (Vol. IV, p. 49).

ply, if such was sent to him by the General. Upon his release he made the same offer of service to Howe's successor as Commander-in-chief, Sir Henry Clinton. At the request of the Loyalists, Governor Franklin set sail in August, 1782, for England, accompanied by a letter of instructions from the Loyalists and refugees in the City of New York, apparently protesting against the grant of American Independence.

There is a long description of his valuables, his elegant furniture, pictures and other treasures, including his large library of scarce books and curious manuscripts relating to the first settlement of America, which he had been collecting from his youth, and which were destroyed in the great fire in New York in September, 1776, and a long account of his real estate in New Jersey and elsewhere. During the Revolution he sold lands in New York to discharge a debt of £1,500, due to and demanded by his father, Dr. Benjamin Franklin, a debt "which would not have been demanded had he not been on the British side."

The Governor mentions J. F. Davenport (q. v.), High Sheriff of the county and city of Burlington, New Jersey, and Collector of Customs, who was deprived of his offices on account of his loyalty and died towards the end of the war. (Ibid, ff. 43-4). He also states that Chief Justice Frederick Smyth (q. v.) received the whole of his salary as Chief Justice, though he took no active part in the Revolution (f. 50).

Franklin was exchanged on November 1, 1778, for John McKinley and proceeded to New York and offered his services to the Commander-in-Chief. The King, on January 22, 1779, expressed appreciation of his loyal attachment and zeal and ordered him an allowance of £500 a year until restored to his former dignity as Governor of New Jersey, or otherwise provided for. (British Museum: Addl. MSS., 11514, f. 178).

The Board of Associated Loyalists (which included Daniel Coxe, q. v.), mentioned above was appointed in April, 1780, for the purpose of employing the zeal of the Loyalists and "annoying the coasts of the revolted Provinces and distressing their Trade either in co-operation with your Majesty's Land and Sea

Forces, or by making diversion in their favor when they were carrying on operations in other Parts." The Associated Loyalists collected forage, acted as guides and pioneers, annoyed the enemy by raids, and collected intelligence. Many New Jersey Loyalists were among them. Their frequent enterprises so annoyed the Americans as to compel them to employ a part of their forces, together with a body of French troops, to attack Fort Franklin at Lloyd's Neck, the principal post held by the Associators, by whom the attacking force was repulsed with considerable loss. So obnoxious did the Board become that the Directors were subjected by law to attainder and to the penalty of death, if captured. (F. O. 4:1; C. O. 5:175, ff. 451, 453.)

Franklin, in a letter dated August 12, 1782, denies the rumor that he had given orders in his own house for the execution of the American soldier, Joshua Huddy in 1782. He says that the Loyalist refugees were determined on reprisals for the murders of their brethren, but that the Board of Associated Loyalists had no power to give orders for retaliatory measures without the consent of the British Commander-in-Chief, who was extremely averse from such measures. (C. O. 5:107, ff. 9-17). Captain Richard Lippincott (q. v.) was tried by court-martial for the murder. A majority of the Board declared that his trial was illegal and unjustifiable. According to a deposition of James Putnam, the younger (a son of the distinguished Massachusetts lawyer and Loyalist of the same name) Huddy had declared just before his execution that if the Loyalists would spare his life, he would be their friend and a loyal subject. (C. O. 5:107, f. 29). Governor Franklin, in a previous letter of April 27, had expressed his disapproval of reprisals. If the British (he adds) could not afford the Loyalists better protection, they would leave the country or join the Rebels. ("Earl of Dartmouth's MSS." II: 469).

Joseph Galloway, the eminent lawyer and loyalist, of Pennsylvania, in evidence in London stated that never a spark of disloyalty entered into the breast of Governor Franklin (C. O. 5:107, f. 60); and General Sir Henry Clinton added that he did not think that the conduct of the Board of Associated Loyalists in New York, of which Franklin was an active member, was proper in the execution of Huddy, though the motives were chiefly from resentment. He could not say how far the Governor himself was concerned in the affair (C. O. 5:107, ff. 63-4).

Reports would seem to have been current in London that the political disagreements between Dr. Franklin and his son, the Governor, were purely collusive. The Commissioners of American Loyalists' Claims, though they placed no credence in these rumors, were nevertheless obliged to satisfy the Government on the subject by hearing the Governor's denial in person. They were not astonished to hear his denial, and forthwith recommended that his zeal and distinguished services, as well as his sufferings in the cause of loyalty, should be compensated in a worthy manner, so long as a shilling remained in the national treasury of Great Britain.

In an interesting secret letter, dated from New York, November 6, 1781, to Lord George Germain, Franklin says that but for the unfortunate surrender of Lord Cornwallis at Yorktown, it was the resolve of a great majority of the people of Virginia and other Colonies, both Rebels and Loyalists, to take up arms, not so much to support the British army as to compel Congress or the Colonial Legislatures to consent to an accommodation with Great Britain. In this spirited letter the Governor asserts that if the Loyalists had been taken into the confidence of the British Generals and Admirals and the measures suggested by them pursued, this catastrophe would have been avoided. A Virginia correspondent of the Governor says that previous to the disaster to Cornwallis it "was confidently asserted that nine-tenths of the people were in favor of reunion with the mother country." (C. O. 5:175, f. 475).

From his large claim of £45,812 he was allowed £1,800, doubtless because his only son, William Temple Franklin, recovered his New Jersey estate. His claim for the loss of his income as Governor at the rate of £960 during the War was awarded in full, and he was granted a pension of £420. (A. O. 12:85; A. O. 12:109).

John Eardley Wilmot says of him that he preserved his fidelity and loyalty to his Sovereign from the commencement to the conclusion of the contest, notwithstanding powerful incitements to the contrary.

The Governor was admitted to the Middle Temple on February 11, 1750-1, and was called to the English Bar by that Inn on November 10, 1758.

His attempt at reconciliation with his father brought forth an affectionate letter from Dr. Franklin, dated August 16, 1784, from Passy, saying that he ought not to blame his only son for differing with him in political questions and expressing appreciation of his son's view of his duty to his King and regard for his country. (British Museum; Addl. MSS., 11514, f. 173).

With Sir William Pepperell he heads the group of Loyalists in the picture, now lost, "The Reception of the American Loyalists by Great Britain in 1783," painted by his fellow-countryman, Benjamin West, of which an engraving by H. Moses may be seen in J. Eardley Wilmot's "Historical View of the Commission for Enquiring into the Losses . . . . of the American Loyalists." (1815).

Governor Franklin's portrait was executed in a medallion by Wedgwood. His motto was: "Pro Rege et Patria." (A. O. 12:104, f. 10).

The long and interesting will of Governor Franklin, made in Norton street, in the parish of St. Marylebone, London (where he died on November 16, 1813), contains a request to be buried in St. Pancras churchyard, where his wife was buried. He left certain property to be held in trust for Helena, commonly called Ellen Franklin, and bequests to his four godsons, William Franklin Bonnell, of Digby, Nova Scotia; Leonard Coxe, son of Daniel Coxe (q. v.); William Franklin Odell, son of the Rev. Jonathan Odell (q. v.); and Francis Barlow, son of William and Ellen Barlow. To the following he bequeathed money to purchase memorial rings: his much esteemed friends, Mrs. Anne Henley and Miss Hester Whitingdale, of No. 11, Manchester street, London; to his friends, Catherine Floyer, widow of Charles Floyer, Esq., of Portland Place, Arthur Cooke, Esq., Miss Teresa Jones, of Chelmsford, County Essex, Mrs. Mary Byrne, Miss Anna Byrne, Miss Mary Odell, daughter of the above Rev. Jonathan Odell, Miss Mary Porden, Miss Vardill, Major Thomas Gamble, Mrs. Burnet, wife of Lieut.-Colonel Burnet, Miss Frances Chalmers and Miss Sarah Lane. Having a right to a very considerable share of a grant of lands called "the Indiana" on two frontiers of Pennsylvania and having assigned one half to William Temple Franklin (his son), he left the other half to this son, if he could recover it or any compensation for it from the United States Government. To his son he bequeathed one-third of the debt due to him from the estate in the State of New York of Colonel George Croghan, deceased, formerly Deputy Superintendent of Indian Affairs in America. He left £40 for the eldest sons of his kinsman, Jonathan Williams, Esq., of Philadelphia, and in a codicil directs his executors to provide clothes for three years for a child, named Mary Jones, bound apprentice to Margaret Heanley, mantua maker, and afterwards to give her £25. The will is dated April 15, 1813, and was proved February 28, 1814. (P. C. C., 63 Bridport).

FRANCIS FRASER (Lieutenant)

He was of Scottish descent and was born in New Jersey. He was married, January 26, 1769, to Diodema Morris, at Woodbridge, N. J., according to the rites of the Church of England. He joined the British army as a volunteer in 1776, and in the winter of that year was taken prisoner in an action between New Brunswick and Amboy. On September 29, 1778, he was exchanged for Lieutenant Matthew Wideman, of Col. Atlee's Continental troops. The date of his commission as Lieutenant in the 3rd New Jersey Volunteers is February 21, 1777, when, according to his own account, he was a prisoner. He died on April 20, 1823, at Parrsborough, Nova Scotia, at the age of 89, leaving a widow, one son and two married daughters. (W. O. 42:F16; Ind.: 5605).

THOMAS S. FRASER (Major)

A Scotsman, who served throughout the War in a Loyalist Corps and, on August 10, 1780, was appointed Major of the South Carolina Royalists, at the age of 25. The War did not deter him from marrying, on November 7, 1782, Anne Loughton Smith, at Charleston, the ceremony having been performed by the Rev. Edward Jenkins, Chaplain to his Regiment. She was the niece of Miss Mary Inglis and sister of Mrs. Harriet B. Crafts, both of Charleston. He died at Philadelphia on May 31, 1820, and was buried in the graveyard of the historic Christ Church.

The name of Major Fraser is included in these pages because of the family connection of his widow with New Jersey, where she died on August 6, 1835, at the country place of her son-in-law, Prince Lucien Murat, at Bordentown. (W. O. 42:F13; Ind.: 5604-5-6; A. O. 12:3, ff. 327-340).

ADOLPHUS FRENCH (Lieutenant)

He was born in America about 1741 and was a Lieutenant in the New Jersey Volunteers. His name is on the Seconded List at the end of the War. (Ind.: 5605).

GILBERT GIBERSON (GUISBERTSON) (Captain)

He is described as a farmer, of Monmouth county, New Jersey, where he was born. Here he was appointed, in 1775, Captain of American militia and continued in this service until the Declaration of Independence, when he resigned. The documents in A. O. 13:18, consist of:

1. An official description of his tract of land, which was left by will of his father, Guisbert Guisbertson, to be divided between this son, Gilbert (or Guisbert) and another son, William. 2. A copy of the will of Guisbert Guisbertson, yeoman, in which are mentioned his wife, Hannah; the children of his son, John; Guisbert Guisbertson, son and heir of his son, John, deceased; and his two sons, above named, dated April 13, 1758. 3. The original deed, dated October 26, 1764, between Oliver de Lancey and Henry Cuyler, Junior, merchants in the city of New York, for property in Monmouth county, New

Jersey, sold to "Guis Guibertson and William Guibertson." 4. The original release of certain property by William Guibertson to Guisbert Guibertson, dated March 8, 1768. 5. A schedule of this Loyalist's confiscated real property, which was sold in Monmouth county, N. J., for £3.950 in 1779, and a copy of the inquisition.

In 1786 he was residing in Pennsylvania. (A. O. 12:63, f. 48; A. O. 12:15, ff. 376-381).

JAMES GORDON

At one time a gardener and overseer on the estate of Lord Stirling at Basking Ridge, N. J. He was a Scotsman, who emigrated in 1769. He then settled on a plantation of his own on the banks of the Raritan river. For three months early in the War he served in the American militia, but escaped and joined the Royal Navy, in which he acted as steward's mate in H. M. S. "Monmouth" until August, 1783.

The Commissioners in rejecting his claim for an allowance as a Loyalist, were severe upon him for serving in the American militia. By better fortune he obtained a comfortable situation in the Royal Navy. (A. O. 12:100, f. 186).

DAVID GOSLING

This Englishman emigrated in 1751 and settled at Perth Amboy, New Jersey, as a planter. He died in 1778 on service with the British army in New York, in the capacity of butcher, leaving a widow, Elizabeth; his eldest son, James; and another son, born in 1776 and named Howe Carleton Gosling, after the two British Commanders-in-Chief; and other children. His widow married one Henry Potter and the family were living at Cornwallis in Nova Scotia in 1786. (A. O. 13:19; A. O. 12:16, ff. 9-17; A. O. 12:63, f. 101). She claimed £709.11s., for the loss of the Gosling property in New Jersey and was awarded £320. (A. O. 12:109).

PHILIP GRANDIN (Major)

He was the son of Daniel and Margaret Grandin (Daniel, himself, said to have been a Loyalist officer). Philip gave an affidavit in proof of the loyalty and ownership of property of

Christopher and John Vought (q. v.), dated New York, October, 1783. He is described therein as "gentleman," of Hunterdon county, N. J., formerly Major in the Royal militia in New Jersey. He was presumably a Loyalist. (A. O. 13:19). He is said to have lived near present Lansdown, in Hunterdon county, and died Feb. 23, 1791. His wife, Eleanor, died Mar. 1, 1791, both being buried at Quakertown, N. J. They had two sons and five daughters. (Snell's "Hunt. & Som.," p. 542).

JAMES GRAY (Major)

He was a Scotsman who joined the Earl of Loudoun's Highland Regiment in 1745, was commissioned Ensign on May 23, 1746, and served until the reduction of this Regiment in 1749. In 1756 he was appointed Lieutenant in the 42nd Regiment, accompanied Lord Loudoun to America and served in the capture of Martinique and Havana, where he was rewarded by the grant of a Captain's commission. In the siege of Havana he contracted a serious illness, which compelled him to retire from the army. He retired to America in 1763 and married there, settling first in Essex county, New Jersey, where he bought, in 1765, a farm of 300 acres for £2,000 from Colonel John Low and built a house. In 1771 he removed to Stone Hook, five miles from Albany, New York, and rented a farm from Stephen Schuyler.

Early in the Rebellion he was offered, by a person high in the esteem of the Americans, the command of a Regiment of Continental troops and also the appointment of Chief Engineer on the Expedition against Canada. As one who was unalterably attached to the King's person and to the British Government the Scottish soldier rejected both offers.

He now consulted Sir John Johnson, Superintendent of Indian Affairs, and other prominent men in the district, and it was agreed among them to enlist 1,000 men to suppress the Rebellion, a scheme which was frustrated by the arrival in January, 1776, of Schuyler and a large force of men. Gray was captured at his own home and sent to Albany, but was allowed later to return. On May 9, 1777, he escaped with

200 men to Canada and joined the Regiment formed by Sir John Johnson, the King's Royal Regiment of New York, which, according to Gray, was the first Provincial Regiment raised in the Revolution.

At his farm near Albany he had six English-blooded breeding mares and his house was "genteelly furnished."

James Gray was awarded £1,650 from his claim of £3,414, and received half-pay as Major of the 1st Battalion of the King's Royal Regiment of New York. (A. O. 12:109; Ind.: 5606; A. O. 13:109; A. O. 12:14, ff. 180-191; Army Lists).

ELIJAH GROOM

He was born in America and lived in Monmouth county, New Jersey. He served for six years in the New Jersey Volunteers, and for a time as a privateer. He mentions in his memorial the names of Jacob Cooper and Ezekiel Groom, probably Loyalists, as witnesses to his loyalty, and includes a schedule of his property lost in New Jersey. In 1786 he was residing in First township, above Cataraqui, Canada. (A. O. 13:18; A. O. 12:16, ff. 426-7; A. O. 12:63, f. 125).

WILLIAM GROVER

He was born in New Jersey and lived on a plantation in Upper Freehold township, Monmouth county, New Jersey, with his four brothers, Joseph, Barzillai, Thomas and Samuel, all of whom went into the British lines at Allentown, N. J., in 1776. In 1780 he was banished to Morristown, New Jersey, having been taken prisoner and tried for his life. Samuel was shot by accident in July, 1783; Barzillai remained on Staten Island; Joseph was somewhere in New Jersey and Thomas near Philadelphia. William's share of the property was confiscated and sold in Monmouth county, N. J., with that of Barzillai, as also was Joseph's. William was granted £10 for relief in 1789 and his expenses back to America from England. (A. O. 12:102, f. 182).

PATRICK HAGGERTY (Captain)

This Loyalist was appointed Lieutenant on June 29, 1778, and was promoted Captain on December 25, 1781, in the 1st

New Jersey Volunteers. His original commissions, signed by Sir Henry Clinton, Commander-in-Chief in America, are in W. O. 42:H1.

Early in June, 1772, at the age of 20, he was married in Sussex county, N. J., to Sarah (aged 20), daughter of Joseph Dennis, by Samuel Crowel, magistrate for that county, in the presence of his sister, Margaret, wife of Stephen Haggerty, of Frankford in the same county. He died on May 29, 1810, at his residence in William street, New York, and was buried in a vault in the graveyard of St. Paul's.

Captain Haggerty had seven sons, John, Patrick, Joseph, Bonnel, Redman, Ludlum and Morris, and three daughters, Hannah, Nancy and Polly. His widow was alive on June 1, 1819, when she made an affidavit, sworn to before Cadwallader D. Colden, Mayor of New York, that she was a widow, without pension, allowance or provision from the British Government, probably with the intention of applying for a pension or an allowance from the Compassionate Fund. (W. O. 42:H1; Ind.: 5604-5-6). Captain Haggerty had been a member of the first Masonic Lodge at Digby in Nova Scotia (where he went after the Peace), which Lodge was founded in September, 1784, and of which some other New Jersey Loyalists mentioned in these pages were members.

JACOB HALL

A Loyalist farmer in Hopewell township, Cumberland county, New Jersey. (A. O. 13:96; A. O. 13:110).

IBBETSON HAMER (Captain)

An Englishman who had served for over ten years in the Royal Marines before he was appointed in 1772 as Lieutenant in the 7th Regiment of Foot (Royal Fusiliers). In 1773 he accompanied this Regiment to Canada, where he was taken prisoner by the Americans early in the War of Independence. At the end of fourteen months of captivity he was exchanged and, on December 20, 1777, he was commissioned Captain in the 72nd Foot (Royal Manchester Volunteers), in which he served at Gibraltar and afterwards in the American War, where he lost a leg in action.

Meanwhile, on November 30, 1776, Captain Hamer had married, in America, Sarah, (née Hazard) widow of Captain William Howard, formerly of the 17th Foot from 1735, a gentleman of independent fortune, who had retired from the army in 1768 or 1769, and settled on his valuable property near Princeton, called "Castle Howard," a name which suggests a family connection with the Howards, Earls of Carlisle, whose family seat in Yorkshire bears the same name of Castle Howard.

President Witherspoon, of Princeton College, made an affidavit on March 9, 1784, to the effect that Sarah Hazard, late of New York, was married to Captain William Howard and they had lived at Castle Howard, which, including some woodland, contained about 200 acres of land; that Capt. Howard "lived in a genteel manner" and "was generally believed to be wealthy;" that, after his death, his widow lawfully married Capt. Ibbetson Hamer, then a Lieutenant in the 7th Regiment of Foot; that Capt. Howard's property was left by him to his widow; that their possessions were seized by the State and sold at public vendue; and that he, Dr. Witherspoon, believed the property worth what Capt. Hamer estimated to the Commissioners. (A. O. 13:61). In addition there are letters from Dr. Witherspoon to Capt. Hamer in 1785 and 1786 and various documents relating to the fact that at the sale Dr. Witherspoon purchased the estate and then sold it to Rev. Philip Stockton, and it was questionable if Capt. Hamer ever benefitted by the transaction. The deed of sale of Castle Howard to Rev. Mr. Stockton recently came to light in a private collection in Princeton.

In addition to the above documents in A. O. 13:61 there are the following: The original inventory of the furniture and other effects at Castle Howard on December 24, 1776, most of which were to be sold at New York in the spring of 1777. It included five family pictures, a large organ and many books, which were apparently left at Castle Howard; an abstract of Captain Hamer's title to lands, etc., called Castle Howard;

certificates in his favor from Lord Cornwallis, General Sir Henry Clinton, General Sir William Howe and the Rev. T. B. Chandler (q. v.); Lord Lisburne's certificate, February 18, 1778, that Captain Hamer had lost a leg by a musket shot while serving under General Vaughan; and a printed advertisement of the sale on December 15, 1776, of Castle Howard, printed by Hall & Sellers, of Philadelphia. He was allowed £584 from his claim of £3,048.

Captain Howard, who died in 1776, was a strong Whig and ordered the warning, "No Tory talk here," to be painted over his mantelpiece for the benefit of his wife, a warm Loyalist. A contemporary description of the Castle Howard property is in "New Jersey Archives" (2nd Ser., Vol. I, p. 233).

One of Captain Ibbetson Hamer's letters is sealed with a coat of arms: A bend between two lions rampant. Crest: A demi-lion. (A. O. 13:61; A. O. 12:109; A. O. 13:109; A. O. 12:14, ff. 289-297; A .O. 12:85; A. O. 12:104, f. 5).

Dr. JOHN HAMMELL

A physician who was born in America about 1755. He served as surgeon on the American side in the beginning of the Revolutionary War. On July 24, 1776, he was commissioned on the American side as surgeon's mate in Colonel Philip Van Cortlandt's Battalion of Heard's Brigade of New Jersey Militia, taking part as surgeon in the Battle of Long Island in August, 1776. The precise date of his transfer to the Loyalist side has not so far been ascertained; but he had accepted a commission as surgeon in the New Jersey Volunteers as early as November 25, 1776, and continued to serve for the remainder of the War. On Nov. 30, 1777, when he had been taken prisoner on Staten Island, he was committed to jail in Trenton, N. J., but subsequently was released or escaped. He was in receipt of half-pay until 1801. (Ind.: 5605-6; Stryker; Sabine).

REUBEN HANKINSON (Ensign)

This American-born Loyalist (born in 1758) joined the New Jersey Volunteers as a private in September, 1776, and passed through from Sergeant to Ensign in the 1st Battalion on August 14, 1781. He was married on December 18, 1785, to Gitty ———, and died on May 20, 1819, at Sissiboo, Nova Scotia, leaving a widow and 13 children. His original commission as Ensign, bearing the signature of Sir Henry Clinton, is in W. O. 42:H6. (Ind.: 5604-5-6; W. O. 42:H6). He was taken prisoner on Staten Island in 1777 and sent to Trenton. (Sabine).

ABRAHAM C. HARING

He was a yeoman, of Bergen county. Theunis Blauvelt and Cornelius Herring (Haring), previously of Bergen county, and probably Loyalist refugees, testified at New York in August, 1783, to their knowledge of his property, which was advertised under confiscation in 1778. (A. O. 13:96; A. O. 13:110).

CHARLES HARRISON (Captain)

An Irishman, born about 1740, who settled at Trenton, New Jersey. He served in the Provincial Corps through much of the War, apparently as Captain in the 2nd New Jersey Volunteers, in which he was placed on half-pay. He was in prison in Philadelphia and at York, Pa., 1777-'78, in which latter year he was again in the British service. He died about 1803. (Ind.: 5605-6). He was a grantee of land at St. John, New Brunswick. (Stryker; Sabine).

CHRISTOPHER HARRISON

He went in 1772 from England to New Jersey as groom to John Allen, Esq., of Hunterdon county. Richard and Abraham Bowlby, in a certificate, dated in Nova Scotia, January 9, 1784, state that Harrison was their neighbor in New Jersey; that he was loyal from the beginning of the Revolution; that he had suffered persecution and imprisonment, and that he accompanied Richard Bowlby into the British lines in December, 1776. His schedule of property includes two English-bred mares and a colt, which he had doubtless taken with him from England in 1772. He was living at Annapolis in Nova Scotia in 1786. (A. O. 13:18; A. O. 12:63, f. 20). He was allowed £45 from his claim of £260.14s. (A. O. 12:109).

JAMES HARRISON (Lieutenant)

An Irishman who was appointed Ensign in the 6th New Jersey Volunteers in 1777 and was transferred to the 3rd Battalion in 1778, and, on May 28, 1778, was promoted Lieutenant.

On April 9, 1788, he was married in Sunbury county, Province of New Brunswick, to Charity Cowperthwaite, probably a daughter of Hugh Cowperthwaite (q. v.). Two children are mentioned: Elizabeth, born September 2, 1800, and William, born October 16, 1804, both baptised by the Rev. Joshua Marsden, Methodist minister at Sheffield in Sunbury county. James Harrison died on March 11, 1806, at that place, in the presence of Sarah Cowperthwaite, described as a Quaker. His wife survived him. (W. O. 42:H9; Ind.: 5604-5-6; Stryker).

CHARLES HART

He was of New Jersey and traded in different American Colonies after he left England in 1763. He was at Shelburne, Nova Scotia, in 1784. (A. O. 13:96; A. O. 13:110).

ROBERT and EZEKIEL HARTSHORN

Their estate was not confiscated, and they were in possession of it in 1787. It probably suffered considerably from plundering by Americans and British. (A. O. 12:85). They may have been of Shrewsbury, N. J.

JOHN HASLOP or HYSLOP (Adjutant)

This Englishman, born about 1755, served throughout the War, part or whole of the time as Lieutenant in the 3rd New Jersey Volunteers, and also as Adjutant in that Corps. He was struck off the 60th Regiment (orginally known as the Royal American Regiment) in 1805, a fact which suggests that he may have seen service in the army in the Wars arising from the French Revolution. (Ind.: 5605-6).

BARNES HATFIELD

He was of New Jersey and received a military allowance of £70 from October 24, 1783, an allowance indicating that he had served as an officer in an irregular Corps, which had not been "put on the regular Establishment," and therefore not entitled to half-pay. (Ind.: 5606).

CORNELIUS HATFIELD, Jr. (Captain)

He managed the farm of his aged father, Cornelius Hatfield, Sr., at Elizabethtown, where he joined the British in December, 1776. In February, 1779, he was appointed by Sir Henry Clinton a Captain of refugees. He lost a sloop and cargo in 1778 at Middletown Point, worth £2,500, on his way from New York. He operated from Staten Island and was one of the most daring Loyalists of the region. His estate, in Essex county, N. J., was confiscated in July, 1779. Cortlandt Skinner (q. v.), in his certificate to the character and the services of Hatfield in the War, stated that he had "given very essential information and had succeeded in many bold attempts." The Commissioners made him, "with great satisfaction," a temporary allowance of £50. He received a military allowance of £70 from June 24, 1786, and died on August 13, 1823; Stryker says in England. (Ind.: 5606. See also John Smith Hatfield, infra).

A Loyalist of this name absconded to Nova Scotia, or Prince Edward Island, to escape writs for debt. Many references to these debts are in the "Am. MSS. in Roy. Inst.," IV.

According to Stryker, Hatfield returned to the United States after the War (in 1789), was arrested for the murder of a Mr. Ball, but escaped punishment by reason of the terms of the Treaty of Peace. (Stryker's "N. J. Volunteers," p. 49).

JAMES HATFIELD

He was of Elizabethtown, (his father died in 1772), joined the British army in 1776 and acted as guide in every expedition into New Jersey. His claim is sealed with a seal showing a ship in full sail. One Morris Hatfield in a letter (much torn), also apparently from New Jersey, regarding papers as to James Hatfield's property, states that one Daniel March would not do the work (not mentioned) under £50. With James Hatfield's memorial is a deposition of Jacob Tucker and John Ogden, refugee Loyalists from New Jersey, dated from Shelburne, Nova Scotia, January 19, 1784, testifying to the loyalty of Hatfield. Two younger brothers were also living in that Province. There is also an official document regarding the sale of his confiscated property in 1779 for £170. (A. O. 13:18). He was allowed £70 from his claim of £112. 10s. (A. O. 12:109).

JOHN HATFIELD (Captain)

He was appointed Captain in the 3rd New Jersey Volunteers on April 15, 1777. He was married, on June 28, 1778, to Mary Lockerman, at Trinity Church, New York, by the Loyalist Rev. Charles Inglis (q. v.), Rector and a Chaplain in this Regiment. (W. O. 42:H2).

A Captain of this name, born in England about 1740, had served for 28 years in the British army before or after the American Revolution and seven years in Provincial Regiments, and was put on half-pay of Lieutenant-Colonel Robert Rogers' King's Rangers in 1792. (Ind.: 5605-6; W. O. 24:751). This date suggests that he had served in the regular army between 1783 and 1792.

JOHN SMITH HATFIELD

A carpenter, of Elizabethtown, who was born in that place and joined the British on their landing on Staten Island. As all the creeks were known to him, he was employed as a pilot for the ships of the Royal Navy and also acted as a guide for the army. With Cornelius Hatfield, Jr. (q. v.), and another Loyalist, Samuel Man, he went to Springfield in New Jersey and captured Colonel Matthias Ogden and Captain Jonathan Dayton, of the Light Infantry under Gen. Lafayette and took them prisoners to New York, where these American officers were exchanged later for a British Captain and 96 rank and file. Hatfield was also extremely instrumental in capturing Matthias Halstead, "a Rebel Justice," one Colonel Thomas and a Captain Smith, as well as a number of "other notorious Rebels and persecutors of the Loyalists, so that all of them dreaded and hated him."

One other feat was accomplished by this adventurous Loyalist, namely, that he piloted a sloop, (which he had assisted in seizing from Americans by marching overland), under heavy fire of the enemy, to Elizabethtown, for the purpose of making a bridge across the sound to facilitate the march of General Knyphausen's troops.

His estate was confiscated and ordered to be sold in February, 1779. He went into exile in the Province of New Brunswick, with his wife and five children, and there owned a packet boat, sailing to and from New York, which he lost in a storm. In January, 1789, he sailed from St. John to New York, to try to rescue some of his property in New Jersey and to recover some debts, but he was arrested and taken to New Jersey and there confined in gaol in Newark and Bergen for eight months. A handsome certificate to his loyal services was given by Brigadier-General Cortlandt Skinner.

According to Sabine, Hatfield revenged the execution of a British spy by hanging an American, named Ball; but this act of revenge is attributed by Stryker to Cornelius Hatfield. (F. O. 4:1; A. O. 13:98; A. O. 12:102, f. 235; Sabine; Stryker; Hatfield's "Elizabeth;" Essex Co. Records).

JOHN HATTON

He emigrated at the age of 16, taking with him some money of his own and a legacy of £1,500 left to him by an uncle in England, which he laid out later in buying landed estate in the counties of Gloucester and Cape May, New Jersey. He also built a fine brick house near Swedesboro, his place of residence, all of which estate he valued at £6,000 sterling. In or shortly before 1767 John Hatton was appointed Collector of Customs at Salem and Cohansey. Early in the Revolution he "kept open house for all the King's friends" and was called "King of the Tories."

His only son repaired to the Royal Standard under the Earl of Dunmore, Governor of Virginia, while John Hatton himself was denounced at home in New Jersey by mobs and at length was cast into prison in Philadelphia. He accompanied several detachments of the army and was wounded in the head. Meanwhile, his property was not only confiscated, but his wife, Elizabeth, was treated "with great barbarity and turned out of doors." At the same time, a chest containing his deeds, bonds, silver plate and the Customs books, which had been deposited for safety with Samuel Becket, a Quaker and passive Loyalist, was taken by the Americans. This trunk, with some of the silver and deeds, was, however, in possession of Becket in 1786, when Daniel Cozens (q. v.) visited him. He offered to surrender it upon payment of a debt due to him by Hatton. The "New York Gazette" for April 28, 1784, contains an advertisement of John Hatton's lands in New Jersey.

Governor Franklin stated that, although his loyalty was unquestioned, Hatton had "misbehaved himself" as a Customs officer, without, however, hinting at the form of the misbehavior.

Hatton, who was alive in London in September, 1788, was allowed £1,534 from his claim of £4,180 for the loss of his property, and at the rate of £160 a year during the War for the suspension of his official income, his pension being £90. (A. O. 13:85; A. O. 12:109). His only child was Lieutenant John Hatton (infra). (A. O. 12:17, ff. 9-25; A. O. 12:104, f. 11).

JOHN HATTON (Lieutenant)

The son of John Hatton (supra), and was born about 1756. According to his father he repaired to the Royal Standard under the Earl of Dunmore, Governor of Virginia. He served in a Loyalist Corps throughout the Revolution, part of the time as Lieutenant in the Sixth Battalion New Jersey Volunteers, in which he was commissioned May 28, 1778; later was in the Third and then Second Battalion. He was wounded in the celebrated siege of "96" in South Carolina on May 22, 1781, and wrote an account of the memorable defence of this fort by the Loyalists and of the reduction of New Providence. (Roderick Mackenzie's "Strictures on Tarleton's History of the Campaign in the South").

John Hatton was on half-pay from December 24, 1788, to 1812, and was appointed to the 11th Company of the 23rd Foot, September 25, 1787. (Ind.: 5605-6).

He was apparently the nephew of the Rev. Thomas Hatton, of Waters Upton, Shropshire, England, to whom he wrote on February 17, 1775, from New Jersey, on the disordered state of the country. ("Earl of Dartmouth's MSS.," II, 306).

ISAAC HAULENBECK

Born in America in 1743, he served for seven years in the Provincial Regiments during the Revolution, as Paymaster and Surgeon's mate in the 3rd New Jersey Volunteers. (Ind.: 5605-6). At the Peace he went to Nova Scotia. There are several references to him in "Am. MSS. in Roy. Inst."

SAMUEL HAYDEN (Captain)

He was born on May 26, 1752, and in 1776 joined the British forces, in which he was appointed Captain in the 4th New Jersey Volunteers, on September 27, 1776. This Brigade having been reduced by casualties from six to three Battalions in 1777, he was requested to retire on half-pay until a vacancy should occur in another Corps. After spending some time in New York on duty on courts martial and other services, and desiring more military activity, this officer obtained a warrant to raise a Company in the 1st Battalion of Major Robert Rogers's Rangers. He succeeded in doing so, at great personal expense, and nominated Peter Anderson (q. v.) as his Ensign.

Captain Hayden had served in the Battles of Long Island and White Plains, and in the capture of Fort Washington and New York Island. From March, 1782, he was in command of all the forces on Prince Edward Island, where he had been ordered in that month, with a detachment of Rogers's Rangers, to relieve the force of Lieutenant-Colonel Timothy Hierlihy, the Connecticut Loyalist. He was ordered to refrain from enlisting American prisoners for the British forces and to return the prisoners already enlisted, to the Commissary of Prisoners. ("Am. MSS. in Roy. Inst.," II: 431, 432; III: 149). His considerable real property in this Island was sacrificed and sold to pay a debt.

Samuel Hayden was married on April 22, 1771, to Jemima Carle (born in 1752), daughter of John Carle, by the Rev. Jonathan Elmer, pastor of the Presbyterian Church, New Providence, Essex county, New Jersey. He died on March 13, 1834, at Castine, Maine, where he had lived for seventeen years on half-pay, and his widow died on August 27, 1835, aged 83.

In his memorial of September 16, 1818, to Lord Palmerston, English Secretary of War, he sets forth his services in the American Revolution and hopes that he might nominate his young son, John, to the vacant commission of Lieutenant in his Regiment, so that he (the son) might obtain half-pay. The son was his only surviving child and became a watchmaker in Maine, where Captain Hayden had also tried his hand at this craft. The family Bible, printed in London in 1784, has passed down to a descendant, Mr. Herbert F. Prescott, of Albany, New York, who is also the owner of a miniature portrait in a ring of Samuel Hayden in uniform. (W. O. 42:H13; Ind.: 5606; Ex inform. Mr. H. F. Prescott and Miss K. Davenport).

JOHN HEARD

He was of Woodbridge, N. J. In A. O. 13:18 are the following papers relating to him:

1. A list of deeds, giving the names of William Heard in 1741, John Heard, deceased in 1730-1, and the latter (John's) son, Nathaniel. 2. A copy of the inquisition into his confiscated property, from which it would seem that it was sold for £7,486. 3. 8. 3. A valuation of his estate by Joseph Shotwell and Isaac Freeman, his former neighbors in Woodbridge; also a certificate to his knowledge of John Heard from Jonathan Clawson (q. v.), also a former neighbor. 4. A certificate from Cortlandt Skinner (q. v.) to his loyalty. 5. Two letters from his "near relation," William Taylor (q. v.), a lawyer of Freehold, N. J., dated January 19, 1789, and February 23, 1789, from London.

In the second letter above named this New Jersey lawyer and agent in London for many exiled New Jersey Loyalists, in commenting upon the refusal of the Commissioners of American Claims to grant compensation to John Heard because he remained in the United States after the War, pointed out that his (Taylor's) "near relation" and his eldest son, Nathaniel Heard, had served with the British army for seven years. Such were the misfortunes of this unhappy Loyalist that his mind had been affected and his death occasioned. Moreover, he had left a widow and a large family in extreme indigence in Nova Scotia.

His son, Nathaniel, was granted compensation to the amount of £892 from his claim of £1,478. (A. O. 12:109; A. O. 12:16, ff. 355-9; A. O. 12:63, f. 107).

FREDERICK HENDORFF (Ensign)

A German, born about 1749, who served for four years in the British forces and three years in the Provincial Corps. He was an Ensign in the 3rd New Jersey Volunteers in 1782, and was on half-pay as such until 1798, when he probably died. (Ind.: 5605-6). With Robert Timpany (q. v.) he was a founder of the first Masonic Lodge at Digby, Nova Scotia.

CONRAD HENDRICKS (Captain)

He was born in America, the son of John Hendricks, and was settled as a farmer at the entrance of Whale Creek, Monmouth county. He was seized in 1776 as a Loyalist. He had a warrant as Captain under Lieut.-Colonel John Morris (q. v.). He died in exile in New Brunswick in 1784. His widow (and third wife), Ann (Nancy), married John Sinnott and was living at St. John, New Brunswick, in 1787.

A certificate of Robert Campbell, then late of New Jersey, dated St. John, November 6, 1786, testifies to the loyalty of Hendricks. With this are several official affidavits proving the confiscation of his property (in Monmouth county, May 15, 1779), and a certificate of George Leonard, the Massachusetts Loyalist, dated February 18, 1787, declaring that Hendricks had acted as a Lieutenant on board one of his armed vessels in the war and was brave and loyal. (A. O. 13:18).

Ann Sinnott claimed £1,423. 2s. for the confiscated property of Conrad Hendricks and was awarded £970. (A. O. 12:109; A. O. 12:16, ff. 141-6; A. O. 12:63, f. 116).

PATRICK HENRY (Lieutenant)

An Irishman, born about 1728, was on the seconded list as Lieutenant in the 1st New Jersey Volunteers in 1783 (Ind.: 5605), having been Adjutant from April 1, 1777.

SAMUEL HENRY

He lived in Trenton, New Jersey; is recorded in A. O. 12:110, ff. 23:4.

WILLIAM HICK

An Englishman, settled at Princeton, New Jersey, as an innkeeper in 1763. At the outbreak of the rebellion he suffered persecution and was obliged to remove to Perth Amboy, where he followed the same business until he was driven away for his loyalty. He died in 1780 on the passage to England, leaving a son, William F. Hick, and three other children. This son's claim of £40 was rejected. (A. O. 12:14, ff. 275-7; A. O. 12:109).

JOHN HINCHMAN

An American-born farmer, Quaker, and Judge of the Quarter Sessions of Gloucester county, New Jersey, High Sheriff of that county and member of the House of Assembly from 1769-'75. He took refuge with the British army in 1777 at Philadelphia and accompanied the army later to New York. Here he "persevered in contributing his mite to the assistance of the British cause." He was conspicuous for his loyalty, and, in consequence, his property in New Jersey, inherited from his father and valued at £6,437 sterling, was confiscated and sold by the State. On May 28, 1776, he had drawn up a protest against the election of the Provincial Congress, which was signed by himself and over 100 others, and was read in public at the Court House, presumably in Gloucester county.

He had 1/28 share (bought on February 27, 1769, from Daniel, or Nathaniel, Benezet) in a copper mine in New Jersey, his share being valued at £465. 16s. sterling. One of the witnesses to his loyalty and property was Joshua North, a brother-in-law of one of the Benezets.

This Loyalist settled on his 200 acres of bounty land in Nova Scotia and there built a house, which was destroyed by fire with all the furniture. This misfortune appears to have prompted him to return to New Jersey to solicit the restoration of his property conformably to the Treaty of Peace, but, instead of recovering property, he stated that he "received so much insult and cruel treatment as to cause his wife to lose her senses and himself the use of his right side by a stroke of the palsy, and he with difficulty escaped out of that Province." (A. O. 12:14, ff. 83-95; A. O. 12:101, f. 277; A. O. 13:96). He claimed £6,437 and was allowed £4,034, and also a pension of £60 from 1785. (A. O. 12:109).

John Hinchman was in New Jersey in 1787, very infirm and living on the remains of his wife's property. (A. O. 12:85).

JOHN HIND

A jeweller, of Russell street, London, who appears to have gone out to America between 1770 and 1775 (the date of his death) to take possession of "28,000 acres of land" in West New Jersey, which had been purchased in 1680 or 1681 (actually 1682) by his grandfather, John Hind. He was a jeweller at Philadelphia at the time of his death and left a widow, Mary, who refused an offer of £3,000 for the above land. She received a Loyalist pension of £50 until her death in 1805 or 1806. (A. O. 12:14, ff. 396-8; A. O. 12:99, f. 35; A. O. 462:21; T. 50:7). For the property mentioned above Mary Hind claimed £3,360, but her claim was disallowed. (A. O. 12:109).

BENEZER MURDOCK HINGSTON

He is described as a "gentleman," of Freehold, New Jersey, and second son of the Rev. James Hingston, of Ireland, deceased. His large plantation at Freehold had been transferred to him by his father-in-law, Richard Compton. During the War he served as a guide and a recruiter. In 1784 he was living in Ireland with his wife and children. (A. O. 13:96; A. O. 13:110).

WILLIAM JOHNSON HOLT (Ensign)

He was born in America and joined the British army at the age of 19, having served therein for two years before receiving a commission as Ensign in the Pennsylvania Loyalists on July 1, 1783. He was married on July 30, 1818, to Elizabeth Cuyler, at Trinity Church, Newark, New Jersey, by the Rev. Lewis P. Bayard, Rector. He died on November 19, 1826, aged 64, at Montreal in Canada, where his widow was living in July, 1831, and was appealing to the British Government for a pension. (W. O. 42:H21; Ind.: 5605-6).

ELIAS HOLMES

A farmer, of Hackensack, New Jersey, born in that State, who joined the British forces at Fort Lee in 1776 and served under the Quartermaster-General. He was at Sorel in Canada in 1787. (A. O. 13:83; A. O. 12:16, ff. 412-3; A. O. 12:63, f. 121). He was allowed £35 from his claim of £101. 15s. (A. O. 12:109).

PETER HOLTON

He was born in New Jersey and was a farmer on his own land in the township of Piscataway, in Middlesex county, New Jersey. He joined the British army in 1776.

In A. O. 13:18 are a certificate to his ownership of land, signed by Jonathan FitzRandolph and John Bunyan, of Piscataway, dated Staten Island, October 10, 1783; an original conveyance of land from Benajah Martin, Junior, and his wife, Margaret, to Peter Holton, May 5, 1774; another conveyance from the same Martin, June 6, 1774; a printed "protection" of the British army to Holton, dated December 24, 1776, recommended by Bernardus LaGrange (q. v.); and a copy of the inquisition on his confiscated estate, which had been sold for £1,694. 9s. 6d., doubtless in New Jersey currency. His wife, Mary, was the daughter of Benjamin Drake (q. v.). He was at Digby in Nova Scotia in 1786.

The sum of £170 was awarded to him from his claim of £266. 7s. (A. O. 12:109; A. O. 12:15, ff. 125-9; A. O. 12:63, f. 18).

COTTON HOMFRAY

He was an Englishman, who accompanied his father and family to America in 1767. His father died in 1774, leaving 2,000 acres of unimproved land on Lake Champlain, granted to him in 1771, which was claimed by the State of Vermont at the Revolution. Cotton Homfray settled with his mother at Elizabethtown, New Jersey, and for a few months in 1775 (until compelled by ill-health to resign) enjoyed the important office of secretary to the Governor, William Franklin. He failed to join the British in New York in October, 1776; but, on his second attempt in the following month, he fled to the river, pursued by a Captain of Horse and 25 men, and succeeded in getting into a boat, in which he crossed to the opposite shore, a distance of five miles, with the help only of his hands and some pieces of board. In December he joined General Howe as a volunteer, and from 1777 he served in the Engineers in New York until 1779, when he was made a Deputy Commissary. His only brother died in America in 1781. His claim of £3,519 was disallowed. (A. O. 12:109; A. O. 12:14, ff. 363-7; A. O. 12:100, f. 184).

THOMAS HOOPER

A son of Clement Hooper (who died in 1777) and the owner of a plantation in Windsor township, in Middlesex county, New Jersey, of which there is a description with a copy of the inquisition against him. He also kept a tavern, noted as the place where all public business was transacted. There is an estimate of his losses and a deposition in his favor by Gilbert Giberson (q. v.) and Richard Robins (q. v.), dated December 12, 1783, from Shelburne, Nova Scotia, where he was himself a refugee at that time. (A. O. 13:18; A. O. 12:16, ff. 55-60; A. O. 12:62, f. 67). In 1786 he was living in Prince Edward Island. He was allowed £497 from his claim of £825. (A. O. 12:109).

JOHN HOOTON (Captain)

He was born in America about 1753 and was put on half-pay as Captain in the West Jersey Volunteers. (Ind.: 5606).

JOHN HORNER (Ensign)

A trader and planter, of Upper Freehold, Monmouth county, New Jersey. He was born in America and served in the British army, from 1779, as Ensign in the King's Militia Volunteers. Accompanying his memorial are: A certificate to the valuation of his confiscated property (forfeited May 21, 1779), by Barzilla Grover, late of Monmouth county, dated New York, August 18, 1783; the affirmation of Anthony Woodward, Quaker, of the same county and date; and the official certificate of the confiscation of his property. (A. O. 13:18). He was at Beaver Harbour, New Brunswick, Canada, in 1786. (A. O. 12:16, ff. 82-91; A. O. 12:63, f. 68; "Ontario Archives," pp. 787-9). He was allowed £116 from his claim of £440. 12s. (A. O. 12:109).

THOMAS HUNLOCK (Captain)

He was an American, born in 1751, and served for five years in the Loyalist Corps, the whole of that time probably in the 2nd New Jersey Volunteers, on which he was on half-pay until 1814. (Ind.: 5605-6). He went to New Brunswick at the end of the War. Sabine thinks he returned to the United States. (Stryker; Sabine).

JOHN HUTCHINSON

A yeoman from Yorkshire, who emigrated to New Jersey with his wife, Margaret, in 1774, and bought and settled on a farm in Hanover township, Morris county. As a recent emigrant from the mother country he took an active part from the first on the British side and sent those of his sons who were able to bear arms into the New Jersey Volunteers. His eldest son, William, aged 21, was "done to death in public without trial," for joining the Loyalists and for refusing to abjure his Sovereign. Another son was killed by a horse and a third was drowned, both on service in the New Jersey Volunteers.

John Hutchinson was fined several times for refusing to bear arms against the British, the fines amounting to £356. 17s., doubtless in New Jersey currency. There is a schedule of his property.

The personal safety of John Hutchinson having become more and more precarious, he fled with his wife and daughters to New York in 1780. On the voyage to England, towards the end of 1781, his ship foundered and he was drowned. By his last will, made in New York on Nov. 15, 1781, he left all his remaining property to his wife and children. His widow, Margaret, sought a new home in Nova Scotia, with her son, Francis, a Loyalist, and two daughters, Ann and Margaret. Here she married the Rev. John Wiswall, the distinguished Loyalist from Falmouth (Portland), Maine.

Cortlandt Skinner (q. v.), in his certificate in support of the claim of the Hutchinson family, dated August 29, 1785, states that that part of New Jersey where they settled was inhabited by people "bred in Republican principles," almost all of whom were descendants of emigrants from New England. (A. O. 13:18).

Francis Hutchinson, son, was awarded £850 from his claim of £2,337. 15s. for the loss of his father's estate in New Jersey. (A. O. 12:109; A. O. 13:18; A. O. 12:16, ff. 29-37; A. O. 12:63, f. 61; A. O. 12:101, f. 244).

WILLIAM HUTCHINSON (Captain)

An American-born Loyalist, who served as officer in the New Jersey Volunteers from 1776 until the end of the War, when he was placed on half-pay. With James Moody (q. v.) he enlisted upwards of 500 men. (Moody's "Narrative").

He was married on August 30, 1784, to Catherine Lewis, by the Rev. John Beardsley, the Loyalist exile, at St. John, New Brunswick, and died in March, 1826, at Walsingham in Canada, aged 81. (W. O. 42:H34; A. O. 13:96; Ind.: 5604-5-6; Sabine; Stryker).

Rev. CHARLES INGLIS

The well-known Rector of the historic Trinity Church, New York, finds a place here as the Chaplain to the 1st New Jersey Volunteers, on the list of which he was on half-pay until 1798, nine years after his appointment as first Bishop of Nova Scotia.

In his printed memorial, in A. O. 13:55, he declares that he had always acted from the dictates of his conscience and only did what he conceived to be his duty. Having observed a restless and seditious spirit prevailing, he formed a resolution, in conjunction with some of his intimate friends, particularly the Rev. Dr. T. B. Chandler (q. v.), the Rev. Dr. Myles Cooper, President of King's College, New York, and the Rev. Samuel Seabury, to watch all publications disrespectful to Government or the parent State, or that tended to a breach between Great Britain and her Colonies, and to give them an immediate answer and refutation. He said "he had the strongest predilection in favor of the British Constitution, which he considered as the best political fabric that ever existed; he felt that solicitude for the preservation of the Church of England, which naturally results from full conviction that her doctrines and plan of Government are conformable to Holy Scripture and that of any other Christian church whatever. He was conscious also that the Americans were then in possession of as large a portion of freedom as could well consist with a state of civil society; that if they were not happy, the want of liberty was not the cause; that they could not change but for the worse, and that a separation of the Colonies from the parent State must be highly injurious, perhaps ruinous, to both countries."

In 1774 Mr. Inglis published in the "New York Gazette," printed by Hugh Gaine, a series of papers under the signature of "A New York Farmer," setting forth the then happy state of America, the advantages derived from their connection with the mother country, and refuting the calumnies then industriously propagated that the Government designed to enslave America and to establish Popery. Between then and the beginning of 1776 he had free intercourse with the country, and visited his large estate, dispersed in several parts of the Province of New York, and he endeavored to influence the people of the dangers ahead.

He was the writer in February, 1776, of the "Answer" to the pamphlet, "Common Sense," by Thomas Paine, which was ordered by Governor Tryon to be printed as a pamphlet, but the printing was frustrated by a mob, who went to the printers in New York and committed the whole impression to the flames. His answer was entitled, "The Deceiver Unmasked: or, Loyalty and Interest United." Neither discouraged nor intimidated by the mob, he changed the title to "The True Interest of America Impartially Stated; In Certain Strictures on a Pamphlet, intitled Common Sense," and he wrote out two fair copies himself and his servant a third, and sent the three by different messengers, one being Isaac Ogden (q. v.) to the printer, James Humphreys, in Philadelphia. He became Chaplain of the 1st New Jersey Volunteers April 25, 1781, and so continued until the close of the War.

The assistant Rector (as he then was) of Trinity Church visited the Loyalists in prison in New York in the Spring of 1776, including David Mathews, Mayor of the City, and several other distinguished Loyalists. He continued to animate the members of his flock to persevere in their loyalty, "with such success that they almost all continued loyal, the exceptions being only three or four persons of no note." At this time there were three large congregations of the Church of England in New York, "each consisting of at least 2,000 persons."

In the summer of 1782, when Sir Guy Carleton took command at New York, there was a manifest disposition (according to this zealous Loyalist) among the "leaders of the Rebels" to reach an accommodation with Great Britain, because they dreaded Carleton's influence, talents and activity, and his "prodigious ascendancy" over them. The prisoners taken by the General in Canada, and by him dismissed, including some of the best American officers, refused to fight against him. The affairs of Congress were in a most wretched state now, the paper money was totally ruined and revolts were common in the American army. Such was his statement of affairs and he judged it prudent to publish what he called a moderate, conciliatory paper, pointing out the advantages of union with the mother country; softening, as much as truth would permit, any violence that had happened on either side, and showing the evils likely to arise from independency. This he did in a series of contributions under the signature of "A New York Freeholder," in Rivington's "Royal Gazette," and they were continued until independency was granted. (A. O. 13:55).

In his letter of December 20, 1786, he expresses suspicion that the vindictive spirit prevailing in America might instigate some to take the unjustifiable step of claiming against the estates of the exiled Loyalists. He mentions with grief the low values put on his lands in Dutchess county, New York, partly by one who was not only a magistrate but also a purchaser of confiscated estates, and by one Enos Northrup, a reputed Loyalist and also a purchaser.

In 1783 he went to Halifax, Nova Scotia, and was made first Bishop of Nova Scotia Aug. 12, 1787. He died there Feb. 24, 1816. His portrait is to be found in Lawrence's "Incidents in Early History of New Brunswick." (A. O. 12:100, f. 168; C. O. 5:111, ff. 155, 251-5; "Two Hundred Years of the S. P. G.;" A. W. H. Eaton, in "Acadiensis," July, 1908).

DANIEL JAMES (Quartermaster)

Of Philadelphia, who was appointed Quartermaster of the 2nd New Jersey Volunteers, in February, 1783, in which he served for six years. He was married on September 25, 1796, to Bridget Gaynor, in the Church of England at St. John, New Brunswick. He died at Fredericton in that Province on April 20, 1817, aged 74, leaving a widow. (W. O. 42:J2).

JOHN JENKINS (Adjutant)

He was an Englishman who was Lieutenant from March 20, 1777, and Adjutant in the 3rd New Jersey Volunteers. He was married on August 14, 1781, to Sarah Bradley, at Savannah, in Georgia, by the Rev. James Brown, shortly before (apparently) his appointment as Deputy Muster-Master-General of the "Loyal Southern Corps" in South Carolina. He died on March 25, 1805, at the age of 75, in the Province of New Brunswick, probably at Fredericton, on half-pay of the 2nd New Jersey Volunteers, having served for 17 years in the British army and seven years in the Loyalist Corps.

This officer was one of the first Lieutenants in the King's New Brunswick Regiment, formed on the Declaration of War by France against England in 1793. Joseph Lee, William Chew and William Turner, officers in the 3rd New Jersey Volunteers, joined at the same time. His daughter, Elizabeth, baptised on March 14, 1795, by the Rev. James Milne, Rector of Fredericton, was in great distress in 1820 and was put on the Compassionate Fund for a pension of £8. (W. O. 25:3086).

Captain John Jenkins, who distinguished himself in the capture of Ogdensburgh, in command of the Glengarry Light Infantry in the War of 1812, is believed to have been a son of this Loyalist officer. (Ind.: 5604-5-6; W. O. 42:J5; "Acadiensis," VII, 143; "Judges of New Brunswick," pp. 45-6).

Dr. UZAL JOHNSON

He was born at Newark, New Jersey, on April 17, 1757, being the son of Eliphalet Johnson. The Provincial Congress of New Jersey appointed him, on February 17, 1776, surgeon of the 1st Battalion of the Foot Militia of Essex county. (Force, "American Archives," Series IV, Vol. IV, p. 1595).

At the Declaration of Independence Uzal Johnson seceded from the Revolutionary party and went over to the British side, accepting a commission as surgeon to the 5th New Jersey Volunteers, March 1, 1777. Inquisition against him in Essex county, N. J., was found Jan. 12, 1779. He accompanied his Regiment in the arduous campaigns in South Carolina, where he rendered services to the wounded in the memorable battle of King's Mountain, and where he said he was harshly treated by Colonel Benjamin Cleveland. He was married February 4, 1783, at New York, to Jane Wilmot, spinster, by the Rev. Samuel Seabury, the well-known Loyalist and afterwards first Bishop of the Episcopal Church of America. He resumed practice in Newark and died there on May 22, 1827, and was buried by the Rev. Henry P. Bowers of Trinity Church. His original commission as surgeon to the New Jersey Volunteers is in W. O. 42:J9. (See also Stryker).

HEATHCOTE JOHNSTON

He was born in New Jersey about 1752, the son of Dr. Lewis Johnston, and Martha (Heathcote) Johnston, of Perth Amboy, from whom he and his brother, John Lewis Johnston, inherited property under will of September 26, 1773.

His action in joining the American militia early in the troubles (he was Captain of the 1st Regiment, Middlesex militia) was regarded by Daniel Coxe (q. v.) as a mere matter of form. Governor Franklin declared that in temporising with the Americans at first Heathcote Johnston did so to "keep himself quiet." From his claim of £1,803 for his confiscated estate he was allowed £330. (A. O. 12:109). He was employed in 1787 in the General Post Office in England. He never married and died in England, Dec. 13, 1798.

His brother, John Lewis, mentioned above, entered the College of Philadelphia in 1758 and married Susannah, daughter of John and Gertrude (Johnstone) Barbarie, and received a Loyalist pension of £20 until his death in 1824. (T. 50:8; T. 50:27). A sister was Ann Burnet (q. v.). A younger sister, Margaret, married Bowes Reid, a "Rebel" lawyer of Burlington county, N. J., who was Secretary of State of New Jersey from 1778 until his death, July 27, 1794. (A. O. 13:109; A. O. 12:14, ff. 375-9; A. O. 12:75, ff. 45-50; T. 50:25; Whitehead's "Contrib. to East Jersey History;" Jones's "St. Peter's Ch., Perth Amboy").

JOHN JORDAN

An Irishman, who had settled in New Jersey about 1764 and was director of some ironworks. He raised men for the British army early in the War. He claims to have bought 1,000 acres of land in 1771 in Wyoming, Pa., for £200, towards which he had paid only £20. A military allowance of £25 was granted to him from June 25, 1790, and some time after the War he was granted £35 for his relief and for his passage back to the Bahamas. He was dead in 1804. (Ind.: 5606; A. O. 12:102, f. 194).

Rev. CAVALIER JOUET

A gentleman of Elizabethtown, who was born in the Island of Jamaica of French and British parentage, and lived on a fortune of £800 to £1,000, in New Jersey currency, in a house inherited from his grandfather, Daniel Jouet, who died about 1754. His furniture was of the best mahogany and his library was worth £700.

Persuaded as he was that the "Rebellion" could not last many months, Cavalier Jouet did not solicit a commission in the new Loyalist corps forming (the New Jersey Volunteers), but was content to help the British by "collecting intelligence, discriminating the turbulent, mischievous and dangerous from the loyal and inoffensive," as well as acting as a guide. He had signed an "Association paper," in support of the American cause, but scratched out his name to show his contempt for the document. Two sons joined the New Jersey Volunteers as Ensigns, whom he could not advance in the army by purchase in his distressed condition.

Cavalier Jouet was the great-grandson of Huguenot ancestors who left France after the Revocation of the Edict of Nantes in 1685, and who, after many wanderings, finally settled in Elizabethtown, New Jersey, sometime probably in 1695 to 1700. His father, Daniel Jouet, probably born at Elizabeth, N. J., married, in London, Frances Hargrave, the niece of General William Hargrave, Governor of Gibraltar. She had estates in Jamaica, W. I., and Cavalier had inherited property there under the will of his uncle, Colonel John Cavalier, and thither the young pair went. He was left an orphan at about the age of 5 years; his father left him several slaves and one was to be given her freedom and her return passage to the West Indies after she should have taken Cavalier to his grandparents in Elizabethtown. He was sent there under the tutelage of the Rev. Thomas Bradbury Chandler (q. v.). At the age of 19 or 20 years he married, in 1757, Abigail Hatfield, a descendant of one of the early settlers of Elizabethtown and also of the Patroon Cornelis Melyn, whose grant of land comprised Staten Island. She died in 1770 and was buried in St. John's Churchyard, Elizabethtown. She left seven children.

After her death Cavalier Jouet, in 1770, married Mary Hampton, who died in 1827, a daughter of Jonathan Hampton.

Until this time Cavalier's career had been that of a favorite of fortune, and money, slaves, lands and the consideration attaching to a large fortune were his in good measure. He built a fine house, still standing, which is one of the historical mansions of America, but the Revolution was approaching and all his interests were with the mother country. She had sheltered his people when they had fled from France and he was bound to her with ties of gratitude, and to him its government always appealed as the most enlightened on the face of the earth. Hard it must have been for him to make the decision to remain loyal, for the whole of his life was henceforth changed. For a time he suffered imprisonment and, when on parole, his activities were confined within a prescribed area at Basking Ridge, his moneys were held back and, with his large family of eleven children, he suffered great hardships. After the withdrawal of the British forces from New Jersey he and his family took up their residence within the British lines. The inquisition against him in Essex county, N. J., was found Sept. 15, 1778, and judgment of forfeiture rendered Feb. 17, 1779.

At the close of the war Cavalier Jouet sailed for England, as it was not considered safe for him in America. Shipwrecked off the Isle of Wight, England, he lost what little he had, but escaped with his life. In England, at the advanced age of 49, he studied for the ministry, matriculating at Magdalen Hall (now Hertford College, Oxford) and was ordained a clergyman of the Church of England by the Bishop of London and was curate of Tolles Hunt Major in Essex in 1792.

Cavalier Jouet suffered the resentment of his (second) wife's family, who had in general taken a decided and active part against Great Britain. He was deprived of her property, the legacy of her father, and had the "mortification to see it at the disposal of persons whose political principles are the reverse of his own, and whose private characters alone he conceives it too precarious a security to rely on." As has been stated, his second wife was Mary Hampton, daughter of Jonathan Hampton, a noted partisan of the American cause, who, according to William Luce (q. v.), died from excessive rejoicing at the defeat of General Burgoyne.

Among the debtors of Cavalier Jouet was Philip Livingston, of New York, on a mortgage of £6,000 on an estate in the Island of Jamaica, to which Philip Livingston, the younger, succeeded.

The unfortunate Loyalist was in great distress as an exile in England, more particularly because his elder children had "entirely lost the benefit of a genteel and liberal education."

In 1792 he returned to the United States for a visit, and appeared before the Convention at Philadelphia in order to have his confiscated estates return to him, and all moneys due to him in accordance with the Treaty of Paris. The personal estate was, however, granted to his three daughters by his first wife; possibly his second children may have been thought to have been amply provided for by their grandfather Hampton's will. On this visit he preached in St. John's Church, Elizabethtown, N. J., in which church he had formerly been a vestryman. The font in the church was a gift from him, but the feeling against him was so strong that it was displaced and for forty years it lay neglected in Norris's stoneyard, until in a more kindly day and hour it was brought out and set up in St. John's Church, where it now stands as one of the beautiful accessories. Cavalier, his business before the Convention being accomplished, sailed for England, where he died at Rawreth in Essex, as curate of that parish, on November 6, 1810. He left a large family; the eldest daughter married a British officer and many of her descendants were in the British army.

One of the three sons mentioned above was Xenophon Jouet, born in 1761, for six years Ensign in the 1st New Jersey Volunteers, who became in 1789 High Sheriff of York county, Province of New Brunswick, Lieutenant in the King's New Brunswick Regiment in 1793, Gentleman Usher of the Black Rod to the Provincial House of Assembly for nearly fifty years, and who died at St. John, N. B., in 1843. Another son was John Troup Jouet, born 1763, Ensign in the 3rd New Jersey Volunteers and on half-pay until 1801. ("Colls. of N. Brunswick Hist. Soc.," I, 46).

Cavalier Jouet was granted by the British Government £966 from his large claim of £6,123, which included not only the large debt of Philip Livingston, already mentioned, but also other debts, which were recoverable under the Treaty of Paris. His pension was £120. (A. O. 12:109; T. 50:8; T. 50:22).

For his opinion of the loyalty of Isaac Ogden, his old schoolmate, as he calls him, see the account of Ogden himself, later. Both, it would seem, were educated at King's College, New York (now Columbia University), though Jouet received earlier instruction from the Rev. Thomas Bradbury Chandler (q. v.), as is mentioned above.

In granting him an allowance as a distressed Loyalist, the Commisioners reported favorably on his "spirited opposition to the rebellious measures at the beginning." (A. O. 12:13, ff. 161-179; A. O. 12:100, f. 158; "Am. MSS. in Roy. Inst.," I, 425; Foster's "Alumni Oxon;" "Loyalists' Claims," pp. 269-270; Hatfield's "Elizabeth").

In this connection it may be interesting to quote from an autograph-signed letter by him, dated "New York, May 4, 1783," giving in his own words an account of his reception in America soon after the Armistice of that year, but before a Treaty of Peace had actually been signed and known in America:

"Some little time after the publication of an armistice between the belligerent Powers, I thought it might prove of use to myself and family to pass into the Jerseys, and speculate on the spirit and temper of the times there, in order to determine whether it would be feasible to replace my wife and children in the township where they formerly resided, for the purpose of a more easy maintenance of them, and to be in the way, with the assistance of their friends, of finally recovering their property; and accordingly I pitched upon the neighborhood of Woodbridge to make my entrance, where I had been subject for near three years past in the capacity of a prisoner of war on my parole given to General Washington, in consequence of a parole of like nature given by a certain John Hampton to his Excellency Sir Henry Clinton, at the time of the said Hampton being liberated from the Provost. In this place, where I had received much civility for a course of time, as well from the particular party who captured me as from the inhabitants in general, between whom and myself had passed a reciprocation of good offices, they frequently granting me real indulgences that were not common to every one in a like predicament with myself, and I embracing every opportunity to make all possible acknowledgments consistent with my avowal of the strictest loyalty and fidelity to the cause of my rightful Sovereign; I say, in this place, I received the most outrageous insults, and narrowly escaped the most shameful and degrading abuse. A number of fellows came about me with sticks and whips (the most of whom had formerly treated me with great courtesy) telling me the case was altered now; that, when a prisoner of war, they thought it incumbent to be civil to me, but the Peace had dissolved all paroles, and I had no right or title to come there, and they were determined to give (as they insultingly termed it) a Continental jacket. I expostulated with them whether I had ever injured any of them or others they had heard of in their properties; or had so much as in the slightest manner affronted their persons; in answer to which they told me that I had proved a traitor to my country and had joined the enemy, and they were determined that no such d—d rascals should ever enjoy the benefits of the country again; and had, with the approbation of the Magistrates of the township, entered into an Association for the purpose of expelling every rascal that attempted to come into it in like form as they meant to treat me, by whipping them out again. Near or at this juncture came General Heard, of their militia, and appeared to aggravate the spirit of the mob very much by pointedly asking them what they meant to do with that d—d rascal? And a Justice Freeman coming up shortly after, called aloud, 'Hang him up, hang him up!' A Justice Bloomfield, too, who finally showed a disposition to appease the spirit that had arisen in the people, first told me it was a crime to come here, and, on my enquiring whether their conduct was authorized by the Magistracy, he said so far as that they had entered into an Association, with the knowledge of the Magistrates, to treat persons coming as I had done in such sort, and believed they would find no redress. In short, it was with infinite difficulty I escaped their clutches with all the assistance I could get from a certain Thomas Edgar, who pleaded that he had received favors from one of my sons when a prisoner under his charge, and held himself under obligations to the family, and from the benevolent interposition of their clergyman, Mr. Rowe, who in every instance and respect behaved very much like a Christian and a gentleman. I could mention many other circumstances expressive of a most intolerant spirit prevailing among them, but I have been already too prolix." ("Am. MSS. in Royal Inst.," IV, 69-70; Ex. information from Cavalier Jouet of Roselle, N. J.).

ISAAC JUSTASON

Born in America, he was a farmer living on his own property in Woolwich township, Gloucester county, N. J., inherited from his father and grandfather. Here his neighbors were John Cox (q. v.) and Jesse Richards, both Loyalists. In A. O. 13:18 is an estimate of his property and a copy of the inquisition. An award of £412 was made to him from his claim of £927. 10s. (A. O. 12:109; A. O. 12:15, ff. 303-8; A. O. 12:63, f. 39).

FRANCIS KEARNY (Lieut.-Colonel)

He was born at Perth Amboy in New Jersey, circa 1752, and was in England from 1773 to 1777. Upon his return to America in March he joined the British forces and, on October 14 following, he was commissioned Captain in the Pennsylvania Loyalists, being promoted Major on November 15, 1780. Meanwhile, on May 9, 1778, he was appointed by General Sir William Howe a Deputy Judge Advocate at a court martial at Cooper's Ferry, New Jersey, the original commission of which is in W. O. 42:K1.

For four years he was on duty with his Regiment, the Pennsylvania Loyalists, in West Florida, under Major-General John Campbell, with much honor and reputation to himself, and was beloved by his General and highly esteemed by every officer. During the siege of Pensacola (from March 12 to May 8, 1781), he was in command of his Regiment, and according to his own narrative, the Spaniards had approached to within 500 yards of the British works, when a sortie was ordered and Kearny led the first division and at noon forced the enemy lines, routing them and destroying seven pieces of ordnance. Afterwards he was in charge of the defense of the advanced redoubt, which, unfortunately, was blown up by a shell penetrating the magazine, killing and wounding 50 men, of whom he was one. In consequence, a capitulation immediately took place.

With the papers of Major John Vandyke (q. v.) is a copy of the "Newport Mercury" for July 21, 1781, containing an account of the heroic siege of Pensacola, defended for 57 days by a small force against overwhelming odds. His narrative now proceeds to give an account of a part of Major Kearny's subsequent career. As an exile he made Ireland his residence and was again forming a comfortable establishment, when, in 1793, he was notified of his unsought-for appointment of a Corps then raising in Nova Scotia (the Royal Nova Scotia Regiment) and did not hesitate to give up a lucrative civil appointment. On his arrival in Nova Scotia he unexpectedly found that he had been appointed Lieutenant-Colonel. His letter laments his condition as one who had abandoned his home only to be retired on half-pay as Major, not, as he had expected, as Lieutenant-Colonel, and "conceives that the sacrifices he has made, his unimpeached loyalty and adherence to His Majesty, and His Government for those 46 years past give him some claim to a remuneration; had he employed that period" [during his absence in Nova Scotia] "in planting potatoes he might have been precluded the necessity of thus setting forth so mortifying a case." (W. O. 42:K1).

Francis Kearny was appointed Major of the Loyal Nova Scotia Regiment in 1793, and in 1801 he was Lieutenant-Colonel with Samuel Vetch Bayard. He was married on May 28, 1789, to Anne Herbert, spinster, in the Parish Church of Kinsale, Ireland, and died on March 26, 1828, at Armagh in Ireland, at the age of 76, leaving a widow and six children. His son, James W. Kearney, is mentioned at Armagh in 1828. (W. O. 42:K1).

Major Kearny was allowed £2,056 from his claim of £3,694. (A. O. 12:109). His property had been confiscated in Middlesex county, N. J., in 1778.

This Loyalist was the son of Philip Kearny, eminent counselor-at-law and noted Loyalist, who died at Perth Amboy, New Jersey, July 25, 1775, and in his will, of April 25, 1770, left property to his second wife, Isabella (daughter of Robert Lettice Hooper, q. v.), and to his sons, Philip, Francis, Ravaud and Michael (q. v.). (A. O. 12:14, ff. 328-335; A. O. 12:100, f. 267; A. O. 13:109; Ind.: 5604-6; "Am. MSS. in Roy. Inst.," I:139; Jones's "St. Peter's Church, Perth Amboy," p. 349).

JAMES HUDE KEARNY (Ensign)

He was born at Perth Amboy, N. J., Dec. 27, 1768, son of Ravaud and Ann (Hude) Kearny, and as a mere child was given a commission as Ensign in the Pennsylvania Loyalists, as compensation to his Loyalist relatives, which was a form of appreciation not unusual at the time. He was on half-pay until 1811. (Ind.: 5605-6). He married Catherine Montgomery Parker, daughter of James Parker and Gertrude (Skinner) Parker, had two children and died of yellow fever at Perth Amboy, Sept. 2, 1811.

MICHAEL KEARNY (Captain)

He was born at Perth Amboy, N. J., Sept. 7, 1725, and is described as a Captain in the Royal Navy, who, at the conclusion of the Seven Years' War in 1763, settled as a planter in Morris county, New Jersey. He took an active part in keeping rebellion from his township and by his influence prevented the election of "committee men." At last, the threatened violence to his own person obliged him to quit New Jersey and apparently to set sail for England in 1776. Although he had spent most of his life in the Royal Navy he could obtain no employment in that service and, consequently, he petitioned for a grant of land in West Florida, probably later in the same year. (C. O. 5:115, f. 365). He was, however, appointed in 1776 Regulating Captain at the Port of Cork in Ireland, where he received the freedom of that city in 1778, and held this post until the end of the American War.

The date of entrance of Michael Kearny into the Royal Navy is uncertain, but the naval records show that he was a Lieutenant from 1743 and a Master and Commander from 1759. A tribute was paid to his zealous services in the navy by Chief Justice Frederick Smyth (q. v.). ("Earl of Dartmouth's MSS.," II:301).

Michael Kearny never married. He was the son of Michael Kearny, an Irishman, of Perth Amboy, and his third wife, Sarah, daughter of Lewis Morris, Governor of New Jersey. He died April 5, 1797. (A. O. 13:109; Jones's "St. Peter's Church, Perth Amboy," p. 344).

MICHAEL KEARNY, Jr.

A merchant in Perth Amboy, the brother of Major Francis Kearny (q. v.) and born there Nov., 1751. He was imprisoned for his loyalty for six months in 1776-'7. He was the owner of two farms on the banks of the Raritan river. For five years he served as a volunteer in New York, first in a Company formed in 1778 by Captain Williams and afterwards in the Militia Volunteers. He served also as searcher of imports and exports in New York. He returned to Perth Amboy at the close of the War.

His wife, Elizabeth, whom he married June 30, 1774, inherited property from her grandfather, Samuel Leonard, through her mother, Ann (Leonard) Lawrence, wife of Judge John Lawrence.

This Loyalist was the owner of the boat "York," which was impressed into the American service and used in capturing the vessel "Blue Mountain Valley." (Force, "Am. Archives," Ser. IV, Vol. IV, p. 1492). He died Feb. 24, 1791. He had nine children, one of whom was Commodore Lawrence Kearny, who died Nov. 29, 1868. (A. O. 13:12; A. O. 12:14, ff. 213-229; A. O. 12:101, f. 340; Jones's "St. Peter's Church, Perth Amboy," pp. 348, 353).

PHILIP KEARNY (Lieut.-Colonel)

He was a half brother of Major Francis Kearny (q. v.) and was born at Perth Amboy, N. J., July 27, 1733. He was a wine merchant there and joined the British forces immediately upon their invasion of New Jersey. The only "Association" which he signed was the "constitutional one," drawn up by Brigadier-General Cortlandt Skinner, his brother-in-law. In July, 1776, he was arrested and paroled to remain in Hunterdon county, N. J., but soon joined the King's troops and went in 1777 to New York City and lived there "on his own money until all was spent," when he was granted an allowance of £200 a year by order of General Sir Guy Carleton, an allowance which was regarded by the Commissioners in London as a proof of his worth as a Loyalist, though a civilian at the time.

Philip Kearny was half owner, with Stephen Skinner (q. v.) of the brig "Franklin," which was seized by the Americans and armed. In 1780 he was appointed senior Captain in the Loyal Militia of New York City and afterwards Lieutenant-Colonel. His estate in Middlesex county, N. J., was forfeited in 1779.

Governor Franklin paid tribute to his character and spoke of his handsome confiscated property. He was allowed £1,870 from his claim of £3,115. 14s. (A. O. 12:109), and was allowed a pension of £70 from 1784.

He married, July 4, 1770, Susannah Watts, of New York City, daughter of John Watts, last Royal Recorder of that city, whose statue stands in Trinity churchyard. She died May 6, 1823. Philip Kearny died June 17, 1798, at Newark, N. J., at which place he settled after the War. One of his 14 children was Gen. Stephen Watts Kearny, first Governor of California. (A. O. 12:13, ff. 316-329; A. O. 12:101, f. 169; "Loyalists' Claims," p. 300; Jones's "St. Peter's Church, Perth Amboy," p. 347).

GARRET KEATING (Captain)

He was a Captain in the 1st New Jersey Volunteers in 1777-'79, and was killed, or died, in July, 1780, leaving a widow, Mary, who was put on the pension list with three small children. (Ind.: 8229). She was going to Nova Scotia in the Spring of 1784. ("Am. MSS. in the Roy. Inst.," III:427; IV:196, 455, 461).

STEPHEN KEMBLE (Colonel)

No papers are included in the Loyalist documents of this officer, who was born at New Brunswick, New Jersey, in 1740, the fourth son of Peter Kemble, of Mount Kemble, Morris county; but his commissions in the British army have survived.

His first commission was as Ensign in the 44th Regiment, on May 5, 1757. On January 24, 1765, he was promoted Captain in the 60th (or Royal American) Regiment, and through the influence of his brother-in-law, General Thomas Gage, Commander-in-Chief of the British army in America, he was appointed, on August 7, 1772, Deputy Adjutant-General of the forces in North America and served as such under Gage at Boston, and later in the same rank under Gage's successor, Sir William Howe, through the siege of Boston and at the evacuation of that town by the British in March, 1776. On June 6, 1775, he was promoted Major of the 1st Battalion of the 60th and Lieutenant-Colonel on June 6, 1778.

Captain Stephen Kemble resigned this appointment in October, 1779, because of Sir Henry Clinton's refusal to promote him Adjutant-General, on the resignation of that office by Lord Rawdon, and on November 30 he sailed to rejoin his Regiment, the 60th, in Jamaica. The expedition to the Spanish Main sailed from Jamaica on March 4, 1780, and reached the harbor of St. Juan on the 24th, landing without opposition. Nelson, in H. M. S. "Hinchingbrooke," was in command of the naval force and the expedition reached the Castle of St. Juan, 64 miles up the river and 32 miles from the lake of Nicaragua, on April 11, and invested it, and the enemy surrendered on the 29th. Nelson, one of the heroes with Lieutenant Edward Marcus Despard, fell dangerously ill from fever and was sent home.

Colonel Kemble, then in command of the 1st Battalion, was sent by Major-General John Dalling, Governor of Jamaica, and a veteran of the same Regiment, on April 2, 1780, with a reinforcement and to take chief command as Brigadier-General. The terrible sufferings and heavy mortality of the troops from fever, combined with the desertion of native allies, compelled the destruction of the fort and the abandonment of the expedition, after nearly five months heroic service in the most fatal climate. (See "Annals of the King's Royal Rifle Corps" (60th), by Lewis Butler, 1913, p. 222).

In 1785 he returned once again to the West Indies, in command of the 2nd Battalion of his old Regiment, which he joined in the island of Grenada and served there and in other islands. After three years service he sailed for England and thence, in July, 1788, embarked for New Brunswick in Canada, where he and a brother possessed lands on the river St. John. His sojourn there was short, for he returned within a few months to England, there to retire on his half-pay.

In 1793 Colonel Kemble returned to military life as Deputy Judge Advocate in Canada, and two years later he is mentioned as the holder of the same office in Lord Moira's expedition, ordered by Pitt to proceed to Quiberon and to act as auxiliary to the army of the Count of Artois. He returned in 1805 to his birthplace and lived in the house in which he was born until his death, on December 20, 1822.

The facts of Colonel Stephen Kemble's career are obtained from his Journals, Order Book and Correspondence, 1773-1789, printed in the "Collections of the New York Historical Society" for 1883 and 1884.

Samuel Kemble, his elder brother, spent a few years in the British army before accepting the appointment of Collector of New York in 1773. He was a Loyalist in the Revolution and died in exile in the Island of Sumatra in or about 1796; his younger brother, William, was a Captain in the British army and died in England. His nephew, Peter Kemble, was an Ensign in the 35th Foot until June 23, 1775, when he was transferred to the 4th Foot, in which he was wounded in the Battle of Germantown on October 4th, 1777, having been promoted Lieutenant in May, 1776.

ARCHIBALD KENNEDY (Captain)

A son of Archibald Kennedy (who died June 14, 1763), Scotsman, lawyer, Receiver-General and Collector of the Customs in New York City, and his wife, Mary, daughter of Arent Schuyler, and was born in America. He was superseded in the Royal Navy for refusing to take on board H. M. S. "Coventry" a quantity of stamp paper during the stamp riots of 1765, having succumbed to the threats of violence of the mob. Cadwallader Colden, Lieutenant-Governor of New York, justified Captain Kennedy's conduct by asserting that he did not positively refuse to take charge of the stamp paper, but that he gave reasons for thinking it unnecessary. Indeed, wiser minds in New York regarded the fort of the harbor, strongly fortified as it was, a more suitable place for their custody.

Captain Kennedy would seem now to have retired to the enjoyment of his large and valuable estate called "Pavonia," in New Jersey, adjoining Paulus Hook, on the New Jersey shore, inherited from his father and grandfather. Although smarting under the remembrance of his supersession in the Royal Navy, he openly avowed his sympathies with the mother country at an early stage in the Rebellion and, consequently, was arrested by the Americans in 1776 and retained as a prisoner for four years, until his liberation on parole, when he sailed for England.

Among the losses mourned by this Loyalist was a large silver cup, a gift with a silver salver from the English merchants at Lisbon in Portugal, as a mark of appreciation for his services as Commander of H. M. S. "Flamborough," in saving a convoy of over seventy sail of merchant ships, bound for Portugal from England on April 4, 1760. These treasured pieces of silver were destroyed with other family silver in the destruction of his house by fire by incendiaries in August, 1780. The salver was, however, recovered from the fire, and, with a portrait of Captain Kennedy, is in the possession of the Marquess of Ailsa.

His claim for the loss of his estate amounted to £4,885, and the award as compensation to £1,256 (A. O. 12:109), though, according to John Anstey's report, the New Jersey estate was not confiscated. (A. O. 12:85).

The Kennedy home in the City of New York, No. 1, Broadway, was noted for its historical associations.

Not without interest is his statement that his annual profit from a good bearing apple tree on his estate (Pavonia) was from four to five shillings, and the value of an apple tree was 40 to 60 shillings, doubtless in New Jersey currency.

In October, 1787, Captain Kennedy was living in England on half-pay, with his second wife, Anne, daughter of John Watts, of New York City. His first wife was Catherine, only daughter of Colonel Peter Schuyler, of Petersborough, New York. In 1792 he succeeded to the title of the eleventh Earl of Cassilis in the peerage of Scotland, and died on December 29, 1794.

Captain Kennedy is said to have taken "an uncommon prejudice" against Governor Franklin in 1767, and the Governor on his part entertained suspicions, not unmixed with alarm, that the Captain was an aspirant to replace him in the Governorship. (A. O. 13:65; A. O. 13:109; A. O. 12:24, ff. 388-396; A. O. 12:71, ff. 368-385; A. O. 12:99, f. 239; "New York Hist. Soc. Colls.," 1881, pp. 338, 343, 352; Colden Papers in "New York Hist. Soc. Colls.," 1877, pp. 102-7, 121; "N. J. Archives," First Series, Vol. IX, 640-'1).

STEPHEN KENT

He was born in America and lived at Woodbridge, New Jersey. Both he and his father, David Kent, who died in New York in 1778, joined the British army. At his examination he produced a deed of the property in New Jersey of his great-great-grandfather, Stephen Kent. His three sisters are mentioned: Holday, who was married and lived at Woodbridge in 1786; Rachel, who was dead; and Zernia, who lived with him on the Kennebecasis river in the Province of New Brunswick. There is a copy of the inquisition and a schedule of his estate. (A. O. 13:18; A. O. 12:16, ff. 109-115; A. O. 12:63, f. 74; A. O. 12:110, ff. 97-8). He was allowed £605 from his claim of £1,555. 18s. (A. O. 12:109).

CHARLES KNOWLES

He emigrated from England in 1768 and settled as a soap boiler on property in West Jersey, which had been left to him by a cousin-german. Just before the Revolution he had been offered £525 for this property by one Chalkley James of Philadelphia. For refusing to take the oath to the Americans he was fined twice and imprisoned for nineteen weeks. He escaped from jail and joined the British army on Staten Island, serving in the New York Volunteers during the War, and was wounded four times. He died in England on April 5, 1785, and the balance of his pension was paid to his brother, John, a resident in England. (A. O. 12:101, ff. 24,201).

BERNARDUS La GRANGE

He was a descendant of Huguenots from La Rochelle, France, was baptised on May 11, 1721, in Schenectady, New York, being the son of Jacobus and Engeltje (Veeder) de la Grange. From May 20, 1745, he practised as an attorney-at-law at

Raritan and New Brunswick, N. J., at which latter place he was a member of Christ Church vestry, and where he married, in 1747, Frances Brazier, whose father, Francis, was a vestryman in St. Peter's Church, Perth Amboy. Two of his daughters married officers in the British army and another became the wife of the officer of a Tory Regiment. The name in America has often been written Le Grange, but his own signature was La Grange.

At the outbreak of the Revolution his practice was worth about £400 a year and was larger than that of Daniel Coxe (q. v.). He was the owner of considerable property, including land in New Brunswick, N. J., and 355 acres (actually 352 acres and 17 perches) and a stone house west of Raritan in Somerset county, bequeathed to him by his aunt, Antje Molenaer, widow of Ari Molenaer, by her will of December 27, 1757. From the outset of the Revolution he was active in his opposition to the "Rebel committees," so much so that his effigy was burnt in June, 1775, at New Brunswick. During the occupation of New Jersey by British troops he was employed in administering the oaths of allegiance to the King to recruits and others. Seventeen Hessian officers, with more than twenty servants and carters and as many horses, were quartered upon him. His property in Somerset county was confiscated in 1778 and sold April 13, 1779, the purchaser being Attorney-General William Paterson, for £12,324. 8s. La Grange was probably then in New York City.

This successful lawyer and Loyalist fled to London, England, and at one time had with him four of his children. He died in London, Dec. 10, 1797, and by his will, dated July 1, 1796, proved Jan. 2, 1798, he mentions his son, James Brasier LaGrange (q. v.); his daughters, Susannah, widow of Captain Arthur Wadman (q. v.); Frances, widow of Edward Vaughan Dongan (q. v.); and his granddaughter, Elizabeth Bayley Peters. Another daughter was Lydia, widow of Dr. Henry Dougan (q. v.).

The Commissioners recorded his ownership of "a handsome landed property," and added that they had no hesitation in allowing him £80 per annum to relieve his distress. (A. O. 12:100, f. 31). Later, he was granted as compensation £2,638 from his claim of £8,387. 12s.; and at the rate of £240 a year for the loss of his professional income during the War, together with a pension of £120. (A. O. 12:109; A. O. 461:16; A. O. 459:7; T. 50:8; A. O. 12:13, ff. 275-302; A. O. 12:100, f. 37; A. O. 12:101, f. 282; A. O. 13:83; "Am. MSS. in Roy. Inst.," IV, 107, 268; "Loyalists' Claims," pp. 282-3; Dutch Records, Albany; various N. J. Records).

JAMES BRAZIER La GRANGE (Ensign)

This young Loyalist was the only son of Bernardus La-Grange (supra) and his wife, Frances Brazier. At the beginning of the Revolution, James was a student at King's College, New York (now Columbia University), where he was regarded by one of the Governors of the College, the Rev. Charles Inglis (q. v.) as "regular, studious and his behavior in every respect decent and proper." When barely 16 years of age he was obliged to quit the college on its conversion into a military hospital for the American troops, when he returned home, only to be drafted instantly into the American army, "against his will." On his release, this young Loyalist joined the New Jersey Volunteers and was granted a commission as Ensign in the 3rd Battalion, on December 2, 1776, later being in the 2nd Battalion.

From this well-known Loyalist regiment, James Brazier La-Grange was transferred to the regular British army as Ensign in the 60th Foot, a Regiment originally established in America and known as the Royal American Regiment. The date of his commission was April 3, 1782. Later in the same year he was obliged to resign on account of ill-health. After the Peace he appears to have received an appointment in the Exchequer's Office in London, where his name is recorded in the year 1808. He married the daughter of one Warrington and died in 1822, leaving a son, James Warrington La Grange, who married Harriet Demarest, of Waterford, New York. (A. O. 12:101, f. 83; A. O. 13:110; Stryker; W. H. Benedict's "New Brunswick," N. J.).

GEORGE LAMBERT (Lieutenant)

By birth an Englishman, born in 1757, and he served for six years in a Loyalist Corps, as a Lieutenant in the 2nd and 3rd New Jersey Volunteers. He was on half-pay of this Regiment after the War until his death on December 31, 1828. (Ind.: 5605-6).

ELISHA LAWRENCE (Lieut.-Colonel)

He was born in New Jersey in 1740, the son of John Lawrence, land surveyor and ardent Loyalist, who was in possession of his New Jersey property in 1785. He lived in Monmouth county, of which he was High Sheriff in 1775. Here he formed an Association of Loyalists, of whom 57 joined the British army. At the early age of 26 he was given the command of the 1st New Jersey Volunteers and, in the skirmish between this Regiment and Sullivan's force on Staten Island, on August 22, 1777, he was taken prisoner and his connection with his Corps was finally severed, and his name was added to the list of Seconded officers.

The property of Elisha Lawrence was confiscated and sold in 1779. The schedule of this property includes a farm and cedar swamps. (A. O. 13:18). He was awarded £240 from his claim of £1,200. (A. O. 12:109).

His brother was Dr. John Lawrence (infra). The Lawrence family of Monmouth County was well represented on both sides in the Revolution.

Elisha Lawrence is described in the report of the Commissioners as a Loyalist of great merit from a very early period in the Revolution, and was granted a pension of £80. (A. O. 12:100, f. 306). After the War he removed to Nova Scotia, but he died at Cardigan in Wales in October, 1811, and was buried in the graveyard of St. Mary's Church. (Ind.: 5605; A. O. 12:15, ff. 16-19; A. O. 12:63, f. 144; Stryker; "Ontario Archives," pp. 504-5).

Dr. JOHN LAWRENCE

He was born in Monmouth county, New Jersey, in 1747, a brother to Col. Elisha Lawrence (supra), his father being John Lawrence, and he was graduated from Princeton College in 1764 and at the University of Pennsylvania in 1768, after which he began practice in his native county. He was in Amboy in 1776 as a pronounced Loyalist. In July of that year he was arrested and sent to Elizabethtown; then allowed, on his parole, to be at Trenton and at Morristown. He subsequently went to New York City and practiced there among leading families and took command of a company of volunteers in defense of that city. In 1783 he returned to New Jersey and practiced in Upper Freehold township. He died in Trenton, N. J., April 29, 1830, while playing a game of chess with friends, aged 83 years. He was never married. (A. O. 13:19; Sabine; Wicks' "Hist. of N. J. Medicine," p. 306; "Minutes Com. of Safety, N. J."; "Coll. N. J. Hist. Soc.," Vol. 9, p. 157).

JOHN LAWRENCE (Lieutenant)

A son of William and Margaret Lawrence, of Monmouth county, New Jersey, was born in that State on April 10, 1754, and served seven years in the Provincial forces (as the American Loyalist Corps were called). From 1777 he was an Ensign, and from August 25, 1780, a Lieutenant in the 1st New Jersey Volunteers.

John Lawrence was married on May 4, 1783, to Mary (born March 22, 1766), daughter of Peter and Mary Rezeau, at Richmond, Staten Island, by the Rev. John H. Rowland, the Loyalist Rector of St. Andrew's, Staten Island. The eleven children mentioned are: William, born September 13, 1784; Margaret, born September 25, 1786, who married, June 7, 1810, Joseph Tisdale, of Upper Canada, in 1842; Peter Rezeau, born November 21, 1788, who settled in Upper Canada; John, born October 22, 1791; Mary, born August 26, 1794; Alexander Cairns, born November 23, 1796; Elisha, born February 21, 1800; Charles Earl, born November 27, 1802, a yeoman at Vaughan in Upper Canada in 1842; Abraham Perine, born June 18, 1805; Eliza Ann, born December 10, 1807; and Sarah Catherine, born August 8, 1810. The two last daughters were put on the Compassionate Fund for £11 each in 1824.

He died on December 30, 1821, aged 66, at Vaughan (above named) and was buried by the Rev. William Jenkins, minister of the united congregations of Scarborough, Markham, Vaughan and Whitchurch. His widow died at the same place on September 18, 1842. (W. O. 42:L4; Ind.: 5606).

WILLIAM RICHARD LAWRENCE

He was born in New Jersey and married Elizabeth Oakley, widow of Westchester, New York, where he settled. During the War he was a master carpenter to the British army. After the Peace he was imprisoned. By surrendering his effects (worth £1,244 in New York currency) he was released from prison. Fruitless attempts were made to recover his property by Sir John Temple, then at New York, to Congress and to the Governor of New York. Juries (he said) founded their verdicts against him on a law of New York, passed on March 17, 1783, diametrically opposed to the Treaty of Peace.

In 1788 he was going to Westchester to take the remainder of his family, a wife and nine children, to Nova Scotia, to join his other children. He died on May 25, 1789. One of his executors, Thomas Crowell, appealed to the British Government in 1790 for an allowance for Lawrence's widow and four small children, then in New York, and was granted £60. She received a pension of £20 from 1789 to about January, 1824. (T. 50:11; T. 50:27; A. O. 13:65; A. O. 12:102, ff. 158, 239; A. O. 12:110, ff. 119-120).

GEORGE LEE (Ensign)

He was born in America, probably in New Jersey, about 1773, and was given a commission as Ensign in the 2nd New Jersey Volunteers at the age of seven. This is one of those cases where the son of a zealous Loyalist, probably an officer, was presented with a commission as a form of emolument for the father and a means of maintenance for the holder. He was on the half-pay list until 1814. (Ind.: 5605).

JOHN LEE, Jr.

He lived in Elizabethtown, N. J. (A. O. 13:21). Was a Loyalist, whose estate was confiscated in July, 1779.

JOSEPH LEE (Captain)

Born in England in 1740, he was in charge of some ironworks in New Jersey. In June, 1776, Lee and nearly 60 men employed in these ironworks were repeatedly summoned to attend the trainings of the militia and as often refused. Their refusal subjected them to fines and amercements to great amounts, which they were unable to pay. Determined as he was not to take up arms against his lawful Sovereign, Lee and his men openly opposed the officers of the militia, until, overpowered by numbers, he was taken prisoner and confined in jail in Trenton, where he declared he "suffered every species of barbarity which could be invented." He was arraigned in July, 1776, and fined £200. (A. O. 13:21). Stryker says the fine was £100. In December, 1776, he was Captain in the 6th N. J. Volunteers, later being transferred. He served till the end of the War.

This Loyalist was married on December 10, 1766, to Elizabeth Cypher, a woman of marked character, singularly fearless. Her brother, Peter, was a Sergeant in her husband's Company in the 3rd New Jersey Volunteers, a picked company, known as the "Albert Company," of which he was placed in command. Captain Lee and his company took part in the reduction of Savannah in December, 1778, and in the memorable and successful defense of that town against the combined attacks of Lincoln's army and D'Estaing's naval force in October, 1779. He settled after the War in the Province of New Brunswick, and was Magistrate of York county in 1792.

Once more he took up arms in defense of his adopted country, as one of the first Captains in the King's New Brunswick Regiment, raised in 1793 on the Declaration of War by France on England. (Jonas Howe, in "Colls. of New Brunswick Hist. Soc.," I: 13-59).

Joseph Lee died on October 12, 1812, at Fredericton, while on half-pay of his Regiment. (Ind.: 5605-6; Sabine; "Judges of New Brunswick," p. 45; Stryker).

JOHN LEONARD

He was born in New Jersey and was a farmer in Upper Freehold township, Monmouth county. In June, 1776, he was taken before the Provincial Congress at Trenton on a charge of influencing the people against the measures of Congress and gave a bond for £500 to remain quiet. With nearly 100 friends, all armed, he marched in December, 1776, to join the British army at Trenton, where he was employed in procuring provisions, forage and other supplies. On the evacuation of Philadelphia by the British in 1778 he acted as a guide for General Knyphausen's troops and was present in the Battle of Monmouth.

John Leonard married, first, Magdalen, daughter of John and Ann Riche, or Ritchie, probably the daughter of George Willocks, who left her property at Crosswick in his will of January 3, 1728. This wife died about 1768, leaving issue. He married, secondly, Frances, daughter of John Scooley, owner of an estate in Greenwich and Hanover, New Jersey, and his wife, Frances. John Scooley's will is dated December, 1756. Leonard's estate in Monmouth county was forfeited May 15, 1779. The schedule of his estate includes 140 acres of land in Middlesex county, near New Brunswick, N. J., inherited under the will of George Willocks, deceased, of Perth Amboy, owner of the ferry between Perth Amboy and Staten Island. The beneficiaries under the will (of which there is an abstract) were John Riche, (brother-in-law of George Willocks) and his wife, Ann, and his children, also the children of George Leslie. According to a copy of an indenture, the only children of the above John and Ann Riche (Ritchie) were Magdalen Leonard, wife of John Leonard; Elizabeth, wife of James Lawrence, farmer, of Upper Freehold; and Mary, wife of Jacob Brian, of Chesterfield, New Jersey. (A. O. 13:18).

In 1786 John Leonard and two sons were living at Maugerville, Province of New Brunswick, while his wife was at Hanover in New Jersey. He was proposing to send for her in 1787. (A. O. 12:15, ff. 42-54, 434; A. O. 12:63, ff. 65-6; "Ontario Archives," p. 70).

JOHN LEONARD (Ensign)

He was of Middletown, Monmouth county, N. J.; was born in America about 1758 and served for three years in a Loyalist Corps, as Ensign for whole or part of the time in the New Jersey Volunteers. (Ind.: 5605-6). According to Stryker he died in 1801 in New Brunswick, Canada, but his name survives in the half-pay lists until December, 1816. His estate in New Jersey was forfeited in 1780. He was probably the son of John Leonard, above mentioned.

SAMUEL LEONARD (Captain)

He was American-born and, on December 22, 1776, was appointed Lieutenant in the 1st New Jersey Volunteers. On August 14, 1781, he was promoted Captain. He was married on September 22, 1785, to Nancy Allison, spinster, at Horton, Nova Scotia, by Jonathan Crane, a Justice of the Peace. She was born in 1768 at Newton, Limavady, Ireland, and was taken to Nova Scotia in infancy. From 1807 to 1808 he was a Major in the Nova Scotia militia, which garrisoned the forts at Halifax when the regulars were withdrawn for Wellington's army in Europe.

Samuel Leonard died at Horton on August 20, 1825, aged 69. His widow died in 1858 at Wolfville, Nova Scotia, leaving no children. (W. O. 42:J7; Ind.: 5605-6).

THOMAS LEONARD (Major)

He was born about 1715 and lived at Greenwich Farm, five miles from Freehold, Monmouth county, N. J. For many years he was High Sheriff of Monmouth, his native county, and lived well on his considerable property. He was a prisoner on parole for two years early in the War, apparently while holding the rank of Major in the 1st New Jersey Volunteers.

A schedule of his property includes an estate inherited from his uncle, Thomas Leonard, Esquire, deceased. John Thompson (q. v.) and Cornelius Thompson (q. v.), "gentlemen," of Monmouth county, testified at New York in August, 1783, to their personal knowledge of the Leonard property. His estate in Monmouth county, forfeited May 13, 1779, was sold for £5,456. 14. 9., in New Jersey currency. (A. O. 13:18).

Major Leonard's name is on the list of Seconded officers. (Ind.: 5605). He claimed £1,590 and was allowed £1,210. (A. O. 12:109). His place of residence in 1786 was Parrsborough in Nova Scotia. (A. O. 12:15, ff. 159-169; A. O. 12:63, f. 21; Stryker).

DAVID LEWIS

He probably lived at Shrewsbury, N. J.; was born in New Jersey, eldest son and heir of Jean Lewis, a widow, who died in 1782 and who had been housekeeper to John Williams before his death in 1781. He joined the British forces in 1777 at the age of 16, apparently in the 2nd New Jersey Volunteers. He was a refugee in New York in 1787, but later in the year he was a mariner at Shelburne, Nova Scotia.

Accompanying his memorial are particulars of his property, and an original conveyance of property in New Jersey, conveyed to Mrs. Jean Lewis by the above John Williams, described as an old Loyalist who died at Long Island, a refugee. Thomas and Walter Curtis, Quakers, formerly of Shrewsbury, New Jersey, who were probably Loyalists, affirmed at New York on October 24, 1783, that they were acquainted with the property inherited by David Lewis. He claimed £590. 12s. and was allowed £350. (A. O. 12:109; A. O. 13:18; A. O. 12:16, ff. 391-5; A. O. 12:63, f. 138).

NATHANIEL LEWIS

If this man was, as believed, formerly of Burlington county, N. J., his estate had not been confiscated before John Anstey's visit to New Jersey in 1787. He was at that time a flourishing merchant in Philadelphia. (A. O. 12:85).

RICHARD LIPPINCOTT (Captain)

For trying to conceal a person sent from New York to New Jersey by General Sir William Howe to distribute proclamations he was taken prisoner in October, 1776, but succeeded in escaping from jail in Burlington and joined the British in New York in December following. In the same month he was given a commission as Ensign in the 1st New Jersey Volunteers, which he resigned in April, 1777. In 1780 he recruited a Company of Loyalists, and on February 17, 1781, he was appointed Captain in the Associated Loyalist Refugees in New York.

The name of Richard Lippincott is prominent in the annals of the War as the officer in charge of the party who executed Captain Joshua Huddy, in revenge for the murder of Philip

White, the Loyalist, who, according to Sabine, was the half-brother of Lippincott's wife. A full account of the affair is in Colonel J. J. Graham's "Memoir of General Samuel Graham." Many references to the execution are in the "Amer. MSS. in the Roy. Inst.," Vols II and III, including an address of the inhabitants of Monmouth county, New Jersey, to General Washington, demanding vengeance for the murder. Other full accounts are in Sabine and especially in Stryker's "Capture of the Block House, Toms River," and elsewhere. Daniel Coxe (q. v.) disapproved of the execution of Huddy. ("Am. MSS. in Roy. Inst." II:529; see also under "Governor William Franklin," supra).

The amount of his compensation was £15 from his claim of £200. He received a military allowance of £40 until his death on May 14, 1826. (Ind.: 5606; A. O. 12:109).

Lippincott was born at Shrewsbury, New Jersey, on January 2, 1745, and settled some few years after the War in Vaughan county, Canada, where he was the owner of 3,000 acres of land in what is now the City of Toronto. He died in 1826. His only surviving child, Esther Borden, married, in 1806, Lieutenant-Colonel George Taylor Denison, of Bellevue, Toronto, who served in the War of 1812. (Chadwick, "Ontarian Families," Vol. I, Pt. VII, p. 105; A. O. 13:81; A O. 12:16, ff. 330-3; A. O. 12:63, f. 102; Stryker; "Ontario Archives," p. 307, etc.).

WALTER LOGAN

A Scotsman, who was appointed on November 18, 1767, Comptroller of the Customs at Perth Amboy, at a salary of £50 and fees of £50. In 1770 he was the agent in Massachusetts for Sir Francis Bernard, Governor of the Province, whom he probably accompanied from New Jersey. There is some of his correspondence on the affairs of the Bernard property with the Governor's papers. He was living at Edinburgh, Scotland, with his wife and children, after the War, on a Loyalist pension until 1801, when he probably died. (A. O. 12:104, f. 12; A. O. 459-7; A. O. 451:17; T. 50:6; Sabine).

THOMAS LONG

He was an Englishman who taught school at Rahway, New Jersey, and was a Loyalist. He was charged with crossing over to the vicinity of Rahway from Staten Island in 1781 with a party of 12 to 15 and carrying off seven "leading American Whigs" to the Sugar House in New York City. Later he appeared near Rahway and was captured as a spy, tried by court martial, and executed by hanging at Kinsey's Corner, near there. It was said he was brutally tortured before hanging, and that later his body was dug up and made sport of. (Sworn evidence, in "N. J. Hist. Soc. Proceedings," New Series, Vol. VII, pp. 25, 26; F. O. 4:1). As a reprisal the British captured an American named Ball and executed him. (Stryker's "N. J. Volunteers," p. 49; see also under Cornelius Hatfield, Jr., supra; and John Smith Hatfield, supra).

JOHN LONGSTREET, Jr. (Captain)

He was born about 1746 in Monmouth county, New Jersey, and lived at Freehold as a farmer. His confiscated property, of which there is a schedule, was sold for £3,780. In the spring of 1776 he joined a company of over 70 inhabitants, mostly Loyalists of Freehold, with the declared intention of opposing the British army under Sir William Howe—a device adopted to avoid being called out in the American militia. Many of these Loyalists were afterwards officers in the British forces. In August of the same year he was captured by General Sullivan on Staten Island. He was appointed Captain in the New Jersey Volunteers, July 15, 1776. With his papers is a copy of the inquisition into his affairs and political views. (A. O. 13:18).

Captain Longstreet attempted in 1779 to raise men so as to be appointed on full pay in Colonel Robert Rogers's King's Rangers, but failed and lost two years' half-pay. He was, however, placed on the half-pay list of this Corps in 1792. (W. O. 24:751). He settled at Parrsborough, Nova Scotia. His claim of £2,137.10 was met by a grant of £1,010. (A. O. 12:109).

According to William Taylor (q. v.), his father, John Longstreet, Sr., who remained in New Jersey during the War was not of "general good character," which is another description for a man who was not a Loyalist. (A. O. 12:15, ff. 171-9; A. O. 12:63, f. 22; Ind.: 5605-6).

ISAAC LONGWORTH

He was born in America and lived at Newark, New Jersey, as a shopkeeper. The following papers are in A. O. 13:18:

A schedule of his property which included some which had been left to him by will of his father and to Thomas Longworth, probably a brother. (His Essex county, N. J., estate was confiscated June 12, 1778). A letter to Peter Ogden in London, dated from Newark, New Jersey, October 13, 1787, in which he says that on December 2, 1755, he took a Lieutenant's commission and proceeded to defend the frontiers of New Jersey and took the oath of allegiance to the King, an oath he had never since violated. A letter to his brother-in-law, Hon. David Ogden (q. v.) in London, dated from Newark, November 5, 1787, declaring that if "the King could know what she [his wife] has suffered for Loyalty and with what constancy she has borne it, always declaring she approv'd of the part I had taken in adhering to my allegiance to the King, and that she had rather suffer the loss of all her property than to wrong her conscience and be a rebel." A long letter, unsigned and undated, to Major General West Hyde, Lieutenant-Colonel of the First Regiment of Guards, (who had occupied Isaac Longsworth's house in Newark when the British army entered New Jersey in 1776), on the pitiable condition of himself and his wife Catherine, both devoted Loyalists, old and crippled and penniless in the United States. This letter is endorsed by the General with the date, July 11, 1788, and with the remark that something may be done for their relief. There is also an official account of the sales of the confiscated estates of the following Loyalists, all of Essex county, New Jersey: Thomas Longworth, for £2,230. 3s. 3d.; Caleb Sayres, for £105. 17s. 10d., and Isaac Longworth, for £1,067. 1s. 7d. According to these papers, Isaac Longworth acted as clerk to Mr. Maller, Surveyor-General, during the War. He was allowed £268 from his claim of £636. 1s. (A. O. 12:109).

Catherine, wife of Isaac Longworth, was the daughter of Colonel Josiah Ogden, who died May 17, 1763. He and his wife were in exile at Hartford, Connecticut, until 1786, afterwards in New York until May, 1787, and lastly in Newark, where they tried to sell a little grocery, but apparently without success. They were born in 1726 and 1721 respectively. (A. O. 12:15, ff. 356-362; A. O. 12:63, f. 47).

THOMAS LOOFBOURN (LOOFBOROUGH)

A farmer, born in Woodbridge, N. J., who joined the British forces in 1776, serving in different ships until the end of the War. His farm, apparently inherited from his grandfather, was shared by two brothers. In 1784 he was a refugee in England, earning a shilling a day by chopping wood. Cortlandt Skinner (q. v.) spoke warmly of the loyalty of the Loofbourn (really Loofborough) family. (A. O. 12:101, f. 79).

WILLIAM LUCE (Captain)

This Loyalist was of Elizabethtown, New Jersey, and before the War was Captain of a schooner. Probably he followed the waters by Staten Island during the War. His estate was confiscated Feb. 17, 1779. After the War he was Captain of a British merchant vessel trading to the West Indies. (A. O. 13:112; A. O. 12:100, f. 347). He was allowed £1,285 from his substantial claim of £1,425. (A. O. 12:109).

HENDRICK LUTKINS

He was born in America and lived in New Barbadoes township, N. J., as a small farmer. He served in the New Jersey Volunteers throughout the War, while his only two sons and a son-in-law also served in the British forces.

One Henry Lutkins, of Bergen county, New Jersey, certified that Hendrick Lutkins's estate had been sold for £757. 5. 7. (A. O. 13:18). It was confiscated and sold in 1778. He was living at Clements Precinct, Annapolis, Nova Scotia, in 1786. His claim of £213.17. was met by a grant of £130. (A. O. 12:109; A. O. 12:16, ff. 43-7; A. O. 12:63, f. 64).

Rev. GARRET LYDECKER

The son of Ryck and Mary Lydecker and minister of the English Neighborhood Dutch Reformed Church, Bergen county, New Jersey, 1770-1776. He was born in that county in 1729. He had a farm there of 400 acres, valued at £2,525 sterling, bounded on the Hudson river and Overpeck creek, derived in part by a legacy of Cornelius Lydecker by will of March 6, 1777. This property was confiscated in 1778 and was also advertised in the "New York Gazette" for January 28, 1784. He also received a legacy from Abraham Lydecker. He continued to pray for the King, in face of opposition, and conducted himself from the beginning of the revolt with "true loyalty." He then fled to New York City, where he acted as minister of the Dutch Reformed Church and was engaged by the English Peace Commissioners in America to translate proclamations into German. His mother died about 1760. Samuel Benson Lydecker, a brother, is mentioned.

The Rev. Samuel Seabury, the future first Bishop of the American Episcopal Church, testified to the loyalty, worth and reputation of the Rev. Garret Lydecker ("Am. MSS. in Roy. Inst.," III: 269). He sailed for England in October, 1783 (Ibid, IV: 394), and died there in 1794. He was awarded £1,730 from his claim of £3,175 and a pension of £50. (A. O. 12:109; A. O. 12:14, ff. 9-19; A. O. 12:100, f. 128; Corwin's "Manual").

ENOCH LYON (Lieutenant)

He was born in America about 1753 and served for five years as Lieutenant in the 3rd and 2nd New Jersey Volunteers. He was on half-pay until December, 1816. (Ind.: 5605-6).

JAMES McATEE

A New Jerseyman by birth, who joined the British army in 1776, acted as a guide in obtaining intelligence and took part in many hazardous enterprises. From 1780 until the end of the War he was inspector of Ryerson's Ferry on Staten Island. With pride he announced that he acted as guide to the troops who captured John Hampton, of New Jersey, "a notorious and sanguinary Rebel."

At the conclusion of the War he was arrested on the suit of two persons who claimed to have suffered damage to their boats when he acted as guide to a detachment of the army. In

1790 he was in Nova Scotia and was in receipt of a military year of his death. (Ind.: 5605; A. O. 13:36; A. O. 13:110; A. O. 12:102. ff. 127, 172, 212).

CORNELIUS McCLEESE, or McLEOD (Captain)

He was of the New Jersey Volunteers, who was on the Seconded list of officers in 1783. (Ind.: 5605). Stryker says he was Captain McLeod in the 2nd Battalion until 1780. But under the name of McCleese he had an estate forfeited in Monmouth county, N. J., Feb. 9, 1784. ("N. J. Hist. Soc. Proc.," N. S., Vol. X, p. 319; "Am. MSS. in Roy. Inst," IV: 395).

CREIGHTON McCREA (Ensign)

A brother of Major Robert McCrea (q. v.) and the son of Rev. James McCrea and Catherine (Rosbrugh) McCrea. He was born at Lamington, Somerset county, New Jersey, about 1763. He received a commission as Ensign in his brother's Regiment, the Queen's Rangers Infantry, on April 25, 1781. (Ind.: 5604). In January, 1789, he was serving with the 7th Regiment in the East Indies; and, according to the "History of the Clan Macrae," he became a Captain in the 75th Highlanders and was present at the capture of the fortress of Seringapatam.

Later he returned to the country of his birth, where he owned a large tract of land near Lamington, besides other large tracts in Somerset county. Here he died on December 10, 1818, at the age of 56 and was buried in the graveyard of the Presbyterian Church at Bound Brook. He always remained a bachelor. (For fuller sketch, see "Som. Co. Hist. Quar.," Vol. VII, p. 95).

ROBERT McCREA (Major, etc.)

He was born at Lamington, Somerset county, New Jersey, on November 2, 1754, being the brother of Creighton McCrea (supra), and was studying at Princeton College when the Revolution broke out, and is described as of "an opulent and elevated family" in that Province. As a boy he stepped forth in the cause of his country and earned laurels which he declared, "have always been his greatest comfort, even in his most distressed difficulties." He served in the Queen's Rangers Infantry from the formation of that well-known Loyalist Regiment until its reduction at the end of the War. He was wounded in the Battles of Brooklyn on August 27, 1776, White Plains, and at the Brandywine on September 11, 1777. In the last of these three battles young McCrea lost his right arm and, although incapacitated from further active service in the field, he continued on military service of a non-combatant character.

In picturing the sorrows and sufferings of this Loyalist family, Robert McCrea recalls the "unparalleled misfortunes of his family, more than the common measure of the miseries of Civil War." One of his brothers was killed during the War, while a "youthful sister fell a victim to the dictates of a barbarian polity, and expired under the butchery of the rude tomahawk," (referring to the famed Jane McCrea).

Robert McCrea was appointed in 1785 Captain in an Independent Company, or Royal Veterans, in the Island of Guernsey, where he was promoted Major of the 4th Royal Veteran Battalion and, later, Major Commandant of the 5th Royal Veterans. For sometime he held the honorable office of Governor of Chester Castle in Guernsey.

He married, first, Jane Coutart, a Guernsey lady of Huguenot descent, who was born in 1767 and died on April 8, 1796. His children by this marriage included Catherine Maria, who married Colonel Frederick Barlow, of the 61st Foot, who was killed in leading his Regiment at the Battle of Salamanca on July 22, 1812; Rawdon (named after Lord Rawdon), Captain in the 87th Foot, who was present at the taking of Montevideo in 1807 and was killed at the battle of Talavera on July 28, 1809; Robert Coutart, who became an Admiral and was present under Nelson at Trafalgar in the "Swiftsure;" and Jane, who married Colonel George August Eliot. By his second marriage, on June 12, 1804, to Sophia Le Mesurier, sister of General William Le Mesurier, his children included Robert Bradford McCrea, Captain in the 44th Foot, who was killed at Cabul on November 14, 1841.

Robert McCrea maintained that he was deprived of his expected inheritance of landed property from his maternal grandfather, Robert Rosbrugh, (died in 1783) "the most wealthy man in Somerset county," in consequence of the War, and it passed to Rosbrugh's daughter, Mary, widow of David Henry, and to his great-grandson, Philip, son of his granddaughter, Catherine McCrea (sister of Robert), and her husband, William McDonald, last High Sheriff of Somerset county, N. J., under the Crown. He and his brother, Creighton, (q. v.), claimed jointly the sum of £3,466 for their property and were awarded £1,000 and £500 respectively. (A. O. 12:109). Robert received a pension of £60 from 1784 until his death. (T. 50:8; T. 50:28).

His half brother, Stephen, a physician in New York City, writes somewhat petulantly to Charles Cooke from New York on September 20, 1787, as follows: "I would expect less difficulty in procuring a freehold estate of one thousand pounds in New Jersey than a compliance of what appears by your letter to be requisite for my brother's recovering the moneys and property he loses by his attachment to the British Government." (A. O. 13:118, with papers of William Dunlop). This letter was no doubt written in answer to a request for proofs of the confiscation of the McCrea property in New Jersey and other particulars required by the Commissioners in London in order to assess the amount of compensation.

John McCrea, a half-brother of Robert, was a Colonel in the American army. Stephen, another half-brother, already mentioned, was Surgeon in the same army. Thus, while the children of the Rev. James McCrea by his first marriage to Miss Mary Graham were conspicuous on the American side in the Revolution, others by his second marriage were Loyalists.

Major Robert McCrea, said to have been a man of fine presence, died in Paris on July 2, 1835, and was buried in Pere La Chaise cemetery. (A. O. 13:110; A. O. 13:118; A. O. 12:14, ff. 408-9; A. O. 12:100, f. 156; Alex. Macrae, "Hist. of the Clan Macrae;" Ex inform. Prof. V. Lansing Collins).

JAMES McCULLOCH (Lieutenant)

This Irishman accompanied his Regiment, the 17th Foot, on service as a private to America in 1757. Having obtained his discharge as a Sergeant in 1764 he settled, in 1766, at Hackensack, New Jersey, and married there. About two years later he returned to Ireland and remained there for two years, returning to New Jersey in 1771.

Early in the revolt he was obliged to flee with his two brothers, one of whom, Samuel, a weaver at Hackensack, had emigrated from Ireland in 1773 with a son and daughter. This brother died in 1777 in New York City, leaving a widow and these two children, the son, named James, being about twelve. The widow married again and remained in America, leaving her two children with their uncle, James McCulloch, this zealous Loyalist.

James McCulloch was appointed at New York, on February 2, 1780, a Lieutenant of militia and kept a store there until within twenty days of the evacuation of the city by the British, when he sailed for England, and was there in great distress and obliged to maintain his wife, Martha, and children and his deceased brother, Samuel's, son and daughter. His property in Bergen county, New Jersey, was forfeited October 3, 1778 (name there given as McCollaugh). He was allowed £65 from his claim of £95. 15s. and his nephew £15 from his claim of £40. (A. O. 12:109). He also received a military allowance of £35 from 1786. (Ind.: 5606; A. O. 13:110; A. O. 12:13, ff. 384-392; A. O. 12:100, ff. 119-120; A. O. 12:101, f. 326).

ALEXANDER McDONALD (Captain)

He was a Scotsman who emigrated in 1773 and settled as a storekeeper in Philadelphia. He served throughout the War and was, from 1777, a Captain in the 1st New Jersey Volunteers. He died on December 10, 1817, at the age of 72, at Bridgewater, Somerset, England. (W. O. 42:M6; Ind.: 5605-6; "Ontario Archives," pp. 253-4). Stryker, no doubt in error, says he died in the Province of New Brunswick in 1835, "at the age of 72."

SAMUEL McKENNA

At the advanced age of over 80 he emigrated, in 1775, to New Jersey to join his daughter, Barbara Blain, wife of the

Loyalist William Blain (q. v.), of Woodbridge. He would seem to have inherited or to have bought property there, for his daughter was allowed £253 from her claim of £1,164. 10s. for her father's estate. (A. O. 13:110; A. O. 12:101, f. 143).

THOMAS McKNIGHT

A farmer in Monmouth County, New Jersey, where his property was left by him in charge of his brother, Robert. He served during the War and was taken prisoner several times. (A. O. 13:81).

HANNAH McLEOD

The widow of a Captain McLeod (Cornelius, or Norman), of New Jersey and a Loyalist. Her estate was not confiscated. (A. O. 12:85).

Dr. JONATHAN MALLETT

A Director of the British Military Hospitals during the War. His name is included here only because of his marriage, on September 26, 1778, to Mary Maturin, widow and probably a Loyalist, at Trinity Church, Newark, New Jersey, by the Rev. Isaac Browne (q. v.). He died on November 21, 1806, in Bryanston street, parish of St. Marylebone, London, leaving a widow. (W. O. 25:3101).

———— MARPLE (Captain)

He was of Gloucester township, Gloucester county, New Jersey, and a Captain in the Associated Loyalists in New York from 1781. He was in the Province of New Brunswick in 1787 and his widow, Northrup, was living at St. Andrews in that Province after his death. (A. O. 12:16, ff. 361-5; A. O. 12:63, f. 111). The sum of £108 was allowed her from his claim of £1,280. (A. O. 12:109).

HENRY MARSH (Captain)

He was of Hackensack, New Jersey, and a Captain in the 4th New Jersey Volunteers. He was mortally wounded at the head of his Company in an advance against the Americans at Second river, New Jersey, early in April, 1777, and died shortly afterwards. His estate was sequestered in 1779.

A private in his Company was John Kelly, who was living in the parish of Kingsclear, Province of New Brunswick, in 1822. Marsh's widow, Elizabeth, married Lieutenant Leonard Reed (q. v.). Her memorial is in "Am. MSS. in Roy. Inst," IV:96. (From Reed's papers in W. O. 42:R3).

ANDREW MERCEREAU

A farmer, of Middlesex county, New Jersey, born in that State. He died at Maugerville, Province of New Brunswick, in 1784, leaving a widow, Phebe. By his will he left all his estate for life to his widow, afterwards to Phebe Johnston, daughter of Alexander Johnston, and to Cornelius and Phebe Wilson, children of his wife's brother-in-law, Robert Wilson, all of whom were living in Middlesex county, New Jersey, in 1787, except his widow, Phebe Mercereau, who was at Maugerville. (A. O. 12:16, ff. 280-5; A. O. 12:63, f. 94). She was allowed £198 from her claim of £475. 7s. (A. O. 12:109).

PHINEAS MILLIDGE (Ensign)

The youngest of four sons of Major Thomas Millidge (q. v.). He was born about 1763 and was an Ensign in the 1st and then 3rd New Jersey Volunteers (1780) for three years. (Ind.: 5605-6; Sabine; "N. Bruns. (Can.) Hist. Soc. Coll.," No. 5). He died in Nova Scotia in 1836, aged 71. (Stryker).

STEPHEN MILLIDGE (Ensign)

He was born in or about 1758, the son of Major Thomas Millidge (q. v.), and served for seven years in the Loyalist forces, for part of that time as Ensign in the 1st, 2nd and 3rd New Jersey Volunteers. He was on half-pay until 1810. (Ind.: 5605-6; "N. Bruns. (Can.) Hist. Soc. Coll.," No. 5). According to Stryker he was for some years a surgeon's mate in the 5th New Jersey Volunteers, but on September 14, 1783, was appointed Ensign in the 2nd Battalion.

THOMAS MILLIDGE (Major)

The eldest son of John Millidge, he was born about 1735 and had much property in Hanover, Morris county, New Jersey, his birthplace. On March 23, 1767, he was appointed Deputy Surveyor of the counties of Morris, Sussex, Bergen and Essex, under the Surveyor-General, William Alexander, Earl of Stirling. In the early stages of the revolt he took a moderate attitude. A brother died at Troy in Hanover in 1775. His military title is derived from his commission in the 5th New Jersey Volunteers in 1776 and in the 1st Battalion in 1779.

There is an affidavit of Samuel Tuthill, formerly one of His Majesty's Justices of the Peace and Judge of the Court of Common Pleas in Morris county, who was apparently a Loyalist refugee in New York City in September, 1783. With it is a document, signed by Phineas and John Millidge, dated Digby, Nova Scotia, July 19, 1785. (A. O. 13/19).

Major Millidge's land in Morris county, New Jersey, was early confiscated. He was awarded £1,131 from his claim of £2,777. 6s. and at the rate of £50 a year for the loss of his official income during the War. (A. O. 12:109).

Major Millidge settled in Nova Scotia, where he was a member of the Provincial Assembly and Deputy Surveyor of the Province. He died at Granville on September 8, 1816. His sons were Phineas and Stephen (q. v.). Once only did he return to Morris county, New Jersey, but his "hot" welcome compelled him to retreat. He was regarded as a very honorable man, firm in his convictions of duty and correct in his habits of life. (Stryker; A. O. 12:15, ff. 30-9; A. O. 12:63, f. 5; A. O. 13:85; Ind.: 5604-5-6; Sabine; "Ontario Archives," pp. 67-70; "Am. MSS. in Roy. Inst.," IV:12).

JOHN MONRO

He was born in America on April 23, 1756, the son of Robert Monro, a Scotsman, who had served under the celebrated English General Wolfe and afterwards settled at New Brunswick, New Jersey. On July 6, 1777, he was appointed Lieutenant in the 1st New Jersey Volunteers, by commission of General Sir William Howe, the original of which is in W. O. 42:M39.

He was married, on February 26, 1794, to Sarah Hatheway, of and in Roxbury township, Morris county, New Jersey, in the presence of Ralph Hatheway, yeoman, of that place, and of the latter's father and mother. Within a year of the marriage they removed to Upper Canada, where John Monro died on October 9, 1828, at Walsingham, and was buried by the Rev. Daniel Freeman, minister of the Methodist Episcopal Church at Woodhouse in Upper Canada. His widow was alive in December, 1829, when she was petitioning the British Government for a pension as the widow of a Loyalist officer. (W. O. 42:M39; Ind.: 5605). His brother, Robert Monro, M. D., was living at Charlotteville, Norfolk county, Canada, in 1831. (W. O. 42:M39).

JAMES MOODY (Captain)

One of the most picturesque and gallant figures on the Loyalist side, he was born about 1744 in New Jersey, where he was a farmer in Sussex county, having 500 acres near the Delaware river. He was obliged to leave his property and joined the British, with 74 friends and neighbors, in April, 1777. Such was his zeal in the British cause that not only was he a Lieutenant in the 1st New Jersey Volunteers, but at different times he raised 182 men for the army, at an expenditure to himself of £1,500 sterling, of which only £170 had been refunded to him.

With his papers in A. O. 13:110 is a copy of an order of the British Commander-in-Chief, dated April 24, 1777, encouraging the completion of the Loyalist Corps. Colonels were to receive pay of Lieutenant-Colonels, Majors that of Captains, and Captains no pay, until they should have raised 25 approved men, when they would receive five shillings a day, and full pay upon completion of a Company of three Sergeants, three Corporals, one drummer and fifty privates.

According to a certificate of Brigadier-General Oliver de Lancey, of New York, James Moody was very active and enterprising and was particularly successful in intercepting several important mails from General Washington to Congress, as well as exerting himself by enlisting men. (A. O. 13:110). Among his exploits was the capture of four American field officers, three Captains and two Lieutenants, unfortunately not named. It was not until 1778 that Governor Franklin first met him, in New York, where Moody "bore the character of the most distinguished partizan" on the British side. The Governor afterwards declared in evidence in London that he believed everything in Moody's "Narrative" to be truly stated. General Sir Henry Clinton, whom he had accompanied to England, in a letter to Moody, dated May 2, 1783, thanking him for a copy of his printed "Narrative," expresses a very high opinion of his zealous, active and spirited conduct in the War, adding that he had intended to promote him in the army before quitting his command as Commander-in-Chief in America. He could not understand how the Rev. Charles Inglis (q. v.) could assert that he (the General) had promised to do something beneficial for him. Moody and his associates had already been paid 345 guineas for taking the different mails. (A. O. 13:110).

It would seem from his printed "Narrative" that he was accused of the assassination of a Captain Shaddock and a Lieutenant Hendrickson. To the accusation he replied that American officers, who were witnesses of and participators in the engagement, declared that these two officers had fallen fairly in battle near Black Point. His younger brother, John, perished an ignominious death by execution at Philadelphia in 1781, and, he declared, cost his venerable father (who had himself been a soldier and loved and honored the profession of arms) his reason.

In his "Narrative" Moody says that he was a plain, contented farmer, settled on a large, fertile and pleasant farm of his own, in the best climate and happiest country in the world. However real and great the grievances of the Americans might be, rebellion was not the way to redress them. The great majority of the peasantry had no real grievances.

"Rather would he fight, bleed and die than live to see the venerable Constitution of his country totally lost."

Moody maintained that a very great majority of the people in the Middle Colonies were loyal at the time of writing his story and would still do and suffer almost anything rather than remain under the tyranny of their then present rulers. He complained of the harsh treatment meted out to him by the Americans; he was confined in handcuffs, so made as to be ragged inside next to the wrist. He paid warm tribute to his brother Loyalists, into whose hands he was often obliged to put his life, but not once was he betrayed by them. Generous rewards offered by the Americans for the surrender of so formidable a foe tempted them not from their fidelity to him or their allegiance to their rightful Sovereign, welcome as such rewards would have been in their distressed condition, wondering what their own fate would be.

James Moody was married, on March 21, 1782, to Jane Lynson, widow, of New Jersey, by the Rev. Isaac Browne (q. v.), in the presence of Mary Bell, John Grigg, Hannah Grigg and John Le Chevalier Roome. He died on April 6, 1800 [or 1809], at Sissiboo in Nova Scotia, leaving a widow, who, in December, 1815, was appealing for a pension as the widow of a Loyalist officer. (W. O. 42/M40).

The Rev. Charles Inglis (q. v.), in Nova Scotia, refers to him as reading prayers on Sundays at Sissiboo and describes him as a public benefactor to that settlement, where he and 38 Loyalist families were, in August, 1788, living on the north side of the Sissiboo river and when Captain Moody launched a ship of 250 tons, called the "Loyalist" and was building another. (Bishop Inglis's "Journal").

His claim of £1,719. 10s. was met by an allowance of £1,608, which is ample proof that he had been a man of substance in New Jersey. (A. O. 12:109; Ind.: 5604-5-6; F. O. 4:1; A. O. 12:13, ff. 72-8; A. O. 12:99, f. 4; Moore's "Diary of the Revolution," II:466; Sabine; "Loyalists' Claims," pp. 133-4; "Moody's Own Narrative," first printed in 1781; Salter's "Old Times in Old Monmouth," etc.).

SAMUEL MOORE.

A Quaker, who was born in New Jersey and was a farmer in Woodbridge, where he had bought 75 acres of land and a house from Daniel Shotwell in 1770 for £750 in currency, which was purchased at the sale of his confiscated property by one Ward. He was imprisoned for his loyalty and fled to the British army in New York in June, 1776, and was there joined by his family in September, 1777. His brother, Edward Moore, was living in New Jersey in 1786, while he himself was at Annapolis in Nova Scotia. (A. O. 12:15, ff. 81-4; A. O. 12:110, ff. 23-4). He was awarded £530 from his claim of £588. 7s. (A. O. 12:109).

CHARLES MORGAN

He emigrated from Scotland about 1765 and settled in Bordentown, New Jersey, as a house carpenter and joiner. For six years he served in the Maryland Loyalists. (A. O. 12:100, f. 155; A. O. 13:110).

MAURICE MORGANN

He was Secretary and Clerk of the Council of New Jersey, commissioned on November 13, 1766, by George III (not taking effect until June 18, 1767), serving about two years, when he went to England. In 1775 he granted a lease of all his offices in the Province to John Antill (q. v.). He is remembered for his "Essay on the Dramatic Character of Sir John Falstaff."

Maurice Morgann was Under Secretary of State to William Fitzmaurice Petty, Earl of Shelburne, afterwards first Marquis of Lansdowne; and was Secretary to the embassy for ratifying the Peace with America in 1782. His name appears frequently as Secretary to Sir Guy Carleton, last British Commander-in-Chief in the American War. (A. O. 13:110; "Dict. of Nat. Biog.; "N. J. Archives," First Series, Vol. X, pp. 1, 5, 7, 9, 132).

JOHN MORRIS (Lieut.-Colonel)

This officer was born in America about 1735, probably at Shrewsbury, New Jersey, where he was settled at the outbreak of the Revolution. In the War against the French in North America he had served as Lieutenant in the 47th Regiment of Foot, having been transferred, on December 10, 1756, from the 45th Foot, in which he had served as Ensign from June 30 in the previous year. He was on half-pay as Lieutenant in the regular British army from 1765 until 1785, or 1786.

John Morris was appointed in November, 1776, Lieutenant-Colonel of the 2nd New Jersey Volunteers and continued to serve as such until 1782, when his Battalion was drafted into the other Battalions of that Regiment and his name was added to the list of Seconded officers. He disobeyed orders of the British commander to destroy salt factories in Monmouth county, having spared certain private stores and levied only on public property. (Stryker). His estate in Middlesex county, New Jersey, was forfeited May 17, 1779.

Colonel Morris was at Three Rivers, Canada, in July, 1787, in great distress and in want. With his memorials are papers concerning his property in New Jersey. (A. O. 13:19). He was granted £1,000 from his claim of £1,631. 5s. (A. O. 12:109; Ind.: 5605; A. O. 12:16, ff. 397-403; A. O. 12:63, f. 119; Army Lists; "Ontario Archives," pp. 772, 925-6; "Am. MSS. in Roy. Inst.," IV:298; Sabine).

ROBERT MORRIS (Captain)

He was of the 2nd New Jersey Volunteers, 1777, and on the list of Seconded officers in 1783. (Ind.: 5605). He may have been the Robert Morris of Shrewsbury, New Jersey, whose estate was forfeited May 17, 1779. ("N. Bruns. (Can.) Hist. Soc. Coll.," No. 5; Midd., N. J., Co. Records).

ROBERT MORRIS (Ensign)

An Irishman, born about 1753, who emigrated about 1769 to New York, where he was engaged in the firm of Hugh & Alexander Wallace, merchants, and afterwards prominent Loyalists. Early in the Revolution he removed to Bergen county in New Jersey as a schoolmaster. During the War he was appointed cashier, storekeeper and deputy purveyor to the General Hospital in New York and acted as such until the end. At the evacuation of New York he sought a new home at Shelburne in Nova Scotia, where he received a grant of 600 acres and acted as deputy surveyor of lands; but he was unsuccessful both as a farmer and surveyor. He was granted the half-pay of Ensign, having been commissioned in the 2nd New Jersey Volunteers in 1783.

In 1788 Morris and his wife were in England, appealing to the Government for an allowance of money, an appeal which was refused, despite the handsome certificates to his loyalty. His wife was a native of Newport, Rhode Island, where she inherited property from her Loyalist father, James Sheffield, a representative of that town in the Assembly and a firm advocate for maintaining the connection of the Colonies with the mother country. (A. O. 13:110; A. O. 12:102, f. 128; Ind.: 5605-6; "Am. MSS. in Roy. Inst.," IV:466).

THOMAS MORRISON (Quartermaster)

An Englishman by birth, born about 1744, he was Ensign, Quartermaster and Lieutenant in the New Jersey Volunteers. He was on the Seconded list of officers. (Ind.: 5605; "Am. MSS. in Roy. Inst.," IV:541; Stryker).

ANTHONY LEBERECHT MOSENGEIL (Captain)

He was a German, who emigrated to New Jersey in 1770 to improve certain copper mines, the property of some people in London, of which he became part owner, and which yielded no return on the expenditure of £3,000, in currency, until 1775. His two partners were "Rebels" and lived at Middlebrook, in Somerset county, New Jersey. He joined a party of Loyalists in September, 1776, and recruited men for the New Jersey Volunteers, entitling him to a Captaincy. On January 1, 1779, he was given a commission as Captain in Brigadier-General Cortlandt Skinner's Queen's American Volunteers (which is a title not previously seen for the New Jersey Volunteers). His original commission, signed by General Sir Henry Clinton, is in W. O. 42:M45.

Captain Mosengeil acted as Major and interpreter to two Battalions of Anspach (Hessian) troops and was taken prisoner at Yorktown on October 27, 1781. He remained on the list of active officers until 1789, when he was pensioned. His compensation was £500 from his claim of £1,258. (A. O. 12:109).

He was married, on July 23, 1795, to Dorothea Caroline, daughter of the Rev. ――― Gros, deceased, of Raustadt in the principality of Hollberg Gedern, the ceremony having been performed in the house of his brother, M. Mosengeil, counsellor at the exchequer of the Landgrave of Homburg, Germany. He died on February 18, 1821, aged 76, at Petterweil, near Homburg, where his widow and daughter were living in 1835 in great distress, on a pension of 86 florins from the Landgravine of Hesse-Homburg. (F. O. 4:1; T. 1:339; A. O. 13:110; A. O. 12:14, ff. 345-9; A. O. 12:100, f. 307; "Am. MSS. in Roy. Inst.," III:84).

GEORGE MOUNT

He was a farmer within three miles from Middletown, New Jersey, near the Shrewsbury river. He was born February 8, 1757, and served for a time with his father, master of a schooner in the British service during the War. His father, who had been attainted as a Loyalist, he states, "was murdered by the Rebels" (he died September 27, 1779), and left several children, of whom George was one. His next brother, John (q. v.), born August 22, 1764, was called up by the Americans at the age of sixteen to bear arms, but escaped and joined the British in New York, where he was apprenticed and where he remained until the evacuation. His mother was in New Jersey with a daughter, Oria, in 1786; another brother, Matthias (born 1766), was in New York in that year; his elder sister, Chloe, who in 1781 married James Thearn, was at St. John, New Brunswick; and his second sister, Sarah Pintar (Pintard), was living in the United States in 1786. George Mount and his brother, John, were in New Brunswick, Canada, in 1789. (A. O. 13:19; A. O. 12:16, ff. 128-134, 388-390). He was awarded £241 from his claim of £393. 15s. (A. O. 12:109).

JOHN MOUNT

A brother of George Mount (supra), and is described as a husbandman and a refugee from New Jersey, who had been driven from his home in consequence of his loyalty. His estate at Middletown, New Jersey, was confiscated May 17, 1779. He was unable in 1784 to carry on the business of a farm "in the rough country of Nova Scotia with any success," and appealed to the British Government for relief. (A. O. 13:107).

JONATHAN MUNDAY

He was a native of Woodbridge, New Jersey, and the son of Nicholas Munday, and a brother of Nicholas and Reuben Munday. Early in the insurrection he served in the American militia, "not from choice but from fear." The two brothers named served on the American side. In 1787 he was living in King's county, Province of New Brunswick. His claim of £66 was met by a grant of £60. (A. O. 12:109; A. O. 13:19; A. O. 12:16, ff. 367-370; A. O. 12:63, f. 108).

Rev. HARRY MUNRO

He was a Scotsman and "by birth and education a gentleman," as he proudly describes himself. He went to America in 1757, "not as an adventurer, nor as a missionary of any Society, but as a gentleman and clergyman," already provided for by his purchase of a chaplaincy in a Regiment, commanded by Colonel (the Hon. Archibald) Montgomerie, afterwards Earl of Eglinton. With this Regiment (known as the 77th Foot, or 1st Highland Battalion) he served for six years on active service and had the honor of singing a "Te Deum" after many signal victories by the British troops at the taking of Ticonderoga and Crown Point, at the reduction of Montreal and at the capture of Martinique and Dominica. His Regiment was disbanded in 1764.

From 1765 to 1767 the Rev. Harry Munro was at Philipsburg, New York, a missionary of the Society for the Propagation of the Gospel, and in 1768 he succeeded Dr. Ogilvie as Rector of St. Peter's, Albany, New York, and as a missionary to the Indians. He was also Chaplain to the garrison there.

When many prominent Loyalists were prisoners in the Fort at Albany in 1776 he read prayers and preached to them, "despite continuous threats of violence to him personally," until he himself was taken prisoner and detained for more than fifteen months. On his release he fled for protection to the British army in Canada and was there appointed deputy chaplain to the 53rd and 31st Regiments.

This Scottish divine was the owner of considerable property in New Jersey as well as in New York, but his papers do not indicate whether or where he resided in New Jersey.

On September 1, 1788, he was in ill-health at his then permanent address, Heriot's Entry, Edinburgh, Scotland. One of his letters, dated May 13, 1788, is sealed with arms (defaced), with a bird crest and the motto, "Dread God." (A. O. 13/115). He was granted a Loyalist pension until 1801, when he probably died.

His son, Peter Jay Munro, was at Bedford, New York, in 1785, studying law with John Strang. (A. O. 13:56; A. O. 13:85; A. O. 12:24, ff. 36-46; A. O. 12:103, f. 57; T. 50:6; A. O. 459-7—461-17).

NATHANIEL MUNRO

He was born in Rhode Island, but was settled in the town of New Brunswick, New Jersey, as a carpenter. He was one of the great number of Loyalist exiles who settled at Shelburne in Nova Scotia. (A. O. 13:19; A. O. 12:15, ff. 255-8; A. O. 12:63, f. 31). He was compensated £120 from his claim of £236. 9s. (A. O. 12:109).

JAMES MURPHY

He emigrated from Newry, in Ireland, in 1771, and was employed to instruct lads in weaving somewhere in New Jersey until the end of 1773, when he moved to South Carolina. Here he kept a school for two years, moving at the end of 1775, or early in 1776, to another settlement. Afterwards he kept a store for Dr. Benjamin Durbarow, at

"Ninety-Six," remembered in Loyalist history for the gallant defense of that Fort by the English against Greene's army. Murphy served in other engagements in the War. A witness in his favor stated that he remembered his departure from Ireland with a young woman servant, and was worth £300, being a weaver for himself. (A. O. 12:46, ff. 233-8). He was allowed £75 from his claim of £346. (A. O. 12:109).

JOHN NACTIER

A shopkeeper in Woodbridge and in Elizabethtown, New Jersey, and owner and master of a sloop, which was captured by the Americans and taken to New Haven, Connecticut, where he was detained a prisoner. On his release he joined Captain Robert Chillas's Company in the Loyal Volunteers of New York, on August 2, 1781. On October 8, following, he was enrolled in Captain Vincent Pearse Ashfield's Company of Marine Artillery. At the end of the War he sailed with his wife and five children for Shelburne, Nova Scotia, where he left them in the "most melancholy and pungent distress," and he embarked for England in 1791, to seek relief. (F. O. 4:1). In 1793 he was granted £35 to enable him to go to Cape Breton. (A. O. 461:15).

Two Loyalists are mentioned in his papers, John MacReady and John Willis, who had permits to pass from New Jersey to New York City on November 10, 1776.

JAMES NEALSON (Captain)

He was commissioned Lieutenant and Quartermaster in the 1st New Jersey Volunteers in 1778, and as Captain in the same in September, 1780. His widow, Margaret, and her two children were at Newtown, Long Island, in January, 1783, in great distress. She was granted a pension as an officer's widow. (Ind.: 8229; "Am. MSS. in Roy. Inst.," III:333, 337; Stryker).

ARTHUR SCOTT NEILSON

He lived with and transacted the business of his aged uncle, James Neilson, Esq. (born in 1698), one of the first inhabitants of, and "the most wealthy merchant" in, New Brunswick, New Jersey, a leading man and of high standing in public office. This uncle had sent for him as a boy of eleven from his home in Ireland, with the intention of making him his heir, having no children of his own. His uncle took an active part on the American side in the Rebellion, while he himself was a Loyalist and joined the Royal Navy in 1775, a step which excluded him from the favor of his uncle. His elder brother, Rowley, was also in his uncle's employ and took part with the Americans.

Arthur Scott Neilson served as a midshipman until September, 1781, when he was discharged from the "Heart of Oak." He had previously married in England, in 1777. Several of his letters in 1782 and 1783 disclose his distressed condition in London, fearing arrest for debt. An uncle in Ireland refused to give him a farthing to relieve him of his distress, on account of the part he had taken in America. His father, a Lieutenant in the Royal Navy, was lost at sea in 1758. (A. O. 13:110).

ISAAC NOBLE

He possessed a farm of 170 acres (70 of which were cultivated) with a good house at Ramapo in Bergen county, New Jersey, bought with his savings from his employment in some ironworks. He joined the British early in the revolt and served first in an irregular force of Light Dragoons; afterwards he was a guide to a detachment to ford a river at Aquackanonck, the bridge having been destroyed by the Americans, and in the course of this duty he was wounded and lost an eye, either by accident or by enemy action. He was under care for many months in the New York Hospital, apparently suffering from periodical attacks of insanity, which debarred him from receiving a promised commission as Major in the New Jersey Volunteers. Upon his recovery he was appointed deputy Commissary of Prisoners and met his death at the hands of the Americans, "who had been offered a reward of 500 dollars." His estate in Bergen county was sequestered January 26, 1779.

His knowledge of the German language was exercised in influencing the Germans in New Jersey to remain loyal. His wife, Rachel, suffered much from the hostility of neighbors and was warned that she would be taken prisoner, whereupon she fled on foot one dark night, with an infant of nine months at her breast, leaving three other children behind, who followed her later to New York. She sailed to England in February, 1780, and was supported by her brother-in-law until his death in April, 1781. She was granted a pension of £80 from 1782 to 1804, and £400 from her claim of £973. (T. 50:6; A. O. 461:19; A. O. 12:109; A. O. 13:110; A. O. 12:14, ff. 321-6; A. O. 12:104, f. 21).

Dr. HENRY NORRIS (Captain)

He was born in New Jersey, the son of Henry Norris, of Elizabethtown, and practised medicine in Pennsylvania before the Revolution. Here he was foremost in joining Colonel William Rankin's Corps of Associated Loyalists, formed early in the War in York county, and raised recruits, with the help of the eminent Loyalist, Joseph Galloway, and Colonel Rankin. Norris suffered capture three times. On the last occasion he was tried by court martial and sentenced to pay a fine of £50, and to receive 100 lashes, a punishment which was substituted, by order of General Washington, for a month's hard labor.

He was later employed on important services at great personal risk for the British Commander-in-Chief, Sir Henry Clinton. In July, 1781, having released thirty British prisoners and secreted them, Dr. Norris (or Captain Norris, to give him his military title) proceeded to New York, and there proposed to the Commander-in-Chief that a much larger body of men should be released by force and marched to Lancaster in Pennsylvania, seize the guard, release all the Loyalist and British prisoners and set fire to the magazine and public buildings in that town. But all such tentative arrangements were rendered abortive by the unfortunate military position of Lord Cornwallis, who was to have supplied the necessary force for carrying out Norris's scheme.

At the end of the War Capt. Norris went to London, where he was living in great distress on a military allowance of £90 a year. (Ind.: 5606; A. O. 13:83; A. O. 13:102; A. O. 12:38, ff. 418-429; A. O. 12:100, f. 123).

Rev. JONATHAN ODELL

He was born at Newark, New Jersey, September 25, 1737; was graduated from Princeton College in 1754, and was missionary of the Society for the Propagation of the Gospel for seventeen years from 1767, first at Burlington, in succession to the Rev. Colin Campbell, father of Colin Campbell (q. v.) and at Mount Holly. His church (St. Mary's) at Burlington was closed about the time of, or in consequence of, the Declaration of Independence, but he was allowed to remain in New Jersey until December, 1776, when he was driven away because of his loyalty to the Crown. Early in his life he had practised medicine and was admitted a member of the New Jersey Medical Society in 1774.

According to his account, for his open and decided character as a Loyalist in promoting an abhorrence of such measures as tended to throw the country into confusion and draw the people into rebellion, a "series of persecutions" was commenced against him. The capture of a letter written by him to a friend in October, 1777, caused his arrest by order of the Provincial Congress, before whom he was ordered to appear, and it was endeavored, "by treating him as an enemy of his country, to make him the victim of popular resentment." This proceeding, however, had but little of the intended effect in Burlington, "where the people in general were peaceably disposed." His parole, in which he promised to remain within eight miles of Burlington, New Jersey, was recently found and presented to Princeton University.

This divine, who had been screened by faithful parishioners, fled from his parole and went first to New York and afterwards to Philadelphia, where, during the occupation of that city by the British, he acted as press censor. On January 25, 1778, he accepted the chaplaincy of the Pennsylvania Loyalists, and from this Regiment he was transferred, on May 25, 1782, to the King's American Dragoons. At New York he wrote and published in the newspapers sundry essays and political verses with a view "to secure the interest of truth and loyalty." Here also he was translator of French and Spanish papers, and Assistant Secretary to the Board of Directors of Associated Loyalists, from April, 1781, to November, 1782, and from July 1, 1783, was Assistant Secretary to Sir Guy Carleton, Commander-in-Chief.

At the end of the War he accompanied the great throng of Loyalist refugees to New Brunswick, in Canada, where his personal merits were recognized by other prominent Loyalists, and he was chosen for the important appointment of first Secretary of that new Province, an office in which he was succeeded in 1812 by his only son, William Franklin Odell, godson and namesake of Governor Franklin.

The Rev. Jonathan Odell married, May 2, 1772, Anne, daughter and joint heiress of Isaac de Cou, at St. Mary's Church, Burlington, New Jersey, who, with her sister, Mrs. McKenzie, was possessed of the half share of Rehoboth farm in Burlington county, Isaac de Cou owning the other half. He died on November 25, 1818, at Fredericton, Province of New Brunswick, where his widow died in 1825.

"His principle as a loyalist had in it an invincible honesty, a deathless love, a deathless hate. . . He would not make terms with the Rebels: he still denounced and defied them . . . a proud, guilty member of a political party that had been defeated, but never conquered or convinced." (Tyler, "Hist. of American Literature," II:129). Mr. Tyler in the same work says that as a satirist no one on the Loyalist side approached the Rev. Jonathan Odell either in passionate energy of thought or in pungency and polish of style.

The book plate of the eminent divine consists of his arms: Or, three crescent gules. Crest—A cock. Motto—"Ne quid nimis."

It may be of interest to recall that, still preserved in St. Mary's Church, Burlington, are some old silver vessels of historic interest in which the Rev. Jonathan Odell administered the Sacrament. They are a French chalice of the seventeenth century and an English paten, presented by that remarkable and talented woman, Catherine Boevey, of Flaxley Abbey, Gloucestershire, and a chalice with a patencover, the gift of Queen Anne. (Jones's "The Old Silver of the American Churches;" A. O. 12:16, ff. 296-304; A. O. 12:63, f. 137; A. O. 12:100, f. 290; W. O. 42:02; "Acadiensis," III:239; "Judges of New Brunswick;" Sabine; G. M. Hills, "Hist. of St. Mary's, Burlington," pp. 291-323; Winthrop Sargent, "Loyal Verses of Joseph Stansbury and Jonathan Odell;" "New England Hist. & Gen. Reg.," January, 1892; "Ontario Archives," pp. 298-9).

DAVID OGDEN (Judge)

He was of New England ancestry. His father was Josiah Ogden, a member of the New Jersey Assembly, 1716-25 and 1738-'39. David was born in Newark, New Jersey, in 1707, graduated from Yale in 1728 and became a distinguished lawyer, leader in his profession. He read law in New York and began practice in Newark. He was made sergeant-at-law in 1764 and became an Associate Justice of the New Jersey Colonial Supreme Court May 18, 1772. According to his original memorials he had been Judge of the Supreme Court of New Jersey "for many years until deprived of that office and its salary" on January 5, 1777, and was a member of His Majesty's Council for about 25 years.

On January 6, 1777, the day after his escape with two sons to New York, a regiment of Continental troops went to his house in Newark, New Jersey, and, finding him absent, plundered and destroyed a great part of his most valuable effects. Sometime afterwards the remainder of his personal property and most of his real estate were seized, confiscated and sold. Three of his sons were ordered to be imprisoned if caught.

With these memorials are many papers concerning the distinguished jurist's property; correspondence regarding debts due to him in New Jersey; a brief state of the controversy of the general Proprietors of the Eastern Division of New Jersey against the claim of the first settlers of Elizabeth Town; and a long appraisement of his property. He himself was one of the Proprietors of East New Jersey.

His arms, sealed on some of these papers, are those of John Ogden, granted for faithful services to Charles II, namely, Gyronny of eight or and gules, in the dexter chief an oak branch fructed. Crest—An oak tree, with a lion rampant against it. Motto—"Et si ostendo non jacto." (A. O. 13:110; A. O. 13:111).

John Anstey, on his investigations in New Jersey, confirmed the confiscation of part of the estates of David Ogden in Essex county, the inquisition being dated June 12, 1778. The residue had, however, been conveyed to his son, Abraham Ogden, an active partisan of the American cause in the Rebellion, by an Act of the Assembly. (A. O. 12:85).

In appreciation of his distinguished position in New Jersey before the Revolution he was granted a pension of £200 and was awarded compensation of £9,415 from his claim of £18,414. 11s. for the loss of his property, as well as compensation for the loss of his official income. (A. O. 12:100, f. 100; A. O. 12:109).

Additional information on his support of the Crown may be obtained from another official source. Early in 1776 "he used his utmost efforts to oppose the then measures adopted by the Provincial Congress and, in consequence thereof, became obnoxious to the Americans and, fearful of being apprehended, he abandoned his property in New Jersey and went to New York." There he remained until November, 1783, when he sailed for England.

David Ogden adds that, when General Grant took up his quarters at his house, he (Ogden) used his utmost endeavors to persuade the people to come in and take the oaths to the King, and with so much success that "only 26 people in Newark did not take the oaths." ("Loyalists' Claims," pp. 166-7).

This eminent lawyer and Judge was one of the three Loyalists from New Jersey in these pages who were educated at Yale College, where he preceded by a year his son, Isaac's, father-in-law, the Rev. Isaac Browne (q. v.). The Judge lived in exile in London with his son Peter until 1790, when he returned to America and died on Long Island, New York, in 1802, aged 92.

Judge Ogden was the author of a plan for the government of the Colonies after their expected submission to Great Britain, by which he provided that the American Parliament should "have the superintendence and government of the several colleges in North America, most of which have been the grand nurseries of the late Rebellion, instilling into the tender minds of youth principles favorable to republican, and against a monarchial government, and other doctrines incompatible to the British Constitution." (Dexter, "Biogs. of Graduates of Yale College").

His three sons, Isaac, who became a lawyer in Canada, Nicholas and Peter, were Loyalists, while two other sons, Abraham and Samuel, were active supporters of the American cause and became also distinguished lawyers. He had also one daughter. A brother, Aaron, who fought on the American side, became a United States Senator. (See W. O. Wheeler, "Ogden Family;" Shaw's "Hist. of Essex and Hudson Cos.;" Sabine). Another brother, Jacob, became a physician of eminence. Isaac Longworth (q. v.) was his brother-in-law.

As the agent of the New Jersey Loyalists, Judge Ogden was a signatory to an undated petition for compensation for them. This petition concludes by saying that a great number of those Loyalists remaining in Great Britain were wasting the prime of their lives and dragging out a miserable existence, without being enabled to settle any kind of business whatsoever. A number, through despondency, had died with broken hearts. Others had been arrested, imprisoned and had perished in jail, while others had been driven into insanity and from insanity to suicide, leaving their helpless widows and orphans to subsist on the cold charity of strangers. This petition to the Treasury is signed also by Sir William Pepperell for Massachusetts; John Wentworth, Jr., for New Hampshire; George Roome for Rhode Island; James de Lancey for New York; Joseph Galloway for Pennsylvania; Robert Alexander for Maryland; John R. Grymes for Virginia; Henry Eustace McCulloh for North Carolina; James Simpson for South Carolina, and John Graham for Georgia, most of whom were lawyers. (T. 1:518, f. 51). The Loyalist documents abound in references to arrests and imprisonment for debts contracted by the unhappy exiles in England.

DAVID OGDEN, Jr.

He was not the son of Judge David Ogden, supra. He was a merchant and partner in ironworks and a resident in Newark, New Jersey. In 1775 he was forced to sign "an Association" and, as Captain of an Independent Company, was obliged to call out his Company in the winter of 1775, but, his principles having been doubted by the Americans upon the Declaration of Independence (which he opposed), he was deprived of his command. He was imprisoned for nearly a year and eventually escaped to New York. Here, from 1779 to 1783, he acted as assistant secretary to His Majesty's Post Office, under John Foxcroft, Postmaster-General in America. After the War he continued as secretary to Foxcroft, then director of the packets sailing between New York and England.

The Commissioners reported that David Ogden having resided in New York from the evacuation of the city by the British until 1786, they had reason to think that he intended to become a "subject of the United States." However, his property in Essex county, New Jersey, was forfeited; inquisition was dated June 12, 1778; and he was allowed £257 from his claim of £915. 1s. (A. O. 12:109). With his memorial is a copy of the inquisition into his estate. (A. O. 13:19; A. O. 12:15, ff. 55-61; A. O. 12:63, f. 4; Sabine).

ISAAC OGDEN

A "barrister-at-law, attorney and solicitor," from 1763, as he describes himself, who was the son of Judge David Ogden (q. v.), of Newark, New Jersey. He went into the Provincial Congress from May to August, 1775, and persuaded many of his loyal friends to do the same, with, he said, the privity and approbation of Governor Franklin and Cortlandt Skinner (q. v.). Having found that violent measures could not be stopped by his presence, he resigned from that body in August, 1775. Other members at the same time were Major Robert Drummond (q. v.), William Smith (q. v.), Abraham Van Buskirk (q. v.), and still others who became Loyalists. He was "threatened with death by hanging by General Lee."

In evidence in London, on March 27, 1786, Isaac Ogden said that in November, 1782, he received a message from General George Washington, brought by Ogden's brother, that if the Loyalists would join the American cause their properties should be restored to them. To this message he replied that he had taken the part of an adherent of the Crown from principle and could not, therefore, accede to the proposal.

John Wetherhead, a New York merchant, giving evidence a day later, declared that Isaac Ogden was extremely violent against the British Government early in the Rebellion and harangued the mob in public places to keep up their spirits. To give his conduct "the softest name" he was desirous of popularity. This witness had always understood, not from personal knowledge but from report, that Ogden's conduct in Congress was "violent." In New York he had frequent occasion to rebuke Ogden for his imprudence there, in talking of the King's cause as desperate, long before it was. Wetherhead had never heard of any service rendered by Ogden to the Loyalists. The Loyalists in New York always regarded him as a "Rebel" and were very cautious in discussing affairs before him.

Cornelius Hatfield, Jr., (q. v.), in evidence on the same day, denounced the alleged loyalty of Isaac Ogden, whom he had seen in Newark in 1775 raised on a cask or stage haranguing the populace and encouraging them to persevere in their opposition to Great Britain. He was one of those Loyalists who wished to see the British beaten. Ogden's conduct did not change until the invasion of New Jersey by British troops. Even his own brother, Nicholas Ogden (q. v.), a noted Loyalist, warned Hatfield against him, and he was shunned at British Headquarters in New York. He like him very well personally; he only disliked his political conduct. In cross-examination Cornelius Hatfield admitted that he had had a difference with Ogden, whose explanation of Hatfield's hostility to him arose from his acting as attorney for one Zophir Lyon, who had been plundered of goods by Hatfield.

Cavalier Jouet (q. v.) was also sceptical of the loyalty of Isaac Ogden, said to have been his old schoolmate, and added that Nicholas Ogden, an inflexible Loyalist, had cautioned him against trusting him. Cornelius Hatfield had informed him (Jouet) that if Ogden provoked him he had still powder in store and might blow up a mine, which would clip the wings of Ogden's claim for compensation. Jouet, in answer to questions by the Commissioners, stated that Hatfield was a very zealous Loyalist, much employed at Headquarters, but a loose, drinking sort of man and not of the coolest sense.

Governor Franklin, who was cautious in his answers to questions by the Commissioners, stated that he had regarded Ogden as a Loyalist, but that he went into the Provincial Congress, as many lawyers had done, with a view to promoting his popularity and preventing others from running away with his business. It was against the Governor's opinion that men went into Congress with the object of serving the interests of Great Britain. No admission was made by the Governor that Ogden had gone into Congress with his "privity and approbation," as alleged by Ogden. William Newton's evidence in support of Isaac Ogden was to the effect that it was by the interposition of Ogden that he was liberated from a dungeon in Newark jail.

Daniel Coxe (q. v.), upon expressing surprise to Ogden for going into Congress, received a reply that his motives in doing so were to stop violent measures. His conduct had prevented him (Coxe) from putting any political confidence in Ogden, despite the fact that there were Loyalists in Congress, particularly one Pierson, who enjoyed his confidence, though he could not reconcile his motives in going into that body. He admitted that he approved of Ogden wearing the American uniform. It was only fair to add, said Coxe, that Ogden's conduct in Congress was in consonance with his professions. Moreover, he appeared to be exceedingly zealous in support of Great Britain after he came to New York.

The Rev. John Patterson claimed Ogden as a Loyalist from the beginning. If he had a fault it was that "he was rather too warm." The other witnesses in his favor included the Rev. Charles Inglis (q. v.), the Rev. George Panton (q. v.), and Major Philip Van Cortlandt (q. v.). The last witness was his own father, Judge David Ogden, who stated that Isaac was a member of the "Committee" before and after the Declaration of Independence. Isaac had violently attacked the Whig principles of his own brother, Abraham, and it took him, their father, three days to reconcile the brothers. (A. O. 12:14, ff. 147-178).

Isaac Ogden was Sergeant of the Supreme Court of New Jersey and, during his exile in New York, practised in the Admiralty Court. The Commissioners expressed dissatisfaction with his submission to be a member of that "unlawful assembly," the Congress, which, "in the end overturned the authority of Great Britain." (A. O. 12:101, f. 32). Criticism of his early conduct in the Revolution, however, did not debar him from the important appointment by the British Government of Judge of the Admiralty Court in Quebec. He died in Montreal.

He was allowed £660 from his claim of £2,927, and at the rate of £240 a year during the War for the loss of his professional income of £280 in New Jersey (A. O. 12:109), where inquisition was entered against his estate June 12, 1728.

His first wife, Mary, was a daughter of the Rev. Isaac Browne (q. v.). (A. O. 13:111; Sabine). He had three sons, two of whom were living in Canada and one in the Isle of Man in 1855. (Sabine).

NICHOLAS OGDEN

He was another son of Judge David Ogden (q. v.), of Newark, New Jersey, and in 1775 was a resident of the city of New York. He had been active in opposing the activities of the "Rebels," so much so that he was obliged to seek refuge from their rage in New Jersey. In May of that year, at the risk of his own life, he rescued the Rev. Myles Cooper, President of King's College (now Columbia University) at midnight from a mob and conveyed him to a place of safety.

In 1776 he was apprehended and tried before a Committee of Congress for conspiring against the life of General George Washington, and in December of that year he joined the British army in New York. Inquisition in Essex county, New Jersey, where he had an estate, was entered against him on June 12, 1778.

This member of a distinguished New Jersey family purchased in 1778 a quantity of stores in New York and sailed on board a vessel under cover of the "Jason" for the supply of the British garrison and troops in Georgia, but had the misfortune to be captured by the three American frigates, the "Warren," the "Ranger" and the "Queen of France," and taken to Portsmouth, New Hampshire, and thence to Boston. Ogden remained a prisoner for three months, until ordered by General Washington to be sent to New Jersey to be delivered to Governor Livingston as a State prisoner to take his trial for high treason. He escaped, however, and, after hiding for eighteen days and nights, mostly in the woods, reached New York in greatly impaired health.

In that city Nicholas Ogden was First Lieutenant and Adjutant to the New York Militia, and Assistant Brigade Major until the end of the War. His memorial, embodying the above account, is dated from Quebec, March 19, 1788 (he was at Shelburne, Nova Scotia, in the same year), and is accompanied by a computation of the estate of Henry Cuyler, of New York, his father-in-law, who at his death left his estate, in Sussex and Somerset counties, New Jersey, to be divided equally among six children, of whom Mary Cuyler and Barent Cuyler died before the Revolutionary War. Alida Cuyler died unmarried during the War, as did Henry Cuyler, the son, leaving an infant in New Jersey. The only survivors were Hannah, wife of Nicholas Ogden, and Hester, wife of Captain Nathan Frink, a Loyalist officer of whom there is an account in Sabine. (W. O. 42:F19; F. O. 4:1; Ind.: 5605-6). Joseph Barton (q. v.) was the agent for the Cuyler estate in New Jersey. (A. O. 13:115; A. O. 12:63, f. 136; A. O. 13:19). His large claim of £2,072. 5s. was rejected, except for a grant of £50. (A. O. 12:109).

Henry Cuyler, father-in-law of Nicholas Ogden, was a resident at Newark, New Jersey, in July, 1776, when he was ordered by the Provincial Congress to remove from his house, but in consideration of his illness he was directed to give bond with security in £1,000 for the faithful observance of his parole. ("Min. of Prov. Congress of N. J.," p. 508).

PETER OGDEN

Another son of Judge David Ogden (q. v.), of Newark. New Jersey, who was studying law in Newark at the outbreak of the War. He fled to New York in 1777, then aged 19, and in 1778 was appointed Secretary to the Board of Police there, an office which he held until the end of the War. For some time he was a refugee in London with his father, returning with him in 1790 to America, and was granted a Loyalist pension. (T. 50:28; A. O. 13:85; A. O. 13:111; A. O. 12:100, f. 275).

THOMAS OKERSON (Lieutenant)

He was born in America, perhaps in Monmouth county, New Jersey, about 1749 and, on December 15, 1776, was appointed Lieutenant in the 1st New Jersey Volunteers. On January 15, 1781, he was ordered by Brigadier-General Oliver de Lancey to proceed with a party into the Jerseys to execute a certain plan proposed, namely, to obtain information as to a revolt of the Pennsylvania line. His own humanity was to guide him as to the "treatment he is to receive" and he was ordered on no account to "touch his life."

From the New Jersey Volunteers this officer was transferred to Colonel Robert Rogers's Rangers and was put on half-pay of this Corps in 1792. (W. O. 24:751). The lapse of about nine years since the end of the War and this date suggests that he had been on military service elsewhere. (Ind.: 5605; "Am. MSS. in Roy Inst.," II:235; III:328, 338, 343).

Dr. MATTHEW O'KENNEDY (Captain)

In 1775 he was a practising physician at Salem, New Jersey, though described as of Stow Creek, Cumberland county. His wife, Lucy, a considerable heiress; died in 1782. He raised at his own expense in 1777 two Companies for the Loyal American Rangers, commanded by Lieutenant-Colonel William Odell, and was appointed Captain. With this Corps he served in several actions. (A. O. 13:109).

There is an affidavit of Margaret O'Kennedy, spinster, aged 20, of Bally Phillip, county of Limerick, Ireland, dated December 16, 1789, described as the only child of Matthew O'Kennedy, deceased. (A. O. 12:17, ff. 152-160). His name appears also as Kennedy.

ICHABOD OLIVER

He resided at Rahway, New Jersey, and at the age of 15, in 1776, he was "actuated by the same principles of loyalty that had inspired his father," and left his home to join the Loyalist forces, in which he served as private in the 1st New Jersey Volunteers until the peace. On reaching 18, his estate at Spank Town (Rahway), New Jersey, was confiscated (July, 1779).

Mentioned in the copy of the will of David Oliver, yeoman, of Elizabeth, New Jersey, dated February 27, 1766, are his wife, Zerirah, his three sons, David, Samuel and Ichabod, his three daughters, Jemima Ward, Sarah and Zerirah, and his mother-in-law, Elizabeth Oliver.

Ichabod Oliver was at Annapolis in January, 1786, and David Oliver, doubtless his brother, was in the same place in October, 1788. He was compensated to the amount of £250 from his claim of £1,090. (A. O. 12:109; A. O. 13:19; A. O. 12:63, f. 143).

SAMUEL OSBORNE

He was born in New Jersey, but settled for a time in Dutchess county, New York, where he was esteemed as one of the "neatest farmers." In 1774 and 1775 he was Collector of the township of Freehold, in New Jersey, and was a neighbor of Daniel Van Mater (q. v.).

At the peace he returned to his former home in New Jersey (where he had been fined for not doing military duty), in the hope of recovering his property, which had been forfeited in 1779, but on the advice of friends he quitted the place immediately. According to one report he withdrew his claim for his property, which had not yet been sold (A. O. 12:63, f. 73), but, according to another, he was awarded £1,155 from his claim of £1,947. (A. O. 12:109).

In a letter of December 24, 1788, to the Commissioners, he alleges that Daniel Van Mater (q. v.) sold his real estate for £1,750 in New York currency in 1775 and, at the same time, owed £200, and that, in 1783, when Van Mater was about to leave New York, he was arrested for a debt of £300. Osborne is informed that the heirs of Van Mater were to receive £2,500 sterling as compensation for his confiscated property from the British Government. As to the real estate of Henry Van Mater it was "no better than his [Osborne's] and was in debt," yet he was to be compensated over £600 sterling more than himself, though Osborne personally was satisfied with the amount of his compensation. The letter further alleges that one Gozen Riyerson, a claimant for £1,200, or £1,400, far from being a loser by the War was a great gainer, to the amount of thousands of

pounds. (A. O. 13:19; A. O. 13:112; A. O. 12:14, ff. 121-7;
A. O. 12:101, f. 256).

Rev. GEORGE PANTON

He was born in Scotland and went out to America, in 1771, as a tutor to a young gentleman. Two years later he was appointed Rector of St. Michael's Church, Trenton, New Jersey, and also officiated at Allentown and Maidenhead (Lawrenceville). Previous to hostilities in 1775 he went to Maryland to take charge of Eden School (doubtless so named after Governor Eden), which was intended to be erected as a public seminary, with the assurance of an annexed parish, but the scheme was frustrated by the Battle of Lexington.

It was this clergyman who drew up the petition from the freeholders of the township of Nottingham in Burlington county, to the House of Assembly of New Jersey, on May 20, 1775, expressing their loyal sentiments and attachment to the British Government and desiring that the Assembly would endeavor to promote reconciliation with Great Britain. He gave information and did everything in his power to help the British army, by pointing the proper persons to be trusted and employed in any service, and by giving a sketch of the country to the British officers. Dr. Panton left Trenton upon the Declaration of Independence. He had lodged there with Mr. Justice Pearson, who was killed by the Americans in the surprise of that town.

In conjunction with the Rev. Charles Inglis (q. v.) the Rev. Myles Cooper, President of King's College, New York (now Columbia University), and the Rev. Thomas Bradbury Chandler (q. v.), this Loyalist divine published several essays in support of the British Government. He attended Sir Henry Clinton as a volunteer at the capture of Fort Montgomery and was appointed Chaplain of the Prince of Wales's American Volunteers. From April to November, 1783, he had 23 pupils in his "military and private academy" at Shelburne, Nova Scotia, whither he had sought refuge with a number of exiles and acted as their minister. His memorials and recommendations from several distinguished officers in A. O. 13:62 are printed. His losses by the Revolution included a library of more than 200 books, taken or destroyed by the Americans, exclusive of 40 manuscripts of his own compilation, of essays, sermons, belles lettres, etc.

From 1785 to 1786 he was a missionary of the Society for the Propagation of the Gospel at Yarmouth, Nova Scotia; but in 1786 he was in England soliciting subscriptions for new churches in the new settlement in Nova Scotia. In September, 1788, he was at Kelso, or Roxburgh, in Scotland.

His pension and his half-pay of £57. 10s. as Chaplain was continued until about 1811. (T. 50:11; T. 50:22). His claim of £415. 16s. was rejected. (A. O. 12:109; A. O. 13:19; A. O. 13:83; A. O. 13:85; A. O. 13:93; A. O. 13:111; A. O. 12:15, ff. 8-15; A. O. 12:63, f. 2; Ind.: 5605-6; "Am. MSS. in Roy. Inst.," III:359, 403, 419; Sabine; "Ontario Archives," pp. 53-4).

THOMAS PARK

An Englishman, who emigrated in 1765 and entered the service of Governor Franklin as a very confidential servant Such was his attachment to the Governor that he not only followed his political principles but also attended him through the whole of his confinement in prison. Park took private dispatches from Governor Franklin to Mrs. Franklin at Perth Amboy in August, 1776, and for the British Commander-in-Chief. Again, in December, 1776, he conveyed dispatches to Cortlandt Skinner (q. v.) from his imprisoned master. (A. O. 13:111; A. O. 12:17, ff. 99-103). He was awarded his full claim of £20. (A. O. 12:109).

JOSIAH PARKER (Lieutenant)

He was born in America about 1756 and served throughout the War in the Loyalist forces, part or whole of his service having been as Lieutenant in the 2nd, and later the 3rd New Jersey Volunteers. He was on half-pay until 1801, the probable date of his death. (Ind.: 5605-6).

According to his affidavit, sworn at New York on April 23, 1782, in 1780 he took Joshua Huddy prisoner in Monmouth county, New Jersey, and then Huddy confessed that he had been concerned in hanging Stephen Edwards, around whose neck he had fixed the rope. (C. O. 5:105, f. 323).

WILLIAM PEARCE

He was of Salem county, New Jersey, but lived in Pennsylvania. He was taken prisoner for drinking the King's health, but escaped before a threat of tarring and feathering him could be carried out. He suffered from a wound inflicted in the war. After the Peace he acted as a servant to Colonel Gunning, of the Guards. (A. O. 13:93).

"JUSTICE" PEARSON

Of Trenton, perhaps a Justice of the Peace, who was killed in the surprise attack on that town. It was in his house that the Rev. George Panton (q. v.) lodged. (A. O. 13:93).

WILLIAM PEARSON

Of Westfield, New Jersey, a small farmer, who claimed for a horse, cart and oxen, which were seized by the British in December, 1776, from his son, William, to carry wounded and baggage from Essex county to Springfield. (A. O. 13:92).

JOSEPH PEDDLE

A Quaker and farmer, of Burlington county, New Jersey, who remained in New Jersey during the War. He claimed to have been a Loyalist. The unsettled condition of affairs and his own "bad condition" obliged him, in 1786, to return to his native county of Somerset, in England, leaving behind in America three sons (one married) and four daughters (three married). His religious tenets prevented him from taking up arms on either side; nevertheless his property was seized by the Americans to pay taxes. (A. O. 12:71, ff. 348-356).

JOHN PERINE

A planter of Perth Amboy, New Jersey. He helped James Moody (q. v.) when he went to Philadelphia and brought him safely to the British lines. He was in Canada in 1788. An affidavit of David Stout (q. v.) and John Barclay, then late of Middlesex county, was produced as proof of his ownership of real estate, which was forfeited May 28, 1778. (A. O. 12:19; A. O. 12:16, ff. 67-73; A. O. 12:63, f. 69). His claim of £590 was allowed in full. (A. O. 12:109).

ISAAC PERKINS

He was born at Northcastle, New York, but settled at Hackensack in New Jersey. He served as a guide to Lord Cornwallis at Fort Lee and afterwards joined Colonel James de Lancey's Westchester Refugees. He was at Burton, Province of New Brunswick, in 1787. (A. O. 13:19; A. O. 12:16, ff. 265-8; A. O. 12:63, f. 90). The compensation granted to him was £22 from his claim of £62. 8s. (A. O. 12:109).

WILLIAM PERRINE

He was of Upper Freehold township, New Jersey, but lived on Staten Island, where he was master of a vessel trading between New York and New Brunswick, New Jersey. In 1787 he was at St. John, Province of New Brunswick, commander of the sloop "Return," trading between that port and New York, while his family were in New Jersey. His estate in Monmouth county, New Jersey, was forfeited May 22, 1779. He was awarded £311 from his claim of £1,772. 10s. (A. O. 12:109; A. O. 13:19; A. O. 13:111; A. O. 12:16, ff. 383-7; A. O. 12:63, f. 122; A. O. 12:102, f. 142).

JOHN PERSALL, or PARSELS

He was a small farmer in Bergen county, New Jersey, and bore arms in the War. Inquisition against him was in 1779 (under name of Pearsal). He was at Adolphus-town, in the district of Montreal, Canada, in 1788. (A. O. 13:19; A. O. 12:63, f. 141).

ABRAHAM PETERSON

He was born in Bergen county, New Jersey, and in 1788 was a refugee at Cataraqui in Canada. (A. O. 12:33, ff. 121-2; A. O. 12:63, f. 131). He was awarded £72 from his claim of £122. 12s. (A. O. 12:109).

NICHOLAS PETERSON, Sr.

Of Bergen county, New Jersey, who was a refugee at Cataraqui in Canada in 1787. (A. O. 13:19; A. O. 12:63, f. 128). He was allowed £39 from his claim of £106. (A. O. 12:109).

NICHOLAS PETERSON, Jr.

He was a small farmer in Bergen county, New Jersey, and served in arms under Major Thomas Ward. The witnesses to his claim were Paul and Christian Peterson, of the Bay of Quinty. He was a refugee at Cataraqui, Canada, in 1787. (A. O. 13:19; A. O. 12:63, f. 129). He was granted £18 from his claim of £31. 15s. (A. O. 12:109).

Rev. JOHN LOTT PHILLIPS

He was born in Philadelphia and describes himself as the first graduate of the New Jersey College at Princeton (an error, as the College graduated men in 1748), where he took the degree of B. A. in 1774. He had intended to proceed to England for ordination for the ministry of the Church of England, but, instead, embarked for North Carolina, where he was "entitled to a living" at St. Margaret's Parish in Wake county, the gift of his relative, Mrs. Phebe Warner, of Princeton. His property there also included 573 acres of land, which he had hoped to settle, but the detection of his political principles caused him to escape with difficulty to the coast, leaving this property unsold. At length he obtained permission to sail for Charleston, but, finding no ship sailing for England, he was obliged to go to Savannah, where he suffered imprisonment as a Loyalist for three months.

This clergyman arrived in England in May, 1776, without friends or money, and was relieved by the grant of £50 from the fund raised for the distressed American clergy. Later he was appointed to a curacy at East Ham and was married in England. A pension of £60 was granted to him from 1789 to 1801. His claim of £440 was disallowed for want of satisfactory proof of loss. (A. O. 12:109; A. O. 13:111; A. O. 13:124; A. O. 12:34, ff. 345-9; A. O. 12:99, f. 14; T. 50:11; A. O. 461:17).

ANDREW PICKENS

He was of Hunterdon county, New Jersey, and after the War settled on the Kennebecasis river, Province of New Brunswick, where he was alive in 1787. (A. O. 13:19; A. O. 12:16, ff. 252-5; A. O. 12:63, f. 86). He was allowed £110 from his claim of £465. (A. O. 12:109).

GEORGE PLAYTER

He is described as an English cabinet maker, settled at (former) Nottingham township in Burlington county, New Jersey, where his property, valued at £1,000 in currency, was confiscated and sold. He joined the British at Trenton in 1776 and was employed in repairing a bridge, which "proved of great service." Later he was employed in obtaining intelligence for the army and continued on service until the Peace, when he joined his family in Pennsylvania. (A. O. 12:102, f. 211).

His wife, Hannah, inherited property from her grandmother, Hannah Bickerdike, a copy of whose will is in A. O. 13:111. In this will are mentioned her grandson, Watson Playter (son of this Loyalist); her granddaughters, Anne and Hannah Welding (sisters of Hannah Playter), and her grandsons, Nathan Wright and Watson Welding.

BRERETON POYNTON (Major)

He was an Englishman who had served in the War against the French in North America in important engagements from Louisburg to the reduction of Canada, first as a cornet in the 6th, or Inniskilling Dragoons. He continued to command Indian frontier posts from that time until 1772, when he bought for 1,500 guineas a commission as Captain in the 1st Battalion of the 60th Regiment (originally called the Royal American Regiment), then sailing for Jamaica. He had already been Lieutenant for over 16 years.

This officer's wife, Mary, whom he had married in 1772, was the owner of much property in her native place, Trenton, New Jersey, including a house "opposite the church," and a tavern, which he rented to a distressed relative. She appears to have been the daughter of Elisha Beadles (whose will is dated October 22, 1737) and his wife, Mary, who afterwards married Elijah Bond. She also derived property from her stepfather. The first husband of Mary Poynton was Samuel Rutherford, son of James and Mary Rutherford, of Trenton.

Captain Poynton returned to Trenton from the West Indies in 1774 and had embarked for Jamaica and England before the American War. His wife was told at the outbreak of War that if she wrote to her husband and persuaded him to join the American army he would be made a Brigadier-General; but whether she wrote or not he did not participate in the War on either side. In consequence of ill-health contracted in the West Indies he was obliged to exchange his Company in the 60th (in which he was senior Captain) for a Second Captaincy in the 21st Foot, with which he was serving at Edinburgh in 1783.

Mary Poynton, according to Daniel Coxe (q. v.), was a resolute Loyalist and "rather spoke her mind too plain." She describes her father [stepfather] who was alive in the Rebellion, as "a great Rebel and a great enemy to her." Her younger sister was the wife of Captain Samuel Rutherford of the 60th Regiment in 1784. (See later for an officer of this name). In her memorial of April 8, 1789, she states that a separation was about to take place between her husband and herself. (A. O. 13:111).

The commissions of Brereton Poynton are as follows: Ensign in the 62nd Foot, in America, on December 25, 1755; Lieutenant in the 60th Regiment, also in America, on November 30, 1756; and Captain in the same Regiment on April 13, 1771. The latter commission ante-dates his own statement. His commission of Major does not appear in the army lists.

He was allowed £775 from his claim of £1,764. 6s. (A. O. 12:109; A. O. 12:13, ff. 302-314; "Loyalists' Claims," p. 286).

GEORGE PRICE

His name is recorded in A. O. 12:110, ff. 23-4. Nothing further known, though he is classed as of New Jersey.

MARY PRICE

The widow of Richard Evans, of New Brunswick, New Jersey, who married, in 1772, Dr. Joseph Price, surgeon to the 60th Regiment (2nd Royal Americans). Dr. Price died at St. Vincent on January 14, 1775, on duty with his Regiment. She inherited property from her father at New Brunswick and a house in New York, which was said to be set on fire by the Americans in 1778. A pension of £30 was granted to her from 1782 to 1789, when it was reduced to £24. She also received a pension of £16 as a surgeon's widow, and added to her income in England by doing needlework. (T. 50:11; A. O. 462:23; A. O. 13:111; A. O. 13:116; A. O. 12:13, ff. 394-400; A. O. 12:99, f. 50; "Loyalists' Claims," p. 373).

MICHAEL PRICE

He was born in America, the son of Joseph Price, and lived at Shrewsbury, New Jersey. His estate was forfeited May 15, 1779. He was at Shelburne, Nova Scotia, in 1786. His memorial, with a schedule of his property, is in A. O. 13:19. (A. O. 12:15, ff. 292-7; A. O. 12:63, f. 38). From his claim of £378 the sum of £210 was awarded to him. (A. O. 12:109).

THOMAS G. PRICHARD (Lieutenant)

A Lieutenant in the 2nd New Jersey Volunteers from 1777, who was an Englishman, born in 1736. He was on the list of Seconded officers in 1783. (Ind.: 5605). Stryker gives his name as Thomas T. Prichard.

HUGH QUIGG

He was born in Ireland and emigrated in 1762, settling in Pequannock township, Morris county, New Jersey. He bore arms during the Rebellion. One of his debtors, for £127, was Lord Stirling, the well-known figure in the American forces. Two sons were in the British service, one of whom was killed at Danbury. Two witnesses to his loyalty and to his ownership of real property were George Brown, Loyalist, and former neighbor, and William Cain.

Hugh Quigg was settled on the Kennebecasis in the Province of New Brunswick in 1787. He was awarded £149 from his claim of £382. 11s. (A. O. 12:109; A. O. 12:16, ff. 141-6; A. O. 12:63, f. 96).

JAMES RAYMOND (Captain)

He was of the New Jersey Volunteers and on the list of Seconded officers in 1783. (Ind.: 5605). He appears to have had an earlier commission in DeLancey's Brigade.

JOHN REID (Lieutenant)

He was born in America about 1758 and served for six years in the Loyalist forces, first as Ensign in the 5th New Jersey Volunteers and as Lieutenant in the 1st Battalion from April 1, 1777, to 1781, when he was transferred as Ensign in the Provincial Light Infantry.

He was married, on December 11, 1783, to Mary Philips, who boarded at the house of Jonathan Payson at Annapolis, Nova Scotia, the ceremony having been performed in that house by the Rev. Jacob Bailey in the presence of Jonathan Payson's daughters, Sarah Bancroft (wife of Jeremiah Bancroft, yeoman) and Ann Payson (afterwards Ann Tupper), and his son, Nathaniel Payson. John Reid died on September 21, 1823, at Annapolis, and at the time of his death was an officer in the Canadian Fencibles. (Ind.: 5604-5-6; W. O. 42:R4; "N. Bruns. (Can.) Hist. Soc. Coll.," No. 5).

BENJAMIN REYNOLDS

A small farmer in Deerfield township, Cumberland county, New Jersey. In 1786 he was in or near Montreal, Canada. His claim for compensation was endorsed "Rejected," in 1787. (A. O. 13:81).

BROUGHTON REYNOLDS

An Englishman, who emigrated to New Jersey in 1764 and settled as a farmer at Elizabethtown. He accompanied the British army to New York City in 1777, leaving his wife and seven children "to the mercy of the Rebels," by whom they were kept under guard for three weeks until he was able to remove them into the British lines. His property was seized September 15, 1778, and sold for £507 sterling. He left New York at the evacuation, not daring to remain, and in 1784 he was reduced to extreme want in England. (A. O. 13 :92).

JAMES JEREMIAH RICE (Ensign)

A zealous and active Loyalist and an Ensign, from 1778, in the New Jersey Volunteers, who died on February 16, 1788, leaving a widow, Elizabeth, and a son aged five. His wife was born in America and their marriage took place in 1779 in New York City. She supported herself in England to some extent by needlework, but often suffered bitter distress from poverty. Lord Sydney recommended her for an allowance, which was granted at the rate of £20 a year from 1789 until 1800. (Ind.: 5606; A. O. 461 :16).

CHARLES RICHARDS

A farmer at Elizabethtown, New Jersey, and among the refugees settled at Long Reach on the River St. John, Province of New Brunswick, in 1787. (A. O. 12:16, ff. 262-4; A. O. 12:63, f. 85). He was granted £50 from his claim of £484. 14s. (A. O. 12:109).

NATHANIEL RICHARDS

A son of Thomas Richards and brother of a Thomas Richards. He was born at Newark, New Jersey, where his next neighbor was Judge David Ogden (q. v.). He signed an "Association" and did duty with the American Militia for a month early in 1776. With Jonathan Sayre (q. v.) he had an interest in the sloop "Polly." His property, of which there is an account in A. O. 13:19 (forfeited in 1778) was sold. He served as a carpenter in the Quartermaster-

General's department for the remainder of the War. He was awarded £490 from his claim of £790. 6s. (A. O. 12:109). This Loyalist was living in Shelburne county, Nova Scotia, in 1786. (A. O. 12:15, ff. 218-225; A. O. 12:63, f. 27).

JONATHAN RICHARDSON

This English tailor, settled in Sussex county, New Jersey, after 1764, was unsuccessful in his trade and bought a farm of 50 acres for £80 sterling. He refused in 1775 to take up arms for the Americans and fled to the warship "Asia," and from thence joined the British army in Boston. He was allowed £49 from his claim of £130. (A. O. 12:17, ff. 116-7; A. O. 12:101, f. 65; A. O. 12:109).

THOMAS RICKARDS (Sergeant)

He emigrated from England in 1761 and settled as a farmer in Morris county, New Jersey, where he was the owner of 200 acres, valued at £372 sterling. He refused a commission in the American army and served as a Sergeant in the Prince of Wales's American Regiment and was badly wounded. Captain Bowen of that Regiment of Loyalists gave him a certificate as a "brave and spirited soldier." His wife supported herself in London as a mantua maker, while he was granted the pension of a Chelsea out-pensioner of £12 a year, equal nearly to the full pay of a Sergeant. (A. O. 12:101, f. 124; A. O. 13:111).

CHARLES ROBERTS

He was an Irishman who emigrated in 1751 and settled on his own property at Raritan, New Jersey. A witness to his loyalty and ownership of property was a Cornelius Van Horne, doubtless a New Jersey Loyalist, exiled in the Province of New Brunswick. (A. O. 12:16, ff. 92-3).

OWEN ROBERTS (Lieutenant)

A native of New Jersey but settled in Pennsylvania. On January 12, 1778, he was appointed Lieutenant in the Bucks County Volunteers of Pennsylvania and was twice wounded. He was granted 200 acres of land in Shelburne, Nova Scotia, as a Loyalist refugee. In April, 1790, he sailed for England to prosecute his claim for compensation. (A. O. 13:98; A. O. 12:102, f. 199).

NATHANIEL ROBINS (Captain)

He was of the "Armed Boatmen," a Corps of Loyalists, and was married on August 9, 1783, to Mary ———, at Scotch Plains, New Jersey, by the Rev. Moses Ellmore, in the presence of his sister, Ann Fitz Randolph, who was alive in Jersey City in July, 1831, aged 61. Another sister, Nancy FitzRandolph, who was alive at the same place in July, 1838, aged 68, is also mentioned. He died on March 20, 1831, at Northfield, Staten Island, at the age of 77, and was buried in the graveyard of the Baptist Church. Administration on his property was granted to his widow and to his daughter, Susan Robins.

James Bloomfield, of Woodbridge, New Jersey, a pensioner of the United States, in an affidavit of January 1, 1839, states that he fought against Captain Robins in the Revolution, and that he was "an active and brave officer." From 1788 until his death he received a military allowance of £30. (Ind.: 5606; W. O. 42:R7).

RICHARD ROBINS

A most active Loyalist, resident as a farmer in Monmouth county, New Jersey. He died in 1785 in Prince Edward Island, where his eldest son, John (born about 1756), an Ensign in Lieutenant-Colonel Robert Rogers's King's Rangers from July, 1776, was living in 1786. This son was awarded £60 as compensation for the loss of his father's property in New Jersey, from his claim of £610. 13s. (A. O. 12:15, ff. 364-8; A. O. 12:63, f. 53; A. O. 12:109; Ind.: 5605-6; "Ontario Archives," pp. 649-650, 652).

James Robins, Lieutenant in Major Jessup's Rangers, is believed to have been a son. (Ind.: 5606).

WILLIAM ROBINS (Captain)

He was born in 1759 in New Jersey and, at the outbreak of the Revolution, was living at Quibbletown (now New

Market), Somerset county, with his father, with whom he joined the British forces at Fort Lee in 1776. His father's length of service was but brief, for in the same year he died of wounds received in action.

The young Loyalist—he was only 18—served as a guide under Lord Cornwallis and performed a variety of confidential services, including that of a principal guide at the capture of General Lee, and was present at the engagements at Quibbletown and Princeton. He purchased for £100, in 1780, a commission as cornet in the British Legion Cavalry, known also as Tarleton's Regiment of Dragoons, and in the following year he bought, for £250, a Lieutenant's commission in the same Loyalist Corps, in which he served in every action until the disaster of Yorktown. The young officer was present at the siege of Savannah and at the Battle of Guilford Court House, where he commanded the advance guard and broke the American line three times, for which action he received the public thanks of Lord Cornwallis. General Washington offered a reward of £100 for his capture, dead or alive.

In 1784 William Robins returned to America to see his mother and to reclaim (as he had hoped) under the Treaty of Peace some part of his father's property, which had been seized by two half-brothers, but "instead of meeting with any protection he was seized, tied to a tree and severely flogged," and he also said, was frequently carried to the gallows and threatened with death, and rifled of all his papers.

Lords Cornwallis and Rawdon and other distinguished British officers spoke warmly of the young American's conspicuous services in the War. In recognition of them he was granted in 1788 the sum of £100 to discharge some debts and for other purposes. He was also recommended for an annual allowance, equal to the difference between half-pay and full pay, if ever he should be reduced to half-pay. He claimed £10,100 and was awarded £300. (A. O. 12:109).

In February, 1788, he was on full pay in the 60th Regiment, originally known as the Royal American Regiment, then about to proceed on foreign service. His rank at the time was that of Lieutenant, the commission having been dated November 14, 1787. With this Regiment he was serving in the Island of Antigua in 1790. His later commissions are as follows: On November 7, 1793, he was appointed Captain-Lieutenant and Captain in the 6th Regiment and, on May 12, 1794, he was transferred as Captain in the 43rd Foot. He received another transfer in the same rank on February 27, 1796, to the 49th Foot and was placed on half-pay in the 4th Foot on November 5, 1802, remaining as such until 1826, when he probably died. (A. O. 13:111; A. O. 13:137; A. O. 12:17, ff. 164-180; A. O. 12:102, f. 116; Ind.: 5606; Army Lists).

Rev. DANIEL ROTHWELL

He was a Chaplain to the 3rd New Jersey Volunteers. (From a printed list of officers of the 2nd and 3rd Battalions, with the papers of John Brooks Simson, in A. O. 13:69).

RULOF RULOFSON (Ensign)

He was of Hunterdon county, New Jersey, the son of Harmon Rulofson. He became an Ensign in the 2nd New Jersey Volunteers, and was married in March, 1784, to Mehitable Phinney, at Annapolis, Nova Scotia, by the Rev. Jacob Bailey, Rector, in the presence of her brother, Thomas Phinney, and her sister, Abigail Willett, both of whom were living in Annapolis county in 1841, as was his widow. (W. O. 42:R15). He was a Justice of the Peace for King's county, New Brunswick, in 1809. ("Judges of New Brunswick," p. 164).

Rulof was born December 8, 1754, and had a son, William Harmanes.

SAMUEL RUTHERFORD (Captain)

By his marriage to Ruth Beadles he was possessed of considerable property in Trenton, which was "seized by the Rebels." He was appointed Lieutenant in the 1st Battalion of the 60th Regiment (Royal American Regiment) on February 16, 1774, and later promoted Captain, having served for 23 years in the army. In 1784 he and his wife were in Jamaica in the West Indies. (A. O. 13:92).

PETER RUTTAN (Captain)

He was born in New Jersey and lived at Franklin, Bergen county. He joined the British in December, 1776, and recruited 60 men for the 4th New Jersey Volunteers, in which he was appointed Captain on the 6th of that month. Later he was transferred to the 3rd Battalion. For disobedience of orders he was put under arrest by Brigadier-General Cortlandt Skinner, but not court martialled, and he resigned his commission. Later, by order of the Commander-in-Chief, he was employed in obtaining intelligence, and he recruited 40 men for the King's Orange Rangers. On June 30, 1783, he was in charge of 30 families of Loyalist refugees bound for Canada. He settled on the Bay of Quinty. (A. O. 12:63; "Ontario Archives," p. 429; "Am. MSS. in Roy. Inst.," IV:192). He was awarded £255 from his claim of £926. 5s. (A. O. 12:109).

JOHN FRANCIS RYERSON

He lived in Saddle River township, Bergen county, New Jersey, and was a prosperous farmer and miller on his own property, which he had bought, in conjunction with his brother Richard, from his father, Martin Ryerson, on May 1, 1749. He owned in all 534 acres of land in the township. At the first meeting in his county for choosing committees in support of the American cause, he and two others opposed the appointment of such committees, but their opposition was overruled by a large majority. His own son signed an "Association" without his knowledge. His adherence to the Crown compelled him to hide for many weeks in the woods.

His brother, George, and an uncle, John Ryerson, are mentioned, as are his former neighbors in New Jersey, James Van Buren and Lawrence and John Van Buskirk. The children of his brother Richard were in possession in 1786 of the property mentioned above. He was a refugee near Annapolis in Nova Scotia in 1786.

He was allowed £1,420 from his claim of £3,079. 11s. (A. O. 12:109), his estate having been forfeited in Bergen county, New Jersey, in 1779. (A. O. 12:15, ff. 86-96; A. O. 12:63, f. 12; Bergen Co. Records; see under Major Daniel Isaac Browne).

JOSEPH RYERSON (Colonel)

The son of Luykas Ryerson and his third wife, Joanna Van Duhoff, of New Jersey, and was born February 28, 1761. At the early age of 15 he joined the British forces as a cadet, and, in April, 1783, he was promoted Lieutenant in the Prince of Wales's American Regiment as a reward for his courage and skill as a volunteer in carrying despatches 196 miles into the interior of South Carolina from Charleston.

At the Peace he went to New Brunswick and was appointed Captain of Militia. He removed later to Charlotteville in the county of Norfolk, Upper Canada, where he became a Major and Colonel, Sheriff of London district in 1800 and holder of other public offices.

Once again he took up arms against his native country, this time in the War of 1812, in which he took an active part as Colonel of Militia with his three elder sons.

Joseph Ryerson was married in 1784 to Sophia Mehitabel Stickney (1766-1850), of a New England family, which had removed to New Brunswick in Canada. He died on August 9, 1854, aged 94. His brother was Lieutenant-Colonel Samuel Ryerson (q. v.), and his kinsman was Captain Samuel Ryerson (q. v.). (Ind.: 5605-6; Sabine; Chadwick, "Ontario Families," Vol. I, pp. 15-20).

SAMUEL RYERSON (Lieut.-Colonel)

A son of Luykas Ryerson and his third wife, Joanna Van Duhoff, of New Jersey, and brother of Colonel Joseph Ryerson (q. v.); he was born in 1752 and died on June 12, 1812. On March 25, 1777, he was commissioned Captain in the 4th New Jersey Volunteers, and in 1782 in the Third Battalion. After the Peace he went first to the Province of New Brunswick with other officers of his Regiment, and in 1794 removed to the north side of Lake Erie in Upper Canada at a place near Long Point, which has since borne his ancestral family name, Port Ryerse, county Norfolk. Here he was a Judge of the London District Court and Colonel of Militia. He is said to have been the first Free Mason in Upper Canada, having been master of a military Lodge formed in the 4th New Jersey Volunteers, which derived from a Lodge in the 16th Queen's Light Dragoons. The papers of this Lodge were in the possession of his grandson, George Becher Harris, in 1898.

This Loyalist was married, in 1783, to Sarah Underhill, widow of Captain Davenport. (Ind.: 5604-5-6; Chadwick, "Ontario Families," I:15-20; Sabine).

SAMUEL RYERSON (Captain)

Also of Bergen county, New Jersey, born there about 1751 and served through the War in the Loyalist forces, from March 25, 1777, as Captain in the 4th New Jersey Volunteers. He was wounded and taken prisoner in the celebrated Battle of King's Mountain, in which other men of New Jersey took part on the Loyalist side.

This Loyalist was married, January 22, 1784, to Sarah ———, by and in the house of the Rev. John Sayre, who was then on his death-bed, at Maugerville, the Province of New Brunswick, in the presence of his kinsman, Joseph Ryerson (q. v.). He died on June 12, 1812, at Woodhouse in Upper Canada, leaving a widow. (W. O. 42:R16; A. O. 13:21; Ind.: 5604-5-6; Stryker).

"Dr." PAULET ST. JOHN

An Englishman who emigrated from London in 1770 and settled in Virginia as a physician. There, as he complains, he earned less in the exercise of his profession than in London. He was called upon early in the Revolution to join the American army, but refused and quitted Virginia for North Carolina. Elsewhere he described himself as a Frenchman who had commanded a Corps of horse under General Montcalm in 1758 and after the War settled in Jersey, presumably New Jersey. On his arrival in New York in 1778 he was put into the provost on suspicion of being a French spy. Having been released he was permitted to sail for Europe.

In his original signed memorial (in A. O. 13:32) Paulet St. John, "Med. Doc.," as he called himself, declared that for refusing, through principles of loyalty, to accept a medical department in the American army, he was obliged in 1777 to abandon a considerable property in Virginia. For the same reasons of loyalty he was compelled to quit his property in North Carolina, whither he had fled. In a long and undated letter, mainly on his distressed condition in London, to the Commissioners, he concludes with the remark that he had refused a distinguished employ in the American army, "at the desire and subsequent menaces of General Lee and my own brothers, who have been each rewarded by Congress."

Parker (probably James Parker, a prominent Virginia Loyalist) in evidence said that he saw Paulet St. John with his father at Pierre Point in 1782; that he knew of no such place as Goshen in Orange county in Virginia, where he alleged that he was the owner of property, and that it was odd that after a supposed residence in that colony for eleven years St. John could not claim acquaintance with any of the principal people there. (A. O. 12:100, f. 268).

The Commissioners commented severely upon his alleged professional income of £1,500 in London and the significant absence of certificates in support of his loyalty and character from prominent Loyalists and they strongly suspected him of being a charlatan. (Ibid.).

JAMES SARVENIER, or SERVANIER (Lieutenant)

Resident of Bergen County but born in Germany about 1745, who served for seven years in the Loyalist forces, from January 2, 1777, as Lieutenant in the 4th New Jersey Volunteers, and later in the Third Battalion. He settled with the other officers of this Regiment on his half-pay and on his free grant of land in the Province of New Brunswick, where he died at St. John in 1803. (Ind.: 5604-5-6; A. O.

12:16, ff. 158-161; A. O. 12:63, f. 78; Sabine; Stryker; "Judges of New Brunswick," p. 48). He was allowed £83 from his claim of £245. 5s. (A. O. 12:109).

Rev. JAMES SAYRE

He was born in America, the son of John Sayre, of Philadelphia, where he was educated at the old College, now the University of Pennsylvania, having entered in 1761, graduated in 1765 and took the degree of M. A. in 1770. In 1774 the honorary degree of M. A. was conferred upon him by King's College (now Columbia University), New York. From 1778 to 1783 he was Rector of the Episcopal Church, Brooklyn, New York. Later he served as Chaplain to the 2nd New Jersey Volunteers and received half-pay as such until 1804, though, according to Stryker, he died in 1798, aged 53, at Fairfield, Connecticut. He was a refugee at St. John, New Brunswick, in the early days of that settlement, and from 1786 to 1788 served as a clergyman at Newport, Rhode Island. Before his death he became a Methodist Episcopal clergyman. (Ind.: 5605-6; Sprague, "Annals of the American Pulpit;" Sabine; Stryker; "Catalogue of Matriculates of Philadelphia College").

JONATHAN SAYRE

Born in New Jersey, a "gentleman," who lived in his "new and elegant house" on his plantation in Newark. He produced two claims in support of his loyalty, namely, that he joined Brigadier-General Cortlandt Skinner (q. v.) as a volunteer, and that in March, 1779, he was tried for high treason at Hackensack but was acquitted on giving a bond. Sayre was part owner of the sloop "Polly," with Nathaniel Richards (q. v.).

Colonel Abraham Van Buskirk (q. v.), in evidence, said that he thought Sayre in 1774 "pretty warm in his principles in favor of the Rebels," but that he had altered his principles when he met him in New York in 1777 and gave material information regarding the Americans.

His father left him property at his death in 1752; and he also inherited property in Newark under the will of Jabez

Harrison, who died about 1769. His wife and mother-in-law were living on the Harrison property in 1786. His mother, Martha Sayre, is mentioned.

John Anstey reported in 1787 that Jonathan Sayre had not suffered at all by the Revolution, his wife having bought back his confiscated estate (forfeited, 1778) "for a mere song;" he had returned to Newark after the War and was worth more than ever he was. (A. O. 12:85). An account of his forfeited estates is in A. O. 13:19. He was awarded £612 from his claim of £1,363. (A. O. 12:109; A. O. 12:15, ff. 206-216; A. O. 12:63, f. 34).

JONATHAN SCOFIELD

He was born at Norwalk, Connecticut, but had settled as a farmer in the township of Hardiston, Sussex county, New Jersey. In 1787 he was a refugee with his son, David, on the Kennebecasis river in New Brunswick. (A. O. 12:16, ff. 256-260; A. O. 12:63, f. 89). He was allowed £104 from his claim of £356. (A. O. 12:109).

WILLIAM H. SHAKERLEY

He lived in Elizabethtown, New Jersey, his native province, and, according to the Rev. Dr. T. B. Chandler (q. v.), was descended from a reputable and loyal family. Before or during the War he fitted out a ship for fishing on the Banks of Newfoundland, which was captured by the Americans. Afterwards he was a clerk to a notary public in New York City, and in 1801 he was employed in the Exchequer's office in London. He was apparently in the Bahamas from 1784 to 1801, living with family connections. (A. O. 461:17; A. O. 13:85; A. O. 12:100, f. 9).

DANIEL SHANNON (Ensign)

He was born in America about 1756 and served through the War, first as a private, and, from September 10, 1778, as Ensign in the 2nd and 3rd New Jersey Volunteers. (Ind.: 5605-6; Stryker). A Daniel Shannon is also entered as a Lieutenant in the 5th New Jersey Volunteers on February 12, 1777. These two records maybe, somehow, mixed. ("N. Bruns. (Can.) Hist. Soc. Coll.," No. 5).

SAMUEL SHARP

An American-born Loyalist of Hunterdon county, New Jersey. He was at St. John, New Brunswick, in 1786. A witness to his ownership of property was Richard Seaman, a Loyalist. (A. O. 12:16, ff. 122-6; A. O. 12:63, f. 76). He was granted £200 from his claim of £264. 7s. (A. O. 12:109).

JOHN SIMONSON (Lieutenant)

He was born about 1752 in Richmond county, New York, and served throughout the War in the Loyalist forces. In 1777 and 1778 he was an Ensign in the 3rd New Jersey Volunteers. In 1779 he was a prisoner in Philadelphia.

On March 31, 1798, he was married, according to the rites of the Church of England, at St. John, New Brunswick, to Ann Ness, daughter of John Ness, formerly Lieutenant in the Prince of Wales's American Volunteers and previously, from 1762 to (before) 1775, an Ensign in the 14th Foot.

This Loyalist was one of the exiled officers who accepted commissions in the King's New Brunswick Regiment on the Declaration of War by France on England in 1793, his rank being that of Lieutenant. His father-in-law was also a Lieutenant in this Regiment.

John Simonson died on December 22, 1816, at Maugerville in New Brunswick. His widow died in 1850 at Jacksonville in that Province. His elder son, John Ness Simonson, was born on February 11, 1799. (W. O. 42:S9; Ind.: 5604-5-6; "Acadiensis," III, 267-280; Sabine; Stryker; "New Brunswick Hist. Soc. Colls.," I:13-59).

Sir JOHN SINCLAIR (Baronet; Colonel)

He was born in 1763, the son of Colonel Sir John Sinclair, Quartermaster-General in America (1755-67), and his wife, Elizabeth, daughter and heiress of John Moland, or Moreland, a lawyer of Philadelphia, who were married on March 17, 1762, at Burlington, New Jersey, while that officer was stationed in command of his Regiment, the 26th Foot, in that Province. Their married life was short, for Sir John Sinclair died from the effect of wounds received in action at

Braddock's defeat and was buried at St. John's Church, Elizabethtown, New Jersey. His widow afterwards married, on March 14, 1769, at Elizabethtown, Lieutenant-Colonel Dudley Templer, Sir John Sinclair's successor in command of the 26th Foot.

The subject of this notice states that he and his mother were left the sum of £2,000, which was put into the hands of one Stephens, an American, who appropriated it to his own use. He also inherited 15,000 acres of land in the Province of New York, for which he had been offered £7,000 before it was confiscated by the State because of his loyalty.

Sir John Sinclair joined the 61st (or the South Gloucestershire) Foot as an Ensign in America (the country of his birth) on October 22, 1779, and was promoted Lieutenant on November 5, 1783. His name disappears from the army lists in 1785, but not before he was ordered with his Regiment to Minorca. He was granted an allowance of £100 a year as a Loyalist, from 1783. (A. O. 12:99, f. 58; Hatfield's "Hist. of Elizabeth;" Rev. G. M. Hills, "Hist. of the Church in Burlington," 1885, p. 273; "Penn. Mag. of Hist. & Biog.," IX:1-14).

THOMAS SKELTON

After seventeen years' residence in the Island of Jamaica he sailed for New York in 1771, taking with him money and effects to the value of £3,300 sterling. Having regained his health, impaired by the climate of Jamaica, he married, January, 1772, at Flemington, New Jersey, Elizabeth, daughter of Colonel Thomas Lowrey, and, on March 30, of that year, he entered into partnership with his father-in-law, and purchased a plantation in Amwell from Charity Clarke in June, 1772. Successful in trade and his plantation thriving, Skelton "continued to live in ease and affluence equal to his most sanguine hopes," until the outbreak of War, though he stated his tranquility was not fully disturbed until December 9, 1776.

His share in a certain transaction is not quite clear, though Lord Cornwallis and Brigadier-General Cortlandt Skinner had every confidence in him. It would seem, according to Skelton's statement, that his father-in-law, Thomas Lowrey, had promised to supply some boats belonging to Americans for the British army for crossing the Delaware. Skelton was requested by Lowrey to convey a message to General Skinner for Lord Cornwallis that he (Lowrey) had failed to obtain the boats. An American spy, who had gone to the British headquarters for the ostensible purpose of taking the oath of allegiance, perceived Skelton there and betrayed him, with the result that he was obliged to flee from home to the British army at Trenton. From that place he went to New York and was there employed in a public office by Captain David Laird, Royal Navy, until 1782, his wife and baby having joined him in 1780. On May 13, 1782, he embarked for England.

His confiscated land was bought by his father-in-law, Colonel Lowrey. In a letter of February 5, 1789, to his father-in-law, Skelton accuses him of buying the chief part of his (Skelton's) property underhanded and below its value. (A. O. 12/17, ff. 130-7).

In his evidence, Captain David Laird said that he first met Skelton in Jamaica in 1765 or 1766, when he was a clerk to a Mrs. Ellis. He had not heard that he had been in business for himself there and it was unlikely that he had much property. Captain Laird stated further that Skelton was now better off in England than in New Jersey, having tripled his fortune by the War, and that he ought to be ashamed to make a claim on the British Government. On this evidence the Commissioners reported the claim as fradulent. ("Loyalists' Claims," pp. 4-6; A. O. 12:13, ff. 1-13; A. O. 13:111; A. O. 12:109).

The New Jersey records indicate that Skelton was more or less of a fraud, and that his father-in-law was in no wise a Loyalist. Col. Lowrey was too active in the War on the American side, and held too many civil offices at his home later, to have had real suspicions of loyalty to the British side suggested against him by his neighbors or friends. The story of the "boats," etc., was, doubtless, made up by Skelton to cover up some transaction of his. Skelton, when in England, wrote to America to have his wife join him there. She went and, on arrival found a letter from him that he was in Scotland and she should return to America. She was in ill health and friendless, but started back to New Jersey and died on the way, being buried at sea. (See Dr. Race's Sketch of Lowrey, "The Jerseymen," December, 1891).

CORTLANDT SKINNER (Brigadier-General)

He is described in his memorial as Attorney-General of New Jersey from 1754 and Speaker of the House of Assembly from 1765, and the father of twelve children, who early in the War "were turned out of Perth Amboy, with their mother, by General Mercer."

In his letter of February 10, 1786, he says that Philip Kearny and his own wife were entitled each to one-fourth of their father's property at Six-Mile Run, New Jersey. Their father, after making his will, had disposed of this tract, except 150 acres. This statement is confirmed by a certificate, dated December 7, 1785, of their brother, Ravaud Kearny.

With this letter and certificate is a copy of an order, dated Perth Amboy, July 29, 1776, that the following persons were suspected of being disaffected to the American cause and were ordered by the Convention of New Jersey to be removed into the country, at a distance from all communication with the enemy: Mrs. Cortlandt Skinner and family; Mrs. Antill and family; Mrs. Derbage; Mrs. Homfray and family; Mrs. Kearny and family; Mrs. Holland and family; Peache and wife; Hunter and wife; and Thomas Stevens and wife.

In the same bundle (A. O. 13:111) are: A letter from Cortlandt Skinner, dated March 9, 1786, giving the date of his birth as December 16, 1727, Old Style, and adding that he has three daughters grown up and four sons who call for his assistance; particulars of the estate inherited by his wife from her father; also a schedule of his own property.

Sir William Howe, in a letter dated March 26, 1784, stated that Cortlandt Skinner from his consequence was by him granted a commission to raise a Corps [the New Jersey Volunteers] of four Battalions, which, though not entirely completed, was in great measure effected to Howe's satisfaction. (A. O. 13:79).

The Commissioners in reporting upon his claim declared that he was one of the most respectable men from the Continent of America and had done material services in the War. He was now in want of assistance, and no man was better entitled to ask for it from the British Government. His very modest application, with a large family of twelve, add to their respect for his character. If the Government at any time have any high legal office vacant in the British Dependencies they recommend him as one who would fill it with great honor to himself, and they are very sure that he deserves every reward from England. (A. O. 12:100, f. 31).

In his letter to Lord Sidney he refers to his petition for relief and complains that some Provincial Corps, junior to his, had already been put on the establishment [entitling the officers to half-pay]. He sets forth his military and civil services, and concludes with a gloomy account of his prospects, with nothing left to support his wife and family. (F. O. 4:1).

Cortlandt Skinner was awarded £5,169 from his claim of £10,382, and at the rate of £500 a year during the War for the loss of his official income of £576. (A. O. 12:109).

The above accounts of his career may be supplemented from another official source. In September, 1775, he was called upon before the Town Committee at Morristown and was found guilty of being inimical to the liberties of America, but, on declaring himself generally a friend to liberty, his friends on that Committee "took advantage of these general expressions and obtained his discharge for him." In August, 1775, he was offered the command of the Provincial troops, by Mr. Carter, Secretary to the Provincial Congress, and by Mr. Ellis and Mr. Stewart, acting for the Provincial Congress, with whatever rank in New Jersey he might choose, but he refused the offer. He was obliged to quit in January, 1776, and his wife and family were forced later to leave the Province. The date of his commission as Brigadier-General of the New Jersey Volunteers is September 4, 1776. His library contained 482 volumes. (Loyalists' Claims," pp. 113-5).

Cortlandt Skinner, in evidence in behalf of Philip Kearny in London on February 4, 1785, admitted that he approved of Kearney and other Loyalists signing an "Association paper" drawn up by Skinner himself that they were friends of Liberty and the Constitution. (Ibid., p. 300).

The Brigadier-General, who was a lawyer of marked ability and strict integrity, was the son of the Rev. William Skinner, first Rector of St. Peter's Church, Perth Amboy (originally a Mac Gregor) and his wife, Elizabeth Van Cortlandt, and was the brother of Major John Skinner (q. v.). His mother was a daughter of Colonel Stephen Van Cortlandt, and his wife, Elizabeth, was the daughter of Philip Kearny, lawyer, of Perth Amboy. A son-in-law was William Terrill (q. v.).

He died, March 15, 1799, at Bristol in England, to which country he went after the Peace, and his widow died in 1810 at Belvoir Park, near Belfast, Ireland. His daughter, Catherine, married Sir William Henry Robinson (1765-1836), Commissary-General in the British army, fifth son of Colonel Beverley Robinson, the distinguished New York Loyalist. (T. 50:11; A. O. 461:16; Ind.: 5605-6; A. O. 13:85; A. O. 12:13, ff. 27-60; A. O. 12:74, ff. 83-6; A. O. 12:89, f. 10; Force, "American Archives," Ser. IV, Vol. IV, pp. 363, 1607; "Ontario Archives," pp. 1232-9; Stryker; Sabine. A long account of Rev. William and Gen. Skinner is in Whitehead's "Hist. of Perth Amboy").

His son, Cortlandt, was appointed Ensign in the 70th Foot, on November 11, 1780, and was promoted Lieutenant on December 26, 1787. His name appears in the army lists until 1795. Another son was Lieutenant-General Philip Kearny Skinner (q. v.).

JOHN SKINNER (Lieut.-General)

He was born in New Jersey,[1] but not known to be of any relation to General Cortlandt Skinner (supra). He began his military career in the British army as an Ensign in the 16th Foot on September 4, 1772. In the American War of Independence he served in the campaigns in the Southern colonies, in the actions at Beaufort and Stono Ferry in South Carolina and in the sieges of Savannah and Charleston. He commanded a troop in Tarleton's British Legion (Cavalry) in the Battles of Blackstocks, Cowpens and Guilford Court House.

In 1795 he served in the reduction to submission of the revolting Maroons in Jamaica, and thus saved that Island from the fate of St. Domingo, and in 1804 he commanded the 16th Foot in the expedition against Surinam. He was in command of a brigade at the capture of Guadaloupe in 1810. While holding the rank of Major-General, this American-born officer acted as Governor successively of St. Martin's, Santa Cruz and Guadaloupe.

Three of his sons became officers in the British army, namely, Lieutenant-Colonel Thomas Skinner; John Skinner, an Ensign, who died of yellow fever in Jamaica in 1821; and Captain James Skinner, of the 61st Bengal Native Infantry, who was mortally wounded in India in 1842 by the hand of an assassin. A daughter married Captain Sir Henry Vere Huntly, Royal Navy, Lieutenant-Governor of Prince Edward Island. General Skinner died on October 10, 1827, and in his will he bequeathed all his property to his wife, Anne, whom he left as guardian to his children. His brother-in-law, Donald Maclean, of 37 Brunswick Square, London, is mentioned in his will. (Sabine; Army Lists; original will).

JOHN SKINNER (Major)

He was the son of the Rev. William Skinner, of Perth Amboy, and brother of Brigadier-General Cortlandt Skinner (q. v.). He entered the Provincial service, (circa 1755) at the

---

[1] There was a John Skinner, of Woodbridge, born in 1733, who, in 1799, removed to (present) Franklin Co., Pa., but he was not this John Skinner, nor have his ancestors been traced.

same time as his brother, William (q. v.), and was Lieutenant in the same Company. Both were taken prisoners at Oswego in 1756, and were taken to France and then transferred to England. While waiting in England for a commission in the regular army he volunteered his services in a secret cruising expedition in the Mediterranean, returning in October, 1757.

His commissions in the regular British army are as follows: Ensign in the 3rd Foot (Colonel Howard's), on September 27, 1757; Lieutenant in the 61st (Colonel Grey's) Foot, from December 1, 1758, to 1762, serving therein as stated in the War with the French in North America. On June 25, 1762, he was promoted Captain-Lieutenant in the 119th Foot (Captain Charles Fitzroy's). Promotion as Captain came to him in the 70th Foot on June 10, 1768, and he returned with it to England in 1770. He was made Major in that Regiment on November 17, 1780. In 1784 he retired from the army and settled as a merchant in his native place of Perth Amboy. Here he died in December, 1797, leaving one son, James, by his marriage on February 16, 1774, to Sarah Kearny, daughter of Philip Kearny, the prominent lawyer of Perth Amboy and his second wife, Isabella, daughter of Chief Justice Robert Lettice Hooper. (Army Lists; A. O. 13:83; Whitehead's "Perth Amboy," p. 119).

JONATHAN D. SKINNER (Ensign)

Ensign in the 1st New Jersey Volunteers, on half-pay until 1808, (Ind.: 5605-6). No further account.

PHILIP KEARNY SKINNER (Lieutenant-General)

He was the son of Brigadier-General Cortlandt Skinner (q. v.). On December 21, 1782, he received a commission as Ensign in the 23rd Foot (Royal Welsh Fusiliers), and was promoted Lieutenant in the same Regiment on November 23, 1785.

The young American remained in this Regiment as Captain (October 22, 1793) and Captain-Lieutenant (September 1, 1795), until his promotion as Lieutenant-Colonel in the 56th (or the West Essex) Regiment of Foot on December 11, 1799.

He served in Ireland, 1800-1805. On October 25, 1809, he became Colonel, having served since June 20, previous, as Assistant Adjutant-General.

His next promotion dates from August 1, 1811, when he was appointed Quartermaster-General in the East Indies. He was granted the rank of Major-General on January 1, 1812, and Lieutenant-General in 1825. He became a member of the Consolidated Board of General Officers.

General Skinner's active service includes the expedition to Ostend (where he was taken prisoner), and in the East and West Indies and Spain.

Before his death in Regent street, London, on April 7 (or 9), 1826, he had withdrawn his claim for property at Perth Amboy and elsewhere in America. (A. O. 13:83). In his will, dated April 3, 1826, he bequeathed all his property in trust for his sister, Gertrude (wife of Captain Meredith, of the 70th Regiment), for his nephews, Philip Kearny Skinner and Arthur Skinner (sons of his brother, Cortlandt). Other beneficiaries were his sister, Euphemia, wife of Oliver Barbarie, and her two sons, John and Cortlandt; his sister, Catherine, wife of Sir William Henry Robinson; his sister, Susan, wife of Major Jasper Farmer; his brothers, Cortlandt (q. v.) and Major John Skinner (q. v.); his nieces, daughters of his brother-in-law, William Tyrrell (Terrill) Esq., (q. v.), of New York, and his wife, formerly Isabella Macartney. To his nephew, William Henry Robinson, Ensign in the 72nd Regiment, he left his freehold property at Aylesbury in the county of Bucks, England. (Swabey 237).

STEPHEN SKINNER (Major)

He was a "gentleman and merchant" of Perth Amboy, son of the Rev. William Skinner and brother of Cortlandt Skinner (q. v.), and was bred to the sea. He was, from about 1763, Treasurer of the Province and had also been a Judge of the Court of Common Pleas for Middlesex county. While Treasurer of East New Jersey, in 1768, he reported the robbery of the treasury, and a Committee of the Legislature reported that he was the robber, after which (but not until 1774) he resigned and Governor Franklin, his firm friend, appointed him to the Council.

In the early Spring of 1776 he was privately told that his stay in Perth Amboy was disagreeable to his political enemies and consequently his friends advised him to depart, as his brother, Cortlandt, had fled. Acting upon this warning, and "to avoid the persecution of the Amboy and Woodbridge Committees," he removed to Newark, but could not obtain a house without the recommendation of the Committee of Perth Amboy. He then purchased a house and twenty acres of land outside Newark. In March, however, he went on board a brigantine, of which he was half owner, then lying opposite Newark, accompanied by his wife, ten children, a sister and a few friends, taking with him some furniture, 40 pipes of Madeira and 4 pipes of Lisbon wine. The party were safely landed with the assistance of his friend, Captain Archibald Kennedy (q. v.), at Second River.

By order of Governor Livingston he was made prisoner in July, 1776, and, with Captain Kennedy, sent to the Provincial Congress at Trenton and thence as prisoner to Morristown. Meanwhile, his wife and six small children were treated with severity; their wearing apparel, wagons, horses and a chaise were taken from them and they were turned into a road in a snow storm and obliged to walk four miles to Elizabethtown.

Stephen Skinner served as guide during the British occupation of New Jersey and performed other military services. He removed to New York in the Spring of 1777, and there raised a Company of 100 Loyalists, mostly from New Jersey. In 1778 this Company was joined to a Battalion of which he was appointed Major.

His wife, Catherine, inherited property from her father, Andrew Johnston, who left property to his other children, Gertrude Barbarie, Mary, John, Stephen and William Fennil.

This Loyalist was the owner of much landed property, which is described at length, with a long list of his debtors, in A. O. 13:111. His house at Perth Amboy was occupied by the 33rd Regiment. So considerable was his property that the very substantial sum of £4,764 was awarded to him as compensation for the loss of it from his claim of £6,975. (A. O. 12:109). His confiscated and forfeited lands in the counties of Middlesex and Sussex were advertised to be sold by public auction in the "New Jersey Gazette" for August 9, 1784.

The Skinner family were in great distress at Chester in England in June, 1785, according to a pathetic petition signed by Governor Franklin, David, Isaac and Peter Ogden, Philip Van Cortlandt, Elisha Lawrence, J. Burnet, Vincent Pearse Ashfield and William Taylor. (A. O. 13:111). With this petition is a letter from Stephen Skinner to Governor Franklin, dated Chester, December 3, 1784, in which he says that he was the head of the party at Perth Amboy to oppose Rebel measures and was the only gentleman who appeared in person to oppose the erection of the Liberty pole there. His pension was continued until his death in or shortly before 1809. (Treas. 1: 622; T. 50:8; T. 50:21; T. 50:22). But Sabine says he died at Shelburne, Nova Scotia, in 1790. (A. O. 12:14; ff. 31-59; A. O. 12:100, f. 112; A. O. 12:101, f. 221; Sabine).

THOMAS SKINNER

He was probably related to Lieutenant-General John Skinner (q. v.); was a baker born in New York City and lived in his own house at Perth Amboy from 1725 to 1775, when he was taken prisoner and banished to Cranbury.

His son, John, was in England in 1784, while he himself was in New York in 1788. There is a schedule of Thomas's confiscated estate, for which he claimed £1,348 and was awarded £750. (A. O. 13:111; A. O. 13:113; A. O. 12:13, ff. 331-9; A. O. 12:101, f. 3; A. O. 12:109).

Two sons took part with the Americans. He refused to speak to them and threatened to disinherit them, unless they produced their discharge. One son obtained his discharge after this threat. ("Loyalists' Claims," p. 303).

TIMOTHY SKINNER

He was born in America and lived in Sussex county, New Jersey. He did not go within the British lines during the War, and, therefore, was not exactly regarded as a Loyalist. But he was at Niagara, on the Canadian side, in 1787. (A. O. 13: 81; A. O. 12:16, ff. 421-4; A. O. 12:63).

WILLIAM SKINNER (Lieut.-Colonel)

A brother of Gen. Cortlandt Skinner (q. v.), and third son of Rev. William Skinner. He was born in Elizabeth, New Jersey, and had his first military experience as Captain in the Provincial Regiment of New York. He was at Oswego, N. Y., in August, 1756, became a prisoner under Gen. Montcalm, and was sent to France, being exchanged in the Summer of 1757. On September 21, 1757, he was commissioned Lieutenant in the 24th Foot, and, on August 2, 1759, he was transferred as Captain in the 85th Regiment (or Royal Volunteers), in which he served in the wars against the French and Indians in North America. He was promoted Major on February 11, 1761, and on March 9, 1763, Lieutenant-Colonel in this Regiment, which was disbanded at the Peace in 1763, and he was then placed on half-pay. Three years later Colonel Skinner petitioned for a grant of 10,000 acres of land in America for his services in this War.

A diverting instance of his determined spirit, which had won for him the thanks of his General and a recommendation for promotion, no mean tribute at the time, is illustrated by his determination to present a petition to the King in person at a levee, in face of the opposition of a Yeoman of the Guard, who told this American soldier that, as the Court was in mourning for the Queen of Prussia, he was not properly clad in Court mourning. The young American, however, succeeded in presenting his petition to his Majesty, who afterwards told Lord Barrington, Secretary at War, that he liked Skinner's looks and commanded him to provide a commission for him in the regular army, with the result that within three months he was appointed Lieutenant in Cornwallis's Regiment. But the young soldier was dissatisfied and declined the commission; he wanted something better in the army. He left Lord Barrington in a happier mood upon receiving promise of a better military appointment. ("Docs. relating to Colonial Hist. of New Jersey," IX).

Governor Franklin appears to have been alarmed in 1767 at an alleged plot to deprive him of his high office and darkly hinted at William Skinner as the plotter; but the Governor's suspicions were allayed by the fact that the supposed plotter's prospects in the army were so good, combined with his marriage to a lady of fortune (a daughter of Lady Warren) as to render his alarm unnecessary.

Colonel Skinner did not live to engage in the Revolutionary War. He was in England after about 1763 and, while he desired to get over to America again, for some reason did not. He died in England about 1778. (Whitehead's "Perth Amboy," pp. 112-119).

ABNER SLEUT

He was of Hunterdon county, New Jersey. His name is recorded in A. O. 12:110, ff. 97-8.

JESSE SMITH

He was of Monmouth county, New Jersey, and joined the British army in 1776 at New York. By his father's will he was entitled to 266 acres of cultivated land, which his mother let on rent. He was imprisoned twice, received nine wounds, his right arm was broken and three musket balls remained permanently in his body.

The Commissioners reported strongly on his great services in the War and, as a single man, they granted him a pension of £25 from 1784 until his death in 1823. (T. 50:27; A. O. 12:101, f. 10).

SAMUEL SMITH

He was born in America and was a farmer in Elizabethtown, New Jersey. Although his religious principles as a Quaker would not permit him to bear arms, yet he rendered his Sovereign every service in his power by giving intelligence and acting as guide to the British army in 1776 and 1777. He was at Annapolis, Nova Scotia, in 1786. (A. O. 12:16, ff. 22-8). Inquisition against his property in Essex county, N. J., was made Sept. 15, 1778. From his claim of £1,106 he was allowed £50. (A. O. 12:109).

SAMUEL SMITH

He went out in 1768 as clerk to the American Ironworks Company at Spotswood, New Jersey, of which he was appointed manager in 1772. He was appointed "against his will a Lieutenant in the Rebel militia," but declined to act, though he had mustered. The laborers in these works, to the number of over 50, continued loyal and several went into exile. His property in Monmouth county was taken by inquisition dated May 19, 1779.

In 1785 he was clerk to the Thames and Severn Canal at Stroud in Gloucestershire, England. He was allowed £370 from his claim of £580.10s. (A. O. 12:109; A. O. 12:13, ff. 368-374; A. O. 13:111).

WILLIAM SMITH

He lived at Woodbridge, New Jersey, his birthplace, where he was "happily and independently situated on his valuable estate, with all the comforts of life," as a farmer and grazier. He was taken prisoner in 1776 but later in the same year he joined the British army and accompanied it to Staten Island, his place of residence for the remainder of the War.

According to his evidence he was offered early in the Revolution the office of Treasurer of New Jersey and signed an "Association" to support the civil magistrate in the execution of his duty until a reconciliation with Great Britain could be made in a constitutional manner. He declined, however, to take the oath at a later stage. From May, 1775, he was a member of the Provincial Congress. One Pearson, a Loyalist, informed Smith of the intention of the Whig party to issue paper money with the object of putting the Province in a state of defence. This measure was opposed by Smith and was with difficulty defeated in the House. It would seem from the evidence that he was a Whig early in the Revolution, but became a Loyalist upon the Declaration of Independence.

Cornelius Hatfield maintained that there was not a better cultivated plantation than Smith's between Charleston, South Carolina, and Massachusetts. He had property also at Middletown, N. J., which was seized under forfeiture proceedings of May 18, 1779.

This Loyalist was the son of James Smith, who died in 1772 (will dated September 11, 1766), and his wife, Sarah, who died in 1775. The executors of James Smith were his wife; his son, the above William; his daughter, Sarah Edgar; and his grandsons, Thomas, James and William Edgar. John Anstey's report on his confiscated property at Woodbridge and Middletown Point creek, bought by General Forman, is in A. O. 12:85. A large number of documents concerning his property and his memorial are in A. O. 13:111.

For his substantial estate he claimed £9,418 and was allowed £4,991. (A. O. 12:109; A. O. 12:14, ff. 61-71; A. O. 12:101, f. 254).

FREDERICK SMYTH (Chief Justice)

He was appointed Chief Justice of New Jersey on June 23, 1764, and served until 1776; was a member of the Council on July 20, following. From 1766 to 1771 he occupied the Proprietary house in Perth Amboy, the same that in 1774 became the residence of Governor Franklin. He proved to be a Loyalist in 1775. In 1778 he was appointed one of His Majesty's Council to assist the English Peace Commissioners in America. His house, furniture and library were forcibly possessed by the American and British officers and soldiers, but, having received so much civility from both, he was willing to forget and to forgive all the violences committed in those days of rage in the Revolution, and therefore made no claim for compensation for the same. He was, however, compensated at the rate of £500 a year for the loss of his official income of £600 as Chief Justice during the War and received a pension of £240. (A. O. 12:109). Governor Franklin complained of the payment of his official salary, in view of the fact that he had taken no active part in support of the Crown in the Revolution.

Lord North and Lord George Germain requested the Chief Justice to remain in New York during the War. He removed to Pennsylvania after the War, and was there employed to transact some business for the merchants of Norwich and Yarmouth in England.

Smyth, who was born in England, married a lady of fortune of Philadelphia, namely Margaret Oswald, at Christ Church in that city, on March 21, 1784. (Official records). In 1787 he was living at Roxborough, Philadelphia county. He died in 1815 at Philadelphia. (A. O. 13:111; A. O. 12:14, ff. 269-274; A. O. 12:85; Sabine; Whitehead's "Jud. & Civil Hist. of N. J.," pp. 397-19).

JOHN SMYTH

He was of Perth Amboy, and lived for nearly fifty years in New Jersey, his birthplace in 1722. He was a lawyer, admitted to the New Jersey Bar in August, 1745. He filled many important public offices, as Treasurer of East Jersey from 1774, Register to the Council of Proprietors of East Jersey, Clerk of the Court of Common Pleas for Middlesex county from 1747 and Examiner in Chancery. He was taken prisoner early by order of General Heard and released on parole. At the evacuation of New Jersey by the British he left home, taking only his silver plate and furniture to New York, where his distressed circumstances obliged him to sell his silver, doubtless before his appointment as Treasurer there of the City Funds. With his memorial is a description of his property.

On April 20, 1783, he was directed by Sir Guy Carleton, Commander-in-Chief, to deliver up all records, surveys, files of papers, minutes and maps in his possession, belonging to the Proprietors of East Jersey. (Am. MSS. in Roy. Inst., IV: 41, 44, 46).

John Smyth probably was married twice, as Whitehead says he married Margaret, daughter of Andrew Johnston of Perth Amboy. He died in January, 1786, in London, leaving then a widow, Susannah, and an only child, Andrew, born in 1764, who were granted compensation of £1,633 from their claim of £2,075.

The witnesses to his loyalty were William Smith (q. v.), Thomas Skinner, late of Perth Amboy, and Michael Kearny, all from New Jersey. His Loyalist pension of £150 was continued to his widow as an appreciation of his zeal, high character and heavy losses; this was reduced to £100 in 1784 and paid until 1804, probably the date of her death. (A. O. 461: 19; T. 50:8; A. O. 13:111; A. O. 12:16, ff. 273-8; A. O. 12:17, ff. 67-88, 91-7; A. O. 12:109; A. O. 12:101, f. 225).

JOSEPH SMYTH

He was born in New Jersey about 1737 and claimed to be a merchant and land owner of the township of Knowlton, in Sussex county. In his memorial he states that he had served as a Captain of an Independent Company on the frontier against the Indians in the previous War; that early in the Rebellion he was surrounded by malicious spies at home and escaped to Susquehannah, where he had property, and thence through the woods to Niagara in Canada. Here, in January, 1777, he was presented with a commission as Lieutenant in the King's Royal Regiment of New York and served until November, 1778, when he embarked from Quebec for New York. On the voyage the ship conveying him, named "Mary," was captured by the American privateer, "General Sullivan," commanded by Captain Manning, and he was stripped of everything and treated "with the utmost barbarity, in a manner shocking to humanity, and debarred the necessities of life." On January 6, 1779, this privateer captured the "Weymouth" packet, and, six days later, captured the privateer "Endeavour" from Glasgow, which in turn was ransomed by Captain Marwick, of the "Mary," and all vessels sailed for England. There he married his wife, Caroline, in 1780.

Philip Skene, Lieutenant-Governor of Crown Point and Ticonderoga from 1775, gave him a strong certificate of character and loyalty, but when called upon to give personal evidence in support of Smyth in London, on April 21, 1789, he said that Smyth had deceived him and that the deeds and papers alleging that he was the owner of great property in America were forgeries and the man himself an imposter. (He claimed to have landed property valued at £3,000 sterling in New Jersey and from 30,000 to 40,000 acres in Pennsylvania). In the face of this evidence the Commissioners rejected Smyth's claim for the alleged loss of his property in America. He was at Niagara in 1788.

With his memorial is much correspondence concerning his property. (A. O. 13:111; A. O. 12:17, ff. 105-113; A. O. 12:109). He was probably the "Jos. Smith," the only New Jersey Loyalist who signed the loyal address to George III in 1779. (C. O. 5:7).

HENRY SORREL (Ensign)

He was born in America about 1770 and, as a mere boy, was awarded with a commission as Ensign in the 3rd New Jersey Volunteers, doubtless as a reward for his father's services. He was on half-pay as such until December, 1816. (Ind.: 5605-6). He may have been the son of William Sorrel (infra.).

WILLIAM SORREL

This Englishman was born about 1737; apparently was of Bergen county, New Jersey, and served from December 24, 1776, as Quartermaster in the 3rd and 4th New Jersey Volunteers. He was a prisoner of war in Philadelphia in 1779 and also in 1780. On Oct. 31, 1779, and again on Apr. 20, 1779, his property was advertised under forfeiture in Bergen county. He was on half-pay until 1804. (Ind.: 5605-6; Stryker).

He may have been the father of the above Henry Sorrel. One William Sorrel, of New Barbadoes township, Bergen county, N. J., married, May, 1774, Hannah, daughter of Justus Earle (q. v.), and was probably the William named above.

GEORGE STAINFORTH (Captain)

This Englishman had served for 25 years as an officer in the 18th (Royal Irish) Foot, before his retirement in 1773, of which 17 years were spent on service in America. He bought an estate of 115 acres near Princeton, New Jersey, where his house was well furnished with mahogany and where he took an early and decided part against the Rebellion. In 1778 he was commissioned Captain in the 2nd New Jersey Volunteers and served until 1782, when he set sail for England and was put on the Seconded list in 1783. (A. O. 12:14, ff. 389-394; Ind.: 5605).

His original certificate of December 2, 1777, to the loyalty of Captain Ibbetson Hamer (q. v.) mentions his wife, Ann, and bears the signature of David Mathews, last Mayor of New York under the Crown, and the seal of the City. (A. O. 13: 61). His estate in Middlesex county, N. J., in Windsor township (now in Mercer county) had inquisition taken against it May 3, 1778. (Midd. co. Records).

RICHARD STANTON

This American-born Loyalist was a farmer at Horse Neck in Essex county, New Jersey, and was residing in the United States in 1786. His estate in Acquackanonk township was forfeited in 1778. He was awarded £285 from his claim of £924, 14s. (A. O. 12:15, ff. 334-9; A. O. 12:63, f. 43; A. O. 12:109).

WILLIAM STEELE

In his childhood he was "taught to love his King and the Constitution of England," and "his resolute loyalty in the American Revolution won for him the applause even of his enemies."

He was an Irishman who emigrated in 1761, or 1762, taking with him about £4,000 sterling, which he laid out (with some more money borrowed) in the purchase of over 600 acres of land, negroes and farming requisites, within eight miles of New Brunswick in New Jersey, where his activity resulted in the suppression of smuggling.

His loyalty was manifested early, so much so, that it is stated he was tarred and feathered and "held up to the world as incorrigible." Finally, he was "hunted by a hundred firelocks through the woods," and a reward of 100 dollars was offered for his body, dead or alive; but, although within a few yards of him, he escaped alive.

This Irish Loyalist had taken his mahogany furniture out from England, likewise his silver, which consisted of three quart cups, two pairs of candlesticks, a soup ladle, a milk jug and spoons, all indicating prosperity. There is a long account of his adventures early in the Rebellion, "which," he says, "would be too tedious to set forth in a memorial." (A. O. 12:14, ff. 351-362).

In 1787 he was a widower, living with three adult children at Cork, Ireland, namely, William Henry Steele, born about 1767, and Ann and Grace Steele. His income was derived from a leasehold in Dublin, his Loyalist pension of £100 and his compensation of £1,150 from his claim of £3,129.

Bernardus La Grange (q. v.) said in evidence that, although a Loyalist, Steele did not bear a very good character in New Jersey, an allegation which was ignored by the Commissioners, who reported that he had "infinite merit in persevering in his loyalty under trials which might have staggered very good men." (A. O. 12:104, f. 7; A. O. 12:109).

EDWARD STELLE (Lieutenant)

He was born in America in 1757 and served for six years in the N. J. Loyalist Corps as an Adjutant in 1776 and as Captain-Lieutenant June 24, 1777 (perhaps in the 2nd New Jersey Volunteers), and as Captain-Lieutenant in the 3rd New Jersey Volunteers May 28, 1778. (Ind. 5604).

With other surviving officers of this Regiment he settled on his free grant of land in New Brunswick. On August 26, 1785, he was appointed, with four others, a trustee, or commissioner, for effecting the settlement of Fredericton, the capital of the Province. He represented York county in the first House of Assembly of New Brunswick and was a Judge of the Inferior Court of Common Pleas for that county. He probably died in 1808, the last recorded date of the payment of his half-pay, or the date of his return to the United States. (Ind.: 5605-6; "Judges of New Brunswick," pp. 5, 6, 7).

THOMAS STEPHEN

He succeeded John Barbarie (q. v.), who died in 1770, as Collector of the Customs for East Jersey and Perth Amboy, a post which was worth £400 a year. Here he bought a farm of 60 acres for £500. He died in December, 1777, from the effects of sleeping out in the woods at night in hiding from his political persecutors. Previous to his death he had superintended the preparation of spruce beer, doubtless for the army, for eight months, at a remuneration of 7s. a day, besides perquisites.

His widow, Mary, was of a Dorset (English) family, and, before going out to America with her husband, she had £400 on mortgage, which she withdrew, as she could obtain more interest on it in America. She was "most inhumanly treated" in New Jersey and had lost three sons in America before returning to England with her two young children (daughters). A brother was killed on the British side at Bunker Hill. (A. O. 12:104, f. 22). She was granted a Loyalist pension of £100 from 1782 to 1815. She married again to one Lyte. (T. 50: 6; T. 50:24).

JOHN STEVENSON

A New Jersey Loyalist of Sussex county, who claimed £1,800 and was allowed £900. (A. O. 12:109).

SHORE STEVENSON

He was a resident in Middletown, New Jersey. He probably died before 1786, as his son, John (or Shore), born in 1776, was living with one Mott, his maternal great-grandfather, at Middletown in 1786. (A. O. 12:15, ff. 298-302; A. O. 12: 63, f. 37). The estate of this Loyalist was forfeited in Monmouth county, N. J., under inquisition of March 20, 1780. (Monm. co. Records).

WILLIAM STEVENSON (Lieutenant)

Also of Monmouth county, New Jersey, and was born about 1758. He served for seven years in a Loyalist Corps, having joined the army on December 23, 1776, and was appointed Lieutenant in the 2nd New Jersey Volunteers in 1777, and in the 3rd Battalion July 20, 1781. He was on half-pay of the 3rd Battalion until 1791. (Ind.: 5605-6; W. O. 24:750).

Stryker says that he distinguished himself in the Battle of King's Mountain and at the siege of Charleston in South Carolina, and that he died in 1818 at Weymouth, Nova Scotia.

JAMES STEWART (Captain)

A farmer, innkeeper and blacksmith at Greenwich (perhaps in Sussex county), New Jersey, where he was born about 1737. He was commissioned Captain in the 5th New Jersey Volunteers on November 16, 1776, and at the end of the War received half-pay of that rank. Captain Stewart was living in the parish of Landkey, in Devonshire, England, in 1788. (A. O. 13:111; A. O. 12:14, ff. 206-211; Ind.: 5605). He was awarded £350 from his claim of £606. (A. O. 12:109).

WILLIAM STEWART (Captain)

He was born in America and was possessed of a good estate in New Jersey. In 1778 he was appointed Captain in an Independent troop of cavalry, and in 1782 was transferred with that troop to the King's American Dragoons. He had also served in the Queen's Rangers.

He was married, March 4, 1803, to Mary Thompson, at Fredericton, Province of New Brunswick, where he died, December 17, 1820, aged 69, leaving a widow and two children: William, born in 1810, and Priscilla Anne, born in 1806, both of whom were put on the Compassionate Fund at £9 each per annum from 1822. (W. O. 42:S21; W. O. 25:3088; Ind.: 5604-5-6; Original Corresp. of George III in H. O. 42:3).

WILLIAM STYLE (or STILES)

He was born in 1754, the son of John Style, whose will is dated February 16, 1763, and grandson of John Style, and lived at Newark, New Jersey, where his property was confiscated in 1778 and sold. (Name spelled "Stiles" in confiscation record in Essex county).

He took an oath of allegiance to the Americans early in the Rebellion, but joined the British army on arrival in New Jersey. From the end of 1776 until the Peace he worked as a carpenter in the Engineers in New York and in the South.

The estate of his Loyalist brother, Isaac "Stiles," born in 1757 or 1758, was also confiscated in Essex county in 1778 and sold. His sister, Mary, bought a part of his (William's) property and was living on it with their mother after the War. He was alive in 1786 at Shelburne, Nova Scotia, and was allowed £67 from his claim of £820. (A. O. 12:109; A. O. 12:15, ff 227-236; A. O. 12:63, f. 25).

JAMES STILLWELL

He was of Middletown, New Jersey, and died during the War. His estate in Monmouth county was forfeited in 1779. His eldest son, John, born in 1764, claimed £883 as compensation for the loss of his father's estate and was awarded £306. John was living at Beaver Harbour, New Brunswick, in 1786. (A. O. 12:15, ff. 428-433; A. O. 12:63, ff. 57, 71; A. O. 12:109).

SAMUEL STILLWELL

He resided in Upper Freehold township, Monmouth county, New Jersey, his birthplace, and inherited a plantation there from his father, Samuel, by will of 1753. He settled at Beaver Harbour, New Brunswick. His estate in New Jersey was forfeited in 1779. His uncle, Anthony Woodward, a Quaker, gave evidence in support of his claim, at St. John in that Province (A. O. 12:16, ff. 75-80). He was allowed £853 from his claim of £1,150. (A. O. 12:109).

JOHN STITES, Jr. (or STILES)

He was born in Elizabethtown, New Jersey, but had settled in 1763 in New York City, whence he was obliged to flee to his former home in 1776. Here he bought a small farm and here he trained with the American militia early in the Rebellion. The arrival of the British forces left him free to return to New York, and there he kept a store in Queen street and was part owner, with Thomas Shaw, in three privateers. His Elizabethtown estate was confiscated in 1779.

The only loyal service which he could claim to have rendered in the War was in carrying intelligence to Sir William Howe in December, 1776. He seems to have been a dubious Loyalist and his claim of £2,281 was disallowed. (A. O. 13:111; A. O. 12:14, ff. 231-8; A. O. 12:109; Essex Co., N. J., Records).

ANDREW HUNTER STOCKTON

He was born at Princeton, N. J., Jan. 3, 1760, being the son of Richard Witham Stockton (q. v.). His father purchased a commission for him in the British army and he served from the beginning to the end of the War, for part of the time as Lieutenant in the 1st New Jersey Volunteers. He was made prisoner of war in 1777 and confined in jail at Trenton.

He went to St. John, New Brunswick, after the War and there married, Apr. 4, 1784, Hannah ———. He died at Sussex Vale, New Brunswick, May 8, 1821; his wife died Oct. 1, 1793, aged 25 years. A large number (stated to be 111) of his descendants were living in that Province in 1883. He was on half-pay until 1822. (Ind.: 5605-6; Am. MSS. in Roy. Inst., IV: 326; "Foot-Prints," etc., p. 21).

JOSEPH STOCKTON

A planter, near Princeton, who died as a guide to the British army in March, 1777, leaving a widow, Sarah, and five sons and six daughters. His eldest son, James, who had served with the British army, was living in Bermuda with his sister, Helen, in 1786. The widow, Sarah, was in New Jersey in 1786. Three daughters are mentioned by name, Helen, Elizabeth and Rachel, and two sons, James and John. (A. O. 12: 15, ff. 310-321; A. O. 12:63, f. 41). The widow and four children were granted compensation of £270, their claim being for that sum, while the son, James, received £600 from his claim of £1,763. (A. O. 12:109).

Joseph Stockton seems to have been a son of Samuel and Rachel (Stout) Stockton, whose brothers and sisters were: Major Richard Witham Stockton (q. v.), Jacob, Rachel, who married John Riddell, Ann, and Ruth, who married John Voorhees. Samuel was brother to John Stockton of "Morven" at Princeton. (Information from Mr. Bayard Stockton).

RICHARD WITHAM STOCKTON (Major)

He joined the New Jersey Volunteers in August, 1776, and was commissioned Major in the 6th Battalion on December 3, following. When in command of a post at Lawrence Island on February 18, 1777, he was taken prisoner by Colonel Neilson's party and marched to Philadelphia with a Captain, four subalterns and 100 men, captured at the same time, and was kept a prisoner there and at Carlisle, Pa., for nearly 18 months. (A. O. 13:83).

Major Stockton was tried by court-martial on August 15, 1780, as a party to the murder of Derrick Ammerman, of Long Island, and was found guilty and sentenced to death, but the sentence was remitted. His name is on the list of Seconded officers in 1783. (Ind.: 5605).

This Loyalist, called "Double Dick" by his enemies, was the son of Samuel and Rachel (Stout) Stockton, of Princeton. He was skilled as a guide and was named the "Famous Land Pilot." His wife, Mary, was a daughter of Joseph Hatfield, of Elizabethtown. His daughter, Mary Ann, married Captain John Barbarie (q. v.). He died on May 8, 1801, at St. John, New Brunswick, and is the founder there of what is known as the Canadian branch of the Stockton family. Besides a son, Andrew Hunter Stockton (q. v.), he had also a son, Charles Witham, who saw service on the British side.

DAVID STOUT

He was of Middletown, Monmouth county, New Jersey, whose claim for compensation was rejected. (A. O. 12:15, ff. 405-410; A. O. 12:63, f. 62).

PETER STOUT

He was a farmer on his own property at Middletown, New Jersey, and was native born. His property in Monmouth county is said to have been confiscated. He settled at Beaver Harbor in New Brunswick after the War and was there in 1786 (A. O. 12:15, ff. 327-332; A. O. 12:63, f. 45), but returned later to Middletown, where he died and left a will in 1828. He was allowed £380 from his claim of £562.10s. (A. O. 12:109). He was the son of Jonathan Stout and was born in 1744; his wife was Charity Williams. (Stillwell's "Miscellany," p. 313).

DANIEL STRETCH

He was born in New Jersey and was a farmer in Cumberland county, where he appears to have had three plantations, which were confiscated and sold. He was tarred and feathered in 1776. His wife and nine children were in New Jersey in 1789, while he was apparently returning in that year to Nova Scotia, at the age of 55. (A. O. 12:102, f. 204; "Amer. Archives," Ser. IV, Vol. IV, p. 664).

SAMUEL STRETCH

He was born in America about 1758 and, on March 21, 1778, was appointed Ensign in the West Jersey Volunteers. He was married on August 25, 1779, at New York, to Elizabeth Berry, by the Rev. Garret Lydecker (q. v.). He died on November 14, 1812, at Brooklyn, New York, whence his widow was petitioning the British Government for a pension in February, 1823. (W. O. 42:S23; Ind.: 5605).

PHILIP SUMMERS

A baker, of Bound Brook, New Jersey, who served in the New Jersey Volunteers under Colonel Isaac Allen for seven years. He was at Maugerville, Province of New Brunswick, in 1787. (A. O. 12:16, ff. 287-9; A. O. 12:63, f. 92). £40 was allowed him from his claim of £100. (A. O. 12:109).

GEORGE TAYLOR (Colonel)

He was of Middletown, New Jersey, eldest son of Edward Taylor, and commanded from 1776 the militia in Monmouth county with the rank of Colonel. In June, 1779, he received a warrant to raise a company of Loyalists. In October, 1783, he was a refugee in New York, in receipt of an allowance of £146 in New York currency. He was at St. John, New Brunswick, in 1786. (A. O. 13:21; A. O. 13:112). His estate in Monmouth county, N. J., was confiscated under inquisition of May 14, 1779. (Monm. Co. Records).

JOHN TAYLOR (Captain)

He was the son of John Taylor and grandson of Edward Taylor, and was born near Perth Amboy, New Jersey, May 15, 1742. He lived in Shrewsbury as a farmer, where he was forced to muster with the Militia early in the Revolution. His neighbor was Henry Van Mater (q. v.). Having escaped, he joined the British army on the day on which it landed on Staten Island. Captain Taylor distinguished himself in command of a small Corps of Cavalry under Major Patrick Ferguson in the celebrated Battle on King's Mountain, and subsequent to this defeat of the Loyalists he served in the campaigns in the South. He was promoted Captain in the 1st Battalion of the New Jersey Volunteers on August 26, 1780. Five brothers are mentioned in his memorial, namely, Nathaniel (dead); Asher (died in 1776); Joseph; George and Morford, the latter being killed in action on the British side at Sandy Hook in 1782.

He claimed £3,645 for his valuable estate confiscated by the State of New Jersey in 1779, and was awarded £1,560 (A. O. 12:109).

John Taylor's original commission as Captain, dated August 25, 1780, and signed by General Sir Henry Clinton, is in W. O. 42:73, with a certificate of his marriage on August 6, 1786, to Eleanor Taylor of and at Middletown, New Jersey, by the Baptist minister, in the presence of Edward and Joseph Taylor of the same place. He died on November 13, 1822, aged 81, at Sissiboo, Nova Scotia, where he had a farm of 700 acres and six slaves, leaving a widow, an unmarried daughter, aged 25, and a son, Morris Taylor. (Ind.: 5606; A. O. 13:112; A. O. 12:14, ff. 73-81; A. O. 12:101, f. 258; A. O. 12:111, f. 49).

JOSEPH TAYLOR

A resident of Trenton, New Jersey, and an attorney-at-law, made such April 3, 1770, and brother of William Taylor (q. v.). In November, 1780, he was appointed a Deputy Commissary, and in that capacity accompanied General Leslie on the campaign in Virginia. From thence he went to South Carolina and joined Lord Cornwallis. He returned to New Jersey after the War, and, in 1787, was living at Perth Amboy. (A. O. 13:112; A. O. 12:15, ff. 310-6; A. O. 12:63, f. 40; A. O. 12:85). He was granted £100 from his claim of £432. (A. O. 12:109).

WILLIAM TAYLOR

An attorney-at-law, of Freehold, New Jersey, and a man of reputation in his profession. He was born at Middletown, New Jersey, in 1746. On April. 3, 1770, he became an attorney. When, in June, 1776, a petition was set on foot in Monmouth county in favor of the Declaration of Independence, he and his family zealously opposed it, and such was the Taylor influence that they prevailed upon "a very great majority of the inhabitants of the county to sign counter petitions against the Declaration and William Taylor delivered them himself to a member of Congress."

In November, 1776, General Washington sent a detachment from his army, under the command of Colonel Forman, to take up and secure William Taylor and other Loyalists in Monmouth county, and they took nearly 100 of his relatives and friends, who were removed 300 miles to Fredericktown, Va., and there confined in jail. Taylor himself had, however, escaped previously. (A. O. 13:112).

In examination in London, Taylor admitted that he had belonged to a Grenadier company of American Militia early in the Revolution. ("Loyalists' Claims," p. 317).

He was awarded £250 from his claim of £3,117, 16s., and at the rate of £260 a year, for the loss of his professional income during the War, from his claim of £424. He also received a pension of £130. (A. O. 12:109).

This Loyalist was the son of John Taylor (1716-1798), Sheriff of Monmouth county, himself a prominent Loyalist, and "His Majesty's Lord High Commissioner of New Jersey," appointed by Lord Howe as one of the Commissioners of Peace. John Taylor died at Perth Amboy in 1806. (Salter and Beekman's "Old Times in Old Monmouth," p. 48; Sabine).

William Taylor is said to have married a daughter of Colonel Philip Van Cortlandt and, before his death in 1806, at Perth Amboy, had held the office of Chief Justice of Jamaica in the West Indies, bestowed upon him in recognition of his loyalty. Three sons were officers in the British service, namely, John William, who died in command of a Battalion in the service of the East India Company; Joseph Pringle, a General and a

Knight of the Royal Guelphic Order; and Cortlandt, a Captain in the Madras Artillery. His sister, Mary, married Dr. Absalom Bainbridge (q. v.). Mentioned in his will are his wife, Elizabeth; his brother, Joseph Taylor (q. v.), an executor; and his five children, John William, Catherine Eliza, Joseph Pringle, Cortlandt and Elliot (name said to be George Elliot). John Heard (q. v.) was his "near relation." (A. O. 12:13, ff. 358-367; A. O. 459:7; A. O. 462:21; T. 50:8; Sabine).

WILLIAM TERRILL

A son-in-law of Brigadier-General Cortlandt Skinner (q. v.), and was born in New Jersey. He lived on his property in Piscataway township, Middlesex county. His grandfather was Andrew Johnston, who left him some estate.

As a refugee in New York he was appointed in August, 1777, Warehouse Keeper for the Province. At the end of the War he appears to have gone to Philadelphia, where he was obliged by his poverty to act as a clerk to a merchant. He was, however, in Canada in 1788, and his wife and five young children at Sorel. Their residence in Canada was probably temporary. He was allowed £650 from his claim of £1,870 4s. (A. O. 12:109; A. O. 12:15, ff. 349-355; A. O. 12:63, f. 46; Am. MSS. in Roy. Inst., IV, 8; "Ontario Archives," pp. 125-8).

BARTHOLOMEW THATCHER (Captain)

He was born in New Jersey about 1738 and lived in Kingwood township, Hunterdon county. On September 10, 1778, he was appointed Captain in the 3rd New Jersey Volunteers, his original commission from General Sir Henry Clinton being in W. O. 42:T4.

He was married on December 7, 1806, to Margaret Gamble, of Kingwood, by the Rev. Garner A. Hunt, pastor of the Baptist Church in that place. He died on May 23, 1817, at Kingwood and was buried in the Friends' burial ground, when his half-pay ceased. His widow petitioned the British Government for a pension as an officer's widow. (W. O. 42:T4; Ind.: 5604-5-6).

One Bartholomew and Anne Thatcher were baptized in the Baptist Church of Kingwood (situated at Locktown in Hunterdon county), on April 17, 1763. On a tombstone in a graveyard at the rear of the Baptist church at Flemington is an inscription showing that Margaret Thatcher, daughter of Bartholomew and Ann Thatcher, was buried there in September, 177—. (The last figure is missing). (Ex inform. Mr. Hiram E. Deats).

FRANCIS THOMAS

He was born in Cornwall, England, and settled at Newark, New Jersey, as a farmer on his own land. During or after the War he returned to his native county and resided at Redruth. (A. O. 13:112; A. O. 12:100, f. 165).

CORNELIUS THOMPSON (Lieutenant)

An American by birth, brother of Lewis Thompson (q. v.), born April 9, 1756, who rose from the rank of Ensign in 1776 to that of Lieutenant and Paymaster in the New Jersey Volunteers, and served until the peace. He was Adjutant in the 3rd New Jersey June 29, 1780. (Ind.: 5604).

He was married on May 15, 1785, to Rebecca ———— (born May 3, 1759) at Freehold, New Jersey, though then a permanent resident in Canada. Seven children of this marriage are mentioned: William, born June 17, 1786, who became a magistrate in Toronto; Augustus, born March 20, 1788; Frederick, born April 19, 1790; Amelia, born May 3, 1792; Mary, born December 17, 1793; Cornelius Oliver, born February 17, 1797; and Sally, born January 27, 1800.

Cornelius Thompson died on August 7, 1814, at Grantham, Niagara, whither he had removed in 1810 from New Brunswick. His death is attributed largely to the anxiety of mind arising from the wounding of one son and the capture of two others by the Americans in the War of 1812-1814. His widow was living at Niagara in 1822. Thomas Merigold, a Captain in the militia of Toronto in 1822, had served with him in the New Jersey Volunteers, doubtless as a private. (W. O. 42:T6; Ind.: 5604-5-6).

JOHN THOMPSON (Lieutenant)

He was Ensign from December 1, 1776, and Lieutenant from 1780, in the 1st New Jersey Volunteers. He was born in America about 1751 and, on November 1, 1781, was married to Phoebe Ryers in Richmond county, New York, by the Rev. John H. Rowland, Chaplain to that Battalion and Rector of St. Andrew's in that county. He died on January 23, 1801, in Richmond county, leaving a widow, who had removed to Trenton in New Jersey, whence she was appealing to the British Government for a pension, accompanied by an affidavit of Ozias Ansley (q. v.). (W. O. 42:T7; Ind.: 5605-6). He was from Middlesex county, N. J.

LEWIS THOMPSON (Ensign)

He was born, about 1754, near Freehold, Monmouth county, New Jersey, being the son of Thomas Thompson, and he served for three years as Ensign in the 3rd New Jersey Volunteers, on which he was placed on half-pay until 1814. (Ind.: 5605-6).

He was a noted Loyalist in Monmouth county, whose wife was Anne, daughter of Jacob and Maritje (Schenck) Van Dorn. He and his brother, Cornelius (q. v.), went to Nova Scotia after the War, settling in the Province of New Brunswick on land assigned by the British Government. He was there in 1786, but returned before 1802 and located again near Freehold, where he died previous to 1820. His daughter, Mary, married a Capt. William Stewart, and a son, William (b. 1799 in Nova Scotia, died Mar. 4, 1857) became a prominent lawyer at Somerville, New Jersey. In all Lewis Thompson had eight children. ("Van Doorn Family," p. 157 et seq.; Beekman's "Early Dutch Settlers of Monmouth").

BENJAMIN THOMSON

He was born in 1759, in Somerset county, New Jersey, the son of William Thomson (died in 1765), a lawyer who was a counselor in 1758 and grandson of Benjamin Thomson, a magistrate and Judge of the Court of Common Pleas, both residing at Hillsborough (now Millstone), New Jersey.

Early in the Rebellion he was studying medicine under Dr. John Cochran, a gentleman of eminence in his profession and soon to become the head of the American military hospitals. He (Cochran) used his influence to prevail upon the young Loyalist to join the American service, but his loyalty to His Majesty's person and attachment to the British Government caused him to reject all solicitations and, although under age, to join the Royal army in 1776. Before receiving the appointment of cornet in the Queen's Rangers he had acted as aide-de-camp to Cortlandt Skinner (q. v.). He was present in several actions and lost a limb.

Benjamin Thomson was unable to obtain a settlement of his property, a farm adjoining the Court House in Hillsborough, because his executors were "in rebellion." His uncle was Dr. George Leslie and a brother was named George Thomson.

The Commissioners recorded in his favor that he was a brave and active young man in the War, who could have spared his valuable property in New Jersey by sacrificing his honor. His memorial, certificates, particulars of his considerable property, a copy of the "New York Gazette" and "Country Journal" for March 5, 1784, containing a notice of a sale by auction of his "elegant" farm in Hillsborough, are in A. O. 13:112. He was allowed £800 from his claim of £891. (A. O. 12:109; A. O. 13:109; A. O. 13:137; A. O. 12:17, ff. 1-7; A. O. 12:100, f. 345).

JOHN THORBURN

He was a Scotsman and joiner who emigrated to America as late as 1775 at the age of 19, first to New York (where "everything was confusion") and later to Morristown, New Jersey. (A. O. 13:112; A. O. 12:17, ff. 115-128). He claimed £202 and was allowed £180. (A. O. 12:109).

JOSEPH THORNE

Of Piscataway township, Middlesex county, New Jersey, a farmer, who joined the Loyalists early. "Thanks to his intelligence" the 3rd and 6th Battalions of the New Jersey Volunteers were enabled to withdraw and escape from Sullivan on

Staten Island. He was settled at Beaver Harbor, New Brunswick, in 1787. (A. O. 12:16, ff. 345-9; A. O. 12:63, f. 100). From his claim of £94.2s., the sum of £47 was awarded. (A. O. 12:109).

JOHN THROCKMORTON (Lieutenant)

He was born in New Jersey in 1756 and was settled as a storekeeper at Freehold, New Jersey, before the Revolution. He bore arms in the militia of Monmouth county, called a "Tory Company," and afterwards recruited men, which entitled him to a commission in the New Jersey Volunteers. Some time later he was transferred as Lieutenant to Colonel Robert Rogers's King's Rangers and served until the Peace. In 1777 he was a prisoner of war in Trenton jail. In 1779 his estate in New Jersey was confiscated. In 1786 he was settled on half-pay in Prince Edward Island, where there were other Loyalist refugees from New Jersey and elsewhere.

William Taylor (q. v.) in evidence stated that Throckmorton seemed rather disposed at first to support the measures of Congress, but as soon as he discovered that a separation between the Colonies and Great Britain was aimed at, he left the Americans. ("Ontario Archives," p. 152).

John Throckmorton was awarded £395 from his claim of £568.12s. (A. O. 12:109; Ind.: 5605-6; A. O. 12:15, ff. 397-403; A. O. 12:63, f. 51; Stryker).

One James Throckmorton, of Monmouth county, N. J., married Frances, daughter of John Barbarie and sister of John and Oliver Barbarie (q. v.).

CLAYTON TILTON (Captain)

He lived at Red Bank, New Jersey, and was there engaged in the coasting trade. He was "obliged at first to join a Rebel Association in order to secure his liberty from confinement." In 1776 he joined the British and, on January 15, 1781, was commissioned Captain in the Associated Loyalists in New York. He was farming in the Province of New Brunswick in 1790. (A. O. 13:98; A. O. 13:112; A. O. 12:16, ff. 117-120; A. O. 12:63, f. 75; A. O. 12:102).

According to his affidavit, sworn before William Walton, Magistrate of Police, at New York City on April 23, 1782, Clayton Tilton, when a prisoner in Monmouth county, New Jersey, was carried to Freehold jail and, on the journey thither, his captors stopped at Colts Neck, where two Loyalists, Aaron and Philip White, were prisoners. The property of Philip, including his shoe and knee buckles, was plundered and he was murdered, while his brother, Aaron, was sent ahead with a party. Philip White's sister requested his body for burial in a coffin which she had taken for the purpose to Freehold, but the request was refused. (C. O. 5:108). His estate in Monmouth county was confiscated in 1779. The sum of £56 was allowed him from his claim of £84. 6s. (A. O. 12:109).

Clayton Tilton was shot at Musquash in the Province of New Brunswick, in October, 1808, by a deserter from the 101st Regiment, and died within a few hours. ("Judges of New Brunswick," pp. 106-9).

ROBERT TIMPANY (Major)

He was appointed Major of the 4th New Jersey Volunteers on November 18, 1776, and was on the list of Seconded officers in 1783. (Ind.: 5605). According to Stryker he was an Irishman, who had been educated at the University of Glasgow and had emigrated to America in 1760, living first at Philadelphia and afterwards at Hackensack, New Jersey, where he opened a school. He was a zealous soldier and was wounded on several occasions in the Southern campaign. He died at Yarmouth, Nova Scotia, in 1844, aged 102.

Major Timpany was a founder in 1784, and secretary, of the first Masonic Lodge at Digby, Nova Scotia, where he went in 1783. He was reprimanded for not using the Bible on swearing a man to an affidavit and his conduct was termed by the Governor and Council of Nova Scotia as "indecent, illegal and atrocious." (Rev. Wm. Driffield, "Hist. of Digby Lodge, No. 6, and St. Mary's Lodge, No. 5, Digby," p. 3). Edward K. Timpany and John A. Timpany were prominent Freemasons in 1827 and later. On the records the name often appears as Tenpenny.

Sabine says that his wife was a Sarah Clark, whom he married in 1776, and that several children survived him.

JACOB TUCKER

A native-born Loyalist of Elizabethtown, New Jersey, who joined the British in 1776, and at the Peace settled at Argyll in Nova Scotia. Probably he is the Jacob Tooker, whose estate in Essex county, N. J., was confiscated in 1778. His claim of £281. 5s. was met by a grant of £200. (A. O. 12:15, ff. 149-152; A. O. 12:63, f. 19; A. O. 12:109).

WILLIAM TURNER (Lieutenant)

He was born in America and was commissioned Lieutenant in the 2nd New Jersey Volunteers on September 10, 1778, his original commission from General Sir Henry Clinton being in W. O. 42:T10. He served in the Southern campaigns and was a prisoner in February, 1781. (Am. MSS. in Roy. Inst., IV:17). He also appears as a Lieutenant in the King's New Brunswick Regiment in 1793, and as Commissary in the War of 1812.

He was married on May 2, 1793, to Sarah Smith, by the Rev. Walter Price, Rector of St. Mary's Parish in the Province of New Brunswick, where he died at Wakefield on January 5, 1816, at the age of fifty-nine. Here he was known as "Dr. Turner," and here his widow was living in 1821, when she appealed for and succeeded in obtaining a pension.

The children of this marriage, as mentioned, are: Elizabeth, baptized May 2, 1795; Isabella, baptized September 17, 1803; George Carleton, born June 12, 1805; Frederick Snelling (1), born October 15, 1807; and Marion or Maria, and Frederick Snelling (2), twins, born September 27, 1812. All but the first were baptized at Woodstock, New Brunswick. In consequence of the poverty of their widowed mother the three younger children were allowed £10 each from the Compassionate Fund in 1822. (W. O. 42:T10; W. O. 25:3089; Ind.: 5604-5-6).

THEODORE VALLEAU (Quartermaster)

He was a son of Theodore Valleau and was born in 1752 at Hackensack, New Jersey. He rose from Sergeant Major to the rank of Quartermaster (in 1782) in the 1st New Jersey Volunteers. His original commission in the last rank, signed by General Sir Henry Clinton, is in W. O. 42:vi.

He was married on February 14, 1790, to Elizabeth Burke (who was born December 23, 1769, in Cumberland, Nova Scotia), at Westmorland in New Brunswick, in the presence of Asa Fillimore, of Cumberland, and of Spiller Fillimore, of Hanover, Massachusetts, brother-in-law of Elizabeth Burke.

This Loyalist left New Brunswick in 1805 and settled in New York for the purpose of seeking medical advice, and here he died on September 10, 1812, leaving a widow, who was living in September, 1843, at the age of 73 with her daughter, Mary Louisa Allen, wife of George W. Allen, at Buffalo, New York, whence she addressed an appeal to the British Government for a Loyalist pension. His daughter, Ann, married George L. Fradenburgh and was living at 168 Thirteenth street, New York City, in 1843, at the same time as his sister, Margaret Voorhis, at 21 Morton street in that city. Theodore Valleau's cousin, Mary Morrison, widow of Joseph Morrison, was also residing at 12 Barclay street in that city in 1843. She was the daughter of Falconer Valleau. (W. O. 42:vi; Ind.: 5605-6). Mrs. Elizabeth Valleau, who was on the refugee list in May, 1780, may have been his mother. (Am. MSS. in Roy. Inst., II:116).

HENRY VAN ALLEN (Ensign)

This American-born Loyalist was appointed Ensign in the 3rd New Jersey Volunteers on December 18, 1781. He was married, on December 25, 1785, to Winifred Rapalje, at St. John, New Brunswick, by the Rev. John Beardsley, himself a Loyalist exile. He died on October 30, 1820, aged 55, at Woodhouse, Upper Canada, where his widow was living in 1823. One Abraham A. Rapelje, of London district, Upper Canada, who was in New York in 1824, probably on a visit, was doubtless a family connection of Mrs. Van Allen. (W. O. 42:V5; Ind.: 5605-6).

WILLIAM VAN ALLEN (Captain)

He was born in America about 1744 and was one of those men who had served in the American militia before joining the British. He was appointed Captain in the 4th New Jersey Volunteers on November 23, 1776, and served in that Regiment until the Peace. He is credited with secreting Colonel William Bayard when a reward of £500 was offered for his capture. His property was sequestered in Bergen county, N. J., in 1778. In A. O. 13:19 is an account of his losses and certificates regarding this property, for the loss of which he was awarded £210 from his claim of £334. 19s. (A. O. 12:109). He was living at Burton in New Brunswick in 1787. (A. O. 12:16, ff. 154-7; A. O. 12:63, f. 79; Ind.: 5605-6).

PETER J. VAN BLARCUM

A farmer, of Bergen county, New Jersey, who was a refugee in Nova Scotia in 1786. (A. O. 13:26). His property in Bergen county was forfeited in 1779.

Dr. JAMES VAN BUREN

He was born in New Jersey and settled at Hackensack as a physician and surgeon. Early in the War he prevented his two sons from taking arms with the Americans, by whom they had been called out. In 1776 he attended to the army of General George Washington at his request and acted gratuitously as surgeon to the wounded of both sides. In the same year he acted as guide to the British force under General Grant and was captured by the Americans, who threatened him with death by hanging and kept him a prisoner in a church for eight days, when he was released on the petition of his women patients.

Dr. Van Buren was again imprisoned for his loyalty, but was released upon consenting to take the oath of allegiance to the Americans and abjuration of the King. He remained in New Jersey until 1778, when he again joined the British. His property was seized in Bergen county in 1779.

After the War he settled on his half-pay and Loyalist pension at Clements, near Annapolis, Nova Scotia, where he probably died about April, 1811. He had received as compensation

£280 from his claim of £583. 12s., and at the rate of £90 a year during the War for the loss of his professional income. He likewise received a pension of £45. (A. O. 459:7; T. 50: 43; A. O. 12:15, ff. 112-7; 12:63, f. 11; A. O. 12:109; A. O. 13:19; A. O. 13:83; "Ontario Archives," pp. 543-5).

Dr. ABRAHAM VAN BUSKIRK (Lieut.-Colonel)

A physician, surgeon and apothecary, who was born in New Jersey about 1735. At the desire of Governor Tryon, of New York, he agreed to be chosen the representative of Bergen county in the Provincial Congress, as did other Loyalists mentioned in these pages, but having been accused of being inimical to the United States he resigned. He was tried by four Committees for opposing the measures of Congress.

In his memorial he makes no mention of his appointment by the Provincial Congress on February 17, 1776, as surgeon for a Regiment of militia in Bergen county, nor of payment to him by order of the Provincial Congress for arms sold as late as July 26, 1776. (Force, "Am. Archives," Ser. IV, Vol. IV, p. 1595; "Min. Prov. Cong.," p. 375). Van Buskirk had also signed the first Association drawn up by Major Daniel Isaac Browne (q. v.). But, on November 16, 1776, he was commissioned Lieutenant-Colonel of the 3rd New Jersey Volunteers, with which, according to Stryker, he distinguished himself in the attack on Fort Griswold, New London, Connecticut, when he was highly commended by Benedict Arnold. Lord Cornwallis certified to his merit and to his military services.

Accounts of his forfeited estates in New Jersey are in A. O. 13:19 and A. O. 13:85.

At the end of the War he sought an asylum at Shelburne, Nova Scotia, living on his military allowance of £147. 7. 5., and on his compensation of £1,111, allowed from his claim of £1,827. He was also Mayor of that city.

A son-in-law was Richard Combauld, Commissary and Paymaster to the Royal Artillery, who was in 1785 at Shelburne, where also was his former neighbor in New Jersey, Daniel Jessop, cooper. (A. O. 13:85; A. O. 13:83; A. O. 12:15, ff.

181-190; A. O. 12:63, f. 23; A. O. 12:109; Ind.: 5604-5-6; Sabine).

His daughter, Maria, married, as his first wife, Lynde Walter, son of the Rev. William Walter, Loyalist Rector of Trinity church, Boston, Mass., who was at that time a refugee with this son (Lynde) at Shelburne, Nova Scotia. (Ex inform. Miss Helen C. McCleary, a descendant).

ABRAHAM VAN BUSKIRK (Captain)

A son of Captain Lawrence Van Buskirk (q. v.), and was born about 1753. He was commissioned successively Lieutenant and Captain (October 25, 1778) in his father's Regiment, the King's Orange Rangers. He was drowned toward the end of 1783 in the brig "Argo" (Captain Woodworth) on the voyage to Nova Scotia from New York. (W. O. 24:750).

His widow, Anne Corson, afterwards married Jacob Remsen, who partially wasted her large inherited property near Port Richmond, New York. She married, thirdly, Lewis Ryas, and died in 1825 on Staten Island, childless. (Sabine).

JACOB VAN BUSKIRK (Captain)

A son of Lieutenant-Colonel Abraham Van Buskirk (q. v.), and was born in 1760. He lived in New Jersey. He served for six years in the Loyalist forces, being made Captain in 1780, and was put on half-pay of the 3rd New Jersey Volunteers. He was captured in November, 1777, and was wounded in 1781 at the Battle of Eutaw Springs. In the half-pay list he is described as holding a civil appointment. (Ind.: 5604-5-6; Sabine; Stryker).

JOHN VAN BUSKIRK

There were probably three young Loyalists of this name, doubtless all from Bergen county, New Jersey. One was a John L., and one a John J., indicating they were sons, respectively, of a Lawrence and a Jacob Van Buskirk. One was appointed on May 14, 1778, Lieutenant in the Royal American Reformees, commanded by Lieutenant Rudolphus Ritzema, of New York, and was killed in the War. (Sabine; Raymond). Another, doubtless John L., was the son of Captain Lawrence

Van Buskirk (q. v.), and lived on a rented farm at West Ramapo, New Jersey. He served as a guide and as a volunteer in his father's Regiment, the King's Orange Rangers, with which he was present at the reduction of Fort Montgomery. He settled at Wilmot in Nova Scotia. (A. O. 12:16, ff. 339-343). The third was born about 1755 in America and was on half-pay as Lieutenant of the 3rd New Jersey Volunteers until 1827. (Ind.: 5604-5-6).

One of the above was at Cornwallis in Nova Scotia in 1786 (A. O. 13:19), and one was at Horton, Nova Scotia, in 1787. (A. O. 12:63, f. 103).

LAWRENCE VAN BUSKIRK (Captain)

He was born at Hackensack, New Jersey, about 1729, the son of James Van Buskirk (alive in 1786), but lived on his own estate in Orange county, New York. On January 18, 1777, he was commissioned Captain in the King's Orange Rangers, raised by Lieutenant-Colonel John Bayard in Orange county, and served in the taking of Fort Montgomery, Fort Independence, Stony Point, Red Bank and other actions. The property in Bergen county he must have owned was sequestered in 1779. He settled with his wife, Jane (his cousin), at Round Bay, near Shelburne, Nova Scotia, and was granted a pension of £40 until 1801. She died in 1791 and he died in 1803, aged 74. (Sabine).

Three sons were officers in Loyalist regiments, namely, Abraham, Thomas and John, and a fourth son was lost in a privateer in the British service during the War.

Lawrence's younger brother, James, "a violent Rebel," obtained part of his father's estate intended for this Loyalist, by frightening his father that all the deeds would be seized by the Americans, unless he handed them over to him (James). (T. 50:11; A. O. 461:17; Ind.: 5604-5-6; A. O. 13:70; A. O. 12:102, f. 15; "Ontario Archives," pp. 665-6).

LAWRENCE VAN BUSKIRK

He was of Hanover, Morris county, New Jersey, born in 1724, the son of John Van Buskirk (who was killed during the War). He helped in recruiting for the battalion of Dr. Abraham Van Buskirk (q. v.). He would seem to have settled at Cornwallis in Nova Scotia. On March 9, 1787, his vessel foundered in the Bay of Fundy, but he escaped with his life. The sum of £235 was awarded to him from his claim of £374. 10s. (A. O. 13:19; A. O. 12:16, ff. 335-9; A. O. 12:63, f. 104; A. O. 12:109).

THOMAS VAN BUSKIRK (Lieutenant)

A son of Captain Lawrence Van Buskirk (q. v.), and was born about 1759, probably in Bergen county, New Jersey, and was on half-pay as Lieutenant in his father's Regiment, the King's Orange Rangers, until 1804. (Ind.: 5605-6). Sabine says he returned to New Jersey and died there at the age of about thirty.

PHILIP VAN CORTLANDT (Major)

He was of Hanover, Morris county, New Jersey, born in 1739, and declares in his memorial that his family was "treated in a manner that would disgrace the most savage barbarians;" they "were reduced in the space of three months from affluence to the want of the common necessaries of life," and, finally, "by the orders of General George Washington, inhumanly turned out of doors in a snowstorm to make room for the sick of his army." He was deprived of the property of his aunt, aged 89, to whom he was heir-at-law, it having been conveyed to his relatives in the American service by the influence of his uncle, Lieutenant-Governor Van Cortlandt of New York. His personal losses included one large family picture; the "Dashwood and Argyle" pictures; also other paintings and furniture, which had been "wantonly destroyed by the Americans in their nightly revels." He succeeded in carrying away the family silver, which, however, he was obliged by his necessities to sell in England. (A. O. 13:54).

This member of the well-known New York family of this name was the owner of a pearl-ash factory in New Jersey. Among the family connections mentioned by him are his grandfather, William Ricketts, whose will was dated July 26, 1735, and who left two daughters, Mary and Elizabeth; Anne de Peyster, under whose will, of July 14, 1774, he inherited property; and Gertrude Beekman, who bequeathed property to him and his brother, William Ricketts Van Cortlandt. (Ibid).

A copy of his letter, dated Hanover, New Jersey, June 12, 1775, to the officers of the militia of Morris county, entreats them to "proceed with their proposal to resign their commissions with the greatest caution and circumspection, and so to act with calm deliberation becoming men who are contending for their liberties upon the solid principles of that happy Constitution which is the birthright and boast of Englishmen and the envy and admiration of all the world." He counsels them to await the result of the proceedings of the Continental Congress with patience and discretion, and protests against the resignation of militia commissions. Finally, he hopes that they will treat with respect his honest zeal, which is devoted to the honor of the Corps and to the happiness and welfare of his country, in whose just defence he would be amongst its foremost advocates.

Soon afterwards a deputation waited upon Van Cortlandt and announced that they had brought proposals from Congress that he should join in converting his pearl ash works into nitre works, which, they contended, would yield him an "amazing profit." Another deputation came with an offer of a commission of Colonel in the American army and speedy promotion. Both these offers were treated by him "with contempt." Thereupon, "what could not be effected by fair means the Revolutionary party were determined to accomplish by oppression." He was served with a citation to answer charges of offences against Congressional measures. To these charges he appeared in person in the crowded county hall and pleaded guilty, with this observation that the prospect of losing his life and property would never induce him to draw his sword against his Sovereign and no tortures would ever influence him to change his principles. He was acquitted. Philip Van Cortlandt now left New Jersey for Pennsylvania and Maryland. Upon returning he found the Rebellion more pronounced and the country unsafe for anyone unless clothed in "the uniform of Rebellion." He refused repeatedly to bear arms for the Americans and was fined several times and deprived of his arms. (A. O. 12:22, ff. 96-113).

In a letter from him, dated from Hanover, New Jersey, December 7, 1775, to his friend, the Rev. Isaac Wilkins, D. D., of New York, then in London, he said:

"Gracious heavens, to what a situation are we reduced—not many months ago did we boast of our happy condition in enjoying every earthly felicity in this New World that even the most extravagant fancy could suggest—the tree of peace seemed to have taken deep root in our fertile soil—our commerce extending to every known part of the habitable globe, furnishing us with all the necessarys, nay luxurys, of life—the Sciences were introduced, respected and courted—in short nothing seemed wanting to conspire to make us a flourishing, great and happy people, but our own knowledge of it and gratitude to all bountiful heaven for our happy situation—how alas! is the scene changed. . . . ." (A. O. 13:54).

Philip Van Cortlandt was appointed Major of the 3rd New Jersey Volunteers, December 11, 1776, and acting Brigade-Major in 1777. On the voyage to England his ship was forced by severe weather to land him and his wife and nine children at Madeira, after a voyage of three months, during which most of his personal property was lost or damaged. The British Government sent £100 through his attorney to relieve his distress there and to purchase necessaries. (A. O. 13:112; A. O. 12:100, f. 84; A. O. 12:102, f. 77; Ind.: 5604-5-6; Stryker, op. cit.). He claimed £7,522 and was allowed £1,500. (A. O. 12:109).

His personal estate in Morris county, New Jersey, was sold by the State for £156. 5s. 6d. in Continental money on June 8, 1778, and his confiscated real property for £3,293. 1s. 6d. on March 31, 1779. (A. O. 13:83).

He married, August 4, 1762, Catherine, daughter of Jacob Ogden, who was baptized on November 25, 1746, by the Rev. John Millner, and appears to have had 23 children, of whom ten died young. He died, May 1, 1814, aged 74, at Hailsham, England, where he was Barrack Master, leaving a wife and ten children. His widow was living at St. Helier's in the Island of Jersey in 1816 and was in possession of the family Bible.

She was granted Loyalist pensions of £130 and £144 until her death in 1828 in England. (W. O. 40:26; "Gentleman's Mag.," Vol. 84, p. 624). His two unmarried daughters, Sarah Ogden and Charlotte, were put on the Compassionate Fund at £6 each in 1817. (W. O. 25:3083).

According to the will of Major Van Cortlandt (he is described as "Colonel" in the obituary notice in the "Gentleman's Magazine"), dated April 30, 1814, at Hailsham, and proved July 4, 1814, he left the whole of his property in New York and Nova Scotia—"the wreck of his fortune" as he calls it—to his wife, Catherine. (Bridport, 446).

The sons of this conspicuous Loyalist were as follows: (1) Philip, born in 1766; joined the Provincial Loyalists at the age of 13 and was an Ensign in his father's Battalion of the New Jersey Volunteers. (Ind.: 5605-6). He was appointed, July 3, 1813, Deputy Barrackmaster-General in Lower Canada and died October 3, 1833. He married Mary Addison. (2) Stephen, twin brother of Philip. (3) Jacob Ogden, who was killed in Spain in 1811 on active service with his Regiment, the 23rd Foot (Royal Welsh Fusiliers), of which he was senior Captain. His wife was a daughter of the Rev. Dr. Warrington, of Wrexham, North Wales. (4) Henry Clinton (named after the British Commander-in-Chief in America), who was Major in the 31st Regiment. (5) Arthur Auchmuty, Captain in the 45th Regiment, who died in India.

Of his daughters Mary Ricketts married John M. Anderson; the twins, Elizabeth and Catherine, married (supposed) William Taylor (q. v.) and Dr. William Gourlay, respectively; Margaret Hughes married O. Elliott Elliott, of Binfield Park; and Gertrude was the wife of Vice-Admiral Sir Edward Buller, Bart.

This Loyalist must not be confused with his kinsmen, General Philip Van Cortlandt, of the 2nd New York Continental Regiment (American) and Colonel Philip Van Cortlandt, of Essex County, New Jersey, who was a member of the Provincial Congress of New Jersey and who commanded a Battalion in the American forces in the Battle of Long Island.

ABRAHAM VANDERBECK

A farmer, of Hackensack, New Jersey, born in America and served as Sergeant in the 3rd New Jersey Volunteers. His wife's name was Hannah. He settled at Fredericton in New Brunswick and was alive there in 1787. Some of his property was in possession of his father, Abraham, in the United States in 1787. (A. O. 13:19; A. O. 12:16, ff. 199-203; A. O. 12:63, f. 97; "Acadiensis," VII: 141). £15 was allowed him from his claim of £562. (A. O. 12:109).

WILLIAM VAN DUMONT (Lieutenant)

A Lieutenant in the 2nd New Jersey Volunteers from December 19, 1776, and in the 1st from July 25, 1781. He was born in America about 1752 and was on half-pay until 1827. (Ind.: 5605-6).

The name also appears as Van Dumond.

JOHN VANDYKE (Major)

The eldest son of John and Margaret Vandyke, of Harlingen, Somerset county, New Jersey, and was born at that place April 17, 1747. He was married, November 17, 1761, to his first cousin, Rebecca, daughter of Roeloff Van Dyke (afterwards a member of the Continental Congress) and his wife, Catherine Emans.

Major John Vandyke lived at or near Rocky Hill, N. J., and had considerable landed property there, much of which he farmed himself. In his native county he was a Justice of the Peace and a Judge of the Inferior Court. Like many other adventurous young Americans, he took an active part in the War against the French in the American Colonies and appears to have attained the rank of Colonel before being transferred to the Royal Navy. Of the particular services and rank of John Vandyke in the navy no records have so far been found.

In opposition to the views and wishes of his father and other members of his family he threw in his lot with the British at the outbreak of the Revolutionary War and declined the command of a Regiment in the American service. In December,

1776, he was taken prisoner and sent to General Washington as "a malicious and active Tory," but was exchanged some time later. In March, 1778, he was appointed Lieutenant-Colonel Commandant of the West Jersey Volunteers, a Corps which was disbanded later in the same year, and he and other officers were seconded or attached to other Loyalist Regiments. Vandyke himself went South with the 17th Foot as a volunteer and served there in several campaigns.

His papers in A. O. 13:112 include:

An affidavit of Colonel William McDonald, late of Somerset county, and Captain William Stewart (q. v.), to their knowledge of his property, dated New York, September 6, 1783.

A letter from the Deputy Adjutant-General, March 21, 1778, ordering him to repair to Billingsport, to take command of the Jersey Volunteers, who were to embark on the following day for that Fort under Major de Veber. Vandyke is here described as "late Captain in the Queen's Rangers."

A copy of the "Newport Mercury," R. I., July 21, 1781, containing an account of the siege of Pensacola. The besieged consisted of 1,051 men, including 595 seamen, and 62 seamen at The Clifts. The Spaniards were 23,200 strong, including seamen, and had 50 pieces of brass cannon and other guns, 11 Spanish and 4 French ships of the line, 4 Spanish and 4 French frigates, and other vessels. The British losses during nine weeks of the siege were: Killed, Lieutenant Carrol, of the 16th Foot; Lieutenant Pinhorn, of Loyal Foresters; Ensign Ussall, of the Waldeckers; 6 sergeants, 6 corporals, 1 drummer, 45 privates, 2 midshipmen and 28 seamen. Major Francis Kearny (q. v.) was wounded in this siege.

Also a certificate of Colonel John W. Watson that John Vandyke was a true Loyalist and a good soldier during his service with the 17th Foot in the South, and several certificates from Lord Cornwallis, Sir William Howe and others. The Commissioners reported that he was distinguished for his uniform conduct and services. (A. O. 12:100, f. 360).

At the Peace Vandyke accompanied the Loyalist refugees into exile in Nova Scotia. Here he remained for a while and, later, returned to the old homestead at Harlingen, where he died on June 23, 1811, leaving several children. He received £1,189 as compensation for the loss of his property, from his claim of £1,341. 7s. (A. O. 12:109; A. O. 12:13, ff. 127-334; Ind.: 5,605; Sabine; "Loyalists' Claims," pp. 189-190; Ex. inform. Dr. William B. Aitken, his great-grandson). During his later life he had the title of "Major," but why does not appear in the English records.

The other members of the Vandyke (Van Dyke) family fought on the American side in the Revolution. His father, a private in the American army, died at the Battle of Monmouth.

JAMES VAN EMBURGH

He was born in America and was a farmer at New Barbadoes Neck in Bergen county, New Jersey. He joined the British in November, 1776, and served as a boatman until March, 1780, and until the end of the War as a sawyer in the British lines. For two years of this time he acted as a spy. His property in Bergen county was forfeited in 1778.

There is a valuation of his real estate by James Walls and Joseph Kingsland, formerly farmers, and probably Loyalists, in Essex county, New Jersey, dated New York, July, 1783; and also an affidavit of his brother, Adoniah Van Emburgh, and Richard Ackerman, both shoemakers, formerly of New Jersey, but in March, 1786, at Shelburne in Nova Scotia, declaring their knowledge of James Van Emburgh's property and to his ownership of 1/12 part of a copper mine. (A. O. 13:19). He was living on the River Tusket in Shelburne county, Nova Scotia, in 1786. (A. O. 12:16, ff. 1-7; A. O. 12:63, f. 56). The sum of £160 was allowed to him from his claim of £573. 17s. (A. O. 12:109).

LAWRENCE VAN HORN

He was a native of New Jersey, resident in the English Neighborhood in Bergen county, as a miller and farmer. He inherited land in Hackensack from his grandfather, Cornelius Christiansen. His property was forfeited in 1778. In 1788 he was living near Annapolis, Nova Scotia. There is an account of his estate in New Jersey in A. O. 13:19. He claimed £2,060 and was allowed £1,045. (A. O. 12:109; A. O. 12:16, ff. 49-53; A. O. 12:63, f. 135).

CHRINEYONCE VAN MATER

He was born in New Jersey, being the son of Joseph and Sarah R. (Schenck) Van Mater, and was a farmer in Middletown, Monmouth county, New Jersey, on land wholly or in part inherited from his (or her) grandfather, Ruloff Schenck; he is also said to have owned Taylor's Mills in the same county. He enlisted in the British army in 1776 and, in consequence of this act of loyalty, he was attainted in 1777 and his property confiscated in 1779. The family of Van Mater were regarded as the best farmers in New Jersey, according to the evidence of a Loyalist, one John Taylor.

In A. O. 13:19 is a copy of bonds due to him and to Ruloff Van Mater, with particulars of his property, and an affidavit to his loyalty from Colonel George Taylor (q. v.), dated from New York in September, 1783. The substantial sum of £1,109 was awarded to him for the loss of his property, from his claim of £2,411. (A. O. 12:109; A. O. 13:82; A. O. 12:15, ff. 340-8; A. O. 12:63, f. 44; Beekman's "Early Dutch Settlers of Monmouth," p. 73 et seq).

He was probably at St. John, New Brunswick, in 1786.

DANIEL VAN MATER

A son of Gysbert Van Mater and Micha (Hendrickson) Van Mater. The father died in 1773 and his will is dated May 29, 1770. Daniel was a storekeeper and farmer in Freehold, and was noted for having the first stud of horses in New Jersey. He went within the British lines in January, 1777, enlisting under Col. Skinner in the "New Jersey Royal Volunteers." His property in Monmouth county was confiscated in 1779.

He died in exile in England on October 4, 1786, leaving an only son and heir, Gilbert Van Mater (q. v.). His three daughters had married prosperous Loyalists, who became citizens of the United States. They were Caty, wife of Henry

Disborough; Sarah, wife of Benjamin Van Mater; and Micah, wife of Daniel Polhemus.

Daniel Van Mater had provided the eldest daughter with a dowry of £250 on her marriage and the other daughters with £150 each, besides which they were presented with "dots" by their mother.

His three brothers, Hendrick (q. v.), Joseph and John, were Loyalists, as were others, but by no means all, of the members of the Van Mater family in New Jersey.

In A. O. 13:112 are several deeds, bonds and papers concerning his property, and a deed of 1771 of property bought by him from Benjamin Van Cleave (Cleaf), of Freehold, a copy of whose will (September 26, 1747) is with this deed. The substantial value of Daniel Van Mater's real estate is confirmed by the award of £2,550 as compensation from his claim of £3,158. (A. O. 12:109). His pension was £40. (A. O. 12:100, f. 301; A. O. 12:14, ff. 301-9; Beekman's "Early Dutch Settlers of Monmouth Co.," p. 73 et seq.; see Samuel Osborne).

GILBERT VAN MATER

Born in 1762 in Monmouth county, New Jersey, he was the only son of Daniel Van Mater (q. v.) and joined the British early in the Rebellion. He arrived in England in 1787, leaving his wife and two children in Long Island, New York, and was granted a Loyalist pension of £36, which was reduced to £20 in 1789, but continued until 1831. (T. 50:11; T. 50:28; A. O. 12:102, f. 78).

HENDRICK VAN MATER

A brother to Daniel Van Mater (q. v.), and a volunteer early, who took six prisoners in one day. He was taken prisoner with his brother, John, at the beginning of the Rebellion and kept in gaol for six months on the frontiers of Maryland, 250 miles from home.

His farm of 450 acres, on the main road from Philadelphia to Shrewsbury, New Jersey, was devised equally between him and his two brothers, John and Joseph, by their father, Gysbert Van Mater, who died in 1773. With his brother, John, Hendrick was a partner in another farm of 230 acres. Their remarkable stud of horses comprised nine head of breeding mares, the stallion "King Herod," which was confiscated and sold by the State of New Jersey for £1,000 currency, and the stallion "Dove." (A. O. 12:14, ff. 310-319).

The personal estate of Hendrick Van Mater was sold for £1,150, the real property in Freehold for £2,725, and the real in Shrewsbury for £3,000, doubtless in New Jersey currency. The forfeiture was in 1779. For the loss of this confiscated property he was awarded £1,828 from his claim of £3,158 and a pension of £30. (A. O. 12:109; A. O. 12:100, f. 355; see Samuel Osborne).

GABRIEL VAN NORDEN

Born in America, he derived his income from his estate in Bergen county, New Jersey. His wife was the only daughter of Stephen Westervelt, who died in 1768. For his loyalty he suffered much imprisonment. Colonel Abraham Van Buskirk (q. v.) testified to his loyalty and to the fact that he was to have had a commission in the New Jersey Volunteers, but declined it in order to support his family. His estate in Bergen county was sequestered in 1779, name being then spelled "Vanorder." There is an account of this confiscated estate in London records. He was a refugee on the River Tusket in Nova Scotia in 1786. (A. O. 13:19; A. O. 12:15, ff. 237-242; A. O. 12:63, f. 28; Bergen Co. Records).

The sum of £700 was allowed to him from his claim of £843. 17s. (A. O. 12:109).

His son, John, was an Ensign in the 3rd New Jersey Volunteers. He settled in Nova Scotia, where he was an instructor at Kings College; he removed later to Bermuda and died there. (Sabine; Stryker).

CHRISTOPHER VOUGHT

He was born in America and lived in Lebanon township, or Kingwood, Hunterdon county, New Jersey. He also owned a plantation of 2,000 acres, with three houses, in Albany county, New York, which he bought on May 19, 1770, from Captain

John Leake of New York, and which was valued at £1,123. 10s. sterling. Three of his family were prisoners of the Americans. He settled at Parrsborough, Nova Scotia, after the War. (A. O. 12:15, ff. 192-9).

He and his son, John (infra), claimed £3,371 and were allowed £1,225 and £496 respectively. (A. O. 12:109).

JOHN VOUGHT (Captain)

A son of the above Christopher Vought, and he resided in Monmouth county, New Jersey, before the War. He raised a Company of Loyalists in New Jersey and was given a commission as Lieutenant in the 2nd New Jersey Volunteers in December, 1776, being promoted Captain in July, 1778. Memorials and particulars of the Vought property (father and son) are in A. O. 13:19.

John Vought was living at Parrsborough, Nova Scotia, on half-pay in 1786. (A. O. 12:63, f. 24).

PETER and JOHN VROOM

These brothers were considerable farmers in New Jersey, residing in Middlesex county. Peter was imprisoned in Somerville jail; was at Clements, Annapolis, Nova Scotia, in 1786, while John was at Annapolis. (A. O. 13:21; 2 Sabine 591).

JOHN WADDINGTON (Quartermaster)

He purchased his commission as Quartermaster in the 1st New Jersey Volunteers for 140 guineas. His widow, Jane, a native of Pennsylvania, petitioned, on November 18, 1782, shortly after his death, that his successor might be allowed to purchase this commission, as she was in distressed circumstances in New York, with three young children. She was put on the pension list. (Ind.: 8229). His estate in Sussex county, N. J., was sequestered.

ARTHUR WADMAN (Captain)

He is described as an Irishman who was appointed Lieutenant in the 26th Foot, then on service at New Brunswick, New Jersey, on November 29, 1760. Here he was married at Christ Church, March 11, 1769, to Susannah, daughter of Bernardus LaGrange (q. v.), and sister of the wives of the two Loyalists, Lieutenant-Colonel Edward Vaughan Dongan (q. v.) and Dr. Henry Dougan (q. v.). He bought a house and lot in Main street, New Brunswick, where he owned a schooner and a pleasure boat.

After many hardships and exile from home and family he was taken prisoner on Lake George on May 10, 1775, on the way to join his company at Ticonderoga, and subsequently was allowed to return home on parole. "Every art and persuasion, and even threats of violence, were used to entice him from his duty and allegiance to his King and country, and any rank which he might desire in the American army was offered to him. Having failed to seduce him from his allegiance he was dragged from his wife and family and banished into the back country, where he suffered incredible hardships and every indignity that revenge or malice could suggest. Meanwhile, his wife and six small children were allowed by the 'Rebels' the use of only one bed in an empty room during his absence in supposed retaliation of his refusal to accept the commands offered to Captain Wadman in the American army."

In bad health Captain Wadman was ordered to England on the recruiting service in 1778 and returned with drafts in nine months. His health continued bad in America and, in 1780, he sold his commission for £18,000 in the 26th Foot and returned to England, after a long service of thirty years in the army, 24 of which were spent in this Regiment.

Captain Wadman lived in England on his private property and a pension, with his wife and six children. His wife survived him and was granted a pension. His claim of £819 was met by a grant of £240. (T. 50:28; A. O. 12:109; A. O. 12:14, ff. 337-343; A. O. 12:101, f. 18).

ROBERT WANNAMAKER

He was of Bergen county, New Jersey, who died a prisoner of war as one of the New Jersey Volunteers in the jail at Philadelphia in 1780, leaving a wife, Elizabeth (born in New Jersey), afterwards an exile at Maugerville, New Brunswick, who later married John Post, a former Sergeant in the New

Jersey Volunteers. (A. O. 13:17; A. O. 12:16, ff. 306-9; A. O. 13:63, f. 95).

THOMAS WARD (Captain)

He was of Newark, New Jersey, but seems later to have resided in Orange county, New York. He is said to have been in the American army at first, deserting to the British army in 1777 at New York, and was engaged frequently on secret intelligence. In 1780 he was appointed Captain of a company of Loyalist refugees without pay and was in command of the Block House on the New Jersey side of the North river, seven miles above Bergen, where, according to Colonel Dundas, he made "a gallant and miraculous defence, which astonished the whole army," at a date not mentioned. His property in Essex county, New Jersey, said to have been worth £1,000, was confiscated and sold.

The Commissioners paid warm tribute to the resolute loyalty to Thomas Ward, supported by eulogistic certificates from Sir Henry Clinton, Commander-in-Chief, the Rev. Charles Inglis (q. v.) and Captain Cunningham. They said he had well earned by his gallantry the grant of 500 acres of land in Nova Scotia, where he settled with his wife and a child. To this free grant was added a pension of £60, "which will support him very comfortably." (A. O. 13:67; A. O. 12:101, f. 171).

UZAL WARD

He was born in New Jersey and resided on his own property in Newark, where he had built a dock and was the owner of stone quarries, and where he carried on the trade of a stonecutter and farmer. He was one of many who had signed an "Association" to support the American cause before joining the British army in 1776. His grandfather, Samuel Ward, from whom he inherited property, died about 1761. His mother was alive in Newark in 1786, as was his uncle, Ebenezer, somewhere in New Jersey. His wife died in 1780; he was her second husband. (A. O. 12:15, ff. 63-73; A. O. 12:63, f. 7; "Ontario Archives," pp. 529-533, 560).

This Loyalist was awarded £942 from his claim of £1,450. 2s. (A. O. 12:109), his property in Essex county, N. J., having been confiscated in 1778. Witnesses expressed their astonishment at his being allowed to remain in New Jersey after the War.

The will of one Samuel Ward, of Newark, dated 1759, mentions his son Ebenezer and his grandson, Uzal Ward. One Uzal Ward, probably the same, was married in November 17, 1746, to Martha Johnson.

JOHN WARDELL

A son of Joshua Wardell (whose will was dated October 6, 1768), and he lived at Shrewsbury, New Jersey, where his house was "the best in the town." He was a Judge of the Court of Common Pleas in his native county of Monmouth. From the dawn of the Rebellion he opposed the views of the "malcontents" and was one of the promoters of and "the first to sign the protest against Independence." He was arrested in November, 1776, on suspicion of recruiting men for the British army and for his loyalty, and was sent to prison in Philadelphia for ten days. Upon returning home he rendered himself obnoxious by receiving the submission of the inhabitants in response to the proclamation of General Sir William Howe. Later he joined the British army in New York, and upon the evacuation of that city by the British he returned to New Jersey to recover his property in accordance with the terms of the treaty, but was immediately arrested and banished, leaving his wife behind with his relatives at Shrewsbury. He had, however, again returned to Monmouth county in or before 1787, as reported by John Anstey, the British investigator into the claims of New Jersey Loyalists. (A. O. 12:85). His property in Monmouth county was confiscated in 1779.

John Wardell was granted £1,570 from his claim of £2,690 and a pension of £40. (A. O. 12:109; A. O. 12:14, ff. 129-137; A. O. 12:101, f. 253).

RICHARD WARE

He was a New Jersey Loyalist, who was allowed £335 from his claim of £2,150 for the loss of his confiscated property. (A. O. 12:109).

FREDERICK WEISER (Lieutenant)

He was born in America and was a tanner at New Brunswick, New Jersey, where he was employed by Lord Cornwallis in establishing a city guard during the War. On November 16, 1777, he was appointed Lieutenant in a Company of volunteers, and on July 1, 1783, Lieutenant of a Company of refugees going to Nova Scotia. He was living at Shelburne in that Province in 1786. (A. O. 12:15, ff. 249-253; A. O. 12:63, f. 30). From his claim of £185. 8s. he was allowed £160. (A. O. 12:109).

JOHN WHEELER

A farmer, of Newark, New Jersey, went into exile in the Province of New Brunswick, where he was living in 1787. (A. O. 12:16, ff. 291-4; A. O. 12:63, f. 106). His property in Essex county, N. J., was forfeited in 1778. His compensation amounted to £90 from his claim of £709. (A. O. 12:109).

DAVID WHITE

He was formerly a planter in the Island of Jamaica before settling (in 1774) in Somerset county, New Jersey, where he married, May 9, 1775, Elizabeth Gould Tucker, by whom he got a fortune of £2,000, which was one-third of the estate of a Mrs. Gould of Exeter (presumably in England), whose other legatees were Mrs. Tucker of Trenton, New Jersey, and Mrs. Murgatroyd, of Philadelphia. The guardian of his wife was William Hawker, of Pauncefote Lodge in Somersetshire, England.

David White was offered a commission of Lieutenant-Colonel in the American army by General Dickinson, but the offer was rejected, despite the inducements held out by his family connections, including his wife's uncle, Samuel Tucker, of Trenton, "a Rebel." He claims to have been the first man in Trenton to declare for the British army when it entered that town on December 8, 1776. For spying and attempting to recruit men for the British he was captured on January 16, 1777, and sent to Washington's camp at Morristown, but was released on parole. Later in the year he went to New York, and from thence he sailed in December, 1777, to his plantation in Jamaica. (This statement is qualified in his evidence, where he stated that he sailed from Bristol in England, in 1779 or 1780, to his (mortgaged) plantation). He had failed to raise the 500 men for which he had been promised a commission as Lieutenant-Colonel in the British forces.

White valued his property, which included a plantation of 600 acres, bought from Cornelius Low with his wife's money, at £5,900. 17.6. sterling, or £9,834. 15s., in currency. The deeds of the plantation were left with Thomas Skelton (q. v.), a doubtful Loyalist and a suspicious character, who sent them to his (Skelton's) father-in-law, Colonel Lowrey.

The Commissioners reported on David White's claim that he had grossly prevaricated and they disallowed the claim. ("Loyalists' Claims," pp. 6-7. A. O. 12:109; A. O. 12:13, ff. 14-25).

AMOS WILLIAMS

He was born in Newark, New Jersey, eldest son of Nathaniel Williams, of that place, who had to abandon his considerable estate and flee for safety to New York, where he died in 1781, "as loyal a man as ever breathed." Amos was at Shelburne in Nova Scotia in 1786, while three of his brothers were with their mother in New Jersey, in possession of a part of his father's property. Another brother, James, a Loyalist, was in New York in 1786, but about to sail for Nova Scotia. (A. O. 12:15, ff. 21-8; A. O. 12:63, f. 3). He was granted £425 from his claim of £1,164. 7s. (A. O. 12:109).

JOSEPH WILLIAMS

He lived in Shrewsbury, New Jersey, on property left to him by his father, a Quaker, who died about 1768, and he was born in New Jersey. He bore arms in the New Jersey Volunteers and, later, in the Associated Loyalists, commanded by Captain Richard Lippincott (q. v.).

His eldest brother, James, was living in New Jersey after the War on the estate of another brother, Obadiah, a Loyalist, who is said to have died from the effects of imprisonment in the Freehold, N. J., jail. Another brother, John, was killed in the British lines by enemy shot. Joseph's estate in Monmouth county, N. J., was forfeited as late as 1784. He appears to have settled at Beaver Harbor, New Brunswick, and was awarded £147 from his claim of £620. (A. O. 12:16, ff. 372-6; A. O. 12:63, f. 117; A. O. 12:109; "Ontario Archives," pp. 317-8).

JOHN WILLIS (Lieutenant)

Born in America about 1747, he resided in Essex county, New Jersey. He was Lieutenant in the 2nd and 3rd New Jersey Volunteers, having been promoted from Ensign in the 3rd. He served from 1776 to 1783, and at the Peace settled, with other officers of this Regiment, on his grant of land in the Province of New Brunswick, where he died at Miramichi on January 11, 1819, leaving a widow, who lived afterwards at Fredericton. (W. O. 42:W15; Ind.: 5605-6; "N. Bruns. (Can.) Hist. Soc. Coll.," No. 5). His estate in New Jersey was confiscated in February, 1779. (Essex Co. Records).

MALCOLM WILMOT (Lieutenant)

He was born in Rhode Island and, at a very early age, was appointed Ensign in the 3rd New Jersey Volunteers, Feb., 1783. From 1793, the year of the declaration of War by France against England, he served as Lieutenant in the King's New Brunswick Regiment, with other former officers of the New Jersey Volunteers, and while on duty he married a daughter of John Bentley, a grantee of St. John. His father may have been Lemuel Wilmot, born in America, who was Captain in the Loyal American Regiment.

Some years before his death, on September 7, 1859, he was settled as a merchant and shipowner at the bend of Petitcodiac in Westmorland county, New Brunswick. (Ind.: 5605-6; "Colls. of N. Brunswick Hist. Soc.," I: 51).

JOHN WILSON

A farmer at Piscataway, Middlesex county, New Jersey, who was born in America and inherited property by the will of his father, John Wilson, who died in 1775. He was at

Miramichi in New Brunswick in 1787. From his claim of £629. 17s. he was allowed £331. (A. O. 12:16, ff. 187-192; A. O. 12:63, f. 115; A. O. 12:109).

SAMUEL RICHARD WILSON

He was an officer on half-pay who went to America in 1777 and, in November of that year, was appointed to a Corps raised in Philadelphia (A. O. 13:100), doubtless the Roman Catholic Volunteers, commanded by Colonel Alfred Clifton, and raised on conditions suggested by that officer and approved by General Sir William Howe on October 7, 1777. Wilson's commission is dated November 26. From this Corps he was transferred in 1779 to the 2nd New Jersey Volunteers, and, on May 10, 1781, to the Royal Garrison Battalion. (Raymond; Stryker).

THOMAS WOODRUFF (Captain)

Apparently a pretended Loyalist. John Anstey in his report states that if this was the man of the same name, of Elizabethtown, his claim for compensation was fraudulent, having been in the American service as Commissary almost the whole War. (A. O. 12:85). The New Jersey records show he was in the War on the American side from Essex county. He was captured by the British at Elizabethtown in January, 1780. (Stryker; "N. J. Archives," Second Series, Vol. 4, p. 153).

ANTHONY WOODWARD

A Quaker, of Monmouth county, New Jersey, who was obliged to abandon his property because of his loyalty. He joined the British army in 1776. He was declared guilty of high treason by the State of New Jersey and his property confiscated in 1779. His losses included several plantations, valued at £5,068 currency, equal to £3,040. 16s. in sterling. A deposition to the truth of his statements regarding his property was made by Henry Edward Knox, Samuel Woodward and Richard Robbins. (A. O. 13:82).

There were two Loyalists of this name (John Anstey's report in A. O. 12:85; Sabine).

JESSE WOODWARD

A Quaker, of Upper Freehold township, Monmouth county, New Jersey, who joined the British force at Trenton. He was a refugee at Beaver Harbor, New Brunswick, in 1783 and later. (A. O. 13:21). According to Sabine he died at St. John; his sons were Jesse, a Loyalist, and John, an Ensign in the 1st New Jersey Volunteers.

JOHN WOODWARD (Ensign)

He was of Monmouth county, New Jersey, of the same family as Jesse Woodward (q. v.), and was American-born, of Quaker parentage. He was Ensign in the 1st New Jersey Volunteers from August 14, 1781, when his age was about 35, and was on half-pay until December, 1816, though Stryker and Sabine record his death as 1805, in the Province of New Brunswick, and Sabine says his family returned to New Jersey. (Ind.: 5605-6; Stryker; Sabine).

ROBERT WOODWARD (Ensign)

He was born in America, probably in New Jersey, about 1756, and served as Ensign in the 3rd New Jersey Volunteers from December 19, 1781, though, according to the records he had been in the Loyalist forces for a year previously. He was on half-pay until 1808. (Ind.: 5605-6).

SUSANNAH WOOLRIDGE

The daughter of one Kelly, a considerable merchant in New Jersey, who died in England about 1773, leaving her over £4,000 and property to her two brothers, both of whom were in the West Indies in 1783, the eldest being a Captain in the 60th Regiment, formerly known as the Royal American Regiment. She was married to one Woolridge in 1771 and had five children. (A. O. 12:99, f. 37). She was granted a Loyalist pension of £60 from 1783 to about 1811. (T. 50:7; T. 50:22).

A William Kelley rose from Ensign in the above Regiment in 1769 to Captain in 1775. He was on service with the 2nd battalion in Jamaica in 1783, and had retired in 1786. (Army Lists).

BENJAMIN WORTH

Believed to be a New Jersey Loyalist, he appears to have found refuge in Nova Scotia after the War. He was allowed £440 from his claim of £523. 3s. (A. O. 12:63, f. 142; A. O. 12:109). He had resided in Bernards township, Somerset county.

WILLIAM WRIGHT

He was born in New Jersey and, in 1783, was given a commission as Captain of militia. He was granted 200 acres of land in the Province of New Brunswick, part of which had been cultivated by him in 1790. (A. O. 12:63, f. 112; A. O. 12:102, f. 229). £120 was awarded to him from his claim of £733. 10s. (A. O. 12:109).

Another Loyalist of this name was born in New York Province and removed early in the Revolution to Chatham, New Jersey. (A. O. 12:16, ff. 95-100).

Appendixes

I. RESIDENCES OF LOYALISTS NOT PREVIOUSLY GIVEN

II. GRENADIER COMPANY IN 1776

III. ADDITIONAL NEW JERSEY LOYALISTS

Appendix I

The following Loyalists named in the main text, but whose residences were not ascertained at the time of publication, appear to have been located in the counties in New Jersey named below, according to the references given herewith. These references are explained in Appendix III.

Anderson, Peter (Major), Sussex county. (2 N. E. 435).

Beers, Joseph (Ensign), Sussex county. (2 N. E. 434).

Campbell, Robert, Middlesex county. (3 N. E. 63).

Cooke, Robert (Major), Burlington county. (2 N. E. 543).

Cyphers, George (Adjutant), Hunterdon county. (3 N. E. 68).

Haggerty, Patrick (Captain), Sussex county. (3 N. E. 165).

Hartshorne, Robert and Ezekial, Monmouth county (so probably at Shrewsbury). (M. C. S. 36).

Hutchinson, William, Sussex county. (N. J. R. C. 47).

Lee, Joseph (Captain), Hunterdon county. (3 N. E. 68).

Leonard, Samuel (Captain), Monmouth county. (4 N. E. 249).

Okerson, Thomas (Lieutenant), Burlington county. (M. P. C. 474, 510).

Osborne, Samuel, Freehold. (3 N. E. 93).

Ryerson, Samuel (Lieut.), Morris county. (3 N. E. 92; 4 N. E. 470).

Stretch, Samuel, Cumberland county. (2 N. E. 496).

Thompson, John (Lieutenant), Middlesex county. (3 N. E. 90, 322).

Appendix II

The following is a list of gentlemen belonging to the Grenadier Company [of American militia] in New Jersey who joined the British army in 1776:

Captains: John Taylor, Samuel Leonard, John Longstreet and John Throckmorton.

Lieutenant: John Thompson, noted as in the United States, after the War.

Ensign: Lewis Thompson, noted as in the United States, after the War.

William Taylor.
Robert Cooke.
Daniel and Henry Van Mater.
Chry. Van Mater.
Samuel Osborne.
John Hankinson } died on Staten Island
Israel Button
Shore Stevenson. Died at Shelburne, Nova Scotia.
Stephen West. Murdered on coming into the British lines.
Timothy Scobey. Taken prisoner, condemned to be hanged, but pardoned through the interest of friends.
James Kearney } Remained behind at the evacuation of New York by the British in 1783.
John Bowne

The above document is in the handwriting of and with the papers of William Taylor (q. v.) in A. O. 13:112.

Appendix III

ADDITIONAL NEW JERSEY LOYALISTS

BY A. VAN DOREN HONEYMAN, PLAINFIELD, N. J.

In the preparation of this Appendix it is to be noted that only such names are included as to whom some actual published reference or references can be given, with a few exceptions. The original records by magistrates and Courts in Revolutionary days would add many more names and facts, but they are totally missing in several counties, and in other counties are difficult of access.

Necessarily the names in this and in the preceding main text go far from completing a record of those Jerseymen who fought on the British side, or whose pronounced sympathies and conduct classified them as Loyalists.

The authorities for the following list are:
1. The "Minutes of the Provincial Congress and the Council of Safety of the State of New Jersey, 1775-'76," published in 1879. 2. The "Minutes of the Council of Safety of the State of New Jersey, 1777-'78," published in 1872. 3. Advertisements of inquisitions, judgments, public sales of forfeited estates, etc., originally published in the "New Jersey Gazette" at Trenton, and republished in the Second Series of "New Jersey Archives," Vols. 1 to 5. 4. Sabine's "Loyalists of the American Revolution," 2 volumes, Edition of 1864. 5. "Collections of the New Brunswick Historical Society," No. 5 (1904), being of that Society located at Saint John, Province of New Brunswick. 6. Stryker's "New Jersey Volunteers (Loyalists)," privately published, 1887. 7. "New York Genealogical and Biographical Record," Vols. 35-40. 8. "New Jersey Revolutionary Correspondence," published in 1848. 9. A few other book sources stated under certain names listed below. 10. Notes on forfeited estates or fines (evidently not full) in Hunterdon, Middlesex, Monmouth and Salem counties, sent us by the courtesy of the County Clerks of Monmouth and Salem, and by Mr. Hiram E. Deats and Mr. William H. Bene-

dict of Hunterdon and Middlesex counties. There have also been used searches by the late Mr. William Nelson in Essex and Bergen records.

Where the Sabine work is mentioned as a reference, in many cases much more may be found given in that work than appears in the present list, as what follows herein is intended to be as tersely abstracted as possible.

As to the proceedings before the Committee of Safety, as hundreds of persons were cited to appear and take oaths of allegiance to the American government, and did so, their names are omitted unless they later proved to have transferred their allegiance to the British. When they refused allegiance to the United States, this fact alone proved them to be Loyalists.

The reader may be cautioned as to the stated county references. Generally they must be correct, but, owing to the incursions of the British forces in various counties, it was permitted, at times, for inquisitions to be had in, and Loyalists to be committed to jail in, counties other than those in which defendants resided. The counties named herein will be therefore, occasionally, no real clue to actual residences; it is otherwise in case of towns or townships.

Except where forfeitures of real estate belonging to women were advertised, names of women Loyalists are not included. Naturally, wives and daughters of Loyalists must generally have been such also.

When the Peace came, thousands of Loyalists went to Nova Scotia or the Province of New Brunswick. In some of the records below no more is known to the compiler of the activities of the person than that they went to these places of refuge, most of them to remain there as valuable citizens; a few, however, to return and to die in New Jersey.

There were a large number of Acts passed by the Legislature between 1776 and the Peace concerning Loyalists and their estates. It is unnecessary to detail them here, except to say that, in 1776 oaths of abjuration of allegiance to Great Britain and of true faith and allegiance to the new Government of the State were prescribed, and persons suspected of disaffection and disloyalty were to be summoned by two Justices of the Peace and the oaths tendered, and, if refused, they were to be bound over to the next Court of General Quarter Sessions, and, if again refusing, to be fined or imprisoned. Later, the Committee of Safety could require bail and commit those refusing oaths to imprisonment. At the same time "traitors and disaffected persons" were to have their personal estate seized and held by appointed Commissioners in each county (not to be sold except in danger of destruction by the enemy) ; and by a law of April 18, 1778, such Commissioners were to take charge of and lease the real estate of Loyalists, and make returns to Justices of the Peace, who would summon juries of inquisition of 24 men, of whom 12 could reach a verdict. But it was not until an Act of Dec. 11, 1778, was passed that matters went far enough to permit of forfeitures of real estate to the State, after inquisition and judgment, followed by actual sales by Commissioners for the benefit of the State. Such sales were not always concluded by the Commissioners before the Peace of 1783, but extended in instances to as late as 1787. Generally speaking, inquisitions took the place of indictments, but not always; certain offenses were indictable, e. g., high treason, etc.

In cases of inquisitions, nothing further being noted, the charges may not have been pressed to judgment, or, as the defendant had no property to be forfeited, no advertisement was published of judgment or sale, or of outstanding claims. In any event, inquisitions, being based on affidavits of officials or neighbors, indicate that the party charged with being a Loyalist as late as 1778 or 1779 must have given grounds for it. Without doubt also, there were many sales under forfeitures not published at the time and so not noted herein.

In nearly all cases of property held by Commissioners after judgment, claims of creditors were duly advertised (sometimes before sale and sometimes afterward), as will often be found from a consultation with the stated references, although not specifically so mentioned in this list. Where claims were advertised, this fact presupposes judgment, and has been so considered in this record. In other words, the judgment itself was not published, but, after the judgment in case of supposed creditors, or in case there was property to be sold, an advertisement to such effect appeared, and such advertisement or advertisements are all that the references stated in the list below will show.

The reason year-dates only are given is to simplify the abstracts. The actual records will often—but not always—be more specific.

The abbreviations, or single words, used in the following list, signify:

    inq.—inquisition.
    com.—committed to jail.
    judg.—judgment of forfeiture upon inquisition.
    sale—advertisement of sale by Commissioners of Forfeited Estates (not actual sale, which could only be learned as a rule by a search in recorded deeds).
    Rec.—Records, usually Court Records of the County stated.
    M. P. C.—Minutes, or Journal, of the Provincial Congress of New Jersey, and Council of Safety for 1775, 1776.
    M. C. S.—Minutes of the Council of Safety of New Jersey, 1777, 1778.
    N. E.—Newspaper Extracts (from volumes in "New Jersey Archives," Second Series, Vols. II-V).
    N. J. R. C.—New Jersey Revolutionary Correspondence.
    N. J. Vols.—New Jersey Volunteers, or Battalion of Volunteers (always of Loyalists).
    C. N. B.—Collections of the New Brunswick (Province) Historical Society.

Abbott, Abdon, Jr., Salem co., judg., 1778-'9. (2 N. E. 470; 3 N. E. 69).

Abel, John, Sussex co., inq., 1779. (3 N. E. 165).

Ackerman, David D., Bergen co., inq., 1779. (3 N. E. 98).

Ackerman, Derrick, New Barbadoes, judg., sale, 1779; to Shelburne, N. S., at Peace. (3 N. E. 98, 526; 4 N. E. 77; see main text under John Van Dyke).

Ackerman, John J., Franklin twsp., Bergen co., judg., sale, 1779; perhaps to Nova Scotia at Peace. (3 N. E. 98, 526; 4 N. E. 77; 2 Sabine 469).

Ackerman, John William, to Shelburne, N. S., at Peace. (2 Sabine 469).

Ackerman, Lawrence A. (or E.), New Barbadoes, order of arrest, 1777; inq., 1779. (M. C. S. 83; 3 N. E. 98).
Ackerson, John, Bergen co., inq., 1778; to Shelburne, N. S., at Peace. (2 N. E. 529; 2 Sabine 469).
Ackerson, Thomas, to Shelburne, N. S., at Peace. (2 Sabine 469).
Ackley, John, Essex co., judg., sale, 1779. (3 N. E. 384, 508, 528).
Adams, Philip, Salem co., judg., 1778-'9. (2 N. E. 470; 3 N. E. 369).
Aker, John, "gone over to enemy," 1777. (M. C. S. 169).
Alias, John, taken in arms, imprisoned, 1777. (M. C. S. 142).
Allen, Benjamin, Gloucester co., imprisoned, 1778. (M. C. S. 247).
Allen, Ethan, "captured Tory," 1777. (N. J. R. C. 84).
Allen, John, Hunterdon co., imprisoned, 1777; judg., 1778-'9. (M. C. S. 103; 2 N. E. 355; 3 N. E. 68).
Allen, Jonah, "captured Tory," 1777. (N. J. R. C. 84).
Allenton, John, Bergen co., inq., 1778. (2 N. E. 529).
Allison, Robert, Sussex co., bound over, 1777. (M. C. S. 23).
Alston, David, Woodbridge, Capt. 3 N. J. Vols., 1777; judg., sale, 1778-'9. (2 N. E. 400; 3 N. E. 95; 5 C. N. B. 238; Stryker's N. J. Vols. 44).
Alston, Jonathan, Woodbridge, Ensign 3 N. J. Vols., 1777-'80; judg., sale, 1778-'9. (2 N. E. 534; 3 N. E. 95; 5 C. N. B. 262; Stryker's N. J. Vols. 62).
Alston, Lewis, Woodbridge, judg., sale, 1778-'9. (2 N. E. 534; 3 N. E. 95).
Alward, John, Middlesex co., high treason, com., 1777. (M. C. S. 82).
Ammerman, Isaac, Sussex co., imprisoned, 1777; inq., 1778. (M. C. S. 138, 142; 2 N. E. 435).
Anderson, John, to Shelburne, N. S. at Peace. (2 Sabine 471).
Andrews, John, "zealous and active Loyalist." (Loyalists' Claims, p. 122).
Anents, Stephen, to Shelburne, N. S., at Peace. (2 Sabine 472).
Annelly, Thomas, to Shelburne, N. S., at Peace. (2 Sabine 472).

Ansley, John, Sussex co., inq., 1778. (2 N. E. 435).
Ansley (see Insley, probably the proper surname).
Antill, John, Major 2 N. J. Vols., 1777-'9. (5 C. N. B. 229; Stryker's N. J. Vols. 31).
Apgar, Peter, Hunterdon co., arrest ordered, 1776. (M. P. C. 478).
Appleby, James, to Shelburne, N. S., at Peace. (2 Sabine 472).
Appleman, Peter, Sussex co., bound over, 1778; judg., 1778-'9. (M. C. S. 273; 2 N. E. 435; 4 N. E. 46).
Archer, George, Sergeant N. J. Vols., captured, 1777. (2 Sabine 472).
Arrowsmith, Joseph, Somerset co., judg., sale, 1778-'9. (2 N. E. 568; 3 N. E. 153).
Ashfield, Vincent Pearce, Essex co., judg., 1779. (3 N. E. 328, 329, 373).
Aston, Thomas, Essex co., judg., 1778-'9. (2 N. E. 519; 3 N. E. 328).
Atkinson, Moses, Salem co., judg., 1778-'9. (2 N. E. 470; 3 N. E. 369).
Atwood, Isaac, Capt. King's Amer. Regt.; to York co., N. B., at Peace. (35 N. Y. Gen. & Biog. Rec. 42).
Auten, John, Middlesex co., judg., sale, 1778-'9. (2 N. E. 400; 3 N. E. 95).
Avis, George, Gloucester co., judg., sale, 1778-'9. (2 N. E. 581; 3 N. E. 131, 451, 650).
Babbington, Charles, 2nd Lieut., 2 N. J. Vols., 1778-'9. (5 C. N. B. 260; Stryker's N. J. Vols. 54).
Bacon, John, Burlington (?) co., leader Tory marauders, killed, 1782. (1 Sabine 200).
Badcock, Simeon, Monmouth co., refused oaths, bailed, 1777. (M. C. S. 35).
Badgely, Mr., joining enemy, high treason, death sentence, 1782. (1 Sabine 201).
Bailey, Joseph, Middletown, judg., sale, 1779-'80. (3 N. E. 94; 4 N. E. 248).
Baker, Conrad, Bergen co., inq., 1779. (3 N. E. 529).
Baker, Philip, Bergen co., judg., 1779. (3 N. E. 525).
Baker, William, Bergen co., judg., 1779. (3 N. E. 525).

Baldwin, Luther, Essex co., judg., 1779. (3 N. E. 328, 329, 373).
Ballanger, Jonathan, Cumberland co., inq., 1779, "Rank Tory." (4 N. E. 1; 2 Sabine 475).
Banghart, Barnabus, Sussex co., inq., 1778. (2 N. E. 435).
Bank, Jonah, Essex co., inq. 1778. (Essex Rec.).
Banks, Joseph, Sergeant N. J. Vols., captured by Americans, 1777. (2 Sabine 475).
Banks, Josiah, Essex co., judg., 1778. (2 N. E. 385, 536, 587).
Banta, Cornelius, Stuckup, Bergen co., arrest ordered, 1777. (M. C. S. 83).
Banta, Cornelius, Winkleman, Bergen co., arrest ordered, 1777. (M. C. S. 83).
(One of above may be a Jr., and one was discharged later on bail, on taking oaths of allegiance; see M. C. S. 116).
Banta, Derick, Winkleman, Bergen co., arrest ordered, 1777. (M. C. S. 83).
Banta, Hendrick, imprisoned, high treason, 1778. (M. C. S. 275).
Banta, Capt. John, Pashack, Bergen co., arrest ordered 1777. (M. C. S. 83).
Barbarie, Andrew, Middlesex co., judg., 1778-'9; sale, 1784. (2 N. E. 401; 3 N. E. 62; 4 N. E. 303, 330; see main text under John Barbarie).
Barbarie, Peter, Middlesex co., judg., sale, 1778-'9, 1784. (2 N. E. 401; 3 N. E. 62, 322; 4 N. E. 303, 330).
Barber, Hugh, Cumberland co., judg., sale, 1778-'9. (2 N. E. 496; 3 N. E. 487).
Barber, John, high treason, com., 1777. (M. C. S. 55, 58, 64).
Barclay, James, captured on Staten Island, 1777. (2 Sabine 476).
Barclay, John, Middlesex co., Lieut., 6 N. J. Vols., 1777. (5 C. N. B. 249).
Bard, Dr. Samuel, Monmouth co., fugitive, judg., 1780; d. 1821. (4 N. E. 249; 1 Sabine 208).
Bardon, John, arrested, improperly released. (1 Sabine 208).
Barker, Michael, N. J. Vols., captured by Americans, 1777. (2 Sabine 476).

Barker, Nathaniel, Shrewsbury, judg., 1780. (Monm. Rec.).
Barnes, Samuel, Ass't Surgeon, 3 N. J. Vols., 1776. (5 N. B. 233).
Barnet, Caleb, Lieut., West Jersey Vols., 1778. (5 C. N. B. 249).
Barnet, Ichabod, Elizabeth Town, adv., then "restored," 1775. (M. P. C. 227); bailed, 1778. (M. C. S. 277).
Barnet, Ichabod Best, Essex co., judg., sale, 1778-'9. (2 N. E. 545; 3 N. E. 92).
Barron, James, to Shelburne, N. S., at Peace. (2 Sabine 477).
Barrott, James, Jr., Cumberland co., judg., sale, 1778-'9. (2 N. E. 496; 3 N. E. 487).
Barton, Benjamin, Capt., took oaths, 1777; joined 2 N. J. Vols., 1778; aso 4 N. J. Vols., 1781. (M. C. S. 127; 5 C. N. B. 239).
Barton, Harry L., Lieut. and Ensign, 1 N. J. Vols., 1780-'2. (2 Sabine 477; 5 C. N. B. 249; Stryker's N. J. Vols. 54; see main text under Joseph Barton).
Barton, Thomas, Colonel, captured 1777; to Nova Scotia at Peace; d. about 1790. (1 Sabine 214; but see Stryker's N. J. Vols. 42).
Bartram, Alexander, Gloucester co., judg., sale, 1778-'9. (2 N. E. 581; 3 N. E. 128, 650).
Batey, Francis, Essex co., judg., 1778-'9. (2 N. E. 519; 3 N. E. 328).
Baugh, Nicholas, Cumberland co., judg., sale, 1779. (3 N. E. 152).
Bayard, William, Bergen co., judg., sale, 1779, 1784. (2 N. E. 529; Hist. Bergen Co., Vol. I, pp. 127, 128).
Beach, Rev. Abraham, D. D., New Brunswick, Loyalist, but inactive; d. 1828. (1 Sabine 218; 9 Coll. Hist. Soc. of N. J. 26).
Beach, Ezekiel, Mendham, published, recanted, 1775; arrested, confessed, 1777; judg., sale, 1778-'9. (M. C. S. 128, 134; 2 N. E. 593; 3 N. E. 92; 2 Sabine 478; Amer. Archives, Ser. IV, Vol. 4, p. 441).
Beatty, George, Morris co., judg., 1778. (2 N. E. 350, 593).

The Loyalists of New Jersey in the Revolution 261

Bedel, Israel, Staten Island and Monmouth co., judg., 1779-'80. (3 N. E. 89; 4 N. E. 249).

Beekman, Charles, Hackensack, judg., sale, 1779. (3 N. E. 98, 526; 4 N. E. 77).

Beekman, Gerardus G., New York and Shrewsbury, judg., sale, 1779-'80. (3 N. E. 94, 368; 4 N. E. 249).

Bell, David, Bridgewater twsp., Somerset co., judg., sale, 1780. (4 N. E. 184).

Benson, Christopher, Bergen co., inq., 1778. (2 N. E. 529).

Benson, James, Cumberland co., inq., 1778. (2 N. E. 496).

Bessonett, Daniel, Capt. 4 N. J. Vols., 1777-'9. (5 C. N. B. 239; Stryker's N. J. Vols. 46).

Bettle, John, Lieut. West Jersey Vols., 1778. (5 C. N. B. 249).

Biddle, Josiah, Gloucester co., judg., 1779. (3 N. E. 650).

Bills, Thomas, Freehold, judg., sale, 1779-'80. (3 N. E. 94, 367; 4 N. E. 249).

Birch, James, Gloucester co., high treason, death sentence, 1778. (2 N. E. 583; N. J. R. C. 137).

Bird, Richard, Monmouth co., Tory "Pine robber." (1 Mon. Hist. 103).

Birdsall, Samuel L., Hunterdon co., oaths refused, fined, 1777. (Hunt. Rec.).

Birdsall, Whitson L., Hunterdon co., oaths refused, com., 1777. (Hunt. Rec.).

Bisset, Asher, trading with enemy, 1781. (5 N. E. 181).

Blackwell, John, Burlington co., high treason, com., 1777. (M. C. S. 41).

Blain, James, Sussex co., judg., 1778-'9. (2 N. E. 435; 3 N. E. 46).

Blauvelt, David, Bergen co., judg., sale, 1778-'9. (2 N. E. 529; 3 N. E. 132, 526).

Blauvelt, Theunis, Bergen co., "active bushranger," judg., sale, 1778-'9; settled in Tuscet, N. S., after the War; died 1830. (2 N. E. 529; 3 N. E. 132, 526; 1 Sabine 232).

Blaworth, Thomas, Bergen co., spy, Lieut. King's Mil. Vols. (Ontario Archives, 554-'6).

Bloom, Frederick, Sussex co., refused oaths, bailed. (M. C. S. 85).

Blundle, James, Essex co., inq., 1779. (3 N. E. 328, 329, 373).
Bocock, William, Billingsport, Gloucester co., judg., sale, 1778-'9. (2 N. E. 581; 3 N. E. 130, 650).
Bogert, Cornelius, Hackensack Pt., arrest ordered, 1777. (M. C. S. 83).
Bogert, Henry, Essex co., com. to jail, 1778. (M. C. S. 228).
Bogert, Jacob, Bergen co., high treason, com., 1777. (M. C. S. 59, 64; N. J. R. C. 107).
Bogert, Jacobus A., Bergen co., inq., 1779. (4 N. E. 90).
Bogert, John C., Bergen co., judg., 1779. (4 N. E. 77).
Bogert, Joost, Bergen co., inq., 1779. (4 N. E. 90).
Bogert, Peter, Winkleman, Bergen co., arrest ordered, 1777. (M. C. S. 83).
Bogert, Peter P., Harrington twsp., Bergen co., judg., sale, 1780, 1787. (5 N. E. 124; Hist. Bergen co., Vol. I, p. 128).
Boice, Jacob, Middlesex co., judg., sale, 1778-'9. (2 N. E. 400; 3 N. E. 95).
Boly, Elias, Middletown, judg., 1780. (4 N. E. 248).
Bond, Nathaniel, Essex co., imprisoned, 1778. (M. C. S. 228).
Bonum, Malachi, Cumberland co., inq., 1778. (2 N. E. 496).
Booten, John, Lower Penns Neck, judg., sale, 1778, 1780. (2 N. E. 470; 4 N. E. 194, 373).
Booth, Benjamin, Newark, judg., 1778-'9. (2 N. E. 385; 3 N. E. 47, 327).
Booth, John, Salem co., inq., 1778. (2 N. E. 470).
Borden, John, Shrewsbury, judg., sale, 1780, 1784. (4 N. E. 191).
Border, John, Gloucester co., judg., sale, 1779-'80. (3 N. E. 527; 4 N. E. 192).
Bough, Nicholas, Cumberland co., inq., 1778. (2 N. E. 496).
Bowen, Ashley, Cumberland co., inq., 1778. (2 N. E. 496).
Bowen, John, Princeton; went to Halifax, 1776; "proscribed and banished" in N. J., in 1778. (2 Sabine 483).
Bowers, Lemuel, Lieut. 3 N. J. Vols., 1776; d. Nov. 4, 1777. (5 C. N. B. 249).
Bowlby, Abraham, Sussex co., judg., 1779. (3 N. E. 46; see main text under Richard Bowlby).

Bowlby, Charles, Morris co., judg., sale, 1780. (2 N. E. 350, 593; 4 N. E. 269).

Bowlby, John, Morris co., judg., sale. (2 N. E. 350, 593; 3 N. E. 92; see main text under Edward Bowlby).

Bowman, Edward, Morris co., judg., 1778. (2 N. E. 350, 593).

Bowne, Andrew, Middletown, judg., 1784. (Mid. Rec.).

Bowne, John, Middletown, judg., sale, 1779-'80. (3 N. E. 94, 368).

Bowne, Obadiah, Middletown, judg., 1784. (Mid. Rec.).

Boyd, James, Cumberland co., inq., 1778. (2 N. E. 496).

Brady, John, imprisoned, 1776. (2 Sabine 484; M. P. C. 487).

Brazilla, Joseph, Upper Freehold twsp., judg., sale, 1779. (3 N. E. 94).

Brinkerhof, John, English Neighborhood, arrest ordered, 1778; inq., 1779. (M. C. S. 83; 4 N. E. 89).

Brinkerhof, Seba, Hackensack Pt., arrest ordered, 1777. (M. C. S. 83).

Brindly, Samuel, Dover twsp., Monmouth co., judg., 1780. (4 N. E. 249).

Brinley, Francis, Amboy, officer in British service, died 1852. (2 Sabine 485).

Britain, Israel, Freehold, Ensign 1 N. J. Vols. 1777; judg., 1779. (3 N. E. 93, 367; 5 C. N. B. 263).

Britain, William, Knowlton, Sussex co., refused oaths, com., 1777; inq., 1778; imprisoned, escaped; to St. John, N. B., 1780; d. about 1811. (2 N. E. 435; 1 Sabine 258).

Brooks, Cornelius, Essex co., judg., 1778-'9. (2 N. E. 519; 3 N. E. 328).

Brooks, William, Essex co., judg., 1778-'9. (2 N. E. 519; 3 N. E. 428).

Brower, Jacob, Essex co., judg., 1778-'9. (2 N. E. 385; 3 N. E. 327).

Brower, Peter, Essex co., judg., 1779. (2 N. E. 385; 3 N. E. 327).

Brown, Hugh, imprisoned, 1777. (M. C. S. 142).

Browne, William, Essex co., N. J. Vols., captured, 1777; judg., 1779. (2 Sabine 486; Essex Rec.).

Brownjohn, William, Essex co., judg., 1778-'9. (3 N. E. 328, 329, 373).
Bruce, David, to Shelburne, N. S., 1783. (2 Sabine 487).
Bruce, George, Bergen co., inq., 1779. (3 N. E. 529).
Bruen, Thomas, Newark, judg., sale, 1778-'9. (2 N. E. 385; 3 N. E. 47, 327).
Bryant, Dr. William, Trenton, Surgeon on half pay. (Am. Archives, Ser. IV., Vol. 4, p. 815).
Bunnel, Isaac, Middlesex co., judg., sale, 1779. (3 N. E. 95).
Burdge, Jacob, Monmouth co., judg., sale, 1780. (4 N. E. 191).
Burdge, John, Monmouth co., judg., sale, 1780. (4 N. E. 191).
Burdge, Jonathan, Tory freebooter, reward offered. (2 N. E. 466).
Burgess, John, N. J. Vols., captured, 1777. (2 Sabine 489).
Burke, Stephen, Tory "Pine robber," killed 1778. (1 Mon. Hist. 103).
Burke, Thomas, Tory "Pine robber." (1 Mon. Hist. 103).
Burling, Samuel, oaths refused, bound over, 1777. (M. C. S. 16, 20).
Burnet, Rev. Matthias, grad. of Princeton, 1769; with enemy on Long Island during war; died in Norwalk, Conn., 1806. (1 Sabine 275).
Burrows, Thomas, Essex co., judg., sale, 1778-'9. (2 N. E. 545; 3 N. E. 92, 384).
Bursley, Daniel, Hunterdon co., oaths refused, fined, 1777. (Hunt. Rec.).
Burton, Jesse, Monmouth co., judg., sale, 1780. (4 N. E. 190).
Burton, John, Cumberland co., refugee, escaped jail, 1780. (2 N. E. 19).
Burwell, James, Morris co., British army, 1776; died in Elgin co., Canada, 1853. (1 Sabine 277).
Bush, Hendrick, New Barbadoes, judg., 1779 (?), sale, 1784. (Hist. Bergen co., Vol. 1, p. 127).
Buskirk (see under Van Buskirk, although "Van" often omitted).
Butcott, John, Sussex co., inq., 1779. (3 N. E. 165).

Butler, James, Bergen co., inq., 1779. (3 N. E. 529; perhaps also 3 N. E. 226, 302, 607, 608).
Butler, John, to Shelburne at Peace. (2 Sabine 490).
Buzhart, Jeremiah, Cumberland co., inq., 1778. (2 N. E. 496).
Byard, William, Bergen co., inq., 1779. (4 N. E. 90).
Cadmus, Thomas, Jr., Essex co., refused oaths, com., 1777. (M. C. S. 74; N. J. R. C. 78, 79).
Cahill, Daniel, Hunterdon co., refused oaths, bailed, 1777. (M. C. S. 103).
Camp, John, Ensign 3rd N. J. Vols., 1777; wounded and discharged, 1778. (5 C. N. B. 263; Stryker's N. J. Vols. 62).
Camp, Matthew, insurgent, imprisoned, 1777. (M. C. S. 138).
Campbell, Archibald, Ass't Surgeon, 1 N. J. Vols. (5 C. N. B. 233).
Campbell, Duncan, Essex co., Capt. Young Royal High Emigrants, 1775; judg., 1779. (5 C. N. B. 239; 3 N. E. 328, 329, 372).
Campbell, James, Teaneck, arrest ordered, 1777. (M. C. S. 83).
Campbell, Patrick, Captain 2 and 4 N. J. Vols., 1777-'82. (2 Sabine 492; Stryker's N. J. Vols. 46; 5 C. N. B. 239).
Carr, Alexander, Jr., Hunterdon co., inq., 1778. (Hunt. Rec.).
Carrell (Carnel), William, Sussex co., judg., 1778-'9. (2 N. E. 434; 3 N. E. 46).
Carter, Benjamin, Gloucester co., inq., 1778. (2 N. E. 581).
Carter, John, Jr., Gloucester co., judg., sale, 1778. (2 N. E. 581; 3 N. E. 650).
Cartwright, Caleb, Cumberland co., inq., 1778. (2 N. E. 496).
Cartwright, Samuel, Cumberland co., inq., 1778. (2 N. E. 496).
Carty, John, Burlington co., inq., 1778. (M. C. S. 136; 2 N. E. 388).
Carty, William, Capt. 3 N. J. Vols., 1778. (5 C. N. B. 240).
Castel, Michael Manuel, N. J. Vols., captured, 1777. (2 Sabine 494).
Castner, George, Hunterdon co., judg., 1777-'9. (M. C. S. 155, 157; M. P. C. 478; 2 N. E. 355; 3 N. E. 68).
Cate, Wardell, Shrewsbury, judg., 1779. (Mon. Rec.).
Cavenaugh, Patrick, N. J. Vols., captured, 1777. (2 Sabine 494).

Cayford, Richard, Cumberland co., published as enemy, 1775; imprisoned, 1776; Capt. N. J. Vols., 1776-'81; judg., sale, 1779. (3 N. E. 152, 487, 488; 1 Sabine 298; 5 C. N. B. 240; Stryker's N. J. Vols. 46; N. J. Archives, Vol. 31, p. 180).

Chandler, Azail, Shrewsbury, judg., sale, 1779-'80. (3 N. E. 94, 368; 4 N. E. 248).

Cheesman, Abijah, Middlesex co., high treason, com., 1778. (M. C. S. 285).

Chestnutwood, Sebastian, Sussex co., fined, com., 1777. (M. C. S. 81).

Chever, George, Sussex co., inq., 1779. (3 N. E. 165).

Chew, David, Gloucester co., inq., 1778. (2 N. E. 581).

Chew, Jonathan, Gloucester co., Capt., West Jersey Vols., 1778; judg., sale, 1778-'9; high treason, death sentence, 1779. (2 N. E. 581; 3 N. E. 129, 560; 5 C. N. B. 240; N. J. R. C. 135).

Chew, William, Lieut., 2 and 3 N. J. Vols., 1777-'82; Royal Garrison Batt., 1782; died 1819, aged 94. (1 C. N. B. 45; 5 C. N. B. 250).

Chosel, Jonathan, Sussex co., inq., 1779. (3 N. E. 165).

Churchward, Richard, joining enemy, com., 1777. (N. J. R. C. 98).

Clarendon, Walter, Loyalist, "house plundered by Whigs," 1777. (1 N. E. 505; 2 Sabine 496).

Clark, Alexander, Freehold, judg., sale, 1779-'80. (3 N. E. 93, 367; 4 N. E. 248).

Clark, Benjamin, Middlesex co., oaths refused, com., 1777. (M. C. S. 175, 176).

Clark, James, Salem co., plea of guilty, com., 1778. (Salem Records).

Clark, John, Cumberland co., published, 1776, as "enemy to his country." (2 Sabine 496).

Clark, John, Middlesex co., oaths refused, com., 1777; to Prov. of New Brunswick, 1783; died there, 1848. (1 Sabine 314; 35 N. Y. Gen. & Biog. Rec. 170; M. C. S. 175, 176).

Clark, Joseph, Gloucester co., judg., sale, 1778-'9. (2 N. E. 581; 3 N. E. 130).
Clark, Samuel, illicit trade with enemy, imprisoned, 1780; at St. John, N. B. at Peace; died 1804. (1 Sabine 314; 35 N. Y. Gen. & Biog. Rec. 169).
Clark, Thomas, Middlesex co., oaths refused, com., 1777. (M. C. S. 175, 176).
Clarke, Thomas, Salem co., inq., 1778. (2 N. E. 470).
Clawson, Cornelius, Morris co., to join enemy, com. 1777. (M. C. S. 127; N. J. R. C. 98).
Clayton, Joseph, Freehold, judg., 1779-'80. (3 N. E. 93, 367; 4 N. E. 249).
Clement, Jacob, Jr., Gloucester co., inq., 1778. (2 N. E. 581).
Clendenan, John, Sussex co., judg., 1778-'9. (2 N. E. 435; 3 N. E. 46).
Clopper, Peter, Essex co., judg., 1778-'9. (2 N. E. 385; 3 N. E. 328).
Coddington, Asher, to St. John, N. B., 1783; died at Maugerville about 1828. (1 Sabine 323; 35 N. Y. Gen. & Biog. Rec. 277).
Coddington, Isaiah, Middlesex co., judg., sale, 1778-'9. (2 N. E. 534; 3 N. E. 95).
Coke, William (see 1 Sabine 328).
Colden, John, Major 2 N. J. Vols., 1776; De Lancey's Batt.; Capt. 1 N. J. Vols., 1782, etc. (2 Sabine 497; 5 C. N. B. 229; Stryker's N. J. Vols. 32).
Cole, Daniel, Sussex co., inq., 1779. (3 N. E. 165).
Cole, Frederick, Morris co., com., 1778. (M. C. S. 192).
Cole, James, Ensign 4 N. J. Vols., 1777-'9; captured, 1779. (5 C. N. B. 237, 264; Stryker's N. J. Vols. 63).
Cole, Richard, Middletown, judg., 1779-'80. (3 N. E. 94; 4 N. E. 248).
Coleny, John, Essex co., judg., 1779. (3 N. E. 328, 329, 373).
Colgan, Fleming, Quartermaster 5 N. J. Vols., 1777-'8. (5 C. N. B. 234; Stryker's N. J. Vols. 38).
Collins, Elijah, Sussex co., 1777, refused oaths, bailed. (M. C. S. 88).

Collins, James, Jr., Middlesex co., to Shelburne, N. S., at Peace. (2 Sabine 498; perhaps same as James Collins in main text).

Collins, Jonathan, Sussex co., refused oaths, bailed, 1777. (M. C. S. 86).

Collins, Mahlon, Sussex co., refused oaths, bailed, 1777. (M. C. S. 88).

Colvin, James, Essex co., judg., 1778-'9. (2 N. E. 519, 587; 3 N. E. 328).

Colvin, Luther, Jr., Hunterdon co., refused oaths, bailed. (M. C. S. 149).

Colvin, Stephen, Hunterdon co., refused oaths, fined, 1777. (Hunt. Rec.).

Compton, James, Morris co., to join enemy, com., 1777. (M. C. S. 177; N. J. R. C. 98).

Compton, John, Somerset co., judg., 1779. (3 N. E. 591).

Compton, Richard, Somerset co., judg., sale, 1778-'9. (3 N. E. 153).

Compton, Richard, Jr., Somerset co., judg., 1779. (2 N. E. 568; 3 N. E. 49).

Conliff, Joseph, Morris co., judg., 1778. (2 N. E. 593).

Cook, John, Amboy, judg., sale, 1778-'9. (2 N. E. 401; 3 N. E. 62, 63, 435).

Cook, Patterson, Gloucester co., high treason, death sentence, 1778; inq. 1778. (2 N. E. 583; N. J. R. C. 137; Glou. Rec.).

Cook, Silas, Jr., Monmouth co., judg., sale, 1779. (3 N. E. 89, 323).

Cool, Philip, imprisoned, fined, July, 1776. (2 Sabine, 499).

Coombs, Abijah, to St. John, N. B., at Peace. (2 Sabine 499).

Coombs, Dennis, Jr., Middlesex co., judg., sale, 1778-'9. (2 N. E. 400; 3 N. E. 95).

Cooper, Jacob, Monmouth co., joined enemy, captured, 1777. (M. C. S. 55).

Cooper, James, Middletown, judg., sale, 1780. (4 N. E. 191; see main text under Elijah Groom).

Cooper, John, to Shelburne, N. S., at Peace. (2 Sabine 499).

Corrent, William, Sussex co., assisting enemy, 1778. M. C. S. 278).

Corse, Henry, Salem co., inq., 1778. (2 N. E. 470).

Cortreght, Solomon, Sussex co., inq., judg., sale, 1779. (3 N. E. 165, 543).

Cotterel, John, Middletown, judg., sale, 1779-'80. (3 N. E. 94; 4 N. E. 248).

Cotterel, Samuel, Shrewsbury, judg., 1780. (4 N. E. 248).

Courter, John, Essex co., inq. 1779. (Essex Rec.).

Courter, John, Jr., Essex co., judg., 1778-'9. (2 N. E. 587; 3 N. E. 49, 328).

Cowman, John, Salem co., inq., 1778. (2 N. E. 470; 3 N. E. 131, 650).

Cox, Lawrence, Gloucester co., high treason, death sentence, 1778. (2 N. E. 583; N. J. R. C. 137).

Cozins, Joshua, Gloucester co., inq., 1778. (2 N. E. 581; see main text under Daniel Cozens).

Cozins, Samuel, furnishing enemy provisions, 1778. (M. C. S. 219).

Crane, John J., inq., 1779. (3 N. E. 372).

Crine, Vincent, Monmouth co., judg., 1784. (Mon. Rec.).

Cristy, William, Sussex co., inq., 1779. (3 N. E. 165).

Crowel, Richard, gone over to enemy, 1777. (M. C. S. 85).

Cummins, John, Sussex co., judg., 1778-'9. (2 N. E. 435; 3 N. E. 46).

Cunliff, Joseph, Morris co., Lieut. 5 N. J. Vols., 1777, and Capt.-Lieut. 1 N. J. Vols., 1781; judg., 1779. (3 N. E. 92; 2 Sabine 492, 502; 5 C. N. B. 251; Stryker's N. J. Vols. 54).

Curlis, John, Shrewsbury, arrest ordered, 1777. (N. J. R. C. 34, 56).

Curtis, James, Shrewsbury, judg., sale, 1779-'80. (3 N. E. 94; 4 N. E. 248).

Curtis, Samuel, Sussex co., inq., 1779. (3 N. E. 165).

Curtis, William, Shrewsbury, inq., 1782. (5 N. E. 46).

Cuyler, Henry, Newark, bonds given, 1776. (2 Sabine 503; see main text under Nicholas Ogden).

Cyphers, George, Jr., arrest ordered, 1776. (M. P. C. 478).
Cyphers, Peter, Hunterdon co., arrest ordered, 1776. (M. P. C. 478; see main text under Joseph Lee).
Cyphers, Philip, arrest ordered, 1776; with enemy, 1777. (M. C. S. 155, 157; M. P. C. 478).
Dancer, Daniel, com., 1777. (M. C. S. 41).
Dancer, Jacob, Burlington co., high treason, com., 1777. (M. C. S. 41, 42).
Daniel, Joel, Cumberland co., inq., 1778. (2 N. E. 496).
Daniels, John, Salem co., judg., 1778-'9; to Shelburne, N. S., at Peace. (2 N. E. 470; 3 N. E. 369; 2 Sabine 503).
Daniels, Joseph, Salem (?) co., implicated in murder crime. (2 Sabine 503).
Davies, John, N. J. Vols., captured, 1777. (2 Sabine 504).
Davis, James, Morris co., high treason, com., 1778. (M. C. S. 285).
Davis, Jeremiah, Cumberland co., inq., 1778. (2 N. E. 496).
Davis, Jerman, Salem co., judg., 1778. (2 N. E. 470).
Davis, Richard, Middlesex co., judg., 1778-'9. (2 N. E. 401; 3 N. E. 62).
Davis, Samuel, Salem co., judg., sale, 1778-'9. (2 N. E. 470; 3 N. E. 114).
Daws, John, Bergen co., inq., 1779. (4 N. E. 90).
Day, John, Hunterdon co., arrest ordered, 1776. (M. P. C. 478).
Day, Peter, to Shelburne, N. S., at Peace. (2 Sabine 504).
Dean, James, Salem co., judg., 1778-'9. (2 N. E. 470; 3 N. E. 369).
Debauc, John, Bergen co., arrest ordered, 1778. (M. C. S. 83).
DeCamp, Joseph, Middlesex co., bail allowed, 1778. (M. C. S. 284).
DeGroot, Jacob, English Neighborhood, gone to enemy, 1777. (M. C. S. 83, 169).
DeGroot, John, English Neighborhood, arrest ordered, 1777. (M. C. S. 84).
DeGroot, Peter, English Neighborhood, arrest ordered, 1777. (M. C. S. 84).

The Loyalists of New Jersey in the Revolution 271

Demarest, Aaron, Hackensack, judg., sale, 1779. (3 N. E. 526; 4 N. E. 77; Hist. Bergen Co., Vol. I, p. 126).
Demarest, Aaron, Jr., Bergen co., inq., 1779. (3 N. E. 98).
Demarest, Daniel S., Bergen co., judg., sale, 1779. (3 N. E. 98, 526; 4 N. E. 77; Hist. Bergen Co., Vol. I, p. 126).
Demarest, David G., Bergen co., inq., 1780. (5 N. E. 124; perhaps same as David Demare in main text).
Demarest, Garret, Capt., Pashack, Bergen co., arrest ordered, 1777. (M. C. S. 83).
Demarest, Guilliam, Bergen co.; to N. S. after War.
Demarest, Jacob, Morris co., judg., sale, 1778-'9; Bergen co., sale, 1784. (2 N. E. 350, 593; 3 N. E. 92; Hist. Bergen Co., Vol. I, p. 127).
Demarest, John, New Barbadoes, magistrate, arrest ordered, 1777. (M. C. S. 83).
Demarest, Joost, Bergen co., inq., 1779. (4 N. E. 89).
Demarest, Rulif, Bergen co., inq., 1778. (2 N. E. 529).
Demarest, Samuel, Bergen co., inq., 1778. (Bergen Rec.).
DeMott, Jacob, English Neighborhood, arrest ordered, 1777. (M. C. S. 83).
DeMott, John, Bergen and Middlesex cos., and New York, judg., sale, 1779-'80. (3 N. E. 98; 4 N. E. 230).
Dennis, Anthony, Shrewsbury, judg., sale, 1779-'80. (3 N. E. 323; 4 N. E. 248).
Dennis, Ezekial, Ensign 5 N. J. Vols., 1777; resigned, 1778. (5 C. N. B. 264; Stryker's N. J. Vols. 63).
Dennis, Michael, Hunterdon co., judg., 1778. (M. C. S. 155, 157; 2 N. E. 355; 3 N. E. 68).
Dennis, Samuel, to Shelburne, N. S., at Peace. (2 Sabine 505).
DePuyster, Nicholas, Bergen co., judg., sale, 1778-'9. (2 N. E. 529; 3 N. E. 526).
Derik, Prenore, Bergen co., inq., 1779. (4 N. E. 90).
Devanport, Humphrey, Morris co., judg., 1778. (2 N. E. 593).
Devanport, William, Gloucester co., inq., 1778. (2 N. E. 581).
DeVeber, Gabriel, Gloucester co., Major West Jersey Vols., 1778; 3 DeLancey's Brig., 1780; judg., 1778-'80. (2 N. E. 582; 3 N. E. 650; 4 N. E. 192; 5 C. N. B. 229, 251).
DeVeber, Gabriel, Jr., Gloucester co., inq., 1778. (2 N. E. 581).

Dey, Abraham, English Neighborhood, arrest ordered, 1777. (M. C. S. 83).

Dey, Jacob (son of Abraham), arrest ordered, 1777. (M. C. S. 83).

Dilkes, John, Gloucester co., high treason, death sentence, 1778. (2 N. E. 583; N. J. R. C. 137).

Dilkes, Joshua, Gloucester co., high treason, death sentence, 1778. (2 N. E. 583; N. J. R. C. 137).

Dill, Joseph, Gloucester co., high treason, death sentence, 1778. (2 N. E. 583; N. J. R. C. 137).

Dillon, William "Tory burglar," convicted, reprieved, escaped. (2 N. E. 312, 453; Hist. Monmouth & Ocean, p. 81).

Dilts, Christopher, Hunterdon co., arrest ordered, 1776. (M. P. C. 478).

Disborough, Henry, Somerset co., disaffected, com., 1778. (M. C. S. 264, 266).

Doan, Titus, Sussex co., oaths refused, fined, 1777. (M. C. S. 88).

Doan (or Done), John, Middlesex co., judg., sale, 1778, 1779. (2 N. E. 400; 3 N. E. 95).

Dolles, Reuben, Cumberland co., inq., 1778. (2 N. E. 496).

Donaldson, Andrew, Cumberland co., inq., 1778-'9. (M. C. S. 253; 4 N. E. 1).

Donworth, Peter, Ensign 3 N. J. Vols. (5 C. N. B. 265).

Doremus, Hendrick, Saddle River, judg., sale, 1779. (3 N. E. 98, 526; 4 N. E. 77; Hist. Bergen Co., Vol. 1, p. 127).

Dougherty, James, Salem co., inq., 1778. (2 N. E. 470).

Doughty, Bartholomew, Quartermaster, 6th N. J. Vols.; Capt., De Lancey's Brigade. (5 C. N. B. 234; Stryker's N. J. Vols. 38).

Douglas, William, Bergen co., inq., 1779. (3 N. E. 529).

Dowdney, Nathaniel, Cumberland co., imprisoned as "enemy to his country." (1 Sabine 385; Amer. Archives, Ser. IV, Vol. 4, p. 664).

Drake, Imlay, joining enemy, com., 1777. (M. C. S. 142).

Drake, Randolph, Middlesex co., judg., sale, 1779. (2 N. E. 400; 3 N. E. 95).

Dreeler, John, Cumberland co., inq., 1778. (2 N. E. 496).

Drummond, Jane, Acquackanonk, judg., sale, 1779-'80. (4 N. E. 2, 408; see main text under Robert Drummond).
Drury, Wake, Burlington co., Justice of the Peace, imprisoned. (1 Sabine 387).
DuBois, Peter, Second River, oaths refused, com., 1777; judg., 1777-'9. (M. C. S. 74, 83; 3 N. E. 49, 328; N. J. R. C. 78, 79).
Duffield, Benjamin, Gloucester co., inq., 1778. (2 N. E. 582).
Duffield, James, Gloucester co., judg., sale, 1778-'9. (2 N. E. 582; 3 N. E. 129, 650).
Duffield, John. (see 1 Sabine 395).
Dugan, Cornelius, Sussex co., judg., 1778-'9. (2 N. E. 435; 3 N. E. 46).
Dunfield, John, Sussex co., judg., 1778-'9. (2 N. E. 435; 3 N. E. 46).
Dungan, Thomas, Bergen co., inq., 1779. (3 N. E. 98).
Dunham, Daniel, Monmouth co., to St. John, N. B. at Peace. (1 Sabine 399; see main text under Isaac Dunham).
Dunham, John, probably to St. John, N. B., at Peace. (See main text under Isaac Dunham).
Dunham, Moses, Middlesex co., judg., sale, 1778-'9. (2 N. E. 534; 3 N. E. 95).
Dunham, Phineas, Salem co., inq., 1778. (2 N. E. 470).
Dunlap, Samuel, Middlesex co., inq., 1778. (2 N. E. 534).
Dunscomb, John, Bergen co., inq., 1779. (4 N. E. 90).
Dunworth, Peter, Ensign 3 N. J. Vols., 1779. (Stryker's N. J. Vols. 63).
Duryea, Daniel J., Schraalenberg, arrest ordered, 1777. (M. C. S. 83).
Duryea, John, Old Tappen (miller), arrest ordered, 1777; inq., 1779. (M. C. S. 83; 3 N. E. 98).
Duryea, John P., Harrington twsp., judg., sale, 1779. (3 N. E. 526; 4 N. E. 77).
Dutton, William, Cumberland co., refugee, escaped jail, 1780. (5 N. E. 19).
Duwin, Peter, Franklin twsp., Bergen co., judg., sale, 1779. (3 N. E. 526).

Duychinck, Colonel, imprisoned by order of Washington, 1777.
(1 Sabine 401; N. J. R. C. 54).
Duychinck, John, Middlesex co., inq., 1778; judg., sale, 1784.
(2 N. E. 401. If same as "Col. Duychinck," imprisoned
by Washington's order. 1 Sabine 401).
Dykeman, Cornelius, Bergen co., inq., 1780. (5 N. E. 124).
Eagler, Conrad, Hunterdon co., judg., 1778-'9. (2 N. E. 355;
3 N. E. 68; M. C. S. 155, 157).
Eagler (see Eikler).
Earle, John, New Barbadoes, arrest ordered, 1777. (M. C.
S. 83).
Earle, Peter, New Barbadoes, judg., sale, 1778-'9. (2 N. E.
529; 3 N. E. 132, 526).
Earle, Philip, to St. John, N. B., at Peace; d. 1814. (36 N. Y.
Gen. & Biog. Rec. 185).
Eddy, John, Sussex co., high treason, escaped, 1777; judg.,
1779. (M. C. S. 81; 3 N. E. 328; N. J. R. C. 65).
Edison, John, Essex co., bound over; com. for high treason,
1777. (M. C. S. 56, 74, 187; N. J. R. C. 78, 79).
Edwards, Stephen, Monmouth co., executed as spy, 1780. (1
Sabine 403; see main text under Josiah Parker).
Eglinton, Edward, Gloucester co., judg., sale, 1778. (2 N. E.
581; 3 N. E. 130).
Eikler, William, Sussex co., judg., 1778-'9. (3 N. E. 46).
Elliot, Mr., Monmouth co., judg., 1780. (4 N. E. 249).
Ellis, Daniel, refused oaths, bailed, 1777. (M. C. S. 16, 20).
Ellis, Ebenezer, Sussex co., inq., 1779. (3 N. E. 165).
Ellis, Levi, Sussex co., inq., 1779. (3 N. E. 165).
Ellis, Thomas, Sussex co., inq., 1779. (3 N. E. 165).
Ellison, Robert, Sussex co. (magistrate), arrested, recanted,
fined, bail required, 1775-'6. (M. P. C. 333, 334; 2 Sa-
bine 511; Amer. Archives, Ser. IV, Vol. 4, p. 663; N. J.
R. C. 47).
Elston, Thomas, Middlesex co., inq., 1778. (2 N. E. 400).
Elwel, Israel, Salem co., judg., 1778-'9. (2 N. E. 470; 3 N.
E. 369).
Emley, John, Hunterdon co., refused oaths, fined, 1777. (Hunt.
Rec.).

Emmons, Jacob (or Jacobus), Shrewsbury, judg., sale, 1779-
'80. (3 N. E. 94; 4 N. E. 181).
English, Job, to Shelburne, N. S., at Peace. (2 Sabine 512).
Ensley, John, Sergeant, enlisting men for enemy, 1777. (N.
J. R. C. 47).
Etter, Franklin, Lieut., N. J. Vols. (5 C. N. B. 252).
Evans, John, Cumberland co., inq., 1778. (2 N. E. 496).
Everson, Barent, Saddle River, judg., sale, 1779. (3 N. E. 98,
526).
Fagan, "Jake," Monmouth co., "Pine robber," killed, 1778. (1
Sabine 408; Hist. Monm. co., Vol. 1, p. 103).
Fairholm, Johnston, arrested, paroled, 1776. (2 Sabine 513).
Falker, John, Essex co., Quartermaster 3 and 2 N. J. Vols.,
1777; resigned, 1783; judg., sale, 1778-'9. (2 N. E. 545;
3 N. E. 92, 384; Stryker's N. J. Vols. 38; 2 Sabine 515;
5 C. N. B. 235).
Fanker (Forker), Philip, imprisoned, 1776. (2 Sabine 513;
M. P. C. 478).
Farce, Philip, Sussex co., judg., 1779. (3 N. E. 46).
Farnham, John, Monmouth co., "Tory marauder." (1 Sabine
419; Hist. Mon. co., Vol. 1, p. 103).
Farrand, Stephen, Newark, fugitive, judg., sale, 1778-'9. (2
N. E. 385, 3 N. E. 47, 327).
Fennimore, Abraham, Gloucester co., high treason, death sentence, 1778; judg., sales 1779. (2 N. E. 583; 3 N. E.
450; N. J. R. C. 47).
Fenton, Elijah, Sussex co., inq., 1779. (3 N. E. 165).
Fenton, Lewis, Monmouth co., "Tory and robber outlaw,"
killed, 1779. (1 Sabine 420; Hist. Mon. Co., Vol. 1, p.
103).
Finney, George, N. J. Vols., captured, 1777. (2 Sabine 515).
Fisher, George, N. J. Vols., captured, 1777. (2 Sabine 515).
Fisher, Jonathan, Sr., Gloucester co., inq., 1778. (2 N. E.
581).
Fisher, Jonathan, Jr., Gloucester co., inq., 1778. (2 N. E.
581).
Fitzgerald, Ambrose, Cumberland co., judg., sale, 1778-'9. (2
N. E. 496; 3 N. E. 487).

Fitz Randolph, Jacob, Morris co., high treason, com., 1778. (M. C. S. 204).
Flanagan, James, Salem co., inq., 1778. (2 N. E. 470).
Flowers, Martin, Cumberland co., inq., 1778. (2 N. E. 496).
Fonce, Philip, Sussex co., inq., 1778. (2 N. E. 435).
Ford, Oswald, Woodbridge, judg., 1778; died during War. (2 N. E. 534; Mid Rec; see main text under John Ford).
Forman, Aaron, Hunterdon co., oaths refused, fined. (Hunt. Rec.).
Forsman, William, Gloucester co., judg., sale, 1779-'80. (3 N. E. 450, 650; 4 N. E. 192).
Foster, Frederick, to Grand Manan, N. B., at Peace; d. 1834. (36 N. Y. Gen & Biog. Rec. 189).
Foster, Lawrence, Monmouth co., to St. John, N. B., at Peace; d. 1823. (36 N. Y. Gen. & Biog. Rec. 189; see main text under Ebenezer Foster).
Foust, Jacob, gone to enemy, 1777. (M. C. S. 155, 157).
Fowler, Thomas, Monmouth or Burlington co., high treason, com., 1777. (M. C. S. 25, 87; N. J. R. C. 53).
Fox, George, Hunterdon co., refused oaths, fined, 1777. (Hunt. Rec.).
Fox, Hendrick, Bergen co., judg., 1779. (3 N. E. 98, 525; 4 N. E. 77).
Fox, Jacobus, Franklin twsp., Bergen co., judg., sale, 1779. (3 N. E. 98, 526; 4 N. E. 77; Hist. Bergen co., Vol. 1, p. 127).
Fox, Mattines, Bergen co., judg., 1779. (3 N. E. 526, 529).
Foy, Moses, to Shelburne, N. S., at Peace. (2 Sabine 516).
Franklin, John, Gloucester co., high treason, death sentence, 1778; judg., sale, 1779-'80. (2 N. E. 581, 583, 588; 4 N. E. 192; N. J. R. C. 137).
Frazee, James, Essex co., judg., sale, 1778-'9. (2 N. E. 545; 3 N. E. 92, 384).
Frazee, James, Jr., Essex co., judg., sale, 1779. (3 N. E. 384, 508, 528).
Frazer, Rev. William, Hunterdon co., refused oaths, fined, 1778. (Hunt. Rec.).

Fredericks, Conrad, Bergen co., judg., 1779. (3 N. E. 98, 525).
Fredericks, Hendrick, Bergen co., judg., 1779. (3 N. E. 98, 525).
Freeman, Edmund, Hunterdon co., refused oaths, fined, 1778. (Hunt. Rec.).
Freeman, Isaac, Woodbridge twsp., gone to enemy, 1777. (M. C. S. 124).
Freeman, Lewis, Hunterdon co., bound over, 1777. (M. C. S. 176).
French, Joseph, Essex and Morris cos., judg., sale, 1779-'80. (3 N. E. 328, 329, 373; 4 N. E. 269).
French, Philip, New Brunswick, judg., 1778. (2 N. E. 400, 401; Benedict's New Brunswick Hist., p. 32).
Friend, Charles, Hunterdon co., com., 1777. (M. C. S. 176).
Fritts, Frederick, Hunterdon co., arrested, fined, 1776. (M. P. C. 478, 527; 2 Sabine 517).
Fullerton, William, Cumberland co., inq., 1778. (2 N. E. 496).
Furman, Dr. Aaron, Hunterdon co., refused oaths, joining enemy, imprisoned, 1777. (M. C. S. 102, 142).
Fusman, Daniel, Gloucester co., high treason, death sentence, 1778. (2 N. E. 583; N. J. R. C. 137).
Fusman, William, Gloucester co., judg., sale, 1778-'9. (2 N. 2 581; 3 N. E. 131).
Gach, Philip, Middlesex co., fugitive, judg., sale, 1778-'9. (M. C. S. 187; 2 N. E. 400; 3 N. E. 95).
Gaine, Hugh, Newark (publisher), fugitive, judg., 1778-'9. (2 N. E. 593; 3 N. E. 49, 328).
Galbreaith, Thomas, Essex co., fugitive, judg., 1778. (2 N. E. 385; 3 N. E. 328).
Gardner, Jacob, imprisoned on confession, 1777. (M. C. S. 59).
Gardner, Thomas, New Barbadoes, judg., sale, 1778-'9. (2 N. E. 529; 3 N. E. 132, 526).
Garrabrant, Garrabrant, Essex co., judg., 1778. (2 N. E. 385, 536, 587).
Garrabrant, Garrabrant, Jr., Essex co., judg., 1779. (3 N. E. 327).

Garrabrant, Nicholas, Essex co., judg., 1778-'9. (2 N. E. 519, 587; 3 N. E. 328).
Garrison, Jacob, Salem co., inq., 1778. (2 N. E. 470).
Garvie, Alexander, Sergeant-Major N. J. Vols., captured, 1777. (2 Sabine 518).
Garvie, John, N. J. Vols., captured, 1777. (2 Sabine 518).
Garvie, William, N. J. Vols., captured, 1777. (2 Sabine 518).
Gault, Robert, Essex co., judg., sale, 1779. (3 N. E. 384, 508, 528).
Gesner, Abraham, in British army, 1776-'9; to Nova Scotia. (Hist. of Annapolis, N. S., 417).
Gibbs, Lucas, Gloucester co., pub. as "enemy to country," 1776. (2 Sabine 519).
Giberson, Benjamin, Upper Freehold, judg., sale, 1779-'80. (3 N. E., 95, 368; 4 N. E. 249).
Giberson, John, Monmouth co., Tory "Pine robber." (1 Mon. Hist. 103-4).
Giberson, Malachi, Upper Freehold, judg., sale, 1779-'80. (3 N. E. 94).
Giberson, William, Jr., Upper Freehold, judg., sale, 1779-'80. (3 N. E. 94, 368; 4 N. E. 249; M. P. C. 539).
Gilian, William, Monmouth co., "Tory marauder," killed. (1 Sabine 473).
Glan, Gabriel, Cumberland co., inq., 1779. (4 N. E. 1).
Godbier, William, Middlesex co., judg., sale, 1778-'9. (2 N. E. 400; 3 N. E. 95).
Goelet, Peter, Hackensack twsp., judg., sale, 1778-'9. (2 N. E. 529; 3 N. E. 132, 526).
Golden, George (alias John), Burlington co., judg., 1778-'9. (2 N. E. 544; 3 N. E. 417).
Goodman, Robert, Sussex co., judg., 1779. (3 N. E. 46).
Goodwin, Isaac, high treason, 1778. (M. C. S. 275).
Goodwin, Jacob, Sussex co., high treason, 1777. (M. C. S. 18, 26).
Goodwin, Robert, Sussex co., inq., 1778. (2 N. E. 435. Possibly same as Richard Goodman, supra).
Gordon, John, N. J. Vols., captured, 1777. (2 Sabine 521).

Gorman, John, Sussex co., with enemy, judg., 1778-'9. (M. C. S. 188; 2 N. E. 435; 3 N. E. 46).
Goslin, David, Middlesex co., judg., sale, 1779. (3 N. E. 322; 4 N. E. 303).
Gouveneur, Nicholas, Newark, arrest ordered, 1777. (M. C. S. 83).
Graham, Robert, Middlesex co., judg., sale, 1780. (4 N. E. 230).
Grames, (Grimes) Robert, Middlesex co., judg., 1778-'9. (2 N. E. 401; 3 N. E. 62).
Grandin, Daniel, Monmouth co., Ensign 3 & 6 N. J. Vols., 1777-'8; refused oaths, bound over, 1777; to Nova Scotia at Peace. (5 C. N. B., 265; Stryker's N. J. Vols., 63; M. C. S. 33).
Grandin, Thomas, Ensign N. J. Vols., 1777; 6 N. J. Vols., 1778, when court-martialled; to Shelburne, N. S., at Peace. (DeLancey's Brig. Orderly Book, p. 49).
Grandin, William, Monmouth co., bound over, 1777. (M. C. S. 35).
Greames, James, disaffected, com., 1776. (M. P. C. 487; 2 Sabine 522).
Green, Reuben, Sussex co., judg., 1778-'9. (2 N. E. 435; 3 N. E. 46).
Green, Samuel, Hunterdon co., refused oaths, fined, 1777. (Hunt. Rec.).
Green, William, Sussex co., fined, com., 1777; judg., sales, 1779. (M. C. S. 81; 3 N. E. 328, 553).
Greenfield, Lewis, Newark, judg., sale, 1778-'9. (2 N. E. 385; 3 N. E. 47, 327).
Grover, Barzilla, Upper Freehold, judg., 1779-'80. (3 N. E. 368; 4 N. E. 249).
Grover, Joseph, Upper Freehold, judg., 1779. (4 N. E. 249).
Grover, Samuel, Upper Freehold, judg., sale, 1779. (3 N. E. 94).
Grover, Thomas, Upper Freehold, judg., sale, 1779. (3 N. E. 94).
Gruff, John, Gloucester co., to Nova Scotia at Peace; judg., sale, 1778-'9. (2 N. E. 582; 3 N. E. 129, 650; 2 Sabine 524).

Guillon, William, Monmouth co., judg., sale, 1780. (4 N. E. 191).
Habblings, Thomas P., merchant, to Shelburne, N. S., at Peace. (2 Sabine 524).
Hadden, Isaac, Lieut. and Adjutant, 5 N. J. Vols., 1777, and 1st N. J. Vols., 1778; Prov. Light Infantry, 1780; became Clerk House of Assembly, Prov. of New Brunswick. (Ind.: 5604; 5 C. N. B. 237, 352; 1 Sabine 504; Stryker's N. J. Vols. 36).
Hagle, John, Martin, Bergen co., inq., 1778. (2 N. E. 529).
Halfpenny, Mr., trading with enemy, 1777. (N. J. R. C. 59).
Hall, Elisha, Salem co., inq., 1778. (2 N. E. 470).
Hall, Isaac, Cumberland co., inq., 1778. (2 N. E. 496).
Hall, Levi, Cumberland co., inq., 1778. (2 N. E. 496).
Hall, William, Middlesex co., inq., 1778. (2 N. E. 401).
Hallens, Cornelius, Bergen co., inq., 1779. (4 N. E. 90).
Hallet, Joseph, Essex co., fugitive, judg., 1778-'9. (2 N. E. 385; 3 N. E. 328).
Halstead, William, Elizabeth Town, "engaged with Lippincott in murder of Huddy;" settled at Tuscet, N. S., after War. (2 Sabine 525).
Hamilton, Joshua, Adjutant 4th N. J. Vols. (5 C. N. B. 237).
Hammet, William, Gloucester co., high treason, death sentence, 1778. (2 N. E. 583; N. J. R. C. 137).
Hampton, John, Shrewsbury, judg., sale, 1779-'80. (3 N. E. 94, 368; 4 N. E. 248).
Hancock, Joseph, Sussex co., joined enemy, 1778. (M. C. S. 246).
Hand, John (carpenter), Aaron and Samuel, to St. John, N. B., at Peace; then to Bellevue, Charlotte co., N. B. (2 Sabine 525; 5 C. N. B. 276; 37 N. Y. Gen. & Biog. Rec. 12).
Handorff, Frederick, Ensign 4th N. J. Vols., 1782. (5 C. N. B. 266).
Hankinson, John, Shrewsbury, judg., sale, 1779. (3 N. E. 94).
Hanks, John, Cumberland co., "murderer," inq., 1778. (2 N. E. 496; 1 Sabine 516).
Hannah, Nathaniel, to Shelburne, N. S., at Peace. (2 Sabine 526).

Hannisey, James, Gloucester co., judg., sale, 1778-'9. (2 N. E. 581; 3 N. E. 129, 650).

Hannison, Henry J., Bergen co., inq., 1779. (3 N. E. 98).

Harber, Jacob, Shrewsbury, judg., sale, 1779. (3 N. E. 94).

Harding, Robert, to Shelburne, N. S., at Peace. (2 Sabine 526).

Haring, John C., Harrington twsp., judg., sale, 1779. (3 N. E. 98, 526; 4 N. E. 77; Hist. Bergen Co., Vol. I, p. 123).

Haring, Peter J., Bergen co., magistrate, arrest ordered, 1777. (M. C. S. 83).

Haring, Peter T. (or I.), Harrington twsp., judg., sale, 1779. (3 N. E. 98, 526; 4 N. E. 77).

Haring, Cornelius, Captain, Bergen co., arrest ordered, 1777. (M. C. S. 83).

Harned, Benjamin, Sussex co., judg., 1778-'9. (2 N. E. 435; 3 N. E. 46).

Harned, John, Middlesex co., judg., sale, 1778-'9. (2 N. E. 400; 3 N. E. 95).

Harned, Nathaniel, Middlesex co., judg., sale, 1778. (2 N. E. 400; 3 N. E. 95; 4 N. E. 303, 330).

Harris, Edmund, high treason, com., 1777. (M. C. S. 31, 32).

Harris, John, Bridgewater twsp., Somerset co., judg., sale, 1779. (3 N. E. 96, 591).

Harrison, Samuel, Essex co., fugitive, judg., 1778-'9. (2 N. E. 519; 3 N. E. 328).

Hartpence, John, Hunterdon co., oaths refused, fined, com., 1776-'7. (M. P. C. 478; Hunt. Rec.).

Hartshorne, Isaac, refused oaths, com., 1777. (M. C. S. 35, 36).

Hartshorne, Lawrence, Shrewsbury, merchant; to Halifax, N. S. at Peace; member of House of Assembly of Nova Scotia; died 1822, aged 67. (1 Sabine 521).

Hartshorne, Robert, refused oaths, com., 1777. (M. C. S. 35, 36).

Hartshorne, Thomas, Jr., Monmouth co., judg., sale, 1780. (4 N. E. 191).

Hassen, Felix, Sussex co., fined, com., 1777. (M. C. S. 81).

Haten, Nathaniel, "enemy to country," 1775. (2 Sabine 527).
Hatfield, Abel, Essex co., inq., 1778. (2 N. E. 545, 594).
Hatfield, Cornelius, Essex co., refugee, inq., 1779. (3 N. E. 109, 441; Essex Rec.).
Hatfield, Job, Essex co., judg., 1778-'9. (2 N. E. 545; 3 N. E. 384).
Hathaway, Simon, captured, 1777. (2 Sabine 528).
Havens, John, Essex co., joining enemy, 1777. (M. C. S. 74; N. J. R. C. 78, 79).
Havens, Stout, high treason, com., 1777. (M. C. S. 64; N. J. R. C. 107).
Heard, John, Woodbridge, with enemy, 1777; judg., sale, 1784. (M. C. S. 124; N. J. Gazette, 1784).
Hedger, John, Somerset co., bound over, 1777. (M. C. S. 176).
Hedges, Stephen, Middletown, inq., 1782. (5 N. E. 46).
Helme, Benjamin, bound over, 1777. (M. C. S. 26).
Hempstead, Jeremiah, Middlesex co., judg., sale, 1778-'9. (2 N. E. 400; 3 N. E. 95).
Henchman, John, Gloucester co., magistrate, com. for disloyalty, 1777. (M. C. S. 48, 49, 53, 57, 58).
Hendricks, Baker, Essex co., bound over, 1777; suspended as Capt. of war vessels, 1780. (M. C. S. 168; 5 N. E. 459).
Hendricks, John, Essex co., bound over, 1777. (M. C. S. 168).
Hendrickson, Daniel, Monmouth co., refused oaths, bound over, 1777. (M. C. S. 37).
Henry, Herbert, high treason, 1778. (M. C. S. 272).
Heslop, John, Adjutant and Lieut., 3 & 4 N. J. Vols., 1777, 1781. (5 C. N. B. 237, 253).
Hewitt, Jacob, Gloucester co., judg., 1778. (2 N. E. 581; 3 N. E. 131, 650).
Hewitt, Job, Gloucester co., judg., sale, 1779. (Glouc. Rec.).
Hewlings, Joseph, Mt. Holly, fugitive, judg., sale, 1777-'79. (M. C. S. 47; 2 N. E. 543; 3 N. E. 115, 369).
Hewlings, Thomas P., inq., 1777-'8. (M. C. S. 20; 2 N. E. 543).

Hewlings, William, committed to jail, 1778. (M. C. S. 219).
Heyden, Samuel, Capt. 4th N. J. Vols., captured, paroled, 1777. (Stryker's N. J. Vols., 50).
Hicks, Oliver, Shrewsbury., judg., sale, 1779-'80. (3 N. E. 94, 368; 4 N. E. 248).
Hiler, Jacob, Morris co., gone to enemy, 1777; judg., 1778. (M. C. S. 46; 2 N. E. 593).
Hiler, Nicholas, gone to enemy, 1777. (M. C. S. 46).
Hilton, Joseph, Salem co., inq., 1778. (2 N. E. 470).
Himeon, Adam, Bergen co., judg., 1779. (3 N. E. 98, 526).
Himeon, George, to Nova Scotia after Peace. (1 Sabine 529).
Himeon, Hendrick J., Saddle River, judg., sale, 1779; to Shelburne, N. S., after the Peace. (3 N. E. 98, 525, 526; 1 Sabine 529).
Himeon, Jacob, Bergen co., judg., 1779. (3 N. E. 98, 525).
Himeon, Philip, Bergen co., to Shelburne, N. S., after Peace. (1 Sabine 529).
Hoagland, Obadiah, Sussex co., judg., 1778-'9. (2 N. E. 435; 3 N. E. 46).
Hoffman, Christopher, Sussex co., judg., 1778. (2 N. E. 435; 3 N. E. 46).
Hoffman, Nicholas, Essex and Morris cos., judg., sale, 1779-'80; Bergen co., sale, 1786. (3 N. E. 49, 165, 328; 4 N. E. 269; Hist. Bergen Co., Vol. I, p. 128).
Holcomb, John, Hunterdon co., refused oaths, fined, 1777. (Hunt. Rec.).
Holcombe, Jeremiah, Hackensack, farmer, to St. John's, N. B., at Peace. (2 Sabine 531; 5 C. N. B. 266).
Hole, John, Sussex co., bound over, 1777. (M. C. S. 88).
Hollinshead, Anthony, Lieut. 3 N. J. Vols. to 1779; judg., 1778. (Stryker's N. J. Vols. 56; 2 N. E. 593).
Holmes, Joseph, to Shelburne, N. S., at Peace. (2 Sabine 531).
Homer, Fuller, Upper Freehold, judg., sale, 1779-'80. (3 N. E. 94, 368; 4 N. E. 249).
Hones, John, Bergen co., inq., 1779. (3 N. E. 529).

Honeyman, John, Somerset co., inq., judg., etc. (3 N. E. 96; M. C. S. 176, 177, etc.).[1]

Hopkins, Silas, Capt. 5th N. J. Vols., 1776, 1777. (M. C. S. 85; 5 C. N. B. 242).

Hopper, Garret A., Bergen co., inq., 1780. (5 N. E. 124).

Hornbeck, Isaac, Morris co., judg., sale, 1778-'9. (2 N. E. 593; 3 N. E. 92).

Horner, Asher, of N. J. Vols., captured, 1777. (2 Sabine 532).

Horner, Hugh, of N. J. Vols., captured, 1777. (2 Sabine 532).

Horner, James, of N. J. Vols., liquor dealer, 1776. (2 Sabine 532).

Horner, Joseph, Middlesex co., oaths refused, com., 1777. (M. C. S. 175).

Howard, George, Middlebrook, judg., 1777-'9. (M. C. S. 103; 3 N. E. 49, 153, 591).

Howard, Sheffield, Essex co., judg., 1779. (3 N. E. 328, 329, 373).

Howard, William, Morris co., judg., sale, 1778-'9. (2 N. E. 593; 3 N. E. 92).

Hudnot, Samuel, Essex co., Capt. 3 N. J. Vols., 1777; judg., 1779. (3 N. E. 49, 328; 5 C. N. B. 242; Stryker's N. J. Vols. 50).

Hulett, Daniel, Monmouth co., judg, sale, 1780. (4 N. E. 191).

Hulett, Michael, Monmouth co., judg., sale, 1780; to Shelburne, N. S. at Peace. (4 N. E. 191; 2 Sabine 533).

Humbert, Stephen, to St. John, N. B., at Peace; held office in N. B. Assembly, etc.; died 1849. (1 Sabine 554; 37 N. Y. Gen. & Biog. Rec., 132).

---

[1] He was in the Secret Service of Gen. Washington; resided at Griggstown, N. J., and, from his occupation within and without the British lines, was believed by his neighbors to be a Loyalist. Both inquisitions and indictments were found against him, and personal and real property advertised, but nothing was actually sold, and at the Peace he resumed his occupation at Griggstown. Particulars, more or less, appear in many publicatons, including Stryker's "Battles of Trenton and Princeton," p. 87, Stockton's "Stories of New Jersey," Van Dyke's "The Raritan," "Our Home," 1873, "The Honeyman Family," etc.

Humphries, Dr. Nicholas, Surgeon, N. J. Vols., to Prov. of New Brunswick at Peace; d. 1822. (1 Sabine 554).
Hunt, Daniel, Hunterdon co., arrest ordered, 1776. (M. P. C. 498).
Hunt, John, Hunterdon, arrest ordered, 1776. (M. P. C. 478).
Hunt, Jonathan, Hunterdon co., arrest ordered, 1776. (M. P. C. 478, 487; 2 Sabine 534).
Hunt, William, Jr., Hunterdon co., arrest ordered, 1776. (M. P. C. 478).
Hurlet, William K., Ensign 2 N. J. Vols., 1778. (Stryker's N. J. Vols. 63).
Hurst, George, N. J. Vols., captured, 1777. (2 Sabine 535).
Husk, Thomas, Morris co., judg., 1778. (2 N. E. 350, 593).
Iliff, James, imprisoned and hanged, 1777. (1 Sabine 561; 2 N. E. 12, 13, 14).
Iliff, William, enlisting men for enemy, hanged, 1778. (2 N. E. 82).
Ingland, William, Jr., Gloucester co., inq., 1778. (2 N. E. 581).
Inglish, John, Gloucester co., inq., 1778. (2 N. E. 581).
Inglish, John, Jr., Gloucester co., inq., 1778. (2 N. E. 582).
Ink, John, joining enemy, 1777. (M. C. S. 142).
Insley, Christopher, Sussex co., Lieut. 5th N. J. Vols., 1776; Rogers's King's Rangers, 1779; killed in 1781; judg., 1778-'9. (2 N. E. 434; 3 N. E. 46; 1 Sabine 566; 5 C. N. B. 254).
Insley, Jacob, Sussex co., judg., 1778-'9. (2 N. E. 434; 3 N. E. 46).
Insley, John, Sussex co., judg., 1779. (3 N. E. 46).
Irons, John, Dover twsp., judg., 1779-'80. (4 N. E. 249).
Izalton, Robert, Newark, imprisoned, 1778. (M. C. S. 202).
Jacklin, John, to Shelburne, N. S., at Peace. (2 Sabine 536).
Jackson, Samuel, to Shelburne, N. S., at Peace. (2 Sabine, 536).
Jackson, William, to Shelburne, N. S., at Peace. (2 Sabine 536).

Jacobus, Garret, Acquackanock, judg., sale, 1779. (3 N. E. 48, 328).
James, Robert, Freehold, judg., sale, 1779; high treason, death sentence, 1781. (3 N. E. 323; 5 N. E. 191).
Jameson, Samuel, Salem co., judg.; to Shelburne, N. S., at Peace. (2 N. E. 470; Salem Records; 2 Sabine 536).
Jaquish, David, Middlesex co., judg., sale, 1779. (3 N. E. 95).
Jauncey, James, Essex co., judg., 1779. (3 N. E. 328, 329, 373).
Jefferis, John, Cumberland co., inq., 1778. (2 N. E. 496).
Jenkins, Griffen, Newark, judg., sale, 1778-'9. (2 N. E. 385; 3 N. E. 47, 327).
Jenkins, Trivis, Salem co., inq., 1778. (2 N. E. 470).
Jessup, Daniel, New Barbadoes, judg., sale, 1778-'9; to Shelburne, N. S., at Peace. (2 N. E. 529; 3 N. E. 132, 526; 4 N. E. 1; Hist. Bergen co., Vol. 1, p. 127; 2 Sabine 537).
Jessup, Jeremiah, to Shelburne, N. S., at Peace. (2 Sabine 537).
Joans, Edward, Bergen co., inq., 1779. (3 N. E. 98).
Johnson, Eliphalet, Essex co., refused oaths, com., 1777. (M. C. S. 74; N. J. R. C. 78, 79).
Johnson, George, Salem co., judg., 1778-'79. (2 N. E. 470; 3 N. E. 369).
Johnson, Ichabod, "Tory plunderer," killed in 1783. (1 Sabine 588).
Johnson, Isaac, 1 N. J. Vols., captured, 1777. (2 Sabine 537).
Johnson, Peter, Gloucester co., judg., sale, 1779. (3 N. E. 450, 650).
Johnston, Robert, Sussex co., joining enemy, 1778. (M. C. S. 246).
Jones, Andrew, Gloucester co., inq., 1778. (2 N. E. 581).
Jones, Edward, Saddle River, judg., sale, 1779. (3 N. E 526).
Jones, Thomas, Bergen co., confessed, bound over, 1778. (M. C. S. 219, 227).
Kaign, James, N. J. Vols., captured, 1777. (2 Sabine 539).

Kaign, Thomas, N. J. Vols., captured, 1777. (2 Sabine 539).
Kearney, Isabel, Middlesex co., inq., 1778. (2 N. E. 534).
Kearney, Peter, Salem co., inq., 1778. (2 N. E. 470).
Kearney, Thomas, Monmouth co., held to bail, 1777. (M. C. S. 36).
Kelly, John, Gloucester co., 4 N. J. Vols.; inq., 1778. (2 N. E. 581; see main text under Henry Marsh).
Kemp, John Tabor and wife, Grace (dau. of Daniel Coxe), Essex, Hunterdon and Sussex cos., judg., sales, 1779-'80. (3 N. E. 328, 329, 373, 393; 4 N. E. 46, 278, 393; Hunt. Rec.).
Kenact, Matthias, Bergen co., inq., 1779. (3 N. E. 98).
Kent, David, Middletown, judg., sale, 1778-'9. (2 N. E. 400; 3 N. E. 95).
Kent, Erasmus, Jr., Salem co., judg., 1778. (Salem Rec.).
Kent, William, Middlesex co., inq., 1779. (3 N. E. 90).
Ketcham, Richard, Cumberland co., inq., 1778; to Shelburne, N. S., at Peace. (2 Sabine 540; 2 N. E. 496).
Ketteltos, Winant, Bergen co., inq., 1779. (4 N. E. 90).
Kichline, Philip, Sussex co., judg., 1778. (2 N. E. 435; 3 N. E. 46).
Kilbourn, Elijah, N. J. Vols., captured, 1777. (2 Sabine 540).
Kiker, Tobias, Shrewsbury, judg., sale, 1779-'80. (3 N. E. 94, 368; 4 N. E. 248).
Kindal, Joseph, Salem co., judg., 1778-'9. (2 N. E. 470; 3 N. E. 369).
King, Andrew, to Shelburne, N. S., at Peace. (2 Sabine 540).
King, Benjamin, N. J. Vols., captured, 1777. (2 Sabine 540).
King, James (alias Lippincott), Shrewsbury, judg., sale, 1779, 1784. (3 N. E. 89, 323; Mon Rec.).
King, John, Bergen co., inq., 1779. (Bergen Rec.).
King, Joseph, oaths refused, com., 1777. (M. C. S. 149).
Kingsland, Charles, New Barbadoes, judg., sale, 1779. (3 N. E. 132).
Kingsland, Charles, Jr., Bergen co., judg., 1779. (2 N. E. 529; 3 N. E. 526).
Kingsland, Cornelius, to Shelburne, N. S., at Peace. (2 Sabine 540).

Kingsland, Henry, New Barbadoes Neck, arrest ordered, 1777. (M. C. S. 83).

Kingsland, Isaac, Essex co., judg., sale, 1778-'9. (2 N. E. 519; 3 N. E. 48, 328).

Kingsland, Joseph, Newark, judg., sale, 1778-'9. (2 N. E. 385; 3 N. E. 47, 327; see main text under James Van Emburgh).

Kingsland, William, Jr., Bergen co., judg., sale, 1779. (3 N. E. 132, 526).

Kipp, Isaac N., Bergen co., inq., 1779. (4 N. E. 90).

Kipp, Nikasey (Nicholas ?), Bergen co., inq., 1778. (2 N. E. 529).

Kirby, John, Gloucester co., joining enemy, imprisoned, 1778. (M. C. S. 247).

Kitchen, Andrew, Sussex co., judg., 1778-'9. (2 N. E. 434; 3 N. E. 46).

Kitchen, John, Sussex co., joining enemy, imprisoned, 1777; judg., 1778-'9. (M. C. S. 139; 2 N. E. 434; 3 N. E. 46).

Kline, Jacob, Sussex co., judg., 1778-'9. (2 N. E. 435; 3 N. E. 46).

Kline, Philip, Sr., Sussex co., judg., 1778-'9. (2 N. E. 434; 3 N. E. 46).

Kline, Philip, Jr., Sussex co., inq., 1778. (2 N. E. 434).

Konkle, Hanadam, Sussex co., bound over, 1778. (M. C. S. 275).

Konkle, Mathias, Sussex co., bound over, 1778. (M. C. S. 275).

Laight, Edward, Essex co., inq., 1779. (4 N. E. 2).

Lake, Mr., Middlesex co., trading with enemy, 1777. (N. J. R. C. 59).

Lamb, Thomas, Salem co., judg., 1778-'9. (2 N. E. 470; 3 N. E. 369).

Lambert, Isaac, N. J. Vols., captured, 1777. (M. C. S. 142; 2 Sabine 542).

Lambert, John, Lieut. 3 N. J. Vols., captured, 1777. (2 Sabine 542; 37 N. Y. Gen. & Biog. Rec. 212).

Lambert, Lancelot, N. J. Vols., captured, 1777. (2 Sabine 542).

Langley, Henry, Salem co., inq., 1778. (2 N. E. 470).
Langley, Reuben, Salem co., judg., 1778-'9. (2 N. E. 470; 3 N. E. 369).
Large, Aaron, Hunterdon co., oaths refused, fined and com., 1777. (M. C. S. 103; Hunt. Rec.).
Laquier, John, Hunterdon co., oaths refused, fined, 1777. (Hunt. Rec.).
Lawrence, Daniel, bound over, 1777. (M. C. S. 28).
Lawrence, John, Monmouth co., distinguished N. J. lawyer; member of Council, 1771-'5; imprisoned; went to Upper Canada. (2 Sabine 3).
Lawrence, Thomas, Major N. J. Vols. (2 Sabine 543).
Lawrence, William, Shrewsbury, Ensign 1st N. J. Vols., 1776; resigned, 1780; judg., sale, 1779. (5 C. N. B. 267; 3 N. E. 94; Stryker's N. J. Vols. 64).
Lawton, Lewis, to Shelburne, N. S., at Peace. (2 Sabine 543).
Layton, Samuel, Shrewsbury, judg., sale, 1779-'80. (3 N. E. 94; 4 N. E. 191).
Lee, John, Essex co., inq., 1779. (Essex Rec.).
Leezear, Nicholas, Bergen co., inq., 1778. (Bergen Rec.).
Lefferty, Bryan, Somerset co., bailed, paroled, 1776. (2 Sabine 543; M. P. C. 519).
Leffettre (Lefferty?), Daniel, Shrewsbury, judg., sale, 1779. (3 N. E. 94, 368; Mon. Rec.).
Leinbach, Frederick, Sussex co., oaths refused, bound over, 1777. (M. C. S. 84).
Lemmon, Michael, Essex and Sussex cos., inq., 1778. (2 N. E. 435; 3 N. E. 46).
Lemmon, Peter, Middlesex co., inq., 1779. (3 N. E. 366).
Lennox, David, Middlesex co., judg., sale, 1778-'9. (2 N. E. 400; 3 N. E. 95).
Lennox, Richard, Middlesex co., judg., sale, 1778-'9. (2 N. E. 400; 3 N. E. 95).
Lent, Abraham, Bergen co., judg., sale, 1779. (3 N. E. 98, 526; 4 N. E. 77).
Lent, Peter, Bergen co. (and Orange co., N. Y.), judg., sale, 1779. (3 N. E. 98, 526; 4 N. E. 77).

Leonard, Joseph, Middletown, judg., sale, 1778-'80. (3 N. E. 323; 4 N. E. 190).
Leseter, Daniel, Shrewsbury, judg., 1780. (4 N. E. 248).
Lessheir, Jacob, Essex co., provisions to enemy, bound over, 1778. (M. C. S. 228).
Letts, Francis, Middlesex co., trading with enemy, 1777. (N. J. R. C. 59).
Lewis, Daniel, N. J. Vols., captured, 1777. (2 Sabine 544).
Lewis, Timothy, Saddle River, judg., sale, 1779. (3 N. E. 98, 526; 4 N. E. 77).
Linn, John, Belvidere, carpenter, died 1841, aged 108. (2 Sabine 17).
Lippincott, Elias, judg., sale, 1779. (3 N. E. 89, 323).
Lippincott, Jacob, to Shelburne, N. S., at Peace. (2 Sabine 545).
Lippincott, James, to Shelburne, N. S., at Peace. (2 Sabine 545).
Lippincott, Jedediah, to Shelburne, N. S., at Peace. (2 Sabine 545).
Liponer, Anthony, Bergen co., inq., 1779. (4 N. E. 90).
Lisk, Stacy, Middlesex co., judg., sale, 1779. (3 N. E. 90, 322).
Lloyd, David, Gloucester co., high treason, death sentence, 1778. (2 N. E. 583; N. J. R. C. 137).
Logan, Patrick, N. J. Vols., captured, 1777. (2 Sabine 546).
Long, Joseph, Gloucester co., judg., sale, 1778-'80. (2 N. E. 581; 3 N. E. 130, 450, 650; 4 N. E. 192).
Long, Silas, Gloucester co., inq., 1778. (2 N. E. 581).
Longworth, Isaac, Jr., Essex co., fugitive, judg., 1778-'9. (Essex Rec.).
Longworth, Thomas, Newark, fugitive, judg., sale, 1779. (2 N. E. 385; 3 N. E. 48, 327).
Lord, Asa, Gloucester co., judg., sale, 1778-'9. (2 N. E. 581; 3 N. E. 130).
Lord, Isaac, Gloucester co., high treason, death sentence, 1778. (2 N. E. 583; N. J. R. C. 137).
Loshier, Nicholas, Hackensack twsp., judg., 1778, sale, 1784. (2 N. E. 529; Hist. Bergen Co., Vol. I, p. 128).
Loshier (see Lessheir).

Lott, Andrew, Morris co., bound over, 1778. (M. C. S. 249).
Lowrey, Joseph, Sr., Sussex co., judg., 1778-'9. (2 N. E. 435; 3 N. E. 46).
Lowrey, Joseph, Jr., Sussex co., inq., 1778. (2 N. E. 435).
Lowry, David, tailor, "ducked, and tried afterward." (2 Sabine 547).
Lowry, James, to Shelburne, N. S., at or before Peace. (2 Sabine 547).
Lowry, William, N. J. Vols., captured, 1777. (2 Sabine 547).
Ludlow, George, Morris co., judg., sale, 1780. (4 N. E. 269).
Ludlow, William W., Morris co., judg., sale, 1780. (4 N. E 269).
Lufburrow, John, Middletown, inq., 1782. (5 N. E. 46).
Lufburrow, Nathaniel, "Rider" in N. J. Vols.; captured, 1777; settled at Pennfield, N. B., at Peace. (2 Sabine 35).
Lundy, Jacob, Sussex co., oaths refused, bound over, 1777. (M. C. S. 86).
Lundy, Reuben, Sussex co., bound over, 1777. (M. C. S. 88).
Lundy, Samuel, Sussex co., oaths refused, bound over, 1777. (M. C. S. 86)
Lundy, Thomas, Sussex co., oaths refused, bound over, 1777. (M. C. S. 85).
Lurton, William, Middlesex co., judg., sale, 1778-'9. (2 N. E. 534; 3 N. E. 95).
Lutkins, Hermanus, Bergen co., inq., 1779-'80. (4 N. E. 90; 5 N. E. 124).
Lutkins, John, New Barbadoes, judg., sale, 1778-'9, 1784. (2 N. E. 529; 3 N. E. 132, 526; Hist. Bergen Co., Vol. I, p. 127).
Lycan, Enoch, Lieut. West Jersey Vols. and 3 N. J. Vols., 1778. (5 C. N. B. 255).
Lydecker, Samuel, English Neighborhood, arrest ordered, 1777. (M. C. S. 83).
Lyon, Thomas, Bergen co., judg., 1779. (3 N. E. 98, 525).
M'Carty, Duncan, Middlesex co., judg., 1778-'9. (2 N. E. 401; 3 N. E. 62).
McCleary (McCleney), John, Mansfield Woodhouse, Sussex co., N. J. Vols., captured, 1777. (2 Sabine 551; Amer. Archives, Ser. IV., Vol. 4, p. 1590).

MacCord, John, Hunterdon co., arrest ordered, 1776. (M. P. C. 478).
McEowin (McCowin), John, Oxford, judg., 1778-'9. (2 N. E. 435; 3 N. E. 46).
McEvers, Charles, Hunterdon co., judg., sale, 1779. (Hunt. Rec.).
McFadden, Cornelius, N. J. Vols., captured, 1777. (2 Sabine 553).
McGalvin, William, Somerset co., bound over, 1778. (M. C. S. 267).
McGee, Francis, Sussex co., fined, com., 1777. (M. C. S. 81).
McGinness, John, Essex co., joining enemy, com., 1777. (M. C. S. 74; N. J. R. C. 78).
McGinnis, Richard, Ensign West Jersey Vols., 1778, and 3 N. J. Vols. 1779; Lieut. 1780; killed, 1780. (5 C. N. B. 268; Stryker's N. J. Vols., 65).
MacKinzey, Kenneth, Bergen co., inq., 1779. (4 N. E. 90).
M'Koy, (McCoy), Alexander, Bergen co., inq., 1779. (3 N. E. 98).
McLean, Hector, Ensign 1st N. J. Vols., 1778-'9. (Stryker's N. J. Vols. 65).
McLeod, Donald, Lieut. King's Orange Rangers, 1782. (2 Sabine 554).
McLeod, Duncan, to Prov. of New Brunswick at Peace. (2 Sabine 554).
McLeod, John, to Prov. of New Brunswick at Peace; died 1805. (2 Sabine 554).
McLeod, Norman, Capt. 2nd N. J. Vols., 1778; Capt. Prov. Light Infantry, 1781; Capt. 4th (or 3rd) N. J. Vols., 1781. (Ind.: 5604; 2 Sabine 554; 5 C. N. B. 245; Stryker's N. J. Vols. 52).
McLeod, Roderick, Lieut., King's Amer. Regt. (2 Sabine 554).
McLeod, William, Elizabethtown, arrest ordered, 1775; Ensign 52nd Reg't, 1775. (2 Sabine 70; Amer. Archives, Ser. IV, Vol. 2, p. 1591).
M'Minn, John, Middlesex co., inq., 1778. (2 N. E. 534).

McMullen, Robert, Monmouth co., condemned for burglary, reprieved, joined enemy. (2 N. E. 312, 453).
McPherson, Donald, Lieut. 4th N. J. Vols., 1777-'8; Capt. British Legion. (5 C. N. B. 256; Stryker's N. J. Vols. 57).
McPherson, Nathaniel, Hunterdon co., oaths refused, com., 1777. (M. C. S. 103).
McVane, Colin, Ensign 4th N. J. Vols., 1777-'9. (5 C. N. B. 269; Stryker's N. J. Vols. 65).
Maddox, Arthur, Capt. and Adjutant, 4th N. J. Vols., 1777. (5 C. N. B. 237, 243; Stryker's N. J. Vols. 37).
Maish, Henry, Bergen co., inq., 1778 (2 N. E. 529).
Makus, James, Bergen co., inq., 1779. (4 N. E. 90).
Man, Matthias, Middlesex co., judg., sale, 1779. (3 N. E. 95).
Mann, Samuel, to Shelburne, N. S., at Peace. (2 Sabine 549).
Margison, Richard, high treason, com., 1777. (M. C. S. 55, 58, 64).
Marr, Lawrence, of James Moody's party; imprisoned, tried as spy and executed, 1781. (2 Sabine 48; Moody's Narrative, 2nd Ed.).
Marsh, Benjamin, Middlesex co., judg., sale, 1778-'9. (2 N. E. 534; 3 N. E. 95, 323; 4 N. E. 303).
Marsh, Elias, Newark, com., 1778. (M. C. S. 202).
Marsh, Esther, high treason, com., 1778. (M. C. S. 189).
Marsh, John, Essex co., inq., 1779. (3 N. E 384).
Marsh, Joseph, Essex co., judg., sale, 1779. (3 N. E. 508, 528).
Marshall, George, Essex co., judg., sale, 1779. (3 N. E. 384, 508, 528).
Martin, Henry, Hackensack twsp., judg., sale, 1779. (Bergen Rec.).
Martin, Robert, Middlesex co., judg., sale, 1778-'9; to Shelburne, N. S., at Peace. (2 N. E. 401, 557; 3 N. E. 62, 63, 435; 2 Sabine 550).
Martin, Runyon, to Shelburne, N. S., at Peace. (2 Sabine 550).
Masterson, David, New Barbadoes, judg., sale, 1779. (3 N. E. 98, 526).

Maxwell, William, Essex co., fugitive, inq., 1778. (2 N. E. 385).

Mead, Richard, Salem co., judg., 1779. (3 N. E. 369).

Mee, John, tried and hanged for treason, 1777-'8. (2 N. E. 82; 2 Sabine 76; Moody's Narrative, 2nd Ed., p. 8).

Melvin, Daniel, trading with enemy, 1781. (5 N. E. 181).

Merrill, Joseph, Hunterdon co., judg., sale, 1778-'9. (2 N. E. 355; 3 N. E. 68, 113; 4 N. E. 46).

Merrill, Richard, Middlesex co., inq., 1778. (2 N. E. 400).

Merselis, John, Hackensack twsp., judg., sale, 1779. (3 N. E. 98, 526; 4 N. E. 77; Hist. Bergen Co., Vol I, pp. 126, 127).

Meyer, Johannes G., Bergen co., inq., 1780. (Bergen Rec.).

Meyers, John, New Barbadoes, judg., sale, 1778-'9; to Shelburne, N. S., at Peace. (2 N. E. 529; 3 N. E. 132, 526; 2 Sabine 56).

Meyers (see Myer, Myers).

Mian, John, Bergen co., inq., 1778. (Bergen Rec.).

Millack, William, Sussex co., judg., 1778-'9. (2 N. E. 435; 3 N. E. 46).

Millenburg (Miltenberry), Lewis, Bergen co., judg., 1779; sale, 1784. (3 N. E. 98; Hist. Bergen Co., Vol. I, p. 128).

Miller, George, Bergen co., inq., 1779. (3 N. E. 529).

Miller, John, Ensign 3 N. J. Vols., 1776, and in British Legion, 1782. (Ind.: 5604; 5 C. N. B., 267).

Miller, Michael, Salem co., judg., sale, 1778-'80. (2 N. E. 470; 3 N. E. 528; 4 N. E. 373).

Miller, Richard, Essex co., judg., 1778-'9. (2 N. E. 545; 3 N. E. 92, 384).

Millham, Herman, Hunterdon co., arrest ordered, 1776. (M. P. C., 478).

Mills, Henry, Sussex co., judg., 1778-'9. (2 N. E. 434; 3 N. E. 46).

Mills, Isaac, Essex co., judg., sale, 1779. (3 N E. 384, 508, 528).

Mills, John, gone to enemy, 1777. (M. C. S. 155, 157).

Minor, Samuel, Middlesex co., discouraging enlistments, bound over, 1778. (M. C. S. 227).
Monden (Mongan), Rev. Charles, Chaplain, 2nd and 3rd N. J. Vols., 1782-'3. (2 Sabine 557; 5 C. N. B. 231).
Money, Matthew, Salem co., inq., 1778. (2 N. E. 470).
Moody, Bonnell, Sussex co., hanged as spy. (2 Sabine 98).
Moody, John (brother of James), Sussex co., tried as spy, executed, 1781. (2 Sabine 97; see main text under James Moody).
Moore, Daniel, Hunterdon co., oaths refused, fined, 1777. (Hunt. Rec.).
Moore, Daniel, Essex co., judg., sale, 1778-'9. (2 N. E. 545, 594; 3 N. E. 92, 384).
Moore, James, Essex co., judg., sale, 1778-'9. (2 N. E. 545; 3 N. E. 92, 384).
Moore, John, Sussex co., bound over, 1778. (M. C. S. 275).
Moore, Joseph, Hunterdon co., oaths refused, fined, 1777. (Hunt. Rec.).
Moore, Michael, Bergen and Hunterdon cos., inq., 1778, judg., sale, 1779. (2 N. E. 529; 3 N. E. 396).
Moore, Thomas, Hackensack, "Chairman Loyalist meeting." (2 Sabine 558).
Moote, George, Sussex co., bound over, 1778. (M. C. S. 275).
Morden, James, Sussex co., judg., 1778-'9. (2 N. E. 435; 3 N. E. 46).
Morgen, Dr. Lewis, Assistant Surgeon, 1776; Capt.-Lieut., 1776; Capt. 3 N. J. Vols., 1777; perhaps went to Bahamas in 1783. (5 C. N. B. 244, 248; Am. MSS. in Roy. Inst., IV, 294, 227).
Morris, Eva, Middlesex co., oaths refused, bound over, 1778. (M. C. S. 285).
Morris, Israel, Hunterdon co., oaths and bail refused, com., 1778. (M. C. S. 254).
Morris, James, Sussex co., high treason, com., 1777. (M. C. S. 82).
Morris, Noah, Cumberland co., refugee, com., escaped, 1780. (5 N. E. 19).

Morrow, John, Salem co., judg., sales, 1778-'9. (3 N. E. 115, 369).
Morse, John, Essex co., judg., sale, 1778-'9, 1784. (2 N. E. 545; 3 N. E. 92, 384; N. J. Gazette, 1784).
Morse, Joseph, Jr., Essex co., bound over, 1778. (M. C. S. 202).
Mount, James, Shrewsbury, judg., sale, 1779-'80. (3 N. E. 94, 368; 4 N. E. 248).
Mount, Richard, to Shelburne, N. S., at Peace. (2 Sabine 559).
Mountain, Richard, Sussex co., 1778-'9. (2 N. E. 435; 3 N. E. 46).
Mourisson, Francis, joining enemy, com., 1777. (M. C. S. 46).
Mowrison, Peter, Newark, fugitive, judg., sale, 1778-'9. (2 N. E. 385; 3 N. E. 48, 328).
Mullin, Andrew, N. J. Vols., captured, 1777. (2 Sabine 559).
Mullin, James, N. J. Vols., captured, 1777. (2 Sabine 559).
Munday, Hopewell, Middlesex co., judg., sale, 1778-'9. (2 N. E. 400; 3 N. E. 95).
Munday, John, Jr., Middlesex co., judg., sale, 1778-'9. (2 N. E. 534; 3 N. E. 95).
Munday, Joseph, Middlesex co., judg., sale, 1778-'9. (2 N. E. 400; 3 N. E. 95).
Munday, Nathaniel, Middlesex co., inq., 1778. (2 N. E. 400)
Munday, Nicholas, Jr., Middlesex co., judg., sale, 1778-'9. (2 N. E. 400; 3 N. E. 95).
Munday, Reuben, Middlesex co., inq., 1778. (2 N. E. 534).
Murphy, Edward, to Shelburne, N. S., at Peace. (2 Sabine 560).
Mushback, John, oaths refused, bound over, 1777. (M. C. S. 85).
Myer, George, Sussex co., judg., 1778-'9. (2 N. E. 434; 3 N. E. 46).
Myer, Peter, Ensign N. J. Vols., 1778; killed, 1779. (2 Sabine 118; Stryker's N. J. Vols. 65).
Myers, Thomas, to Shelburne, N. S., at Peace. (2 Sabine 561).
Nelson, Ananias, Salem co., inq., 1778. (2 N. E. 470).

Newman, William, high treason, com., 1777. (M. C. S. 58, 64).
Nightengale, Thomas, Gloucester co., high treason, death sentence, 1778; judg., sale, 1779-'80. (2 N. E. 581, 583, 588; 4 N. E. 192; N. J. R. C. 137).
Nix, Peter, Bergen co., judg., 1779. (3 N. E. 98, 525).
Noble, Anthony, Salem co., inq., 1778. (2 N. E 470).
Norwood, Andrew, Middlesex co., inq., 1778. (2 N. E. 401).
Nutman, James, Captain, Essex co., oaths refused, com., 1777. (N. J. R. C. 78, 79; 2 Sabine 121).
O'Brien, Edward, to Shelburne, N. S., at Peace. (2 Sabine 562).
O'Bryant, John, Gloucester co., judg., sale, 1779. (2 N. E. 582; 3 N. E. 450, 650).
Ogden, James, South River, tried and hung as spy, 1781. (2 Sabine 127).
Ogden, John, Essex co., with enemy, 1778; to Shelburne, N. S., at Peace. (M. C. S. 192; 2 Sabine 562).
Ogden, Jonathan, to Prov. of New Brunswick at Peace; died at Greenwich, that Province, 1845, aged 97. (2 Sabine 126).
Ogden, Nathaniel, Essex co., judg., 1778-'9. (Essex Rec.).
Ogden, Robert, burned in effigy as Loyalist. (2 Sabine 123).
Ogden, Samuel, with enemy, personal forfeited, 1778. (M. C. S. 274).
Okeson, John, Hunterdon, Middlesex and Monmouth cos., judg., sale 1778-'80. (2 N. E. 355; 3 N. E. 93, 367; 4 N. E. 249).
Okeson, Samuel, Upper Freehold, judg., sale, 1779. (3 N. E. 95).
Oldwater (Outwater), Thomas, Harrington twsp., judg., sale, 1779, 1785. (3 N. E. 98, 526; 4 N. E. 77; Hist. Bergen Co., Vol. I, p. 127).
Oliver, Caleb, Hunterdon co., oaths refused, fined, 1777. (Hunt. Rec.).
Oliver, David, Essex co., judg., sale, 1778-'9; at Annapolis, N. S., after Peace. (3 N. E. 92, 384; see main text under Ichabod Oliver).

Oliver, Jonathan, Essex co., judg., sale, 1778-'9. (2 N. E. 545; 3 N. E. 92, 384).
Oliver, Samuel, Jr., Essex co, inq., 1778. (2 N. E. 545, 594).
Orr, John, to Shelburne, N. S., at Peace. (2 Sabine 563).
Overt, Peter, Middlesex co., trading with enemy, 1777. (N. J. R. C. 59).
Owen, James, Cumberland co., refugee, com., escaped, 1780. (5 N. E. 19).
Pace, William, Morris co., provisioning enemy, com., 1778. (M. C. S. 204).
Pack, Benjamin, to Nova Scotia at Peace. (2 Sabine 563).
Pack, John, Middlesex co., inq., 1778; to Shelburne, N. S., at Peace; then to St. John, N. B. (2 Sabine 563; 38 N. Y. Gen. & Biog. Rec. 254; 2 N. E. 401).
Park, Ozias, Sussex co., inq., 1778-'9. (2 N. E. 434; 3 N. E. 46).
Park, William, Sussex co., judg., 1778-'9. (2 N. E. 435; 3 N. E. 46).
Parker, James, Hunterdon co., oaths refused, jailed, bound over, 1777. (M. C. S. 117, 122; 9 Coll. Hist. Soc. of N. J. 173).
Parker, James, Cumberland co., inq., 1778. (2 N. E. 496).
Parker, Nathaniel, Shrewsbury, judg., sale, 1779. (3 N. E. 94).
Parker, Thomas, bound over, 1777. (M. C. S. 88).
Parr, John, Morris co., "Tory robber;" imprisoned, 1782. (2 Sabine 149).
Parsons, John, N. J. Vols., captured, 1777. (2 Sabine 564).
Patterson, David, to Shelburne, N. S., at Peace. (2 Sabine 564).
Patterson, Robert, shipmaster, to Shelburne, N. S., at Peace. (2 Sabine 564).
Patterson, William, Surgeon 1st N. J. Vols., 1776; 2 N. J. Vols. (2 Sabine 564; 5 C. N. B. 232).
Paulison, John, Hackensack Pt., arrest ordered, 1777. (M. C. S. 83).
Paulson, William, joining enemy, com., 1777. (M. C. S. 139).

Peak, Jacobus, Schraalenberg, imprisoned, judg., sale, 1777-'79. (M. C. S. 83; 3 N. E. 98, 526; 4 N. E. 77).
Peak, Samuel, Schraalenberg, arrest ordered, judg., sale, 1777-'79). (M. C. S. 83; 3 N. E. 132, 526; 4 N. E. 77).
Peaker, Philip, Bergen co., inq., 1779. (3 N. E. 98).
Peaker, William, Bergen co., inq., 1779. (3 N. E. 98).
Peck, David, Schraalenberg, Capt. N. J. Vols., judg., sale, 1778-'9. (2 N. E. 529; 3 N. E. 132, 292, 526; Hist. Bergen Co., Vol. I, p. 126).
Pell, John, Hackensack twsp., judg., sale, 1778-'9. (2 N. E. 529; 3 N. E. 132, 526).
Perine, John, Jr., Upper Freehold, judg., sale, 1779. (3 N. E. 62, 63, 368; may be same as John Perine in main text).
Perkin, Nathaniel, Monmouth co., judg., sale, 1780. (4 N. E. 191).
Persel, Abraham, Bergen co., judg., 1778-'9. (2 N. E. 529; 3 N. E. 526).
Peterson, Robert, Lieut. 1st N. J. Vols., 1777; imprisoned, 1777; Lieut. N. Y. Vols., 1783. (5 C. N. B. 257; Stryker's N. J. Vols. 59).
Peterson, Dr. William B., Elizabethtown, Surgeon 1st N. J. Vols., 1776; captured, 1777; 3rd N. J. Vols., 1779. (M. C. S. 83; 2 Sabine 565; 5 C. N. B. 232; Stryker's N. J. Vols. 41).
Pettit, Nathaniel, Sussex co., Judge, Member of Assembly, 1772-'5; arrested, fined, com., bailed, 1776. (M. P. C. 81, 333, 334; Amer. Archives, Ser. IV, Vol. 4, p. 663).
Pew, James, Middletown, with enemy, 1778; judg., sale, 1779-'80. (M. C. S. 243; 3 N. E. 94, 368; 4 N. E. 248).
Phillips, Thomas, Essex co., judg., 1779. (3 N. E. 328, 329, 372).
Phipps, John, Cumberland co., judg., sale, 1778-'9. (2 N. E. 496; 3 N. E. 487).
Pierce, Joseph, high treason, com., 1777. (M. C. S. 58, 64; N. J. R. C. 107).
Pierson, Aaron, Essex co., judg., 1779. (3 N. E. 49, 328, 587).

Pierson, Benjamin, Essex co., judg., 1778-'9. (2 N. E. 385, 536, 587; 3 N. E. 328).
Pierson, Daniel, Essex co., judg., 1779. (3 N. E. 328, 329, 373).
Pilgrim, Francis, Cumberland co., judg., sale, 1778-'9. (2 N. E. 496; 3 N. E. 487).
Pintard, John, Shrewsbury, judg., sale, 1779-'80. (3 N. E. 94, 368; 4 N. E. 248).
Pinyard, William, Gloucester co., judg., sale, 1778-'9. (2 N. E. 581; 3 N. E. 450, 650).
Polhemus, John, Monmouth co., high treason, death sentence. (2 N. E. 312).
Polhemus, John, Jr., Monmouth co., judg., sale, 1778-'9. (3 N. E. 94).
Porter, John, N. J. Vols., captured, 1777. (2 Sabine 567).
Potter, Eliazer, Middlesex co., inq., 1778. (2 N. E. 400).
Potter, Robert, Sergeant, N. J. Vols., captured, 1777. (2 Sabine 567).
Potts, Stacy, Hunterdon co., oaths refused, fined, 1777. (Hunt. Rec.).
Poynton, Mary (wife of Brereton), Hunterdon co., judg., sale, 1778-'9. (2 N. E. 356).
Pratt, Joseph, Gloucester co., inq., high treason, death sentence, 1778. (2 N. E. 581, 583, 588; N. J. R. C. 137).
Pray, John, Middlesex co., judg., sale, 1778-'9. (2 N. E. 534; 3 N. E. 95).
Prevost, James Marcus, Bergen co., inq., 1780. (5 N. E. 124).
Price, James, Shrewsbury, judg., sale, 1779-'80. (3 N. E. 94, 368; 4 N. E. 248).
Price, Joseph (son of William), Shrewsbury, judg., sale, 1779-'80. (3 N. E. 89, 323; 4 N. E. 191).
Price, Joseph (son of Joseph), Shrewsbury, judg., 1780. (Mon. Rec.).
Price, William, Shrewsbury, judg., sale, 1779. (3 N. E. 94).
Prickman, Rinehart, Bergen co., inq., 1779. (Bergen Rec.).
Prideaux, Edward, Lieut. 2nd N. J. Vols., 1778. (5 C. N. B. 257).

Proctor, Nathaniel (or Nathan), Shrewsbury, judg., 1784. (Mon. Rec.).
Prosser, Jeremiah, Gloucester co., judg., sale, 1778-'9. (2 N. E. 582; 3 N. E. 650).
Prue, Michael, Shrewsbury, judg., 1779. (3 N. E. 368).
Puckman (Prickman), Rinehart, Bergen co., inq., 1779. (3 N. E. 98; Bergen Rec.).
Pulisfelt, Christian, Franklin twsp., Bergen co., judg., sale, 1779, 1784. (3 N. E. 98; Hist. Bergen Co., Vol. I, p. 128).
Quackenbush, Abraham A., Hackensack twsp., judg., sale, 1779. (3 N. E. 98, 526; 4 N. E. 77; Hist. Bergen Co., Vol. I, p. 127).
Quinlin, James, N. J. Vols., captured, 1777. (2 Sabine 568).
Raines, David, to Shelburne, N. S., at Peace. (2 Sabine 569).
Ramsay, James, to Shelburne, N. S., at Peace. (2 Sabine 569).
Randall, Amos, to Shelburne, N. S., at Peace. (2 Sabine 569).
Randolear, Christopher, Salem co., judg., 1778-'9. (2 N. E. 470; 3 N. E. 369).
Randolph, Thomas, Middlesex co., "tarred and feathered" as Loyalist, 1775. (2 Sabine 209; N. J. Archives, Vol. 31, p. 235).
Rapalje, Garret, Sussex co., fugitive, imprisoned, bailed, 1777-'8. (M. C. S. 49, 50, 57, 203).
Rappelje, George, Middletown, com., 1777; judg., sale, 1779-'80. (M. C. S. 51; 3 N. E. 89, 323; 4 N. E. 248).
Rapelje, Richard, with enemy, 1777. (M. C. S. 138).
Rattan, John, Sussex co., inq., 1779. (3 N. E. 165).
Rattan, Samuel, Sussex co., inq., 1779. (3 N. E. 165).
Rawson, William, Gloucester and Salem co., imprisoned, 1777; judg., sale, 1778-'9. (M. C. S. 219; 2 N. E. 470; 3 N. E. 115, 369).
Reed, Lewis, Salem and Cumberland cos., inq., 1778. (M. C. S. 219; 2 N. E. 470).
Rees, Thomas, joining enemy, com., 1777. (M. C. S. 142).
Retter, Henry, Middletown, judg., 1779-'80. (3 N. E. 89; 4 N. E. 248).

Retter, Wair, Monmouth co., judg., sale, 1779. (3 N. E. 323).
Rice, John, Sussex co., judg., 1778-'9. (2 N. E. 435; 3 N. E. 46).
Rice, William, Sussex co., judg., 1778-'9. (2 N. E. 435; 3 N. E. 46).
Richards, John, Bergen co., arrested, paroled, 1776; killed, 1778; judg., sale, 1778-'9, 1786. (M. P. C. 498, 505; Sabine, 213; 2 N. E. 529; 4 N. E. 90; Bergen Rec.).
Richardson, Thomas, Sussex co., judg., 1778-'9. (2 N. E. 435; 3 N. E. 46).
Richmond, James, New Brunswick, inq., 1778. (2 N. E. 400, 401).
Richmond (Ritchman), John, Hunterdon and Middlesex cos., bound over, judg., 1778-'9. (M. C. S. 227; 2 N. E. 401; 3 N. E. 62).
Rickman, John, Bergen co., judg., 1779. (Bergen Rec.).
Rider, Stephen, New Barbadoes, judg., sale, 1778-'9. (2 N. E. 529; 3 N. E. 132).
Riding, Richard, Middletown, judg., 1780. (4 N. E. 248).
Ridner, Abel, Bergen co., judg., 1779. (3 N. E. 98, 526).
Ridner, Conrad, Bergen co., inq., 1779. (3 N. E. 529).
Ridner, Hendrick, Bergen co., inq., 1779. (3 N. E. 98).
Ridner, John, Bergen co., inq., 1779. (3 N. E. 98).
Riggins, Thomas, Cumberland co., inq., 1778. (2 N. E. 496).
Rightmyer, Conrad, Sussex co., judg., 1778-'9. (2 N. E. 435; 3 N. E. 46).
Riker, Jacob, Bergen co., inq., 1779. (4 N. E. 90).
Roberts, Silas, fugitive to enemy, 1777. (M. C. S. 46).
Robertson, John, Bergen co., inq., 1779. (3 N. E. 98).
Robeson, John, Gloucester co., judg., sale, 1778-'9. (2 N. E. 582; 3 N. E. 129, 650).
Robins, John, Ensign 1st N. J. Vols., 1776-'7; captured, 1777; Rogers' King's Rangers. (5 C. N. B. 269; Stryker's N. J. Vols., 65).

Robinson, John, Essex co., oaths refused, com., 1777. (M. C. S. 74; N. J. R. C. 78, 79).
Rodney, George, Somerset co., judg., 1777-'9. (2 N. E. 568; 3 N. E. 49).
Rodrow, John, Gloucester co., judg., sale, 1778-'9. (2 N. E. 581; 3 N. E. 650).
Roelofson, Martin, Bergen co., inq., 1779. (3 N. E. 98).
Roome, Henry, New Barbadoes, judg., sale, 1778-'9. (2 N. E. 529; 3 N. E. 132, 526).
Roome, Lawrence, Bergen co., inq., 1779. (4 N. E. 90).
Roome, William, Bergen co., inq., 1779. (4 N. E. 90).
Rope, Christian, Hunterdon co., judg., 1778-'9. (2 N. E. 355; 3 N. E. 68).
Rosbrugh, Robert, Sussex co., fined, com., 1777. (M. C. S. 81).
Rose, William, Monmouth co., judg., 1779. (1 Mon. Hist. 103-4).
Rosin, Harmon, spy., 1778. (M. C. S. 192).
Rowett, Thomas, to Shelburne, N S., at Peace. (2 Sabine 573).
Rowland, Rev. John Hamilton, Chaplain, 2nd N. J. Vols., 1778-'81. (5 C. N. B. 231; Stryker's N. J. Vols. 43).
Runyon, Reune, Sr., Piscataway, judg., sale, 1778-'9. (M. C. S. 184; 2 N. E. 400; 3 N. E. 322).
Rush, Martin, Bergen co., judg., 1779. (3 N. E. 98, 525).
Russell, Thomas, Middlesex co., gone to enemy, 1777, judg., sale, 1778-'80. (M. C. S. 144; 3 N. E. 366, 574; 4 N. E. 230).
Rutherford, Walter, Hunterdon co., oaths refused, bound over, 1777. (M. C. S. 117, 122).
Ruttan, David, to Shelburne, N. S., at Peace. (2 Sabine 574).
Ryckman, John, Hackensack, judg., sale, 1779. (2 N. E. 529; 3 N. E. 132, 526).
Ryder, Stephen, Ensign, 3 N. J. Vols., 1781-'2. (Ind.: 5604; 5 C. N. B. 270; 2 Sabine 74; Stryker's N. J. Vols. 66).
Ryerson, George, Bergen co., Ensign 4th N. J. Vols., 1778; joined enemy, 1777. (M. C. S. 108; Stryker's N. J. Vols. 66).

Ryerson, John J., Bergen co., inq., 1779. (3 N. E. 529).
Ryerson, Martin, Lieut. 4th N. J. Vols., 1777; died circa July, 1780. (5 C. N. B. 257; Stryker's N. J. Vols. 59).
St. Clair, John, Hunterdon co., oaths refused, fined, 1777. (Hunt. Rec.).
Saltar, Joseph, com., 1777. (M. C. S. 15, 16).
Sanders, Egbert, Tory prisoner, 1777. (N. J. R. C. 84).
Saunders, Abraham, Salem co., inq., 1778. (2 N. E. 470).
Saunders, John, Elizabeth Town; to Hampton, N. B., at Peace. (2 Sabine 258; 39 N. Y. Gen. & Biog. Record 245).
Sayler, William, Cumberland co., inq., 1778. (2 N. E. 496).
Sayres, Caleb, Essex co., fugitive, judg., sale, 1778-'9. (2 N. E. 385; 3 N. E. 328; see main text under Isaac Longworth).
Schooly, Andrew, Sussex co., judg., 1778-'9. (2 N. E. 435; 3 N. E. 46).
Schooly, William, Sussex co., judg., 1778. (2 N. E. 435; 3 N. E. 46).
Schuyler, Aaron P., New Barbadoes Neck, arrest ordered, 1777. (M. C. S. 83.)
Schuyler, Derick, Essex co., fugitive, judg., 1778-'9. (2 N. E. 385; 3 N. E. 328).
Scoby, Timothy, Shrewsbury, judg., sale, 1779. (3 N. E. 94).
Scott, John B., Sussex co., judg., sale, 1779. (3 N. E. 544).
Seamon, John, Ensign 3 N. J. Vols., 1779; served one year. (Stryker's N. J. Vols. 66).
Sears, John, high treason, com., 1777. (M. C. S. 55, 64; N. J. R. C. 107).
Seeley, Job, Cumberland co., inq., 1778. (2 N. E. 496).
Seguglet, Henry, Jr., Monmouth co., judg., sale, 1780. (4 N. E. 191).
Sergeant, Cecil, Middlesex co., inq., 1779. (3 N. E. 90).
Service, James, Ensign 6 N. J. Vols., 1778. (Stryker's N. J. Vols. 66).
Shaw, Arthur, Sussex co., inq., 1779. (3 N. E. 165).
Shaw, Daniel, Cumberland co., treating with enemy, 1777; inq., 1778. (N. J. R. C. 90; 2 N. E. 496).

Shaw, Hezekiah, Cumberland co., inq., 1778. (2 N. E. 496).
Shaw, James, Capt. 5 N. J. Vols., 1776; 1st N. J. Vols., 1778; Provincial Light Infantry, 1781 (but see Stryker's N. J. Vols. 52); inq. 1779. (5 C. N. B. 246; 2 Sabine 576; 3 N. E. 165).
Sherbrook, Miles, Essex co., judg., sales, 1779-'80. (3 N. E. 328, 329, 373, 574; 4 N. E. 230).
Shoemaker, Baltus, Bergen co., inq., 1779. (3 N. E. 529).
Shotwell, James, Middlesex co., inq., 1779. (3 N. E. 90).
Shotwell, Joseph (4th), Morris co., high treason, com., 1778. (M. C. S. 284).
Simmons, Edmund, Hackensack, judg., sale, 1778-'9, 1784. (2 N. E. 529; 4 N. E. 90; Hist. Bergen Co., Vol. I, p. 128).
Simonson, Simon, Old Hackensack, arrest ordered, 1777. (M. C. S. 83).
Sisse, Nicholas, Bergen co., inq., 1779. (3 N. E. 529).
Skelton, Joseph, Middlesex co., oaths refused, bound over, 1777. (M. C. S. 177).
Skenact, Mattenes, Bergen co., judg., 1779. (3 N. E. 526).
Skinner, B. G., Colonel, 1st N. J. Vols., 1781. (2 Sabine 309).
Skinner, Cortlandt, Jr., commissioned in British army, 1782. (2 Sabine 306; see also main text, under Cortlandt Skinner).
Skinner, Elisha (bro. of Cortlandt), Lieut.-Colonel, N. J. Vols. (2 Sabine 308).
Slater, Samuel, Hunterdon co., oaths refused, com., 1776-'7. (M. C. S. 148; M. P. C. 478).
Sleight, Matthew, Middlesex co., "Tory robber," inq., 1778. (2 N. E. 401, 539).
Slone, John, Essex co., judg., sale, 1779. (3 N. E. 384, 508, 528).
Slover, James, Middlesex co., trading with enemy, 1781. (5 N. E. 181).
Smith, Daniel, Secaucus, magistrate, arrest ordered, 1777; judg., 1778. (M. C. S. 84; 2 N. E. 529).
Smith, Ezekiel, Middlesex co., bound over, 1777. (M. C. S. 176).

Smith, Freeman, Middlesex co., judg., sale, 1780. (4 N. E. 303, 330).

Smith, James, Hunterdon co., Tory prisoner, 1777; judg., sale, 1778-'9. (2 N. E. 355; 3 N. E. 68; Hunt. Rec.; N. J. R. C. 84).

Smith, Job, Secaucus, arrest ordered, 1777. (M. C. S. 84).

Smith, John, Sr., Sussex co., judg., 1779. (2 N. E. 435; 3 N. E. 46).

Smith, John, Jr., Sussex co., judg., 1779. (2 N. E. 435; 3 N. E. 46).

Smith, John, Somerset co., judg., sale, 1778-'9. (2 N. E. 568; 3 N. E. 49, 153, 591).

Smith, John, Middletown, judg., sale, 1779. (3 N. E. 323; Mon. Rec.).

Smith, Joseph, Hunterdon co., N. J. Vols., captured, 1777; fugitive, 1779; judg., sale, 1778-'80. (M. C. S. 139; 2 N. E. 355; 3 N. E. 396; 4 N. E. 393; 2 Sabine 579).

Smith, Michael, English Neighborhood, Lieut. 4 N. J. Vols., 1777-'8. (Stryker's N. J. Vols. 59; 5 C. N. B. 258; M. C. S. 83).

Smith, Richard, bound over, 1777; inq., 1778. (M. C. S. 26; 2 N. E. 470).

Smock, John White, Sussex co., judg., 1779. (3 N. E. 46).

Snowden, Richard, Gloucester co., oaths refused, com., 1777. (M. C. S. 57).

Snyder, Elias, high treason, death sentence, 1777; pardoned by Gov. Livingston on conditions. (2 Sabine 322).

Souder, Peter, Jr., Cumberland co., judg., sale, 1778-'9. (2 N. E. 496; 3 N. E. 488; 4 N. E. 2).

Soup, Henry, Bergen co., inq., 1779. (3 N. E. 529).

Sparks, John, Salem co., inq., 1778. (2 N. E. 470).

Sparks, John, Jr., Salem co., inq., 1778. (2 N. E. 470).

Spear (Spier), John, Hackensack twsp., judg., sale, 1778-'9, 1784. (2 N. E. 529; 3 N. E. 132; Hist. Bergen Co., Vol. I, p. 127).

Spinning, Benjamin, Essex co., com., 1778. (M. C. S. 228).

Spinning, John, Essex co., com., 1778. (M. C. S. 228).

Stacey, Matthew, to Shelburne, N. S., at Peace. (2 Sabine 580).
Stager, Cornelius, Essex co., judg., 1779. (3 N. E. 328, 329, 372).
Stager, Henry, Newark, fugitive, judg., sale, 1778-'9. (2 N. E. 519; 3 N. E. 48, 328).
Stagg, Nicholas, Capt. 3 N. J. Vols., 1777. (5 C. N. B. 246).
Stagg, Richard, enabling escapes, 1777. (M. C. S. 46).
Stallcope, John, Salem co., inq., 1778. (2 N. E. 470).
Stanbury, Isaac, Essex and Middlesex cos., judg., sale, 1778-'9. (2 N. E. 545; 3 N. E. 92, 384).
Steirman(?), Samuel, Hunterdon co., oaths refused, fined, 1777. (Hunt. Rec.).
Stevenson, Arthur, oaths refused, fined, 1777. (Hunt Rec.).
Stevenson, Edward, Hunterdon co., oaths refused, fined, 1777. (Hunt. Rec.).
Stevenson, James, Middletown, judg., sale, 1780. (4 N. E. 190).
Stevenson, Samuel, Middletown, judg., sales, 1779-'80. (3 N. E. 89, 323; 4 N. E. 190).
Steward, John, Morris co., judg., sale, 1778-'9; to Shelburne, N. S., at Peace. (2 N. E. 593; 3 N. E. 92; 2 Sabine 582).
Stiles, Isaac, Essex co., fugitive, judg., sale, 1779. (3 N. E. 49, 328; see main text under William Style).
Stockley, Painter, refugee, escaped, 1780. (5 N. E. 19).
Stockton, Charles Witham, Ensign 1 N. J. Vols., 1777; captured, 1777. (5 C. N. B. 270; 2 Sabine 583; see main text under Richard W. Stockton).
Stor, Michael, Bergen co., inq., 1779, (3 N. E. 98).
Stout, Abram, Middletown, judg., 1780. (Mon. Rec.).
Stout, John Clark, Monmouth co., judg., sale, 1780. (4 N. E. 191).
Stout, Jonathan, Middletown, judg., sale, 1779-'80. (3 N. E. 94, 368; 4 N. E. 248).
Stout, Louis, Middletown, judg., 1784. (Mon. Rec.).
Stout, Philip, Gloucester co., inq., 1778. (2 N. E. 581).

Stout, Robert, Shrewsbury, judg., sale, 1779-'80. (3 N. E. 94, 368; 4 N. E. 248).
Stout, William, Middletown, judg., sale, 1780. (4 N. E. 191; Mon. Rec.).
Stretch, John, Cumberland co., inq., 1778. (2 N. E. 496).
String, Charles (or Christopher), Gloucester co., high treason, death sentence, 1778. (2 N. E. 583, 558; N. J. R. C. 137),
Stuart, Lieut. of Cavalry. (2 Sabine 583).
Stur, Michael, Bergen co., judg., 1779. (3 N. E. 525).
Suran, David, Gloucester co., judg., sale, 1778-'9. (2 N. E. 581; 3 N. E. 650).
Sutherland, Daniel, to Shelburne, N. S., at Peace, 1783. (2 Sabine 584).
Sutton, Rev. David, Kingwood, Hunterdon co., oaths refused, fined, 1777. (Hunt. Rec.).
Sutton, Jacob, Salem co., judg., 1778. (2 N. E. 470; Salem Rec.).
Sutton, James, Salem co., judg., 1778-'9. (2 N. E. 470; 3 N. E. 369).
Sutton, John, Salem co., judg., 1778-'9. (2 N. E. 470; 3 N. E. 369).
Sutton, Moses, Salem co., inq., 1778. (2 N. E. 470).
Sutton, Thomas, Salem co., judg., 1778-'9. (2 N. E. 470; 3 N. E. 369).
Sutton, Thomas Coat, Salem co., judg., pleaded guilty, imprisoned. 1778. (Salem Rec.).
Swanton, George, Gloucester co., Ensign West Jersey Vols. and 3 N. J. Vols., 1778; judg., sale, 1778-'9. (Ind.: 5604; 5 C. N. B. 271; 2 N. E. 582; 3 N. E. 650).
Swanton, John, Ensign 1st N. J. Vols., 1778; 2 N. J. Vols., 1782. (2 Sabine 584; Stryker's N. J. Vols. 66).
Swartfeller, Matthias, Sussex co., bail allowed, 1778. (M. C. S. 275).
Sweeny, John, Bergen co., harboring Tories, bound over, 1778. (M. C. S. 235, 237).
Swezey, Aaron, Bergen co., inq., 1779. (3 N. E. 529).

Swezy, Caleb, Jr., joined British, "atrocious robber," shot by captors. (2 Sabine 344).
Swindle, Thomas, arrest ordered, 1776. (M. P. C. 478).
Tack, John, Middlesex co., judg., 1779. (3 N. E. 62).
Talman, Christopher, Shrewsbury, judg., sale, 1779-'80. (3 N. E. 94, 368; 4 N. E. 248).
Talman, Jeremiah, to Shelburne, N. S., at Peace. (2 Sabine 585).
Talman, Oliver, Shrewsbury, judg., sale, 1779-'80. (3 N. E. 94, 368; 4 N. E. 248).
Talman, Steven, Monmouth co., bound over, 1777. (M. C. S. 25).
Taylor, Edward, Hunterdon co., arrest ordered, 1776; imprisoned as spy, refused oaths, bound over, 1777; judg., 1778-'9. (M. C. S. 29, 168; M. P. C. 478; 3 N. E. 68; N. J. R. C. 80, 96).
Taylor, George, Jr., Middletown, judg., sale, 1779. (3 N. E. 94; perhaps same as George Taylor in main text).
Taylor, Matthias, Cumberland co., inq., 1778. (2 N. E. 496).
Taylor, Morford, Shrewsbury, judg., sale, 1779. (3 N. E. 94, 368; see under John Taylor in main text).
Taylor, Samuel, refugee, captured, escaped, 1780. (5 N. E. 19).
Tedford, Jacob, to Shelburne, N. S., at Peace; settled at Yarmouth. (2 Sabine 349).
Tedford, Samuel, to Shelburne, N. S., at Peace; settled at Yarmouth. (2 Sabine 349).
Templeton, William, Morris co., bound over, 1778. (M. C. S. 238).
Thomas, Ezekiel, Cumberland co., inq., 1778. (2 N. E. 496).
Thomas, Job, Gloucester co., inq., 1778. (2 N. E. 581).
Thompson, James, Gloucester co., judg., sale, 1779-'80. (3 N. E. 527; 4 N. E. 192).
Thompson, Robert, Sussex co., judg., sale, 1778-'9. (2 N. E. 435; 3 N. E. 46).
Thomson, John, Newark, com., 1778. (M. C. S. 202).
Thorn, Jacob, Morris co., high treason, com., 1777. (M. C. S. 146).

Thorne, Abraham, Essex co., bound over, 1778. (M. C. S. 285).

Thorne, John, Monmouth co., judg., sale, 1780. (4 N. E. 191).

Thorne, Samuel, Middletown, judg., sale, 1780. (4 N. E. 191).

Thorne, Thomas, Middletown, judg., sale, 1779-'80. (3 N. E. 94, 368; 4 N. E. 248).

Thornton, John, Morris co., judg., sale, 1779. (3 N. E. 92).

Thorpe, Morris, Newark, com., 1778. (M. C. S. 202).

Tiers, Abraham, fugitive to enemy, 1777. (M. C. S. 46).

Tillford, Mr., gone over to enemy, 1777. (M. C. S. 69).

Tilton, Ezekiel, Middletown, judg., sale, 1778-'80. (M. C. S. 243; 3 N. E. 94, 368; 4 N. E. 248).

Tilton, John, Middletown, with enemy; judg., sale, 1778-'80. (M. C. S. 243; 3 N. E. 94, 368; 4 N. E. 248).

Tise, John, Bergen co., inq., 1779. (3 N. E. 98).

Tise, Peter, Bergen co., judg., 1779. (3 N. E. 98; 4 N. E. 77).

Troup, John, Lieut. 3 N. J. Vols., 1777; killed in Battle of Eutaw Springs, 1781; judg., sale, 1778-'9. (M. C. S. 231; 2 N. E. 593; 3 N. E. 92; 2 Sabine 362; 5 C. N. B. 259; Stryker's N. J. Vols. 60).

Tubman, Ananias, Cumberland co., judg., sale, 1778-'9. (2 N. E. 496; 3 N. E. 152).

Tubman, Sylvanus, Cumberland co., judg., sale, 1778-'9. (2 N. E. 496; 3 N. E. 152, 487; 4 N. E. 487).

Tucker, Samuel, Hunterdon co., sheriff, State Treasurer, Justice Sup. Ct., Loyalist late in 1776. (Whitehead's Jud. Hist., 400).

Tudas, John, Salem co., inq., pleaded guilty, imprisoned, 1778. (Salem Rec.).

Turpan, Thomas, Sussex co., judg., 1778-'9. (2 N. E. 435; 3 N. E. 46).

Tuthill, Benjamin, Sussex co., with enemy, 1777; inq., 1779. M. C. S. 46; 3 N. E. 165).

Updike, George, Hunterdon co., arrest ordered, 1776. (M. P. C. 478).

Urion, Gideon, Gloucester co., inq., 1778. (Glouc. Rec.).
Van Allen, Andrew, Bergen co., inq., 1779. (3 N. E. 529).
Van Amber (Van Emburgh?), John, to Shelburne, N. S., at Peace. (2 Sabine 589).
Van Blarcum, Abraham, Bergen co., inq., 1780. (5 N. E. 124).
Van Blarcum, Hendrick, Bergen co., judg., 1779. (3 N. E. 98, 526).
Van Blarcum, Herman, Paramus, judg., sale, 1779. (3 N. E. 98, 526; 4 N. E. 77; Hist. Bergen co., Vol. I, p. 128).
Van Blarcum, John J., Bergen co., inq., 1779. (3 N. E. 98).
Van Buskirk, Andrew, New Barbadoes, arrest ordered, 1777; judg., sale, 1779. (M. C. S. 83; 3 N. E. 98, 526; 4 N. E. 77; N. J. R. C. 93).
Van Buskirk, Cornelius, Bergen co., inq., 1778. (2 N. E. 529).
Van Buskirk, Daniel, Kinderkameck, arrest ordered, 1777. (M. C. S. 83).
Van Buskirk, David, New Barbadoes, judg., sale, 1779. (3 N. E. 98, 526; 4 N. E. 77).
Van Buskirk, Garret, to St. John, N. B., at Peace; then to Aylesford, N. S.; died 1843, aged 87. (2 Sabine 376).
Van Buskirk, Jacob, Lieut., captured, high treason, com. (M. C. S. 167).
Van Buskirk, Peter, Bergen co., judg., 1778-'9. (2 N. E. 529; 4 N. E. 90).
Van Camp, Thomas, Morris co., provisioning enemy, fined, com., 1778. (M. C. S. 204; 2 N. E. 55).
Vanderhoff, Henry, Essex co., judg., 1779. (3 N. E. 328, 329, 373).
Vanderhoven, John, Middlesex co., inq., 1778. (2 N. E. 534).
Van Dine, Dennis, Middletown, judg., sale, 1780. (4 N. E. 191).
Van Dine, Hendrick, Monmouth co., judg., sale, 1780. (4 N. E. 191).
Van Emburgh, Abraham, New Barbadoes; to St. John, N. B., at Peace; judg., sale, 1778-'9. (2 N. E. 529; 3 N. E. 132, 526; Hist. Bergen Co., Vol. I, p. 127; 40 N. Y. Gen. & Biog. Rec. 30).

Van Emburgh, Adoniah, Bergen co., to Shelburne, N. S., at Peace. (2 Sabine 590; see main text under James Van Emburgh).
Van Emburgh, Gilbert, to Shelburne, N. S., at Peace. (2 Sabine 590).
Van Giesen, Abraham, Essex co., with enemy, confessed, 1777; inq., 1778. (M. C. S. 118; 2 N. E. 385; N. J. R. C. 84).
Van Giesen, Abraham, Jr., Newark, judg., sale, 1778-'9. (3 N. E. 48, 328).
Van Giesen, Cornelius, Tory prisoner, 1777. (N. J. R. C. 84).
Van Giesen, Garret, Secaucus, arrest ordered, 1777. (M. C. S. 83).
Van Giesen, Isaac, Tory prisoner, 1777. (N. J. R. C. 84).
Van Horn, Cornelius, Hackensack twsp., judg., sale, 1778-'9. (2 N. E. 529; 3 N. E. 132, 526).
Van Horn, Cornelius L., Bergen co., inq., 1779. (4 N. E. 90).
Van Horne, Barent, Pamrapo, Loyalist, house plundered by Whigs, 1777. (1 N. E. 505; 2 Sabine 590).
Van Horne, Mindert, to Shelburne, N. S., at Peace. (2 Sabine 590).
Van Houten, John, Bergen co., judg., 1779. (3 N. E. 526).
Van Houten, John H., inq., 1779. (3 N. E. 98).
Van Mater, Clarence, Middletown, judg., 1784. (Mon. Rec.).
Van Mater, Cyrenus, Monmouth co., information to enemy, fined, escaped, 1778. (2 N. E. 283).
Van Mater, Jacob, Salem co., judg., sale, 1778-'9. (2 N. E. 470; 3 N. E. 114, 369).
Van Mater, John, refused oaths, bailed, 1777. (M. C. S. 33; see main text under Daniel Van Mater).
Van Norden, David, high treason, com., 1778. (M. C. S. 194).
Van Norden, Henry, high treason, com., 1778. (M. C. S. 194).
Van Norden, James, New Barbadoes, judg., 1779. (3 N. E. 526).
Van Norden, John (son of Gabriel), Bergen co., Ensign 4th N. J. Vols., 1777; Lieut. 3 N. J. Vols., 1780, and Prov. Light Infantry; inq., 1779; to Shelburne, N. S., at Peace; in-

structor in King's College, Nova Scotia; removed to Bermuda. (2 Sabine 379, 590; 5 C. N. B. 259, 271; 3 N. E. 529; Stryker's N. J. Vols. 61; see also under Gabriel Van Norden in main text).

Van Norden, John, Jr., Middlesex co., inq., 1778. (2 N. E. 401).

Van Note, Peter, Shrewsbury, judg., sale, 1779-'80. (3 N. E. 94, 368; 4 N. E. 249).

Van Saen, Cornelius, com., 1777. (M. C. S. 66, 67).

Van Saen, Isaac, com., 1777. (M. C. S. 66, 67).

Van Tuyl, Michael, Bergen twsp., judg., sale, 1778, 1787. (2 N. E. 529; Hist. Bergen Co., Vol. I, p. 128).

Van Voorhees, David, to Shelburne, N. S., at Peace. (2 Sabine 590).

Van Vorst, Aaron, to Shelburne, N. S., at Peace. (2 Sabine 590).

Van Vorst, Cornelius, Bergen co., judg., 1778. (2 N. E. 529).

Van Wagoner, John, Essex co., judg., 1778-'9. (2 N. E. 385; 3 N. E. 327).

Van Winkle, Jacob, Franklin twsp., Bergen co., judg., sale, 1779. (3 N. E. 98, 526).

Van Winkle, Jacob S., Bergen co., judg., 1779. (4 N. E. 77).

Villou, Theodore, Quartermaster 1st N. J. Vols. (5 C. N. B. 236).

Voorhees, Jacobus (James), Rider in N. J. Vols.; captured, 1777; judg., sale, 1778-'80. (2 N. E. 552; 4 N. E. 87, 184; 2 Sabine 591).

Vreeland, Derick, English Neighborhood, arrest ordered, 1777; judg., 1778. (M. C. S. 84; 2 N. E. 529).

Vreeland, Nicholas, Morris co., judg., 1778. (2 N. E. 593).

Vreeland, Peter, Bergen co., bound over, 1778. (M. C. S. 223).

Waddell, Rev. Henry, D. D., of Lincoln's Inn, London; New Jersey attorney, 1767; Episcopal minister Shrewsbury, Middletown and Trenton after the War; died at Trenton, 1811. (2 Sabine 389; Jones's American Members of the

Inns Court, p. 212; Schuyler's "Hist. St. Michael's Church, Trenton, p. 138 et seq.).
Wager, Allen, Sussex co., with enemy, 1777; inq., 1779. (M. C. S. 85; 3 N. E. 165).
Wake, Drury, Salem co., com., 1776. (M. P. C. 513).
Walker, Mesbeck, Essex co., high treason, com., 1777. (M. C. S. 113).
Walker, Thomas, Middlesex co., judg., sale, 1778-'9. (2 N. E. 400; 3 N. E. 95).
Wall, Jesse, Hunterdon and Burlington cos., judg., 1778-'9. (2 N. E. 356; 3 N. E. 68).
Wallace, Hugh, Essex and Hunterdon cos., judg., 1779-'80. (3 N. E. 328, 329, 373; Hunt. Rec.).
Waller, Joseph, Lieut. 5th N. J. Vols., 1776. (5 C. N. B. 259; Stryker's N. J. Vols. 61).
Waller, Robert, high treason, com., 1778. (M. C. S. 285).
Walls, George, Newark, judg., 1778; to Shelburne, N. S., at Peace. (2 Sabine 592; 3 N. E. 48, 328).
Waln, Richard, refused oaths, bound over, 1777-'8. (M. C. S. 143, 276).
Walton, William, New York and Shrewsbury, judg., sale, 1779-'80. (3 N. E. 94, 368; 4 N. E. 249).
Wanamaker, A., Bergen co., inq., 1779. (4 N. E. 90).
Ward, Ebenezer, Jr., Essex co., fugitive, judg., 1778-'9. (2 N. E. 385; 3 N. E. 327).
Ward, Richard, Salem co., inq., 1778. (2 N. E. 470).
Warde, John, Shrewsbury, judg., sale, 1779. (3 N. E. 94).
Wardel, Ebenezer, Shrewsbury, Capt. 1st N. J. Vols., 1776; judg., sale, 1779-'80. (5 C. N. B. 247; 3 N. E. 94, 368; 4 N. E. 248).
Wardel, Jacob, arrest, furnishing provisions to enemy. (2 Sabine 592).
Wardel, Joseph, arrested, bailed, 1776. (2 Sabine 592).
Wardel, Peter, Shrewsbury, judg., sale, 1779-'80. (3 N. E. 94; 4 N. E. 191).
Wardel, William, Shrewsbury, judg., sale, 1779. (3 N. E. 323).

Warne, Samuel, Middlesex co., judg., 1779. (2 N. E. 401; 3 N. E. 62, 435).
Warner, George, Essex co., judg., 1779. (3 N. E. 328, 329, 373).
Warren, Samuel, Middlesex co., inq., 1778. (2 N. E. 557. May be same as Samuel Warne, supra).
Waterhouse, Ambrose, Hunterdon co., fined, 1778. (Hunt. Rec.).
Waterhouse, Henry, Hunterdon co., oaths refused, fined, 1777. (Hunt. Rec.).
Waterhouse, Ingram, Hunterdon co., oaths refused, fined, com. 1777. (Hunt. Rec.).
Watkins, David, Cumberland co., judg., sale, 1778-'9. (2 N. E. 496; 3 N. E. 487).
Watson, Alexander, Woodbridge, judg., sale, 1778-'9. (2 N. E. 400, 401; 3 N. E. 62, 63, 95, 435, 590, 591; 4 N. E. 320).
Watson, William, Gloucester co., inq., 1778. (2 N. E. 581).
Watts, George, Essex co., high treason, com., 1777. (M. C. S. 74; N. J. R. C. 78, 79).
Wear, John, Sussex co., refused oaths, bound over, 1777. (M. C. S. 88).
Welcher, John, fugitive to enemy, 1777. (M. C. S. 46).
Welcher, Robert, fugitive to enemy, 1777. (M. C. S. 46).
Welcher, Thomas, fugitive to enemy, 1777. (M. C. S. 46).
Welding, Benjamin, Cumberland co., escaped jail, 1780. (2 N. E. 19).
Welding, Jesse, refugee, imprisoned, escaped, 1780. (5 N. E. 19).
Wells, Daniel, Gloucester co., inq., 1778. (2 N. E. 581).
Wells, George, Essex co., fugitive, judg., 1778. (2 N. E. 385, 587).
Wells, Harrison, Gloucester co., high treason, death sentence, 1778; judg., sale, 1779. (2 N. E. 581, 583; 3 N. E. 131, 650; N. J. R. C. 136).
Wells, James, joining enemy, 1777. (N. J. R. C. 88, 98).
Wells, William, Gloucester co., judg., sale, 1778-'9. (2 N. E. 581; 3 N. E. 130, 650).

Wessigh, Ludwick, Sussex co., judg., 1778-'9. (2 N. E. 435; 3 N. E. 46).
West, Beriah, to Shelburne, N. S., at Peace. (2 Sabine, 594).
West, Jonathan, Monmouth co., "Tory robber in Pine barrens," killed. (2 Sabine 413; Hist. Mon. co., Vol. I, p. 126).
West, Joshua, to Shelburne, N. S., at Peace. (2 Sabine, 594).
West, Stephen, Monmouth co., Tory robber, killed, 1778. (3 N. E. 53).
West, Uriah, Gloucester co., high treason, com., 1778. (M. C. S. 247, 269).
Westervelt, Casparus, Pashack, arrest ordered, 1777. (M. C. S. 83).
Wetherby, Henry, Monmouth co., bound over, 1777. (M. C. S. 38).
Wetherby, Matthew, N. J. Vols., captured, 1777. (2 Sabine, 594).
Whilenack, John, Sussex co., inq., 1778. (2 N. E. 435).
Whitaker, Robert, Salem and Gloucester cos., judg., sale, 1778-'9. (2 N. E. 470, 581; 3 N. E. 116, 369, 650).
White, Aaron, to Shelburne, N. S., at Peace. (2 Sabine 595).
White, Britain, Shrewsbury, judg., sale, 1779-'80. (3 N. E. 94, 368; 4 N. E. 248).
White, John, Essex co., fugitive, judg., 1778-'9; to Shelburne, N. S., at Peace. (2 N. E. 519, 587; 3 N. E. 328; 2 Sabine 595).
White, Josiah, Shrewsbury, judg., sale, 1779. (3 N. E. 94).
White, Robert, Middlesex co., bound over, 1777. (M. C. S. 175, 176).
White, Thomas, Essex co., judg., 1779. (3 N. E. 328, 329, 373).
Whitney, Joseph, N. J. Vols., captured, 1777. (2 Sabine 595).
Wiem, Peter D., Bergen co., inq., 1779. (3 N. E. 98).
Willet, Thomas Stike, Middletown, judg., sale, 1779. (3 N. E. 323).
Willets, John, Sussex co., oaths refused, bound over, 1777. (M. C. S. 88).
Williams, Daniel, N. J. Vols., captured, 1777. (2 Sabine 596).

Williams, Edmund, Monmouth co., com., 1777. (M. C. S. 24).
Williams, Ezekiel, Monmouth co., Tory robber, captured, 1778; killed. (3 N. E. 53).
Williams, Giles, joining enemy, 1777. (N. J. R. C. 60).
Williams, John, Shrewsbury, Capt. 5 N. J. Vols., 1778, judg., sale, 1779-'80. (3 N. E. 94, 368; 4 N. E. 191, 248; 2 Sabine 596; Stryker's N. J. Vols. 53).
Williams, John, Jr., judg., sale, 1779-'80; to Shelburne, N. S., at Peace. (3 N. E. 89, 94, 323, 368; 4 N. E. 248).
Williams, Nathaniel, Newark, fugitive, judg., sale, 1778-'9. (2 N. E. 385; 3 N. E. 48, 327).
Williams, Obadiah, Shrewsbury, judg., 1782; sale, 1784. (Mon. Rec.; see also main text under Joseph Williams).
Williams, Thomas, com., 1777. (M. C. S. 50).
Williamson, Cornelius, prisoner in jail, July, 1776. (2 Sabine 597).
Willson, Alexander, Burlington co., encouraging disaffection, com., 1777. (M. C. S. 42).
Willson, John, Sussex co., refused oaths, bound over, 1777. (M. C. S. 88).
Wilson, Ebenezer, Sussex co., refused oaths, bound over, 1777. (M. C. S. 88).
Wilson, Jacob, high treason, com., 1778. (M. C. S. 285).
Wilson, James, Essex co., judg., 1779. (3 N. E. 328, 329, 373).
Wilson, Joseph, high treason, com., 1778. (M. C. S. 285).
Wilson, Jesse, Cumberland co., escaped jail, 1780. (2 N. E. 191).
Wilson, Richard, Monmouth co., bound over, 1777. (M. C. S. 37).
Winslow, Rev. Edward, Chaplain 1st N. J. Vols., 1777-'80; died in New York City, 1780. (5 C. N. B. 231; Stryker's N. J. Vols. 44).
Winters, Garret, Essex co., inq., 1778. (Essex Rec.).
Wiser, Frederick, Jr., Middlesex co., judg., sale, 1779; to Shelburne, N. S., at Peace. (3 N. E. 62, 63, 435; 2 Sabine 597).
Wiser, Jacob, Jr., Middlesex co., inq., 1778. (2 N. E. 401).

Witchell, John, N. J. Vols., captured, 1777. (2 Sabine 598).
Woller, Joseph, Sussex co., inq., 1779. (3 N. E. 165).
Wood, Ezekiel, gone to enemy, 1777. (M. C. S. 46).
Wood, John, Tory "Pine robber." (1 Mon. Hist. 103-4).
Wood, Obadiah, Salem co., judg., 1778. (2 N. E. 470).
Woodland, William, Cumberland co., judg., sale, 1778-'9. (2 N. E. 496; 3 N. E. 487).
Woodley, Asa, to Shelburne, N. S., at Peace. (2 Sabine 598).
Woods, Peter, Essex co., judg., 1778-'9. (2 N. E. 385; 3 N. E. 328).
Woodward, Abraham, to Pennfield, N. B., at Peace. (40 N. Y. Gen. & Biog. Rec. 120).
Woodward, Anthony, Jr., to Pennfield, N. B., at Peace. (40 N. Y. Gen. & Biog. Rec. 120).
Woodward, Isaac, to Beaver Harbor, N. S., at Peace. (2 Sabine 455; 40 N. Y. Gen. & Biog. Rec. 120).
Woodward, Jacob, to Pennfield, N. B., at Peace. (40 N. Y. Gen. & Biog. Rec. 120).
Woodward, Nimrod, to Pennfield, N. B., at Peace. (40 N. Y. Gen. & Biog. Rec. 120).
Woodward, Thomas (son of Anthony), Gloucester co., com., 1777. (M. C. S. 60).
Wooley, Benjamin, Shrewsbury, judg., sale, 1779-'80. (3 N. E. 94, 368; 4 N. E. 248).
Woolverton, Thomas, Sussex co., fined, com., 1777; judg., sale, 1779-'80. (M. C. S. 81; 3 N. E. 165; 4 N. E. 229).
Woortman, John, high treason, com., 1778. (M. C. S. 272).
Worth, Alexander, spy, burnt in hand, 1778. (2 N. E. 22).
Worth, James, going to enemy, 1777. (N. J. R. C. 98).
Worthley, John, to Shelburne, N. S., at Peace. (2 Sabine 599).
Wouters, Garret, Essex co., fugitive, judg., 1778-'9. (2 N. E. 385; 3 N. E. 328).
Wrench, Matthew, Hunterdon co., com., 1777. (M. C. S. 176).
Wright, Austin, Morris co., bound over, 1778. (M. C. S. 194).

Yates (Yeats), Richard, Acquackanonk and Saddle River, judg., sale, 1778-'9. (2 N. E. 385; 3 N. E. 48, 328, 526; 4 N. E. 77).
Young, Christopher, Sussex co., judg., 1778-'9. (2 N. E. 435; 3 N. E. 46).
Young, David, Sussex co., judg., 1778-'9. (2 N. E. 435; 3 N. E. 46).
Young, Peter, Hunterdon co., judg., 1778-'9. (M. C. S. 46, 59, 155, 157; 3 N. E. 68).
Young, William, to Shelburne, N. S., at Peace. (2 Sabine 600).
Younglove, Ezekiel, Sussex co., joined enemy, 1778. (M. C. S. 246), inq., 1779. (3 N. E. 165).
Youren, John, Salem co., inq., 1778. (2 N. E. 470).
Yule, James, to Shelburne, N. S., at Peace. (2 Sabine 600).
Zabriskie, Albert, Schraalenburg, judg., sale, 1778-'9, 1785. (2 N. E. 529; 3 N. E. 132, 526; Hist. Bergen Co., Vol. I, p. 126).
Zabriskie, Christian A., Franklin twsp., Bergen co., judg., sale, 1779. (3 N. E. 526; 4 N. E. 77).
Zabriskie, John, New Bridge, magistrate, arrest ordered, 1777; judg., sale; forfeited estate given to Baron von Steuben. (2 Sabine 465; M. C. S. 83).
Zabriskie, John I., Bergen co., inq., 1780. (5 N. E. 124).
Zimmerman, Matthew, Sussex co., judg., 1779. (3 N. E. 46).

INDEX TO NAMES AND PLACES

[Military and other titles are omitted, unless where first name is not given, but exception is made in cases of physicians and clergymen, as the prefixes "Dr." and "Rev." serve to distinguish them].

INDEX TO NAMES AND PLACES

Abbott, Abdon, Jr., 256
Abel, John, 256
Ackerman, David D., 256
  Derrick, 256
  John, 257
  John J., 256
  John W., 256
  Lawrence A., 257
  Richard, 234
  Thomas, 257
Ackley, John, 257
Acquackanonk, 65, 153, 206, 273, 286, 319
Adams, Philip, 257
Addison, Mary, 231
Adolphus-town (Can.), 171
Ailsa, Marquess of, 120
Aitken, Dr. William B., 234
Aker, John, 257
Albany (N. Y.), 17, 60, 83, 84, 95, 150, 151, 237
Alexander, Robert, 160
  William, 142
Alexandria township, 26
Alias, John, 257
Allen, Anne, 10
  Benjamin, 257
  Charlotte, 10
  Ethan, 257
  Frances, 10
  George W., 223
  Hannah, 10
  Isaac, 7, 8, 9, 10, 40, 213
  James, 11
  John, 10, 88, 257
  Sir John, 10
  Jonah, 257
  Joseph, 11
  Margaret, 10
  Mary L. V., 223
  Sarah, 10
  Sarah C., 40
  William, 10, 46
Allenton, John, 257
Allentown, 47, 84, 168
Allison, Nancy, 129
  Robert, 257
Alston, David, 12, 74, 257
  John, 12
  Jonathan, 12, 257
  Lewis, 12, 257
Alward, Asa (or Asher), 11
  Benjamin, 12
  John, 257
  Silas, 12
Amboy, 268 (See Perth Amboy).
Ammerman, Derrick, 212
  Isaac, 257
Amwell, 48
Anderson, John, 257
  John M., 231
  Mary R. V. C., 231
  Peter, 12, 94, 251
Andrews, John, 257
Anents, Stephen, 257
Annapolis (N. S.), 9, 32, 35, 36, 71, 88, 134, 146, 167, 176, 181, 182, 200, 224, 234, 238, 278, 297
Annelly, Thomas, 257
Ansley, John, 258
  Ozias, 12, 218
  Rev. Thomas, 13

Anstey, John, 6, 120, 130, 158, 202, 241
Antigua (W. I.), 52
Antill, Edward, 13
  Eliza W., 15
  Henry, 14
  Jane, 46
  John, 13, 46, 146, 258
  John C., 14
  Margaret C., 14
Apgar, Peter, 258
Appleby, James, 258
Appleman, Peter, 258
Archer, George, 258
Argyle (N. S.), 222
Armagh (Ire.), 40, 63, 114
Arnold, Benedict, 225
Arrowsmith, Joseph, 258
Ashfield, Vincent P., 152, 198, 258
Aston, Thomas, 258
Atchison, John, 15
  Sarah C., 15
Atkinson, Moses, 258
Atlee, Colonel, 80
Atwood, Isaac, 258
Auchmuty, Rev. Samuel, 37
Augusta (Ga.), 65
Australia, 15
Auten, John, 258
Avis, George, 258
Aylesbury (Eng.), 196
Aylesford (N. S.), 45, 311

Babbington, Charles, 258
Bacon, John, 258
Badcock, Simeon, 258
Badgely, Mr., 258
Bahamas, 107, 295
Bailey, Rev. Jacob, 176, 181
  Joseph, 258
Bainbridge, Abigail, 15, 16
  Dr. Absalom, 15, 216
  Sir Arthur, 15
  Edmund, 15, 16
  John, 16
  Joseph, 16
  Mary, 16
  Mary T., 216
  Peter, 16
  Sarah, 16
  William, 16
Baker, Conrad, 258
  John, 16
  Philip, 258
  William, 258
Baldwin, Luther, 259
Ball, Mr., 90, 92
Ballanger, Jonathan, 259
Bally Phillip (Ire.), 166
Bancroft, Daniel, 17
  Dr. Daniel, 17
  Jeremiah, 176
  Mary V., 17
  Sarah P., 176
Banghart, Barnabus, 259
Bank, Jonah, 259
Banks, James, 17
  Joseph, 259
  Josiah, 259
  William, 17
Banta, Cornelius, 259
  Derick, 259
  Hendrick, 259

Index

John, 259
Sieba, 18
Weart, 17, 18
Barbadoes Island, 18
Barber, Hugh, 259
John, 259
Barberie, Andrew, 19, 259
  Cortlandt, 20, 196
  Euphemia S., 20, 196
  Frances, 220
  Gertrude, 19, 197
  Gertrude J., 18, 107
  John, 18, 19, 20, 107, 196, 207, 212, 220, 259
  Mary Ann S., 212
  Mary S., 19
  Oliver, 18, 19, 196, 220
  Peter, 259
  Susannah, 107
Barclay, James, 259
John, 171, 259
Bard, Dr. Samuel, 259
Bardon, John, 259
Barker, Michael, 259
  Nathaniel, 260
Barlow, Catherine McC., 137
  Ellen, 79
  Francis, 79
  Frederick, 137
  William, 79
Barnes, John 20
  Mary, 21
  Samuel, 260
  Sarah, 21
Barnet, Caleb, 260
  Ichabod, 260
  Ichabod, B. 260
Barrington, Lord, 199
Barron, Ellis, 21
  James, 260
  Samuel, 74
  Dr. Samuel, 44, 61
Barrott, James, Jr., 260
Barton, Benjamin, 260
  Henry L., 22, 260
  James, 22
  Joseph, 7, 22, 165, 260
  Thomas, 260
Bartram, Alexander, 260
Basking Ridge, 82, 109
Batey, Francis, 260
Batwell, Bithia, 23
  Rev. Daniel, 23
Baugh, Nicholas, 260
Bayard, John, 227
  Rev. Lewis P., 99
  Samuel V., 114
  William, 224, 260
Beach, Rev. Abraham, 260
  Ezekiel, 260
Beadles, Elisha, 174
  Mary, 174
  Ruth, 181
Beardsley, Rev. John, 47, 69, 102, 223
Beatty, George, 260
Beaufort (S. C.), 194
Beaver Harbour (N. B.), 101, 210, 212, 220, 244, 246, 318
Beccles (Eng.), 49
Becket, Samuel, 93
Bedell, Israel, 261
  Stephen, 24
Bedford (N. Y.), 151
Beekman, Charles, 261
  Gerardus G., 261
  Gertrude, 229

Joseph, 24, 251
Margaret, 24
Margaret H., 24
Maria, 24
Matilda, 24
Thomas, 24
William, 24
Beers, Henrietta C., 24
Bell, Andrew, 25
  Cornelia, 26
  David, 261
  John, 25
  Mary, 145
  Susannah M., 26
Bellevue (N. B.), 280
Belvidere, 290
Benedict, William H., 123, 253
Benezet, Daniel, 97
  Nathaniel, 97
Bennetts Neck, 67
Benson, Christopher, 261
  James, 261
  Matthew, 26
  Peter, 11
Bentley, John, 244
Bergen County, 16, 18, 26, 28, 34, 35, 38, 59, 66, 69, 88, 92, 134, 139, 142, 147, 153, 171, 172, 182, 183, 184, 205, 224, 225, 226, 227, 228, 234, 237, 239, 254, 256—319
  Neck, 11
  Township, 313
Bermuda Island, 211, 237, 313
Bernard, Sir Francis, 131
Bernards township, 247
Berry, Elizabeth, 213
Bessonett, Daniel, 261
Bettle, John, 261
Bickerdike, Hannah, 173
Bickle (Pickle), Nicholas, 26
Biddle, Josiah, 261
Bigelow, Captain, 11
Billingsport, 36, 51, 52, 233, 262,
  Fort at, 55
Bills, Thomas, 261
Binfield Park, 231
Birch, James, 261
Bird, Richard, 261
Birdsall, Samuel L., 261
  Whitson L., 261
Bisset, Asher, 261
Blaau (Bleau), Eleanor, 28, 29
  Uriah, 28
  Waldron, 28
Blackwell, John, 261
Blackwood, Samuel, 54
Blagg, Alderman, 17
Blain, Barbara, 27
  Barbara McK., 139
  James, 261
  William, 27, 140
Blakeney, Thomas, 28
Blauvelt, David, 261
  Theunis, 88, 261
Blaworth, Thomas, 261
Bleaching Green (Pa.), 9
Bleau (See Blaau)
Bloom, Frederick, 261
Bloomfield, James, 179
  Justice, 112
Blue (See Blaau)
Blundle, James, 262
Blunt, Joanna, 29
Board, James, 35
Bocock, William, 262

Boevey, Catherine, 157
Bogert, Cornelius, 262
  Henry, 262
  Jacob, 262
  Jacobus A., 262
  John C., 262
  Joost, 262
  Peter, 262
  Peter P., 262
Boggs, Ezekial, 29
  Dr. James, 26, 29
  Mary M., 29
Boice, Jacob, 262
Boly, Elias, 262
Bond, Elijah, 174
  Mary, 174
  Nathaniel, 262
Bonnell, Grace F., 30
  Isaac, 30
  Nathaniel, 30
  William F., 30, 79, (See Bunnell)
Bonum, Malachi, 262
Booten, John, 262
Booth, Benjamin, 262
  John, 262
Borden, John, 262
Bordentown, 81, 146
Boston (Mass.), 47, 118, 164, 178, 226
Boudinot, Elias, 46
Bough, Nicholas, 262
Bound Brook, 136, 213
Bowen, Captain, 178
  Ashley, 262
  Daniel, 30
  John, 262
  Sarah D., 31
Bowers, Rev. Henry P., 106
  Lemuel, 262
Bowlby, Abraham, 32, 88, 262
  Charles, 263
  Edward, 31, 263
  George, 31
  John, 31, 263
  Richard, 31, 88, 262
  Thomas, 31
Bowman, Edward, 263
Bowne, Andrew, 263
  John, 252, 263
  Obadiah, 263
Boyd, James, 263
Braddock, General, 56
Bradford, Colonel, 18
Bradley, Sarah, 105
Brady, John, 263
Brandywine (Pa.), 137
Brazier, Francis, 122
  Frances, 123
Brazilla, Joseph, 263
Brian, Jacob, 128
  Mary R., 128
Bridgewater (Eng.), 139
Bridgewater Township, 25, 261, 281
Brighton (Eng.), 54
Brindly, Samuel, 263
Brinkerhof, John, 263
  Seba, 263
Brinley, Francis, 263
Bristol (Eng.), 243
Brittain, Eleanor B., 32
  James, 32
  Israel, 33, 263
  Joseph, 33
  William, 33, 263

Broderick, James, 22
Brookhaven (L. I.), 35
Brooklyn (N. Y.), 69, 137, 213
Brooks, Cornelius, 263
  William, 263
Brower, Jacob, 263
  Peter, 263
Brown, (Browne), Daniel, 35
  Daniel I., 8, 33, 36, 183, 225
  Elizabeth, 33
  Francis, 35
  George, 176
  Hugh, 263
  Rev. Isaac, 33, 34, 35, 36, 140, 145, 159
  Rev. James, 105
  John, 33
  Margaret, 33
  Mary, 164
  Mary E., 35
  Rev. Nathaniel, 13
  Dr. Peter, 36
  William, 263
Brownjohn, William, 264
Bruce, David, 264
  George, 264
Bruen, Thomas, 264
Bryant, Dr. William, 264
Buccleuch Park, 37
Bucks County (Eng.) 196
Buffalo, (N. Y.), 223
Bulwer, Sir Edward, 231
  Gertrude V. C., 231
Bunker Hill (Mass.), 208
Bunnel, Isaac, 264 (See Bonnell)
Bunyan, John, 99
Burdge, Jacob, 264
  John, 264
  Jonathan, 264
Burford (Can.), 31
Burgees, John, 264
Burgoyne, General, 110
Burke, Elizabeth, 223
  Stephen, 264
  Thomas, 264
Burkett, Hannah, 37
  William, 36
Burling, Samuel, 264
Burlington, 38, 59, 76, 130, 155, 156, 157
  County, 38, 40, 48, 58, 59, 107, 130, 168, 170, 173, 258-319
Burnet, Ann, 37, 80
  Ann J., 107
  John, 37, 80, 198
  Rev. Matthias, 264
Burrows, Thomas, 264
Bursley, Daniel, 264
Burton (N. B.), 11, 171, 224
Burton, Jesse, 264
  John, 264
  William, 37
Burwell, James, 264
Bush, Hendrick, 264
Buskirk, (See Van Buskirk)
Butcott, John, 264
Butler, Eleanor, 32
  James, 265
  John, 265
  Lewis, 118
Button, Israel, 252
Buzhart, Jeremiah, 265
Byard, William, 265
Byrne, Anna, 80
  Mary, 80

Cadmus, Abraham, 38
  Thomas, Jr., 265
Cadwallader, 14, 46, 85, 119
  Jane, 14, 70
  John, 46, 267
  Margaret, 14
  Thomas, 46
Cahill, Daniel, 265
Cain, William, 176
California, 117
Callagher, Donald, 38
Cambridge (Eng.), 23, 49
Cameron, John, 38
  William, 38
Camp, John, 265
  Matthew, 265
Campbell, Archibald, 40, 55, 265
  Bayan, 40
  Charles, 39
  Rev. Colin, 38, 39
  Colin, 38, 39, 155
  Donald, 39, 265
  Duncan, 265
  James, 265
  John, 40, 113
  Margaret, 40
  Margaret E., 39
  Patrick, 265
  Peter, 10, 15, 40
  Robert, 41, 96, 251
  Sarah, 40
  Thomas, 10, 40
Canby, Thomas, 10
Cape Breton, 152
Cape May County, 92
Cape St. Vincent (Por.), 74
Cardigan (Wales), 124
Carle, Jemima, 94
  John, 94
Carlisle (Pa.), 23, 212
Carlton, Sr Guy, 14, 25, 29, 60, 104, 116, 146, 156, 203
Carr, Alexander, Jr., 265
Carrell (Carnel), William, 265
Carrol, Lieut., 233
Carter, Benjamin, 265
  John, Jr., 265
Cartwright, Caleb, 265
  Samuel, 265
Carty, John, 265
  William, 265
Cassilis, Earl of, 120
Castel, Michael M., 265
Castine (Me.), 95
Castle, Howard, 86, 87
Castner, George, 265
Cataraqui (Can.), 16, 26, 64, 172
Cate, Wardell, 265
Cavalier, John, 108
Cavenaugh, Patrick, 265
Cayford, Richard, 266
Ceylon Island, 14
Chaleur Bay (Can.), 50
Chalmers, Frances, 80
Chandler, Azail, 266
  Mary G., 42
  Rev. Thomas B., 7, 36, 41, 43, 87, 103, 108, 111, 168
  William, 42, 43
Charleston (S. C.), 9, 40, 58, 81, 172, 183, 194, 201, 208
Charlotte County (N. B.), 39, 280
Charlottetown (P. E. Is.), 24
Charlotteville (Can.) 143, 183
Chatham, 247
Cheesman, Abijah, 266

Chelmsford (Eng.), 80
Cherry Valley (P. E. Is.), 24
Chester (Eng.), 198
Chester Castle (Guer.), 137
Chesterfield, 128
Chestnutwood, Sebastian, 266
Chever, George, 266
Chew, David, 266
  Jonathan, 266
  William, 68, 106, 266
Chillas, Robert, 152
Chosel, Jonathan, 266
Christiansen, Cornelius, 234
Churchward, Richard, 266
Clarendon, Walter, 266
Clark (Clarke), Alexander, 266
  Benjamin, 266
  George, 44, 55
  James, 266
  John, 266
  Joseph, 267
  Samuel, 267
  Sarah, 222
  Thomas, 267
  William, 43
Clawson, Cornelius, 267
  John, 44
  Jonathan, 44, 95
Clayton, Joseph, 267
Clement, Jacob, Jr., 267
Clements (N. S.), 224, 238
Clendenan, John, 267
Clendenning, James, 44
Cleveland, Benjamin, 106
Clifton, Alfred, 245
Clinton, Sr Henry, 25, 43, 76, 77, 85, 87, 88, 90, 111, 118, 144, 148, 154, 168, 214, 216, 222, 223, 240
Clopper, Peter, 267
Cloud, John, 45
  Rebecca, 45
Cochran, John, 46
  Dr. John, 219
  Richard, 45
Coddington, Asher, 267
  Isaiah, 267
Cohansey, 92
Coke, Daniel P., 5
  William, 267
Colden, Alexander, 14
  Alice, 46
  Anne W., 46
  Elizabeth N., 14
Coldenham (N. Y.), 46
Cole, Daniel, 267
  Frederick, 267
  James, 267
  Richard, 267
Coleny, John, 267
Colgan, Fleming, 267
Collins, Elijah, 267
  James, 46, 268
  James, Jr., 268
  Jonathan, 268
  Mahlon, 268
Collver, Rev. Jabez, 32
Columbia University, 111, 123, 164, 168
Colts Neck, 221
Colvin, James, 268
  Luther, Jr., 268
  Stephen, 268
Combould, Richard, 225
Combs (Coombs), Abijah, 268
  Alice O., 47

Index

Dennis, 47
Dennis, Jr., 268
John, 47
Martha V., 47
Nathan, 48
Nathaniel, 47
Compton, James, 268
John, 268
Richard, 98, 268
Richard, Jr., 268
Conliff, Joseph, 268
Connecticut, 35, 42, 47, 75, 94, 134, 225, 264
Cook (Cooke), Arthur, 80
Charles, 48, 138
Mrs. Graham K., 49
Isabella, 49
John, 268
Mary, 49
Michael, 49
Patterson, 268
Robert, 48, 251, 252
Rev. Samuel, 49
Silas, Jr., 268
Thomas, 49
Cool, Philip, 268
Cooper, Jacob, 84, 268
James, 268
John, 268
Rev. Myles, 103, 164, 168
Richard, 50
Cooper's Ferry, 113
Cordue, John, 50
Cork (Ire.), 207
Corlin, William, 50
Cornwall (Eng.), 217
Cornwallis (N. S.), 82, 227, 228
Cornwallis, Lord, 16, 28, 52, 78, 87, 154, 171, 180, 214, 225, 233, 242
Corrent, William, 269
Corse, Henry, 269
Corson, Ann, 226
Cortreght, Solomon, 269
Cotterel, John, 269
Samuel, 269
Cougler, John, 50
Courter, John, 269
John, Jr., 269
Coutart, Jane, 137
Cowgill (Cougle), John, 50
Cowman, John, 269
Cowperthwaite, Charity, 51, 89
Hugh, 50, 55, 89
Sarah, 89
Cox, (Coxe), Abigail, 53, 54
Anne, 54
Daniel, 8, 9, 51, 52, 76, 79, 107, 122, 131, 163, 174, 287
Grace, 287
George, 54
John, 51, 113
Dr. John R., 54
Lawrence, 269
Leonard, 79
Leonard S., 54
Sarah R., 54
Cozens, Daniel, 51, 52, 54, 93, 269
Elizabeth, 54, 55
Jacob, 55
Joshua, 55, 269
Martha, 55
Samuel, 269
Crafts, Harriet B., 81
Cranbury, 30, 198
Cranmer, Sarah, 15

Crane, John J., 269
Jonathan, 129
Creighton, James, 55
Crine, Vincent, 269
Cristy, William, 269
Croghan, George, 80
Crosswicks, 48, 128
Crowe, Eyre E., 56, 57
Richard 56
Crowell, Joseph, 57, 58
Richard, 269
Samuel, 57, 85
Thomas, 44, 57, 126
Crown Point (N. Y.), 150, 204
Cumberland (N. S.), 223
Cumberland County, 30, 31, 54, 85, 166, 176, 213, 259-319
Cumberland County (Pa.), 23
Cummins, John, 269
Cunliffe, Joseph, 59, 60, 269
Cunningham, Capt., 240
Cupar's Ferry, 45
Curlis, John, 269
Curtis, James, 269
Samuel, 269
Thomas, 130
Walter, 130
William, 269
Cuyler, Alida, 165
Barent, 165
Elizabeth, 99
Hannah, 165
Henry, 165, 269
Henry, Jr., 81
Hester, 165
Mary, 165
Cyphers, Elizabeth, 127
George, 58, 251
George, Jr., 58, 270
Peter, 127, 270
Philip, 270
Sarah E., 58

Dagworthy, Capt. John, Jr., 20
Dailing, Gen. John, 118
Danbury, (Conn.), 176
Dancer, Daniel, 270
Jacob, 270
Daniel (Daniels, Joel, 270
John, 270
Joseph, 270
Sarah, 31
Davenport (Devenport), Captain, 184
Humphrey, 271
Josiah F., 58, 76
Miss K., 95
William, 271
Davies, John, 270
Jeremiah, 270
Jerman, 270
Davis, James, 270
Richard, 270
Samuel, 270
Daws, John, 270
Day, John, 270
Peter, 270
Dayton, Elias B., 43
Jonathan, 91
Dean, James, 270
Dear, Jonathan, 71
Deats, Hiram E., 217, 253
Debauc, John, 270
Debnam, William, 59
DeCamp, Joseph, 270

de Cou, Anne, 156
  Isaac, 9, 156
Deerfield Township, 176
DeGroot, Jacob, 270
  John, 270
  Peter, 270
de Lancey, James, 51, 160, 171
  Oliver, 23, 81, 143, 165
Delaware, 29
Demare, David, 59, 271
Demarest, Aaron, 271
  Aaron, Jr., 271
  David G., 271
  Daniel S., 271
  Garret, 271
  Guilliam, 271
  Harriet, 123
  Jacob, 271
  John, 271
  Joost, 271
  Rulif, 271
  Samuel, 271
Demayne, William, 59
De Menezes, John, 60
DeMott, Jacob, 271
  John, 271
Denison, Esther L., 131
  George T., 131
Dennis, Anthony, 271
  Ezekial, 271
  Joseph, 85
  Michael, 271
  Samuel, 271
  Sarah, 85
de Peyster, Abraham, 61
  Anne, 228-229
  Catherine, 61
  Frederick, 61
  James, 61
  Nicholas, 271
  Pierre, 38, 60
Derik, Prenore, 271
Desbrisay, Rev. Theophilus, 24
Despard, Edward M., 118
DeVeber, Gabriel, 51, 233, 271
  Gabriel, Jr., 271
Devonshire (Eng.), 209
Dey, Abraham, 272
  Jacob, 272
Dickinson, General, 242
Digby (N. S.), 22, 30, 37, 56, 64, 79, 85, 96, 99, 142, 221
Dilkes, John, 272
  Joshua, 272
Dill, Joseph, 272
Dillon, William, 272
Dilts, Christopher, 272
Disborough, Caty. V. M., 235
  Henry, 236, 272
Doan, John, 272
  Titus, 272
Doleay, Pierre, 66
Dolles, Reuben, 272
Dominica, (W. I.), 55
Donaldson, Andrew, 272
Dongan, Edward, 61
  Edward V., 7, 8, 61, 63, 122, 239
  Frances La G., 61, 63, 122
  Walter T., 62
Donworth, Peter, 272
Doremus, Hendrick, 272
Dorset (Eng.), 208
Dougan, B., 63
  Dr. Henry, 61, 62, 122, 239
  James, 63
  Lydia, 63

Leydia La G., 61, 63, 122
Lydia M., 63
Margaret, 63
Susannah, 63
Douglas, (N. B.), 58
Douglas, William, 272
Dougherty, James, 272
Doughty, Bartholomew, 272
Dover Township, 11, 263, 285
Dowdeswell, Thomas, 63
Dowdney, Nathaniel, 272
Drake, Benjamin, 64, 99
  Fitz Randolph, 64
  Imlay, 272
  Mary, 64, 99
  Rachel, 64
  Randolph, 272
  William, 26, 64
Dreeler, John, 272
Driffield, Rev. William, 56
Drummond, Jane, 273
  Jennie V., 66
  Robert, 65, 161, 273
Drury, Wake, 273
Dublin (Ire.), 207
Dubois, Catherine de P., 61
  Peter, 273
Duffield, Benjamin, 273
  James, 273
  John, 273
Dulyea, Peter, 66
Dumont, John, 66
Duncombe, Dennis, 67
Dundas, Colonel, 240
Dunfield, John, 273
Dungan, Cornelius, 273
  Thomas, 273
Dunham, Asher, 67
  Azariah, 68
  Daniel, 68, 273
  Isaac, 67, 273
  John, 68, 273
  Josiah, 67, 68
  Phineas, 273
Dunlap, Samuel, 273
Dunlop, William, 138
Dunmore, Earl of, 92, 93
Dunn, Benjamin, 68
  Hugh, 68
  James, 68
Dunscomb, John, 273
Dunworth, Peter, 273
Durbarow, Dr. Benjamin, 151
Durham (Eng.), 15
Duryea, Daniel J., 273
  John, 273
  John P., 273
Dutchess County (N. Y.), 105, 167
Dutton, William, 273
Duwin, Peter, 273
Duychinck, Colonel, 274
  John, 274
Dykeman, Cornelius, 274

Eagler, Conrad, 274
Earle, Dr. Charles, 68
  Edward, 69
  Hannah, 70, 205
  John, 69, 274
  Justus, 69, 205
  Peter, 274
  Philip, 274
  Sichy, V. D., 69
  Silvester, 69
East Ham (Eng.), 113
East Windsor (Conn.), 75

Index

Eddy, John, 274
Eden, Governor, 168
Edgar, James, 202
  Sarah S., 202
  Thomas, 112, 202
  William, 202
Edinburgh (Scot.), 45, 131, 151, 174
Edison, John, 274
Edwards, Mary, 35
  Stephen, 170, 274
Egerton, H. E., 4
Egg Harbor, 58
Eglinton, Edward, 274
Eikler, William, 274
Elgin County (Can.), 264
Eliot (Elliot), George A., 137
  Jane McC., 137
  Margaret V. C., 231
  O. Elliott, 231
  Mr. 274
Elizabethtown, 30, 41, 42, 43, 50, 58, 60, 61, 62, 71, 90, 91, 92, 100, 108, 110, 125, 126, 134, 152, 154, 158, 166, 177, 197, 199, 200, 210, 212, 222, 245, 260, 280, 292, 299, 304
Ellis, Daniel, 274
  Ebenezer, 274
  Levi, 274
  Thomas, 274
Ellison, Robert, 274
Ellmore, Rev. Moses, 179
Elmer, Rev. Jonathan, 95
Elston, Thomas, 274
Elwel, Israel, 274
Emley, John, 274
Emmons, Catherine, 232
  Jacob, 275
English, Job, 275
English Neighborhood, 263, 270, 271, 272, 291, 306, 313
Ensley, John, 275
Essex County, 24, 43, 80, 83, 90, 95, 106, 109, 110, 133, 142, 158, 160, 164, 170, 200, 206, 209, 222, 231, 234, 240, 242, 244, 245, 254, 257-319
Estey, Aaron, 58
  Sarah, 58
Etter, Franklin, 275
Eutaw Springs (S. C.), 19, 28, 58, 226, 310
Evans, John, 275
  Richard, 175
Everitt, Ruth, 58
Everson, Barent, 275
Exeter (Eng.), 242

Fagan, Jake, 275
Fairholm, Johnston, 275
Falker, John, 275
Falmouth (Me.), 102
Fanker (Forker), Philip, 275
Fanning, Edmund, 66
Farce, Philip, 275, 276
Farmer, Elizabeth, 70
  Jasper, 196
  Susan S., 196
  Thomas, 70
Farnham, John, 275
Farquhar, Elizabeth F., 70
  Jane C., 70
  William, 70
  Dr. William, 70

Farrand, Stephen, 275
Fennimore, Abraham, 275
Fenton, Elijah, 275
  Lewis, 275
Ferguson, Patrick, 61, 214
Fillimore, Asa, 223
  Spiller, 223
Finney, George, 275
Finnimore, Richard, 70
Fisher, George, 275
  Jonathan, Sr., 275
  Jonathan, Jr., 275
Fislar, Felix, 51
Fitzgerald, Ambrose, 275
Fitz Randolph, Ann., 179
  Asher, 71
  David, 70
  Edward, 71
  Jacob, 276
  James, 71
  Jonathan, 99
  Joseph, 70, 71
  Nancy, 179
  Nathaniel, 70
  Robert, 71
Fitzroy, Charles, 195
Flanagan, James, 276
Flatbush (L. I.), 16
Flaxley Abbey (Eng.), 167
Flemington, 217
Florida, 115
Flowers, Martin, 276
Floyer, Catherine, 80
  Charles, 80
Fonce, Philip, 275, 276
Ford, Ebenezer, 72
  John, 12, 72, 276
  Oswald, 72, 276
  Samuel, 72
Forker (See Fanker)
Forman, Colonel, 215
  Aaron, 276
  David, 64, 202
  Ezekiel, 72
Forrest, Arthur, 72
  Augusta, 73
  Cecilia, 73
  Harriet, 73
  Julia, 73
  Margaret, 73
  Thomas, 73, 74
Forsman, William, 276
Fort Franklin, 77
  Griswold (Conn.), 225
  Independence, 227
  Lee, 28
  Montgomery, 227
Foster, Ebenezer, 74, 276
  Frederick, 276
  Lawrence, 74, 276
  Stephen, 74
Foust, Jacob, 276
Fowler, Thomas, 276
Fox, George, 276
  Grace, 30
  Hendrick, 276
  Jacobus, 276
  Mattines, 276
  Thomas, 30
Foxcroft, John, 160
Foy, Moses, 276
Fradenburgh, Ann V., 223
  George L., 223
France, 108, 121
Frankford, Township, 85

Franklin, 182
Franklin, Benjamin, 76, 78, 79
  Ellen, 79
  Helena, 79
  John, 276
  William, 8, 12, 20, 22, 23, 30, 45, 53, 59, 75, 93, 100, 107, 117, 120, 131, 144, 156, 161, 162, 169, 197, 198, 200, 202. (See frontispiece).
  Mrs. William, 75, 169
  William T., 78, 80
Franklin Township, 256, 273, 276, 301, 313, 319
Franklin County (Pa.), 194
Fraser, (Frazer), Anne S., 81
  Diodema M., 80
  Francis, 80
  Thomas S., 81
  Rev. William, 276
Frazee, James, 276
  James, Jr., 276
  Mary D., 64
Fredericks, Conrad, 277
  Hendrick, 277
Fredericton (N. B.), 12, 15, 40, 49, 58, 105, 106, 127, 156, 207, 209, 215, 232, 244
Freehold Township, 49, 95, 98, 129, 132, 167, 215, 217, 218, 220, 221, 235, 236, 244, 251, 261, 263, 266, 267, 286
Freeman, Rev. Daniel, 143
  Edmund, 277
  Isaac, 95, 277
  Justice, 112
  Lewis, 277
French, Adolphus, 81
  Joseph, 277
  Philip, 277
Friend, Charles, 277
Frink, Hester C., 165
  Nathan, 165
Fritts, Frederick, 277
Fullerton, William, 277
Furman, Dr. Aaron, 277
Fusman, Daniel, 277
  William, 277

Gach, Philip, 277
Gage, Thomas, 117, 118
Gaine, Hugh, 103, 277
Galbraith, Thomas, 277
Galloway, Joseph, 77, 154, 160
Gamble, Margaret, 216
  Thomas, 80
Gardner, Jacob, 277
  Thomas, 277
Garrabrant, Garrabrant, 277
  Garrabrant, Jr., 277
  Nicholas, 278
Garrison, Jacob, 278
Garvie, Alexander, 278
  John, 278
  William, 278
Gault, Robert, 278
Gaynor, Bridget, 105
Georgia, 40, 48, 55, 58, 60, 65, 105, 160
Germain, Lord George, 78, 202
Germantown (Pa.), 40, 119
Germany, 149
Gesner, Abraham, 278
Gibbs, Lucas, 278
Giberson (Guisbertson), Benjamin, 278

Guisbert, 81, 82, 100
  Hannah, 81
  John, 81, 278
  Malachi, 278
  William, 81, 82
  William, Jr., 278
Gibraltar, 73, 86, 108
Gifford, William, 11
Gilian, William, 278
Glan, Gabriel, 278
Glasgow (Scot.), 46, 204
  University, 221
Gloucester County, 36, 45, 51, 54, 92, 97, 113, 140, 257-319
  Township, 140
Gloucestershire (Eng.), 157, 201
Godbier, William, 278
Goelet, Peter, 278
Golden, George (alias John), 278
Goodman, Robert, 278
Goodwin, Jacob, 278
Gordon, James, 82
  John, 278
Gorman, John, 279
Gosling, David, 82, 279
  Elizabeth, 82
  Howe C., 82
  James, 82
Gould, Mrs., 242
  Elizabeth, 242
Gourlay, Dr. William, 231
  Catherine V. C., 231
Gouveneur, Nicholas, 279
Graham, John, 160
  J. J., 131
  Mary, 138
  Robert, 279
  Samuel, 131
Grames, James, 279
  Robert, 279
  (See Grimes)
Grand Manan (N. B.), 276
Grandin, Daniel, 82, 279
  Eleanor, 83
  Margaret, 82
  Philip, 82
  Thomas, 279
  William, 279
Grant, Ebenezer, 75, 224
Grantham (Can.), 217
Granville (N. S.), 142
Gray, James, 83
Green, Reuben, 279
  Samuel, 279
  William, 279
Greene, Nathaniel, 28
Greenfield, Lewis, 279
Greenwich (N. B.), 32, 297
Greenwich Township, 128, 209
Grenada (W. I.), 118
Grey, Colonel, 195
Grigg, Hannah, 145
  John, 145
Griggstown, 284
Grimes, Robert, 279
  (See Grymes)
Groom, Elijah, 84, 268
  Ezekiel, 84
Gros, Dorothea C., 149
  Rev. Mr., 149
Grover, Barzilla, 84, 101, 279
  Joseph, 84, 279
  Samuel, 84, 279
  Thomas, 84, 279
  William, 84

Index

Gruff, John, 279
Grymes, John R., 160
Guadalupe (W. I.), 194
Guernsey, Island, 137
Guibertson, (See Giberson)
Guillon, William 280
Gummersall, Thomas, 59, 60
Gunning, Colonel, 170

Habblings, Thomas P., 280
Hackensack, 10, 17, 33, 69, 99, 139, 140, 171, 221, 223, 224, 227, 232, 234, 261, 271, 283, 295, 303, 305
  Point, 262, 263, 298,
  Township, 278, 290, 293, 294, 299, 301, 306, 312
Hadden, Isaac, 280
Haggerty, Bonnel, 85
  Hannah, 85
  John, 85
  Joseph, 85
  Ludlum, 85
  Margaret, 85
  Morris, 85
  Nancy, 85
  Patrick 84, 85, 251
  Polly, 85
  Redman, 85
  Sarah D., 85
  Stephen, 85
Hagle, John M., 280
Hailes, Harris W., 49
  Isabella C., 49
Hailsham (Eng.) 230, 231
Halfpenny, Mr., 280
Halifax (N. S.), 26, 29, 56, 105, 129, 262, 281
Hall, Elisha, 280
  Isaac, 280
  Jacob, 85
  Levi, 280
  William, 280
Hallens, Cornelius, 280
Hallet, Joseph, 280
Halstead, Matthias, 91
  William, 280
Hambleton, David, 46
Hamer, Ann S., 206
  Ibbetson, 85, 206
  Sarah H., 86
Hamilton, John, 20
  Joshua, 280
Hammell, Dr. John, 87
Hammet, William, 280
Hampton (N. B.), 72, 284
Hampton, John, 111, 135, 280
  Jonathan, 109
  Mary, 109
Hancock, Joseph, 280
Hand, Aaron, 280
  John, 280
  Samuel, 280
Handorff, Frederick, 280
Hankinson, Gitty, 88
  John, 252, 280
  Reuben, 87
Hanks, John, 280
Hannah, Nathaniel, 280
Hannisey, James, 281
Hannison, Henry J., 281
Hanover, 67, 128, 142, 227, 228, 229, 230
  Township, 101
Hanover (Mass.), 223

Harber, Jacob, 281
Harding, Robert, 281
Hargrave, Frances, 108
  William, 108
Haring, Abraham C., 88
  Cornelius, 88, 281
  John C., 281
  Peter J., 281
  Peter T. (or I.), 281
Harlingen, 232, 234
Harned, Benjamin, 281
  John, 281
  Nathaniel, 281
Harrington Township, 262, 273, 281, 297
Harris, Edmund, 281
  George B., 184
  John, 281
Harrison, Charity C., 51, 89
  Charles, 88
  Christopher, 88
  Elizabeth, 89
  Henry, 40
  James, 51, 89
  Mary, 40
  Samuel, 281
  William, 89
Hart, Charles, 89
Hartford (Conn.), 134
Hartpence, John, 281
Hartshorn, Ezekiel, 89, 251
  Isaac, 281
  Lawrence, 281
  Robert, 89, 251, 281
  Thomas, Jr., 281
Haslop (Hyslop), John, 89
Hassen, Felix, 281
Haten, Nathaniel, 282
Hatfield, Abel, 282
  Abigail, 108
  Barnes, 89
  Cornelius, 57, 90, 92, 201, 282,
  Cornelius, Jr., 59, 90, 91, 132, 161, 162
  James, 90
  Job, 282
  John, 91
  John S., 90, 91, 132
  Joseph, 212
  Mary, 212
  Mary L., 91
  Morris, 90
Hathaway, Simon, 282
  Ralph, 143
  Sarah, 143
Hatton, Elizabeth, 93
  John, 92, 93
  Nathaniel, 282
  Rev. Thomas, 94
Haulenbeck, Isaac, 94
Havana (Cuba), 56, 83
Havens, John, 282
  Stout, 282
Hawker, William, 242
Hayden, Jemima C., 94
  John, 95
  Margaret, 24
  Samuel, 12, 24, 94, 283
Hazard, Sarah, 86
Heanley, Margaret, 80
Heard, John, 95, 216, 282
  Nathaniel, 95, 96, 112, 203
  William, 95
Heathcote, Martha, 37, 107
Heaton, Mary, 69

Heddon, Margaret, 74
Hedger, John, 282
Hedges, Stephen, 282
Helme, Benjamin, 282
Hempstead, Jeremiah, 282
Henchman, John, 282
Hendorff, Frederick, 96
Hendricks, Ann (Nancy), 96
    Baker, 282
    Conrad, 96
    John, 96, 282
Hendrickson, Lieutenant, 144
    Daniel, 282
    Micha, 235
Henley, Mrs. Anne, 79
Henry, David, 138
    Herbert, 282
    Mary R., 138
    Patrick, 97
    Samuel, 97
Herbert, Anne, 114
Herring, Cornelius, 88
Hertford College (Eng.), 109
Heslop, John, 89, 282
Hetfield (See Hatfield)
Hewitt, Jacob, 282
    Job, 282
Hewlings, Abraham, 39
    Joseph, 282
    Thomas P., 282
    William, 283
Heyden, Samuel, 283
Hick, William, 97
    William F., 97
Hicks, Oliver, 283
Hierlihy, Timothy, 94
Hiler, Jacob, 283
    Nicholas, 283
Hillsborough Township, 218, 219
Hilton, Joseph, 283
Himeon, Adam, 283
    George, 283
    Hendrick J., 283
    Jacob, 283
    Philip, 283
Hinchman, John, 97, 98
Hind, John, 98
    Mary, 98
Hingston, Benezer M., 98
    Rev. James, 98
Hoagland, Obadiah, 283
Hobart, Bishop, 43
    Mary C., 43
Hoffman, Christopher, 283
    Nicholas, 283
Holcombe, Jeremiah, 283
    John, 283
Hole, John, 283
Hollberg Gedern (Germany), 149
Hollinshead, Anthony, 283
Holmes, Elias, 99
    Joseph, 283
Holt, William J., 99
    Elizabeth C., 99
Holton, Mary D., 99
    Peter, 64, 99
    Rachel D., 64
Holyhead (No. Wales), 20
Homburg (Germany), 149
Homer, Fuller, 283
Homfray, Cotton, 100
Hones, John, 283
Honeyman, A. Van Doren, 4, 253
    John, 284
Hooper, Isabella, 114, 195

Clement, 100
Robert L., 114, 195
Thomas, 100
Hooton, John, 100
Hopewell, 31
    Township, 85
Hopkins, Peter, 22
    Silas, 284
Hopper, Garret A., 284
Hornbeck, Isaac, 284
Horner, Asher, 284
    Hugh, 284
    James, 284
    John, 101
    Joseph, 284
Horse Neck, 206
Horton (N. S.), 129, 227
Howard, Colonel, 195
    George, 284
    Sarah H., 86
    Sheffield, 284
    William, 86, 87, 284
Howe, Jonas, 69, 127
    Richard, 28, 52, 215
    Sir William, 9, 16, 18, 22, 28, 31, 52, 65, 76, 87, 100, 113, 118, 130, 132, 143, 210, 233, 241, 245
Howel, William, 11
Huddy, Joshua, 53, 77, 78, 130, 131, 170
Hude, Ann, 115
Hudnot, Samuel, 284
Hulett, Daniel, 284
    Michael, 284
Hull (Eng.), 61
Humbert, Stephen, 284
Humphreys, James, 104
Humphries, Dr. Nicholas, 285
Hunlock, Thomas, 101
Hunt, Abraham, 9
    Daniel, 285
    Rev. Garner A., 216
    John, 285
    Jonathan, 285
    Nathaniel, 10
    William, Jr., 285
Hunterdon County, 9, 10, 20, 26, 83, 88, 116, 173, 181, 200, 216, 217, 237, 254, 257-319
Huntingdon (Pa.), 23
Huntly, Henry V., 194
Hurlet, William K., 285
Hurst, George, 285
Husk, Thomas, 285
Hutchinson, Ann, 102
    Catherine L., 102
    Francis, 102
    John, 101, 102
    Margaret, 101, 102
    William, 101, 102, 251
Hutton, Captain, 55
Hyde, Gen. West, 133
Hyslop, John, 89, 282

Iliff, James, 285
    William, 285
India, 15, 231
Ingland, William, Jr., 285
Inglis, Rev. Charles, 42, 91, 102, 103, 123, 144, 145, 163, 168, 240
    Mary, 81
Inglish, John, 285
    John, Jr., 285

Index

Ink, John, 285
Insley, Christopher, 285
  Jacob, 285
  John, 285
Ireland, 29, 40, 48, 63, 98, 114, 115, 129, 139, 151, 152, 153, 166, 176, 196, 207
Irons, John, 285
Isle of Man, 164
Izalton, Robert, 285

Jacklin, John, 285
Jackson, Samuel, 285
  William, 285
Jacobus, Garret, 286
Jacquish, David, 286
Jamaica (W. I.), 48, 60, 72, 73, 108, 110, 118, 174, 182, 194, 215, 242, 243, 246
James, Bridget G., 105
  Chalkley, 121
  Daniel, 105
  Robert, 286
Jameson, Samuel, 286
Jauncey, James, 286
Jefferis, John, 286
Jenkins, Rev. Edward, 81
  Elizabeth, 106
  Griffen, 286
  John, 68, 105
  Mrs. Sarah B., 105
  Trivis, 286
  Rev. William, 125
Jersey City, 179
Jersey Island, 230
Jervis, Charles, 10
Jessup, Daniel, 225, 286
  Jeremiah, 286
  Major, 179
Joans, Edward, 286
Johnson, Eliphalet, 106, 286
  Elizabeth, 13
  George, 286
  Ichabod, 286
  Isaac, 286
  Jane W., 106
  Sir John, 83, 84
  Martha, 241
  Peter, 286
  Dr. Uzal, 106
  William F., 197
Johnston, Alexander, 141
  Andrew, 18, 197, 203, 216
  Ann, 107
  Catherine, 197
  Gertrude, 18, 107
  Gertrude B., 197
  Heathcote, 37, 107
  John, 197
  John L., 107
  Dr. Lewis, 37, 107
  Margaret, 107, 203
  Martha H., 37, 107
  Mary, 197
  Phebe, 141
  Robert, 286
  Stephen, 197
  Susannah B., 107
Jones, Andrew, 286
  E. Alfred, 1, 4, 8
  Edward, 286
  Mary, 80
  Teresa, 80
  Thomas, 286
Jordan, John, 107

Jouet, Abigail H., 108
  Cavalier, 112
  Rev. Cavalier, 43, 68, 108
  Daniel, 108
  Frances H., 108
  John T., 110
  Mary H., 109
  Xenophon, 68, 110
Justason, Isaac, 113

Kaign, James, 286
  Thomas, 287
Kearny (Kearney), Ann H., 114, 115
  Catherine P., 115
  Elizabeth, 116
  Francis, 49, 113, 116, 233
  Isabel, 287
  Isabella H., 114
  James, 252
  James H., 115
  James W., 114
  Lawrence, 116
  Michael, 49, 114, 115, 203
  Michael, Jr., 116
  Peter, 287
  Philip, 8, 114, 116, 195
  Ravaud, 114, 115
  Sarah, 195
  Sarah M., 115
  Stephen W., 117
  Susannah W., 117
  Thomas, 287
Keating, Garret, 117
  Mary, 117
Kelly, John, 141, 287
  William, 246
  Mr. 246
Kelso, Rev. Robert, 31
Kelso (Scot.), 169
Kemble, Peter, 117, 119
  Samuel, 119
  Stephen, 117
  William, 119
Kemp, Grace C., 287
  John T., 287
Kenact, Matthias, 287
Kennebecasis River (N. B.), 68, 173
Kennedy, Anne W., 120
  Archibald, 119, 197
  Catherine S., 120
  Mary S., 119
Kennington (Eng.), 59
Kent, David, 121, 287
  Erasmus, Jr., 287
  Holday, 121
  Rachel, 121
  Steven, 12, 121
  William, 287
  Zernia, 121
Kerr, Elizabeth B., 33
  James, 33
Ketcham, Richard, 287
Ketteltos, Winant, 287
Kichline, Philip, 287
Kiker, Tobias, 287
Kilbourn, Elijah, 287
Kindal, Joseph, 287
Kinderkameck, 311
King, Andrew, 287
  Benjamin, 287
  James, 287
  John, 287
  Joseph, 287

Index

Kinsale (Ire.), 114
Kingsclear (N. B.), 32, 40, 58, 141
Kings College, (N. Y.), 43
Kings County (N. B.), 13, 19, 33, 150, 181
Kingsland, Charles, 287
  Charles, Jr., 287
  Cornelius, 287
  Henry, 288
  Isaac, 288
  Joseph, 234, 288
  William, Jr., 288
Kings Mountain (N. C.), 61, 208
Kingston (N. B.), 27, 74
Kingwood Township, 216, 217, 237, 308
Kipp, Isaac N., 288
  Nikasey, 288
Kirby, John, 288
Kitchen, Andrew, 288
  John, 288
Kline, Jacob, 288
  Philip, Sr., 288
  Philip, Jr., 288
Knowles, Charles, 121
  John, 121
Knowlton, 32, 263
Knowlton Township, 204
Knox, Henry E., 245
Knyphausen, General, 92, 128
Konkle, Hanadam, 288
  Mathias, 288

Lafayette, Gen., 91
La Grange, Bernardus, 8, 53, 61, 62, 63, 99, 121, 123, 207, 238, 239
  Engeltje V., 121
  Frances, 61, 63, 122
  Frances B., 122, 123
  Harriet D., 123
  Jacobus, 121
  James B., 61, 122, 123
  James W., 123
  Lydia, 61, 63, 122
  Susannah, 61, 63, 122, 238
Laight, Edward, 288
Lake, Mr., 288
Lake Champlain (N. Y.) 100
Lake George (N. Y.), 239
Lamb, Thomas, 288
Lambert, George, 124
  Isaac, 288
  John, 288
  Lancelot, 288
Lamington, 136
Lancaster (Pa), 154
Landkey (Eng.), 209
Lane, Sarah, 80
Langley, Henry, 289
  Reuben, 289
Lansdown, 83
Laquier, John, 289
Large, Aaron, 289
La Rochelle (France), 121
Lawrence, Abraham P., 125
  Alexander C., 125
  Ann L., 116
  Charles E., 125
  Daniel, 289
  Elisha, 7, 14, 124, 125, 198
  Eliza Ann, 125
  Elizabeth, 116
  Elizabeth R., 128
  Elizabeth O., 126
  James, 128

Dr. John, 124
John, 116, 124, 125, 289
Margaret, 125
Mary, 125
Mary R., 125
Peter R., 125
Sarah C., 125
Thomas, 289
William R., 125, 126, 289
Lawrence Island, 211
Lawrenceville, 168
Lawton, Lewis, 289
Layton, Samuel, 289
Leake, John, 238
Lebanon Township, 237
Lee, Charles, 161, 180
  Elizabeth C., 127
  George, 126
  John, 289
  John, Jr., 126
  Joseph, 32, 68, 106, 126, 251, 270
Lefferty, Bryan, 289
  Daniel, 289
Le Grange (See La Grange)
Leinbach, Frederick, 289
LeMesurier, Sophia, 137
  William, 137
Lemmon, Michael, 289
  Peter, 289
Lennox, David, 289
  Richard, 289
Lent, Abraham. 289
  Peter, 289
Leonard, Ann, 116
  Frances S., 128
  George, 96
  John, 127, 128
  Joseph, 290
  Magdalen R., 128
  Nancy A., 129
  Samuel, 116, 129, 251, 252
  Thomas, 129
Leseter, Daniel, 290
Leslie, General, 214
  Dr. George, 219
Letts, Francis, 290
Lewis, Catherine, 102
  Daniel, 290
  David, 130
  Jean, 130
  Nathaniel, 130
  Timothy, 290
Limerick County (Ire.), 166
Linn, John, 290
Liponer, Anthony, 290
Lippincott, Elias, 290
  Esther B., 131
  Jacob, 290
  James, 287, 290
  Jedediah, 290
  Richard, 77, 130, 243
Lisbon (Portugal), 120
Lisburne, Lord, 87
Lisk, Stacy, 290
Liverpool (Eng.), 40
Livingston, Philip, 110, 111
  William, 8, 62, 164, 197, 306
Lloyd, David, 290
Lloyd's Neck, 77
Lockerman, Mary, 91
Lockhart, Harriet P., 54
  Maria, 54
Locktown, 217
Lodi, 69
Logan, Patrick, 290
  Walter, 131

Index

Cornelia, 29
Stoffel, 29
London (Eng.), 19, 20, 23, 25, 28, 29, 31, 34, 35, 37, 42, 48, 53, 54, 59, 63, 65, 66, 77, 78, 79, 93, 95, 98, 108, 116, 122, 123, 133, 140, 148, 153, 155, 159, 161, 165, 178, 184, 194, 196, 215, 230, 313
Long, Joseph, 290
  Silas, 290
  Thomas, 132
Long Beach (N. B.) 177
Long Island (N. Y.), 31, 33, 34, 55, 65, 87, 94, 130, 159, 212, 231, 236, 264
Longstreet, John, 132, 252
  John, Jr., 132
Longworth, Catherine, 133
  Catherine O., 134
  Isaac, 133, 159, 304
  Isaac, Jr., 290
  Thomas, 133, 290
Loofborough, Thomas, 134
  (See Lufburrow)
Lord, Asa, 290
  Isaac, 290
Loshier, Jacob, 290
  Nicholas, 290
Lott, Andrew, 291
Loudoun, Earl of, 83
Louisburg (N. S.), 56, 173
Low, Cornelius, 243
  Isaac, 50
  John, 83
Lower Penns Neck, 262
Lowrey (Lowry,) Colonel, 243
  David, 291
  James, 291
  Joseph, Sr., 291
  Joseph, Jr., 291
  William, 291
Luce, William, 110, 134
Ludlow, George, 291
  William W., 291
Lufborrow, Catherine, 74
  John, 291
  Nathaniel, 291
  Thomas, 134
Lundy, Jacob, 291
  Reuben, 291
  Samuel, 291
  Thomas, 291
Lurton, William, 291
Lutkins, Hermanus, 291
  Henry, 35, 134
  John, 291
Lycan, Enoch, 291
Lydecker, Abraham, 135
  Cornelius, 135
  Rev. Garret, 28, 134, 213
  Mary, 134
  Ryck, 134
  Samuel, 291
  Samuel B., 135
Lynson, Jane, 145
Lyon, Enoch, 135
  Thomas, 291
  Zophir, 162
Lyte, Mary S., 208

McAtee, James, 135
Macartney, Isabella, 196
M'Carty, Duncan, 291
Maclean, Donald, 194

McCleary, Helen C., 226
  John, 291
McCleese (McLeod), Cornelius, 136
MacCord, John, 292
McCoy, Alexander, 292
McCrea, Catherine, 138
  Catherine M., 137
  Catherine R., 136
  Creighton, 136, 138
  Rev. James, 136, 138
  Jane, 137
  Jane C., 137
  John, 138
  Mary G., 138
  Robert, 56, 136
  Robert B., 137
  Robert C., 137
  Rawdon, 137
  Sophia Le M., 137
  Stephen, 138
McCulloch, Benjamin, 31
  Henry E., 160
  James, 138
  Martha, 139
  Samuel, 139
McDonald, Alexander, 139
  Catherine McC., 138
  Philip, 138
  William, 138, 233
McEowin (McCowin), John, 292
McEvers, Charles, 292
McFadden, Cornelius, 292
McGalvin, William, 292
McGee, Francis, 292
McGinnis, John, 292
  Richard, 292
McKenna, Barbara, 27, 139
  Samuel, 27, 139
McKenzie, Mrs. 156
  Kenneth, 292
McKinley, John, 76
McKnight, Robert, 140
  Thomas, 140
McLean, Hector, 292
Maclean, Rev. John, 16
McLeod, Cornelius, 136, 140
  Donald, 292
  Duncan, 292
  Hannah, 140, 141
  John, 292
  Norman, 140, 292
  Roderick, 292
  William, 292
M'Minn, John, 292
McMullen, Robert, 293
McPherson, Donald, 293
  Nathaniel, 293
Macquarie, John, 15
MacReady, John, 152
McVane, Colin, 293
Maddox, Arthur, 292
Madeira, 230
Maidenhead, 15, 168
  Township, 16
Maine, 95, 102
Maish, Henry, 293
Makus, James, 293
Maller, Mr. 133
Mallett, Dr. Jonathan, 140
  Mary M., 140
Man (Mann), Mathias, 293
  Samuel, 91, 293
Manning, Capt., 204
Manowagonish (N. B.), 12
Mansfield, 59

Index

Mansfield Woodhouse, 291
March, Daniel, 90
Marchinton, Philip, 32
Margison, Richard, 293
Markham (Can.), 126
Marple, Captain, 140
Marr, Lawrence, 293
Marsden, Rev. Joshua, 89
Marsh, Benjamin, 293
  Elias, 293
  Elizabeth, 141
  Esther, 293
  Henry, 140, 287
  John, 293
  Joseph, 293
Marshall, George, 293
Martinique (W. I.), 33, 56, 83
Martin, Benajah, Jr., 99
  Henry, 293
  Margaret, 99
  Robert, 293
  Runyon, 293
Marwick, Captain, 204
Maryland, 160, 168, 236
Massachusetts, 77, 96, 131, 160, 201, 223, 226
Masterson, David, 293
Mathews, David, 22, 104, 206
Maturin, Mary, 140
Maugerville (N. B.), 15, 24, 69, 128, 141, 184, 213, 239, 267
Maxwell, William, 44, 204
Maydown, (Ireland), 40
Mead, Richard, 294
Mee, John, 294
Melville, Alderman, 51
Melvin, Daniel, 294
Melyn, Cornelius, 108
Mendham, 260
Mercer County, 206
Mercereau, Andrew, 141
  Phebe, 141
Meredith, Captain, 196
  Gertrude S., 196
Merigold, Thomas, 217
Merrill, Joseph, 294
  Richard, 294
Merselis, John, 294
Meyer, Johannes G., 294
Meyers, John, 294
Mian, John, 294
Middlebrook, 148, 284
Middlesex County, 12, 21, 30, 44, 46, 47, 62, 66, 68, 70, 99, 100, 114, 117, 128, 141, 147, 171, 196, 198, 203, 206, 216, 218, 219, 238, 244, 253, 254 257-319
Middletown, 49, 57, 128, 148, 149, 150, 201, 202, 208, 210, 212, 213, 214, 215, 235, 258, 262, 267, 268, 269, 282, 287, 290, 291, 299, 301, 302, 306, 307, 308, 309, 310, 311, 312, 313, 316
  Point, 90
Millack, William, 294
Millenburg (Miltenberry), Lewis, 294
Miller, George, 294
  John, 294
  Joseph, 11
  Michael, 294
  Richard, 294
Millham, Herman, 294

Millidge, John, 142
  Phineas, 141, 142
  Stephen, 141, 142
  Thomas, 35, 141, 142
Millner, Rev. John, 230
Mills, Henry, 294
  Isaac, 294
  John, 294
  William, 58
Millstone, 218
Milne, Rev. James, 106
Minor, Samuel, 295
Miramichi (N. B.), 244, 245
Moira, Lord, 119
Molenaer, Antje, 122
  Ari, 122
Monden (Mongan), Rev. Charles, 295
Money, Matthew, 295
Monmonth, Battle of, 25, 48, 128, 234
  County, 11, 16, 49, 57, 81, 82, 84, 96, 101, 124, 125, 127, 128, 129, 131, 132, 136, 140 147, 165, 170, 171, 179, 200, 201, 208, 210, 212, 213, 215, 218, 220, 221, 235, 236, 238, 241, 244, 245, 246, 253, 258-319
Monro, John, 142
  Robert, 142, 143
  Sarah H., 143
  (See Munro)
Montcalm, General, 184, 199
Montevideo (S. A.), 137
Montgomerie, Archibald, 150
Montgomery, Fort, 18
Montreal (Can.), 99, 150, 163, 171, 176
Moody, Bonnell, 295
  James 36, 102, 143, 171, 293, 295
  Jane L., 145
  John, 144, 295
Moore, Mr., 17
  Daniel, 295
  Edward, 146
  James, 295
  John, 295
  Joseph, 295
  Michael, 295
  Samuel, 146
  Susannah, 26
  Thomas, 28, 295
Moote, George, 295
Morden, James, 295
Morgan, Charles, 146
  Rev. Charles, 295
Morgann, Maurice, 146
Morgen, Dr. Lewis, 295
Morris, Mr., 34
  Asa, 67
  Diodema, 80
  Eva, 295
  Israel, 295
  James, 295
  John, 7, 96, 146
  Lewis, 115
  Mary, 29
  Noah, 295
  Robert, 60, 147
  Robert H., 29
  Sarah, 115
Morris County, 24, 31, 59, 67, 101, 115, 117, 142, 143, 176, 178, 227, 228, 229, 230, 260-319

Index

Morrisson, Joseph, 223
  Mary, 223
  Thomas, 148
Morristown, 59, 84, 125, 197, 219, 242
Morrow, John, 296
Morse, John, 296
  Joseph, Jr., 296
Mosengeil, Anthony L., 148
  Dorothea, C. G., 149
  M., 149
Moses, H., 79
Mott, Mr., 208
Mount, Chloe, 149
  George, 149, 150
  James, 296
  John, 149, 150
  Matthias, 149
  Oria, 149
  Richard, 296
Mountain, Richard, 296
Mount Holly, 155, 282
Mount Kemble, 117
Mourisson, Francis, 296
  Peter, 296
Mullin, Andrew, 296
  James, 296
Mulliner (see Molenaer)
Munday, Hopewell, 296
  John, Jr., 296
  Jonathan, 150
  Joseph, 296
  Nathaniel, 296
  Nicholas, 150
  Nicholas, Jr., 296
  Reuben, 150, 296
Munro, Rev. Harry, 150
  Nathaniel, 47, 151
  Peter Jay, 151
  (See Monro)
Murat, Prince Lucien, 81
Murgatroyd, Mrs., 242
Murphy, Edward, 296
  James, 151
Mushback, John, 296
Musquash (N. B.), 221
Myer, George, 296
  Peter, 296
Myers, Thomas, 296

Nactier, John, 152
Nealson, James, 152
  Margaret, 152
Neilson, Arthur S., 152
  James, 152, 212
  Rowley, 153
Nelson, Ananias, 296
  William, 254
Newark, 35, 36, 60, 92, 99, 106, 117, 133, 134, 140, 155, 157, 158, 160, 161, 162, 164, 165, 177, 197, 209, 217, 240, 241, 242, 243, 262, 264, 269, 275, 277, 279, 285, 286, 288, 290, 293, 294, 296, 307, 309, 310, 312, 314, 317
New Barbadoes, 69, 256, 257, 264, 271, 274, 277, 286, 287, 291, 293, 294, 302, 303, 311, 312
  Neck, 234, 288, 304
  Township, 134, 205
New Bridge, 319
New Brunswick, 20, 33, 37, 46, 48, 63, 66, 70, 80, 117, 122, 128, 142, 151, 171, 175, 207, 238, 239, 142, 160, 177, 302
New Brunswick (Prov. of), 10, 12, 13, 19, 28, 32, 33, 39, 40, 47, 49, 50, 51, 52, 58, 67, 68, 69, 70, 72, 92, 96, 101, 105, 106, 110, 118, 121, 127, 128, 139, 140, 141, 149, 150, 153, 156, 171, 173, 176, 177, 178, 181, 183, 206, 209, 210, 211, 212, 213, 217, 218, 220, 220, 223, 224, 232, 235, 239, 242, 244, 245, 246, 247, 253, 254, 256, 266, 280, 285, 292, 297
New Carlisle (Can.), 50
New Castle (Del.), 29
New Dorp (S. I.), 13
New Hampshire, 160, 164
New Haven (Conn.), 35, 152
New London (Conn.), 225
Newman, William, 297
New Market, 179, 180
Newport (R. I.), 148
New Providence, 93, 95
Newry (Ire.), 151
New South Wales, 15
Newton, William, 162
Newton, (Ire.), 129
Newtown (Newton), 22, 50
Newtown (L. I.), 152
New York City, 11, 12, 16, 17, 22, 25, 26, 27, 28, 29, 36, 37, 38, 39, 42, 45, 46, 50, 51, 53, 57, 59, 60, 61, 62, 64, 67, 68, 69, 70, 71, 75, 76, 78, 81, 82, 83, 84, 85, 86, 88, 91, 92, 93, 94, 97, 100, 101, 102, 103, 104, 106, 110, 111, 116, 117, 119, 120, 121, 122, 123, 125, 130, 132, 134, 135, 138, 139, 140, 142, 144, 146, 147, 148, 149, 152, 155, 157, 161, 162, 164, 165, 168, 170, 175, 177, 184, 196, 197, 198, 200, 203, 206, 210, 213, 216, 220, 221, 223, 230, 233, 234, 235, 238, 240, 241, 242, 243, 252, 261, 271, 314, 317
Niagara (Can.), 44, 199, 204, 205, 217
Nicaragua, 118
Nicholls, Elizabeth, 14
Nightengale, Thomas, 297
Nix, Peter, 297
Noble, Anthony, 297
  Isaac, 153
  Rachel, 154
Norfolk County (Can.), 143, 183, 184
Norris, Dr. Henry, 154
North, Joshua, 97
  Lord, 61, 202
North Carolina, 160, 172
Northcastle (N. Y.), 171
Northfield, (S. I.), 179
Northrup, Enos, 105
North Wales, 20, 231
Norwalk (Conn.), 264
Norwich (Eng.), 203
Norwood, Andrew, 297
Nottingham Township, 40, 168, 173
Nova Scotia, 9, 14, 18, 22, 25, 30, 33, 35, 36, 42, 44, 45, 56, 59, 71, 80, 82, 85, 88, 90, 94, 96, 98, 102, 105, 114, 117, 124, 126, 129, 132, 136, 141, 145, 150, 152, 164, 169, 175, 178,

338 *Index*

181, 182, 198, 200, 208, 210, 213, 214, 218, 221, 222, 223, 224, 226, 227, 228, 231, 233, 234, 238, 240, 242, 243, 247, 252, 254, 256, 260, 279, 281, 283, 297, 298, 313

Oakley, Elizabeth, 126
O'Brien, Daniel, 26
  Edward, 297
  Margaret, 26
  Susannah, 26
O'Bryant, John, 297
Odell, Anne de C., 156
  Rev. Jonathan, 7, 15, 38, 79, 80, 155
  Mary, 80
  William, 166
  William, F., 79, 156
Ogden, Aaron, 159
  Abraham, 158, 159, 163
  Catherine, 134, 230
  David, 7, 133, 157, 160, 161, 163, 164, 165, 177, 198
  David, Jr., 160
  Hannah C., 165
  Isaac, 34, 35, 104, 111, 161, 198
  Jacob, 230
  Dr. Jacob, 159
  James, 297
  John, 90, 158, 297
  Jonathan, 297
  Josiah, 134, 157
  Mary B., 164
  Matthias, 91
  Nathaniel, 297
  Nicholas, 159, 162, 164, 269
  Peter, 133, 159, 165, 198
  Robert, 297
  Samuel, 159, 297
Ogdensburgh (N. Y.), 106
Ogilvie, Rev. Mr. 150
O'Kennedy, Lucy, 166
  Margaret, 166
  Dr. Matthew, 166
Okeson, John, 297
  Samuel, 297
Okerson, Thomas, 165, 251
Old Hackensack, 305
Old Tappan, 273
Oldwater (Outwater), Thomas, 297
Oliver, Alice, 47
  Caleb, 297
  Charles, 47
  David, 166, 167, 297
  Elizabeth, 167
  Ichabod, 166, 167, 297
  Jemima W., 167
  Jonathan, 298
  Samuel, 166
  Samuel, Jr., 298
  Sarah, 167
  Zerirah, 167
Orange County (N. Y.), 46, 227, 240, 289
Orr, John, 298
Osborne, Samuel, 167, 251, 252
Oswald, Margaret, 203
Oswego (N. Y.), 195, 199
Outwater, Thomas, 297
Overt, Peter, 298
Owen, James, 298
Oxford, 292
Oxford (Eng.), 109
  University, 41

Pace, William, 298
Pack, Benjamin, 298
  John, 298
Paine, Thomas, 103
Palmerston, Lord, 95
Pamrapo, 312
Panton, Rev. George, 163, 168, 170
Paramus, 311
Park, Ozias, 298
  Thomas, 169
  William, 298
Parker, Catherine M., 115
  Gertrude S., 115
  James, 115, 298
  Josiah, 169, 274
  Nathaniel, 298
  Thomas, 298
Paris (France), 138
Parr, Governor, 14
  John, 298
Parrsborough (N. S.), 56, 80, 129, 132
Parsels, John, 171
Parsons, John, 298
Pashack, 259, 271, 316
Passaic, 65
Paterson, Cornelia B., 26
  William, 26, 122
Patterson, David, 298
  Rev. John, 163
  William, 298
Paulison, John, 298
Paulson, William, 298
Paulus Hook, 120
Payson, Ann, 176
  Jonathan, 176
  Nathaniel, 176
  Sarah, 176
Peak, Jacobus, 299
  Samuel, 299
Peaker, Philip, 299
  William, 299
Pearce, William, 170
  (See Pierce)
Pearson, Mr., 201
  Justice, 168, 170
  William, 170
  William, Jr., 170
  (See Pierson)
Peck, David, 299
Peddle, Joseph, 170
Pell, John, 299
Pennfield (N. B.), 291, 318
Pennsylvania, 9, 38, 40, 46, 53, 72, 77, 80, 82, 99, 154, 160, 170, 204, 238
Pennsylvania University, 125
Pennytown, 32, 52
Pensacola (Fla.), 113, 233
Pepperell, Sir William, 79, 160
Pequannock Township, 176
Perine (Perrine), John, 171
  John, Jr., 299
  William, 171
Perkins, Isaac, 171
  Nathaniel, 299
Persall (Parsels), John, 171
  Abraham, 299
Perth Amboy, 13, 18, 19, 26, 30, 37, 49, 56, 57, 71, 80, 82, 97, 107, 113, 114, 115, 116, 117, 122, 125, 128, 131, 169, 171, 194, 195, 196, 197, 198, 202, 203, 207, 213, 214, 215
Peters, Elizabeth B., 122

Index 339

Petersborough (N. Y.), 120
Peterson, Abraham, 172
   Christian, 172
   Nicholas, 172
   Nicholas, Jr., 172
   Paul, 172
   Robert, 299
   Dr. William B., 299
Petterweil (Germany), 149
Pettit, Amos, 57
   Nathaniel, 57, 299
Petty, William F., 146
Pew, James, 299
Philadelphia, 9, 10, 17, 25, 29, 31, 32, 36, 39, 40, 41, 51, 53, 54, 55, 60, 61, 67, 70, 80, 81, 84, 87, 88, 92, 97, 98, 104, 105, 110, 121, 128, 130, 139, 144, 155, 171, 172, 203, 205, 212, 216, 221, 236, 239, 241, 242, 245
Philadelphia College, 49, 107
Phillips, Rev. John L., 172
   Mary, 176
   Thomas, 299
Phinney, Mehitable, 181
   Thomas, 180, 181
Phipps, John, 299
Pickens, Andrew, 173
Pickle, Nicholas, 26
Pierce, Joseph, 299
Pierson, Aaron, 299
   Benjamin, 300
   Daniel, 300
   (See Pearson)
Pilgrim, Francis, 300
Pinhorn, Lieut., 233
Pintard, John, 300
   Lewis, 45
   Sarah, 149
Pinyard, William, 300
Piscataway, 64, 68, 244, 303
   Township, 99, 216, 219
Pittsgrove, 50
Plainfield, 253
Playter, George, 173
   Hannah, 173
   Watson, 173
Plymouth (Eng.), 37
Polhemus, Daniel, 236
   John, 300
   John, Jr., 300
   Mrs. Micah V. M., 236
Porden, Mary, 80
Porter, John, 300
   Nathaniel, 67
   Reuben, 72
Portland (Me.), 102
Port Richmond (N. Y.), 226
Port Ryerse (Can.), 184
Portsmouth (Eng.), 19
Portsmouth (N. H.), 164
Portugal, 60, 120
Post, Elizabeth W., 239
   John, 239
Potter, Eliazer, 300
   Elizabeth G., 82
   Henry, 82
   Robert, 300
Potts, Stacy, 300
Poynton, Brereton, 173, 300
   Mary, 174, 300
Pratt, Joseph, 300
Pray, John, 300
Prescott, Herbert F., 95

Prevost, James M., 300
Price, George, 175
   James, 300
   Joseph, 175, 300
   Dr. Joseph, 175
   Mary, 175
   Michael, 175
   Rev. Walter, 222
   William, 300
Prichard, Thomas G., 175
   Thomas T., 175
Prickman, Rinehart, 300, 301
Prideaux, Edward, 300
Prince Edward Is. (Can.), 90, 94, 100, 179, 194, 220
Princeton, 15, 16, 45, 67, 86, 97, 180, 205, 211, 212, 262, 264
   University, 15, 16, 45, 86, 124, 136, 155, 172
Proctor, Nathaniel (or Nathan), 301
Prosser, Jeremiah, 301
Prue, Michael, 301
Puckman, Rinehart, 301
Pulisfelt, Christian, 301
Putnam, James, 77

Quackenbush, Abraham A., 301
Quakertown, 83
Quebec (Can.), 51, 56, 164, 204
Queen's County (N. B.), 70
Quibbletown, 179
Quiberon (Can.), 119
Quigg, Hugh, 176
Quinlin, James, 301
Quinty Bay, 11, 66, 172, 182

Rahway, 61, 132, 166
Raines, David, 301
Ramapo, 153
Ramsey, James, 301
Randall, Amos, 301
Randolear, Christopher, 301
Randolph, Reuben, 11
   Thomas, 301
Rankin, William, 154
Rapelje, Abraham A., 223
   Garret, 301
   George, 301
   Richard, 301
   Winifred, 223
Raritan, 122, 178
Ratcliffe (Eng.), 35
Rattan, John, 301
   Samuel, 301
Rawdon, Lord, 118, 137, 180
Rawreth (Eng.), 110
Rawson, William, 301
Raymond, James, 176
   W. A., 4
Red Bank, 220, 227
Redman, Dr. John, 54
   Sarah, 54
Redruth (Eng.), 217
Reed, Elizabeth M., 141
   Leonard, 141
   Lewis, 301
Rees, Thomas, 301
Reid, Bowes, 107
   John, 176
   Margaret J., 107
   Mary P., 176
Remsen, Ann V. B., 226
   Jacob, 226
Retter, Henry, 301
   Wair, 302

Index

Reynolds, Benjamin, 176
  Broughton, 177
Rezeau, Mary, 125
  Peter, 125
Rhode Island, 148, 151, 160, 244
Rhodes Town, 30
Rice, Elizabeth, 177
  James J., 177
  John, 302
  William, 302
Richards, Charles, 177
  Jesse, 113
  John, 18, 302
  Nathaniel, 177
  Thomas, 177
Richardson, Jonathan, 178
  Thomas, 302
Richmond, James, 302
Richmond (S. I.), 24, 62, 125, 218
Rickards, Thomas, 178
Ricketts, Elizabeth, 228
  Mary, 228
  William, 228
Rickman, John, 302
Riddell, John, 211
  Rachel S., 211
Rider, Stephen, 302
Riding, Richard, 302
Ridner, Abel, 302
  Conrad, 302
  Hendrick, 302
  John, 302
Riggins, Thomas, 302
Rightmyer, Conrad, 302
Riker, Jacob, 302
  Tobias, 302
Ringwood, 38
Ritchie, Ann W., 128
  Elizabeth, 128
  John, 128
  Magdalen, 128
  Mary, 128
Ritzema, Rudolphus, 226
Robbins, Richard, 245
Roberts, Charles, 178
  Owen, 178
  Silas, 302
Robertson, John, 302
Robeson, John, 302
Robins, James, 179
  John, 179, 302
  Mary, 179
  Nathaniel, 179
  Richard, 100, 179
  Susan, 179
  William, 179
Robinson, Beverley, 19
  Catherine S., 196
  John, 303
  Sir William H., 196
  William H., 196
Rocky Hill, 232
Rodney, George, 303
  Lord, 73
Rodrow, John, 303
Rogers, Robert, 12, 24, 91, 94, 132, 166, 179, 220
Roome, George, 160
  Henry, 303
  John Le C., 145
  Lawrence, 35, 303
  William, 303
Rope, Christian, 303
Rosbrugh, Catherine, 136
  Mary, 138
  Robert, 138, 303

Rose, William, 303
Roselle, 112
Rosin, Harmon, 303
Ross, George, 50
Rothwell, Rev. Daniel, 181
Round Bay (N. S.), 227
Rowe, Rev. Mr., 112
Rowett, Thomas, 303
Rowland, Rev. John H., 125, 218, 303
Roxborough (Pa.), 203
Roxburgh (Scot.), 169
Roxbury Township, 143
Rulofson, Harman, 181
  Martin, 303
  Mehitable P., 181
  Rulof, 181
  William H., 181
Runnelds, Margaret, 11
Runyon, Reune, Sr., 303
Rush, Martin, 303
Russell, Thomas, 303
Rutherford, James, 174
  Mary, 174
  Ruth B., 181
  Samuel, 174, 181
  Walter, 303
Ruttan, David, 303
  Peter, 182
Ryas, Ann R., 226
  Lewis, 226
Ryckman, John, 303
Ryder, Stephen, 303
Ryers, Phoebe, 218
Ryerson, George, 182, 303
  Gozen, 167
  Joanna V. D., 183
  John, 182
  John F., 35, 182
  John J., 304
  Joseph, 183, 184
  Luykas, 183
  Martin, 182, 304
  Richard, 182
  Samuel, 183, 184, 251
  Sarah, 184
  Sophia S., 183
Ryerson's Ferry (S. I.), 135

Saddle River Township, 182, 272, 275, 283, 286, 290, 319
St. Andrews (N. B), 13, 39
St. Clair, John, 304
St. Helier's (Eng.), 230
St. John, Panlet, 184
St. John (N. B.), 11, 15, 19, 28, 41, 49, 51, 52, 57, 67, 72, 88, 92, 96, 102, 105, 110, 118, 149, 210, 211, 212, 213, 223, 235, 244, 246, 253, 263, 267, 268, 273, 274, 276, 280, 283, 284, 298, 311
St. Juan, 118
Salem County, 44, 50, 54, 70, 253, 256-319
Saltar, Joseph, 304
Sanders, Egbert, 304
Sandy Hook, 57, 214
Santa Cruz (W. I.), 194
Sarvenier (Servanier), James, 185
Saunders, Abraham, 304
  John, 304
Savannah (Ga.), 9, 40, 55, 58, 60, 65, 105, 127, 180, 194
Sayler, William, 304
Sayre, Rev. James, 186

Index

Rev. John, 184
Jonathan, 177, 186
Sayres, Caleb, 304
Scarborough, (Can.), 126
Schenck, Maritje, 218
  Ruloff, 235
  Sarah R., 235
Schenectady (N. Y.) 121
Schooly, Andrew, 304
  William, 304
Schraalenberg, 273, 299, 319
Schuyler, Aaron P., 304
  Arent, 119
  Catherine, 120
  Derick, 304
  Mary, 119
  Peter, 120
  Philip, 61
  Stephen, 83
Scobey, Timothy, 252, 304
Scofield, Jonathan, 187
Scooley, Frances, 128
  John, 128
Scotch Plains, 179
Scotland, 39, 120, 131, 146, 151, 168, 169
Scott, John B., 304
Seabury, Rev. Samuel, 103, 106, 135
Seamon, John, 304
Sears, John, 304
Secaucus, 305, 306, 312
Second River, 197, 273
Sedgeberrow (Eng.), 63
Seeley, Job, 304
Seguglet, Henry, Jr., 304
Sergeant, Cecil, 304
Seringapatam (India), 15
Servanier (See Sarvenier)
Service, James, 304
Setauket (L. I.), 35
Sexton, Jared, 10
Shaddock, Captain, 144
Shakerley, William H., 187
Shannon, Daniel, 187
Sharp, Samuel, 188
Shaw, Arthur, 304
  Daniel, 304
  James. 305
  Hezekiah, 305
  Thomas, 210
Sheffield, James, 148
Sheffield (N. B.), 89
Shelburne (N. S.), 18, 47, 57, 70, 89, 91, 100, 130, 148, 151, 152, 164, 168, 175, 178, 198, 210, 225, 226, 227, 234, 242, 243, 252, 256, 257, 258, 260, 264, 265, 268, 270, 271, 275, 276, 279, 280, 281, 283, 284, 285, 286, 287, 289, 290, 291, 293, 294, 296, 297, 298, 301, 303, 307, 308, 309, 311, 312, 313, 314, 316, 317, 318, 319
Shelburne, Earl of, 5
Sherbrook, Miles, 305
Shivers, Mary, 54
  Samuel, 54
Shivers Island, 54
Shoemaker, Baltus, 305
Shotwell, Daniel, 146
  James, 305
  Joseph, 95, 305
Shrewsbury, 13, 29, 49, 50, 64, 89, 130, 131, 146, 147, 175, 213, 236, 237, 241, 243, 251, 260, 261, 262, 265, 266, 269, 271, 275, 280, 281, 283, 287, 289, 290, 296, 298, 300, 301, 302, 304, 308, 309, 313, 314, 316, 317, 318
River, 149
Shropshire (Eng.), 94
Simmons, Edmund, 305
Simonson, John, 68, 188
Simon, 305
Simpson, James, 160
Simson, John B., 181
Sinclair, Sir John, 188
Sinnott, Ann H., 96
  John, 96
Sisse, Nicholas, 305
Sissiboo (N. S.), 26, 88, 145, 214
  River (N. S.), 71
Skelton, Joseph, 305
  Thomas, 48, 189, 243
Skenact, Mattenes, 305
Skene, Philip, 204
Skinner, Anne, 194
  Arthur, 196
  B. G., 305
  Catherine, 196
  Catherine J., 197
  Cortlandt, 7, 13, 19, 20, 25, 30, 53, 55, 59, 62, 90, 92, 95, 102, 116, 134, 148, 161, 169, 182, 191, 194, 195, 196, 197, 199, 216, 219, 235, 305
  Cortlandt, Jr., 305
  Elisha, 305
  Euphemia, 20, 196
  Gertrude, 115, 196
  Isabella M., 196
  James, 194, 195
  John, 20, 194, 196, 198
  Jonathan D., 195
  Philip, 20, 195, 196
  Sarah K., 195
  Stephen, 27, 117, 196, 198
  Susan, 196
  Thomas, 194, 195, 203
  Timothy, 198
  William, 195, 199
  Rev. William, 194, 196
Slater, Samuel, 305
Sleight, Matthew, 305
Sleut, Abner, 200
Slone, John, 305
Slover, James, 305
Smith, Captain, 91
  Anne L., 81
  Daniel, 305
  Ezekiel, 305
  Freeman. 306
  James, 202, 306
  Jesse, 200
  Job, 306
  John, 306
  John, Jr., 306
  Joseph, 205, 306
  Michael, 306
  Richard, 306
  Samuel, 200, 201
  Sarah, 202, 222
  William, 161, 201, 202, 203
Smock, John W., 306
Smyth, Andrew, 203
  Caroline, 204
  Frederick, 76, 115, 202
  John, 203
  Joseph, 204
  Margaret, J., 203

Margaret O., 203
Susannah, 203
Snowden, Richard, 306
Snyder, Elias, 306
Somers (See Summers)
Somerset County, 25, 37, 38, 45, 64, 122, 136, 138, 148, 165, 180, 218, 232, 233, 242, 247, 258-319
Somerset (Eng.), 139, 170, 242
Somerville, 218, 238
Sorel (Can.), 38, 99, 216
Sorrell, Mrs. Hannah E., 70, 205
  Henry, 205
  William, 70, 205
Souder, Peter, Jr., 306
Soup, Henry, 306
South Carolina, 55, 58, 65, 81, 93, 105, 106, 151, 160, 183, 194, 201, 214, 208
South River, 297
Spank Town, 166
Sparks, John, 306
  John, Jr., 306
Spear (Spier), John, 306
Spinning, Benjamin, 306
  John, 306
Spotswood, 201
Springfield, 91, 170
Spring Hill (Pa.), 9
Stacey, Matthew, 307
  Richard, 307
Stager, Cornelius, 307
  Henry, 307
Stagg, Nicholas, 307
Stainforth, Mrs. Ann, 206
  George, 205
Stallcope, John, 307
Stanbury, Isaac, 307
Stanford, Rev. John, 39
Stanton, Richard, 206
Staten Island (N. Y.), 12, 19, 21, 22, 43, 58, 59, 61, 62, 65, 71, 84, 87, 88, 90, 91, 99, 108, 121, 124, 128, 132, 134, 135, 171, 179, 201, 214, 220, 226, 252, 259, 261
Steele, Ann, 207
  Grace, 207
  William, 206
  William Henry, 207
Steirman (?), Samuel, 307
Stelle, Edward, 207
  Pontius, 21
  Rachel, 21
Stephen, Mary, 208
  Thomas, 207
Stevenson, Arthur, 307
  Edward, 307
  James, 307
  John, 208
  Samuel, 307
  Shore, 208, 252
  William, 208
Steward, John, 307
Stewart, James, 209
  Mary T., 209, 218
  Priscilla A., 209
  William, 209, 218, 233
Stickney, Sophia M., 183
Stiles, Isaac, 209, 307
  John Jr., 210
  Mary, 209
  William, 209
Stillwell, James, 210
  John, 11, 210

Nicholas, 71
Samuel, 210
Stirling, Captain, 74
  Lord, 82, 142, 176
Stites, John, Jr., 210
Stockley, Painter, 307
Stockton, Andrew H., 211, 212
  Ann, 211
  Bayard, 211
  Charles W., 212, 307
  Elizabeth, 211
  Hannah, 211
  Helen, 211
  Jacob, 211
  James, 211
  Joseph, 211
  John, 211
  Mary Ann, 19, 212
  Mary H., 212
  Rev. Philip, 86
  Rachel, 211
  Rachel S., 211, 212
  Richard W., 19, 67, 211, 307
  Ruth, 211
  Samuel, 211, 212,
  Sarah, 211
Stone Hook (N.Y.), 83
Stono Ferry (S. C.), 194
Stony Brook, 46
Stony Point, 227
Stor, Michael, 307
Stout, Abraham, 307
  Charity W., 212
  David, 171, 212
  John C., 307
  Jonathan, 212, 307
  Louis, 307
  Peter, 212
  Philip, 307
  Rachel, 211, 212
  Robert, 308
  William, 308
Stow Creek, 166
Strang, John, 151
Stretch, Daniel, 213
  Elizabeth B., 213
  John, 308
  Samuel, 213, 251
String, Charles (or Christopher), 308
Stroud (Eng.), 201
Stuart, Lieut., 308
Stur, Michael, 308
Style, John, 209
  William, 209, 307
Suffolk (Eng.), 49
Sullivan, General, 21, 59, 132
Sumatra Island, 119
Summers, Philip, 213
Sunbury (N. B.), 51, 89
Suran, David, 308
Susquehannah, Pa., 204
Sussex County, 12, 22, 31, 32, 44, 50, 57, 85, 142, 143, 165, 178, 198, 204, 208, 209, 238, 256-319
Sussex (N. B.), 19
Sussex Vale (N. B.), 13, 211
Sutherland, Daniel, 308
Sutton, Rev. David, 308
  Jacob, 308
  James, 308
  John, 308
  Moses, 308
  Thomas, 308
  Thomas C., 308

Index

343

Swanton, George, 308
  John, 308
Swarthfeller, Matthias, 308
Swedesboro, 51, 92
Sweeny, John, 308
Swezey, Aaron, 308
  Caleb, Jr., 309
Swindle, Thomas, 309
Sydney, Lord, 177

Tack, John, 309
Talman, Christopher, 309
  Jeremiah, 309
  Oliver, 309
  Steven, 309
Taping, James, 72
Taylor, Asher, 214
  Catherine E., 216
  Cortlandt, 216
  Edward, 213, 214, 309
  Eleanor, 214
  Elizabeth, 216
  Elizabeth V. C., 231
  Elliot, 216
  George, 213, 214, 235, 309
  George, Jr., 309
  John, 8, 16, 213, 215, 235, 252, 309
  John W., 215, 216
  Joseph, 8, 16, 214, 216
  Joseph P., 215, 216
  Mary, 16, 216
  Matthias, 309
  Morford, 214, 309
  Morris, 214
  Nathaniel, 214
  Samuel, 309
  William, 8, 16, 95, 96, 132, 198, 214, 215, 220, 231, 252
Taylor's Mills, 235
Teaneck, 265
Tedford, Jacob, 309
  Samuel, 309
Temple, Sir John, 126
Templeton, William, 309
Terrill, William, 196, 216
Thatcher, Anne, 217
  Bartholomew, 216
  Margaret, 217
  Margaret G., 216
Thearn, Chloe M., 149
  James, 149
Thomas, Colonel, 91
  Ezekiel, 309
  Francis, 217
  Job, 309
Thompson, Amelia, 217
  Anne V. D., 218
  Augustus, 217
  Cornelius, 217, 129, 218, 217
  Cornelius O., 217
  Frederick, 217
  James, 309
  John, 129, 218, 251, 252
  Lewis, 217, 218, 252
  Mary, 209, 217, 218
  Phoebe R., 218
  Rebecca, 217
  Robert, 309
  Sally, 217
  Thomas, 218
  William, 217, 218
Thomson, Benjamin, 218
  George, 219
  John, 309
  William, 218

Thorburn, John, 219
Thorn (Thorne), Abraham, 310
  Jacob, 309
  John, 310
  Joseph, 219
  Samuel, 310
  Thomas, 310
Thornton, John, 310
Thorp, Benjamin, 74
  Morris, 310
Three Rivers (Can.), 147
Throckmorton, Frances B., 220
  James, 220
  John, 220, 252
Ticonderoga (N. Y.), 67, 204, 204, 239
Tiers, Abraham, 310
Tillford, Mr., 310
Tilton, Clayton, 220, 221
  Ezekiel, 310
  John, 310
Timpany, Edward K., 221
  John A., 221
  Robert, 96, 221
  Sarah C., 222
Tisdale, Joseph, 125
  Margaret L., 125
Tise, John, 310
  Peter, 310
Talles Hunt Major (Eng.), 109
Toms River, 131
Tooker, Jacob, 222
Toronto (Can.), 131, 217
Trenton, 9, 19, 20, 21, 40, 50, 52, 87, 88, 97, 125, 127, 128, 168, 170, 173, 174, 181, 211, 214, 218, 220, 242, 246, 264, 313, 314
Trevelyan Sir George O., 75
Troupe, John, 310
Troy (N. Y.), 142
Tryon, Governor, 34, 66, 103, 225
Tubman, Ananias, 310
  Sylvanus, 310
Tucker, Mrs. 242
  Elizabeth G., 242
  Jacob, 90, 222
  Samuel, 242, 310
Tudas, John, 310
Tupper, Ann P., 176
Turner, Elizabeth, 222
  Frederick S., 222
  George C., 222
  Isabella, 222
  Marion (Maria), 222
  Sarah S., 222
  William, 68, 106, 222
Turpan, Thomas, 310
Tuscet (N. S.), 280
Tusket River (N. S.), 234, 237
Tuthill, Benjamin, 310,
  Samuel, 142
Tyrrell, William, 196

Underhill, Sarah, 184
Updike, George, 310
Upper Freehold Township, 84, 101, 125, 127, 128, 171, 210, 233, 246, 263, 278, 279, 283, 297, 299, 311
Urion, Gideon, 311
Vail, Martha, 47
Valleau, Ann, 223
  Elizabeth B., 223
  Falconer, 223
  Mary, 223

344   *Index*

Mary L., 223
Mary M., 17
Theodore, 223
Van Amber (Van Emburgh?), John, 311
Van Allen, Andrew, 311
  Henry, 223
  William, 224
  Winifred R., 223
VanBlarcum, Abraham, 311
  Hendrick, 311
  Herman, 311
  John J., 311
  Peter J., 224
Van Buren, Dr. James, 35, 182, 224
Van Buskirk, Abraham, 7, 161, 225, 226, 227, 228, 237
  Andrew, 311
  Anne C., 226
  Cornelius, 311
  Daniel, 311
  David, 311
  Garret, 311
  Jacob, 226, 311
  James, 227
  Jane, 227
  John, 182, 226, 227
  John J., 226
  John L., 226
  Lawrence, 182, 226, 227, 228
  Maria, 226
  Peter, 311
  Thomas, 227, 228
Van Camp, Thomas, 311
Van Cleef, Benjamin, 236
Van Cortlandt, Governor, 228
  Arthur A., 231
  Catherine, 231
  Catherine O., 230
  Charlotte, 231
  Elizabeth, 231
  Gertrude, 231
  Henry C., 231
  Jacob O., 231
  Margaret H., 231
  Mary A., 231
  Mary R., 231
  Philip, 87, 163, 198, 215, 228
  Sarah O., 231
  Stephen, 231
  William R., 229
Vanderbeck, Abraham, 232
  Hannah, 232
Vanderhoff, Henry, 311
Vanderhoven, John, 311
Van Deursen, William, 66
Van Dine, Dennis, 311
  Hendrick, 311
  Sichy, 69
Van Dorn, Anne, 218
  Jacob, 218
  Maritje S., 218
Van Duhoff, Joanna, 183
Van Dumont, William, 232
Van Dyke, Catherine E., 232
  John 31, 51, 53, 55, 113, 232, 256
  Margaret, 232
  Rebecca, 232
  Roeloff, 232
  Cornelius, 69
VanEmburgh, Abraham, 311
  Adoniah, 234, 312
  Gilbert, 312
  James, 234, 288, 312
  John, 311

Van Giesen, Abraham, 312
  Abraham, Jr., 312
  Cornelius, 312
  Garret, 312
  Isaac, 312
Van Horne, Barent, 312
  Cornelius, 178, 312
  Cornelius L., 312
  Lawrence, 234
  Mindert, 312
Van Houten, John, 312
  John H., 312
Van Mater, Benjamin, 236
  Caty, 235
  Chrineyonce, 235, 252
  Clarence, 312
  Cyrenus, 312
  Daniel, 167, 235, 252, 312
  Gysbert, 235, 236
  Hendrick, 236
  Henry, 167, 214, 252
  Jacob, 312
  John, 236, 312
  Joseph, 235, 236
  Micah, 236
  Micha H., 235
  Ruloff, 235
  Sarah, 236
  Sarah S., 235
Van Norden, David, 312
  Gabriel, 237, 312, 313
  Henry, 312
  James, 312
  John, 237, 312
  John, Jr., 313
Van Note, Peter, 313
Van Saen, Cornelius, 313
  Isaac, 313
Van Tuyl, Michael, 313
Van Voorhees, David, 313
  (See Voorhees)
Van Vorst, Aaron, 313
  Cornelius, 313
Van Wagoner, John, 313
Van Winkle, Jacob, 313
  Jacob S., 313
Vardill, Miss, 80
Varick, Richard, 34
Vaughan (Can.), 125, 126, 131
Vaughan, General, 87
Veal, Abraham, 30
Veeder, Engeltje, 121
Vermont, 100
Villou, Theodore, 313
Virginia, 78, 92, 93, 160, 214, 215
von Steuben, Baron, 319
Voorhees, Jacobus (James), 313
  John, 211
  Ruth S., 211
  (See Van Voorhees)
Voorhis, Margaret, 223
Vought, Christopher, 83, 237, 238
  John 83, 238
Vredenburgh (See Fradenburgh)
Vreeland, Derick, 313
  Elias, 66
  Jennie, 66
  Nicholas, 313
  Peter, 313
Vroom, John, 238
  Peter, 238

Waddell, Rev. Henry, 313
Waddington, Jane, 238
  John, 238

Index

Wadman, Arthur, 61, 63, 122, 238
  Susannah L., 61, 63, 122, 238
Wager, Allen, 314
Wake, Drury, 314
Wake County (N. C.), 172
Wakefield (N. B.), 222
Wales, 124
Walker, Mesbeck, 314
  Thomas, 314
Wallace, Alexander, 147
  Hugh, 147, 314
Wall, Jesse, 314
Waller, Joseph, 314
  Robert, 314
Walls, George, 314
  James, 234
Waln, Richard, 314
  James, 234
Walsingham (Can.), 102, 143
Walter, Lynde, 226
  Maria V. B., 226
  Rev. William, 47, 226
Walton, William, 221, 314
Wanamaker, A., 314
  Elizabeth, 239
  Robert, 239
Wantony Plain, 59
Ward, General, 11, 18
  Ebenezer, 240
  Ebenezer, Jr., 314
  John, 314
  Martha J., 241
  Richard, 314
  Samuel, 240, 241
  Thomas, 172, 240
  Uzal, 240
Wardel (Wardell), Ebenezer, 314
  Jacob, 314
  John, 241
  Joseph, 314
  Joshua, 241
  Peter, 314
  William, 314
Ware, Richard, 241
Warne, Samuel, 56, 315
Warner, George, 315
  Phebe, 172
Warren, Lady, 200
  Samuel, 315
Warrington, Rev. Dr., 231
Washington, George, 18, 111, 131, 144, 154, 161, 164, 180, 215, 224, 228, 233, 274, 284
Washington Fort, 94
Waterhouse, Ambrose, 315
  Henry, 315
  Ingram, 315
Waterford (N. Y.), 123
Waters Upton (Eng.), 94
Watkins, David, 315
Watson, Miss, 10
  Alexander, 315
  John W., 233
  William, 315
Watts, Anne, 120
  George, 315
  John, 117, 120
  Susannah, 117
Wear, John, 315
Weiser, Frederick, 242
  (See Wiser)
Welcher, John, 315
  Robert, 315
  Thomas, 315
Welding, Anne, 173
  Benjamin, 315
  Hannah, 173
  Jesse, 315
  Watson, 173
Wells, Daniel, 315
  George, 315
  Harrison, 315
  James, 315
  William, 315
Wentworth, John, Jr., 160
Wessigh, Ludwick, 316
West, Benjamin, 79
  Beriah, 316
  Jonathan, 316
  Joshua, 316
  Stephen, 252, 316
  Uriah, 316
Westchester (N. Y.), 126
Westervelt, Casparus, 316
  Stephen, 237
Westfield, 170
Westfield (Mass.), 17
West Indies, 118, 134
Westmorland (N. H.), 223, 244
West Ramapo, 227
Wetherby, Henry, 316
  Matthew, 316
Wetherhead, John, 161
Wetmore, Luther, 57
Weymouth (N. S.), 208
Whale Creek, 96
Wheeler, John, 242
Wheelock, Capt., 74
Whilenack, John, 316
Whitaker, Robert, 316
Whitchurch (Can.), 126
White, Aaron, 221, 316
  Anthony, 37
  Britain, 316
  David, 242
  Elizabeth, 37
  Elizabeth T., 242
  John, 316
  Josiah, 316
  Philip, 130, 131, 221
  Robert, 316
  Thomas, 316
White Plains (N. Y.), 94, 137
Whitingdale, Hester, 79
Whitney, Joseph, 316
Wideman, Matthew, 80
Wiem, Peter D., 316
Wight, Isle of, 109
Wilkins, Rev. Isaac, 230
Willett, Abigail, 181
  Alice C., 46
  Anne, 46
  Thomas S., 316
  William, 46
Willets, John, 316
Williams, Captain, 116
  Amos, 243
  Charity, 212
  Daniel, 316
  Edmund, 317
  Ezekiel, 317
  Giles, 317
  James, 243
  John, 130, 244, 317
  John, Jr., 317
  Jonathan, 80
  Joseph, 243, 317
  Nathaniel, 243, 317
  Obadiah, 243, 317
  Thomas, 317
Williamson, Cornelius, 317
Willis, John, 152, 244

Willocks, Ann, 128
 George, 128
Wills, Eliza, 15
Willson, Alexander, 317
 Andrew, 57
 John, 317
 (See Wilson)
Wilmot, J. Eardley, 5
 Jane, 106
 John E., 79
 Lemuel, 244
 Malcolm, 244
Wilmot (N. S.), 31, 227
Wilson, Cornelius, 141
 Ebenezer, 317
 Jacob, 317
 James, 317
 Jesse, 317
 John, 244
 Joseph, 317
 Phebe, 141
 Robert, 141
 Richard, 317
 Samuel R., 245
 (See Willson)
Windsor Township, 100, 206
Windsor (N. S.), 36
Winkleman, 259, 262
Winslow, Rev. Edward, 317
Winters, Garret, 317
Wiser, Frederick, 47, 242
 Frederick, Jr., 317
 Jacob, Jr., 317
Wiswall, Rev. John, 102
 Margaret H., 102
Witchell, John, 318
Withern (Eng.), 25
Witherspoon, John, 45, 86
Wolfe, General, 142
Wolfville (N. S.), 129
Woller, Joseph, 318
Wood, Ezekiel, 318
 John, 218
 Obadiah, 318
Woodbridge, 11, 12, 21, 24, 27, 44, 47, 67, 71, 72, 74, 80, 95, 111, 121, 134, 140, 146, 150, 152, 179, 194, 197, 201, 202, 257, 276, 277, 282, 315
Woodhouse (Can.), 143, 184, 223
Woodland, William, 318
Woodley, Asa, 318
Woodruff, Thomas, 245
Woods, Peter, 318
Woodstock (Conn.), 42
Woodstock (N. B.), 222
Woodward, Abraham, 318

Anthony, 161, 210, 245, 318
Anthony, Jr., 318
Isaac, 318
Jacob, 318
Jesse, 246
John, 246
Nimrod, 318
Robert, 246
Samuel, 245
Thomas, 318
Woodworth, Captain, 226
Wooley, Benjamin, 318
Woolridge, Susannah, 246
Woolverton, Thomas, 318
Woolwich (Eng.), 52
Woolwich Township, 51, 113
Woortman, John, 318
Worcestershire (Eng.), 63
Worth, Alexander, 318
 Benjamin, 247
 James, 318
Worthley, John, 318
Wouters, Garret, 318
Wren, Sir Christopher, 66
Wrench, Matthew, 318
Wrexham (No. Wales), 231
Wright, Austin, 318
 Joshua, 71
 Nathan, 173
 William, 247
Wynne, Julius, 63
 Susannah D., 63
Wyoming (Pa.), 107

Yale University, 35, 42, 157, 159
Yarmouth (Eng.), 49, 203
Yarmouth (N. S.), 169, 221, 309
Yates (Yeats), Richard, 319
York, (Pa.), 23, 88
York County (N. B.), 10, 19, 58, 110, 127, 154, 207, 258
Yorkshire (Eng.), 59, 86, 101
Yorktown (Va.), 55, 78, 149, 180
Young, Christopher, 319
 David, 319
 Peter, 319
 William, 319
Younglove, Ezezial, 319
Youren, John, 319
Yule, James, 319

Zabriskie, Albert, 319
 Christian A., 319
 John, 319
 John I., 319
Zimmerman, Matthew, 319

www.ingramcontent.com/pod-product-compliance
Lightning Source LLC
Chambersburg PA
CBHW052057230426
43662CB00036B/1125